# Ecological Counseling

## An Innovative Approach to Conceptualizing Person-Environment Interaction

Edited by

Robert K. Conyne
Ellen P. Cook

American Counseling Association
5999 Stevenson Avenue
Alexandria, VA 22304
www.counseling.org

# Ecological Counseling

*An Innovative Approach to
Conceptualizing Person–Environment
Interaction*

10   9   8   7   6   5   4   3   2   1

**American Counseling Association**
5999 Stevenson Avenue
Alexandria, VA 22304

Director of Publications   •   Carolyn C. Baker

Production Manager   •   Bonny E. Gaston

Copyeditor   •   Chris Howland

Cover design   •   Bonny E. Gaston

**Library of Congress Cataloging-in-Publication Data**

Ecological counseling : an innovative approach to conceptualizing
person–environment interaction / edited by Robert K. Conyne,
Ellen P. Cook
   p.   cm.
Includes bibliographical references and index.
   ISBN 1-55620-199-0 (alk. paper)
   1. Counseling.   2. Environmental psychology.   I. Conyne, Robert K.
II. Cook, Ellen Piel, 1952–

BF637.C6E26 2003
158′.3—dc22

                  2003014837

# Table of Contents

## Section I
### *Conceptual Foundations of Ecological Counseling*

# Section II
## *Ecological Counseling Interventions*

# Acknowledgments

To my former colleagues at Illinois State University's Student Counseling Center, where ecological applications were in full force, and to my long-time colleagues in the University of Cincinnati counseling program, who are all represented in this work ... thank you.

—Robert K. Conyne

Thank you to the many colleagues, students, and staff members who have provided a supportive and stimulating environment for many years; to many others in my ecosystem whose contributions to this book were crucial although unrecognized; and, finally, to those closest to my heart who have given my life meaning, especially David, Jenny, and Laura.

—Ellen P. Cook

# Preface

First, a story. The Tarahumara Indians live freely in and around the Copper Canyon region of the state of Chihuahua in Mexico, in an area about 7,000 feet above sea level. Many of them live within the canyons, traversing up and down the steep elevations. Their name, Tarahumara, can be translated loosely into English as Lightfooted People. The running prowess of the Tarahumara, both in speed and long distance, is the stuff of legends; thus, the lightfooted people appellation.

Not long ago, reportedly, representatives of a major running shoe company learned about the great running skills of the Tarahumara and visited the canyons hoping to contract some of the best runners to join their team. Of course, they brought with them samples of their advanced technology running shoes as an attractor. The shoe company representatives succeeded in identifying some prospects, gave them shoes, and asked these runners to try them out. Shortly following the tryout, the Tarahumara runners returned the shoes, explaining that they slowed them down and that they much preferred their customary flat sandals.

This, in fact, is an ecological story, one that counselors should heed. Ecology, at its simplest level, relates to the old bromide of "If the shoe fits, wear it," or its corollary, "If it doesn't fit, don't!" The Tarahumara runners found that the wonderfully advanced running shoes simply did not fit. That is, although the shoes may have physically matched the size of their feet, they did not fit them as runners. The shoes probably did not fit the gait they used to accommodate sandals, meaning they likely slowed them down! The technologically sophisticated shoe was also out of place with centuries of tradition and culture within the Tarahumara community surrounding the practice of running. Such shoes may have appeared as out of place to the Tarahumara as wearing bunny slippers with a tuxedo might appear to us. As the old Chinese proverb goes, "Only the foot knows if a shoe fits."

*Ecology* is a big word with many meanings. A standard definition is that ecology is the science of the relationship between organisms and their environments. When ecology is merged with the word *counseling*, which itself holds a variety of understandings, it can result in many possibilities and much confusion. One important perspective links ecological counseling within the tradition of ecopsychology (e.g., Roszak, Gomes, Kanner, Hillman, & Brown, 1995), of ecological psychotherapy (Kurato, 2000), or of "deep ecology" (Capra, 1996). These approaches are concerned with the ethical interconnections of humans with all aspects of the environment, including nature, and maintaining a synergistic relationship between personal and planetary health.

Although this orientation is connected with our view of ecological counseling, we are more focused on interactions between people and human systems. Kurt Lewin (1936) helped us to understand the basics of an ecological perspective as applied within psychology. He suggested that Behavior is dependent on how People interact with their Environment ($B = P \times E$). The resulting fit of $P \times E$ is a dynamic process constructed by participants. This formula can be used to help understand many life situations, such as the Tarahumara shoe story, as well as to guide the ecological counseling process.

An ecological approach to counseling is both simple and complex, as you will see in the ensuing chapters. That is, it seems quite natural and direct to view all of counseling ecologically—that people, environments, and their interaction are all important. However, when one begins to delve more deeply into this approach—for example, to consider the multiple levels of interaction potentially available for counselor intervention—a certain amount of complexity is quickly discovered. Obviously, many concepts are packed into this definition. This book is intended to unpack these concepts and to provide concrete illustrations of how ecological counseling interventions can be implemented at multiple contextual levels of the ecosystem.

Ecological counseling is a comprehensive and metatheoretical approach that includes multiple factors. We define *ecological counseling* as contextualized help-giving that is dependent on the meaning clients derive from their environmental interactions, yielding an improved ecological concordance.

We decided to develop this book on ecological counseling because we could find no single existing source that addressed it. We had created a six-course doctoral seminar series in ecological counseling at the University of Cincinnati as one way to fulfill our program vision, which revolves around an ecological theme. In looking for reading sources for the seminar series, we had to resort to pulling together readings from a range of disciplines into reading packets. Students encouraged us to try filling the void. This book is the result.

Chapter authors are both internal and external to the University of Cincinnati. Those internal include each faculty member of the university's counseling program (i.e., Bob Conyne, Ellen Cook, Lynn Rapin, Mei Tang, Al Watson, Bob Wilson, and Geoffrey Yager), a current doctoral student in the program (Cheryl Savageau), two recent doctoral graduates (Bill O'Connell and Joe Stewart-Sicking), and a faculty member from Educational Foundations (Roger Collins). The external experts who contributed to the book include Fred Bemak, Krista Chronister, Felicia Collins Correia, Mary Heppner, Ed Herr, Shoshana Kerewsky, Alan Mabry, Benedict McWhirter, Mary Lee Nelson, Susan Neufeldt, and Karen O'Brien. We thank each one for their contributions.

Section I of this book contains five chapters that focus on conceptual foundations important for ecological counseling. Chapters 1 and 5 represent our thinking of how an ecological mindset is connected with counseling. In chapter 1, we define and describe ecological counseling and the several important foundations on which it rests, such as individual within ecosystem, collaboration, interaction, and meaning making. We also begin the example of Jamie, which continues in chapter 5. The fifth chapter (by Ellen Cook, Bob Conyne, Cheryl Savageau, and Mei Tang) contains a description of the processes of ecological counseling, to provide readers with an understanding of how the familiar pathways of counseling (e.g., goal setting, assessment) are addressed ecologically. In these and all book chapters the authors begin their chapter with chapter highlights and conclude with a set of learning activities, all of which are intended to help make the ideas expressed more accessible.

Elsewhere in Section I, the book focuses on conceptual foundations, addressing significant forces that have contributed to the development of ecological counseling. In chapter 2, Ed Herr demonstrates how social, political, and economic events can strongly influence the contexts within which we operate and the sense we make out of our lives. Joe Stewart-Sicking (chapter 3) and Susan Neufeldt and Mary Lee Nelson (chapter 4) position ecological thinking within a philosophical evolution concerning the nature of human life and knowing. Their emphases on the interconnection of people and environment (Stewart-Sicking) and on the importance of constructivism and meaning making within life experience (Neufeldt and Nelson) capture central aspects of ecological counseling.

Ecological counseling is much more than facilitating individual adjustment. Section II of the book contains eight chapters that examine a variety of counseling interventions from an ecological perspective. Ecological psychotherapy involves developing a niche comprised of complex interpersonal processes, as Bob Wilson writes in chapter 6. In addition, students and others can be trained in counseling skills from an ecological perspective (Geoffrey Yager, chapter 7). Also, as Fred Bemak and Bob Conyne write in chapter 8, the concept of an ecologically centered group is based on assumptions and premises qualitatively different from traditional practice, aligned more closely with multicultural, collectivist, and systemic orientations.

In chapter 9, Ellen Cook, Karen O'Brien, and Mary Heppner write that career interventions from an ecological perspective are described as emerging from an appreciation of the myriad social and cultural contexts in which we all live. Advocacy efforts aimed at empowering individuals or groups are of growing importance in general within counseling, and chapter 12 by Albert Watson, Roger Collins, and Felicia Collins Correia illustrates how an ecological perspective affords a considerable advantage to these efforts. In chapter 11, Lynn Rapin discusses how developing organizations need to be more effective and supportive from an ecological perspective, which is a significant ecological counseling intervention. In chapter 10 (Bill O'Connell and Alan Mabry), the challenges and supports faced by community counseling agencies are analyzed ecologically, with some useful suggestions for counselors and administrators. And last, but certainly not least, prevention efforts go hand-in-hand with an ecological perspective. As Krista Chronister, Benedict McWhirter, and Shoshana Kerewsky remind us in chapter 13, this may require many of us to expand our skill repertoire in order to be truly effective as change agents.

This book concludes with a brief afterword in which the coeditors provide their perspective on the book's contents.

So, we have organized the book to focus on conceptual underpinnings of ecological counseling and on counseling interventions embracing an ecological orientation. Both theory and practice are critically important in counseling, of course, and so it is with ecological counseling.

We hope you will read and discuss this book actively, seeking to connect theory and practice. Allow the chapter highlights to guide you as a kind of preorganizer. Take advantage of the learning activities. Some important questions include What might ecological counseling mean for your personal and professional development? How might you apply any of this material? How does it fit with other approaches to counseling you find important? In other words, what meaning can you make from it, and how does it fit within the environment of your own professional practice? How might it change your interactions with clients?

And, now, on to chapter 1.

—Robert K. Conyne and Ellen P. Cook

# References

Capra, F. (1996). *The web of life: A new scientific understanding of living systems*. New York: Doubleday.

Lewin, K. (1936). *Principles of topological psychology*. New York: McGraw-Hill.

Kurato, Y. (2000). Toward a human ecological psychotherapy. In *Proceedings of the Eighth International Counseling Conference: Counseling and Human Ecology*. (pp. 71-76). San Jose, Costa Rica.

Roszak, T., Gomes, M., Kanner, A., Hillman, J., & Brown, L. (1995). *Ecopsychology: Restoring the earth, healing the mind*.

# About the Editors

**Robert K. Conyne**, PhD, is a professor and the director of the counseling program at the University of Cincinnati. An AB (cum laude) graduate of Syracuse University, Bob received his master's and doctoral degrees from Purdue University, where he was an NDEA Title IV Fellow. After completing a postdoctoral internship in counseling psychology at the University of California—Berkeley Counseling Center, he spent 9 years at Illinois State University as a professor of counselor education, in addition to serving as staff psychologist and coordinator of group services and consultation in the Student Counseling Service. Following a year as a visiting scholar at the University of Michigan's Community Psychology Program and Counseling Service, he joined the University of Cincinnati, where he has spent the past several years in his present role. He has also held positions as department head and associate vice provost at the university.

Bob holds clinical counselor and psychologist licenses, and multiple certifications (e.g., Approved Clinical Supervisor). He is a fellow of the Association for Specialists in Group Work (ASGW), the American Psychological Association (APA), and the American Psychological Society (APS); has served in numerous professional leadership roles at the national level (e.g., president of ASGW, editor of *The Journal for Specialists in Group Work*); and has received various awards (e.g., ASGW Professional Advancement Award). His scholarly work, encompassing 9 books and more than 250 referenced articles and presentations, focuses on group work, preventive counseling, consultation, and ecological approaches to counseling.

**Ellen P. Cook**, PhD, is a professor in the counseling program at the University of Cincinnati. She graduated with a BA (summa cum laude) from the University of Toledo, having been a member of the university honors program and named Psychology Student of the Year. She received a PhD in counseling psychology from the University of Iowa in 1977, with a minor in clinical psychology. She spent 1 year as visiting assistant professor at the University of Nebraska, and since 1978 has been a full-time faculty member at the University of Cincinnati.

This is her third book. Her two earlier books were on gender issues in psychology and counseling, one of which (*Psychological Androgyny*) was the alternate selection of the Behavioral Sciences Book Club. Her numerous publications and presentations are in the areas of ecological counseling, career development, and gender issues. She holds professional licenses as a clinical counselor and psychologist in the state of Ohio and is a fellow of the American Psychological Association. Ellen is the editor of the *The Career Development Quarterly*. She has also served as a contract psychologist for a local mental health center and as director of the University of Cincinnati counseling program. Currently she leads adult education programs and women's retreats at her church. An emerging area of interest is enhancing psychological development within church communities using an ecological perspective.

# About the Contributors

**Fred Bemak**, EdD, is a graduate of the University of Massachusetts. He is a professor and program coordinator of the counseling and human development program in the Graduate School of Education at George Mason University.

**Krista M. Chronister,** PhD, is a graduate of the University of Oregon counseling psychology program.

**Roger L. Collins**, PhD, is a graduate of Harvard University. He is a professor of educational foundations at the University of Cincinnati.

**Robert K. Conyne**, PhD, is a graduate of Purdue University. He is a professor and director of the counseling program at the University of Cincinnati.

**Ellen P. Cook**, PhD, is a graduate of the University of Iowa. She is a professor in the counseling program at the University of Cincinnati.

**Felicia Collins Correia** received her MPH from Columbia School of Public Health. She is executive director of Domestic Violence Intervention Services in Tulsa, Oklahoma.

**Mary J. Heppner**, PhD, is a graduate of the University of Missouri. She is an associate professor of education (counseling psychology) and a counseling psychologist in the Career Center at the University of Missouri.

**Edwin L. Herr**, PhD, is a graduate of Teachers College, Columbia University. He is Distinguished Professor of Education (Counselor Education and Counseling Psychology) Emeritus and Associate Dean Emeritus at Pennsylvania State University.

**Shoshana D. Kerewsky**, PsyD, is an assistant professor in the counseling psychology and family and human services programs at the University of Oregon.

**Alan Mabry**, PhD, is a graduate of the University of Pittsburgh. He is executive director of Core Behavioral Health Centers in Cincinnati, Ohio.

**Benedict T. McWhirter**, PhD, is a graduate of Arizona State University. He is an associate professor of counseling psychology at the University of Oregon.

**Mary Lee Nelson**, PhD, is a graduate of the University of Oregon. She is an associate professor of counseling psychology at the University of Wisconsin.

**Susan Allstetter Neufeldt**, PhD, is a graduate of the University of California at Santa Barbara. She is clinic director and lecturer in the counseling/clinical/school psychology program in the Gevirtz Graduate School of Education at the University of California at Santa Barbara.

**Karen M. O'Brien**, PhD, is a graduate of Loyola University at Chicago. She is an associate professor in the counseling psychology program at the University of Maryland.

**William O'Connell**, EdD, is a graduate of the University of Cincinnati. He is an assistant professor of counseling at Xavier University.

**Lynn S. Rapin**, PhD, is a graduate of the University of Illinois. She is a psychologist in private practice in Cincinnati, Ohio, and adjunct professor in the counseling program at the University of Cincinnati.

**Cheryl Savageau** is a doctoral student in the counseling program at the University of Cincinnati.

**Joseph A. Stewart-Sicking**, EdD, is a graduate of the University of Cincinnati. He is a project associate at Virginia Theological Seminary, Alexandria, Virginia.

**Mei Tang**, PhD, is a graduate of the University of Wisconsin. She is an associate professor in the counseling program at the University of Cincinnati.

**Albert L. Watson**, PhD, is a graduate of the University of Michigan. He is an associate professor in the counseling program at the University of Cincinnati.

**F. Robert Wilson**, PhD, is a graduate of Michigan State University. He is a professor in the counseling program at the University of Cincinnati.

**Geoffrey G. Yager**, PhD, is a graduate of Michigan State University. He is a professor in the counseling program at the University of Cincinnati.

# Section I

*Conceptual
Foundations
of Ecological
Counseling*

Chapter 1

# Understanding Persons Within Environments: An Introduction to Ecological Counseling

*Robert K. Conyne and Ellen P. Cook*

---

*Chapter Highlights*
- *Ecological counseling is defined and set within a context.*
- *Fourteen fundamental principles underlying ecological counseling are described.*
- *An extended example involving Jamie is shown.*

---

Jamie is in trouble at school. An energetic and outgoing 8-year-old, she loves to interact with others and will readily strike up conversations with strangers. Because of her limited intellectual capacities, she spends most of her school day in the special education classroom. Her time with her peers in the general classroom and on the bus is very important to her.

Jamie, however, now faces permanent removal from her bus because of persistent misbehavior. She has always ridden directly behind the driver so the driver can keep an eye on her. Despite this monitoring, she frequently gets out of her seat, walks down the aisle, tries to open the window, and even uses bad language. Warnings by the bus driver and assistant principal have not succeeded in changing the situation. She is incapable of explaining reasons for her behavior, and her perplexed parents and special education teacher are out of ideas on how to modify it. The assistant principal has called for a meeting with Jamie's parents to discuss this intractable problem, which he and the bus driver see as potentially dangerous because of how it excites the other children and distracts the driver.

Jamie's problem is of a form commonly encountered by counselors: a client's behavior (or thinking or feelings) seem to be getting him or her into some type of trouble. The obvious solution is to help the client change this problem so that the difficulties cease. The target of the behavior change process is the client; the problem is some aspect of his or her functioning; the goal of counseling is substitution of a more adaptive way of being. The counselor serves as a remediation expert, skilled at identifying the nature of one's personal dysfunction and helping the client develop alternatives that are more satisfying.

This characterization of counseling has widespread support, and for good reason: it has helped countless clients live happier lives. Yet this view is only part of a broader perspective on what constitutes, maintains, and changes human behavior. This broader perspective, as we will discuss shortly, has the potential to dramatically increase a counselor's scope for action—and his or her success with a broad range of client concerns.

## Paradigms for Explaining Human Behavior

Counselors often tend to view the world by using person-oriented lenses. Confront counselors with a problem to be solved and their predictable focus will be on variables attached to person-level interpretations. This may be more than a tendency, however; it may represent a paradigm.

Here are two brief examples. Our counseling faculty at the University of Cincinnati participated with other faculty in a development training group on problem-based learning. One group consisted of counseling faculty, the other faculty from other disciplines. We were presented with a short case study description and asked to list all the factors that may be important in beginning to understand and work on the problem. The central aspect of the case involved a car that had broken down on the highway, with the driver uncertain about what to do. What factors did the counseling faculty identify and remain concerned with, until the trainer pointed out our narrow viewpoint? That is, our perspective was restricted because we focused only on the feelings of the driver, the thoughts of the driver, the skills of the driver—about everything concerned with the driver. We never thought about the car, what made it behave the way described, what possible solutions might exist to fix it. Notably, faculty members from other disciplines were much more likely to focus on the car itself, not on the driver's experience. An ecological viewpoint would incorporate both driver and car (and more) in a much more comprehensive approach.

In another example, a colleague reported presenting a client case study during a conference for counselors. He had organized his session attendees into three small working groups. The first group was asked to examine the case from a Person orientation; the second from an Environmental orientation; and the third from a Person–Environment Interaction orientation. What happened? All three groups of counselors, regardless of their task assignment, centered their attention on the Person orientation! This example again illustrates how counselors can be myopic in their tendency to restrict their attention to Person level variables. As you will read later, such a limitation needs to be extended.

In the example of Jamie, it is clear that the school personnel view the source of the bus problem as Jamie herself. In their eyes, her cognitive and social limitations coupled with excitability and impulse control issues have made her unable to behave appropriately. Her limitations are inherent and lifelong; her medication has had limited success in curtailing her distracting behavior patterns. Typical consequences for negative behaviors—being warned, scolded, and written up, and sitting near the bus driver—have all been tried with little effect. Because of who she is, in this view, the only option that remains is to remove her from the situation for the benefit of others on the bus.

The implicit paradigm of behavior operative here can be schematized as

$$B = f(P)$$

Behavior is a function of personal characteristics, such as genetic makeup, motivations, emotions, or behavior repertoire. To the extent these characteristics can be changed, the person's targeted behavior can be changed as well. Environmental factors may certainly be influential also, but they are considered mostly in terms of how they might moderate the personal characteristics. For example, riding on an empty bus may make it less likely that Jamie's disruptive behavioral tendencies will occur, but in this paradigm the source of Jamie's problems remains her personal deficits.

The limitations of this person-focused paradigm have become increasingly obvious in recent years. Behaviorists and social psychologists have convincingly demonstrated how human behavior can be modified by a plethora of external factors beyond a person's choice or awareness. Social scientists have analyzed in detail the power of a person's physical or social environment. In recent decades, the pervasive impact on individuals of discrimination because of their biological sex or sexual orientation, race or ethnicity, or age or disability (to cite a few examples) has belatedly attracted counselors' attention. A paradigm emphasizing the preeminent role of environmental factors can be represented as

$$B = f(E)$$

Behavior is a function of a person's environment.

It is apparent that this environment-focused paradigm is an essential addition to, rather than replacement for, the person-focused paradigm. Not all individuals exposed to identical environmental conditions respond to them the same way. Some resilient individuals manage to transcend daunting life circumstances, whereas others in privileged circumstances flounder throughout life. One individual might seem oblivious to blatant personal discrimination, while another might be alert to any hint of bias on the part of others. Individuals can also have an impact on their environments and on others who encounter them daily or from a distance, as illustrated by the scores of people who performed heroic acts during the 2001 terrorist attacks on the World Trade Center. Clearly, some synergy between personal and environmental influences must be recognized.

The third paradigm for human behavior represents this synergy:

$$B = f(P \times E)$$

Most simply, behavior is a function of persons interacting within their environments. This paradigm, first schematized by social psychologist Kurt Lewin (1936), is the basis of the ecological counseling perspective.

## Definition and Features of Ecological Counseling

As we indicated in the preface, *ecological counseling* is defined as contextualized help-giving that is dependent on the meaning clients derive from their environmental interactions, yielding an improved ecological concordance. Ecological counseling draws its defining principles from ecology within the physical world. The following description of human ecology is indebted to numerous sources (e.g., Capra, 1996; Heller, Price, Reinharz, Riger, & Wandersman, 1984; Kelly, 1966; Trickett, Barone, & Watts, 2000).

Human life cannot exist apart from a network of mutually defining and sustaining influences in the animate and inanimate world. All life processes depend on each other and together constitute the "web of life" (Capra, 1996). The Earth has evolved through increasingly intricate patterns of cooperation. Because of this weblike interdependence, natural resources are commonly recycled (e.g., as in photosynthesis) and shared. Human life similarly depends on associations, agreements, and collaboration.

Flexibility is crucial to maintaining complex living systems. The capacity to adapt to changing circumstances is so important that failure to do so can lead to serious dysfunction or extinction, as in the case of the dinosaurs or communism in the former Soviet Union. Resilience within an ecosystem requires both diversity and patterned relationships: In the natural world, if one species is threatened, another may take up its role and function, provided the ecosystem's pattern of complexity and relationship facilitates this. Human systems similarly benefit from support of complexity and relationship within a setting. As Capra (1996) wrote, the "wisdom of nature" has ensured sustainable life for its diverse creatures as they evolved over billions of years. Sustainable changes for humans similarly require a harmonious relationship with the context in which they will live.

Humans share these fundamental processes with other elements of the physical world's ecosystem. To understand the life cycle of both an oak tree and a human, we invoke species-specific and organismic characteristics, characteristics of the environment in which the particular living thing is rooted, and reciprocal interactions with other life forms. Adaptation and change for humans, however, are infinitely more complicated because of one important difference: humans are able to create and respond to their life contexts based on how they understand the world around them. Only humans live in communities structured around abstract ideas (e.g., freedom, justice) and are capable of engineering their own growth. Human ecology is, by its very nature, fundamentally oriented around meaning making.

This extended metaphor of human life as ecological in nature is at the heart of ecological counseling. Human beings are rooted in a physical environment and depend on others for nourishment and support. How each of us understands our place and our significance within this human web of life determines the manner in which we attempt to sustain our unique and communal lives. In the rest of this chapter, we elaborate on this metaphor by introducing principles and concepts linking it to the professional counseling process. The following chart organizes these principles in advance.

### Principles Underlying Ecological Counseling

| | |
|---|---|
| Interdisciplinary | Meaning making |
| Metatheoretical | Concordance |
| Integrated view of people | Full range of targets |
| Individuals in ecosystem | Parsimonious |
| Interactional | Collaborative |
| Considers multiple contexts | Empowering |
| Time is important | Interdependence |

## Ecological Counseling Is Interdisciplinary

The ecological perspective recognizes the value of diverse disciplines for understanding behavior. Several disciplines and professions have contributed to the emergence of the ecological perspective, with no one discipline owning it. For example, medical research has elucidated mind/body connections essential for explaining depression and biological manifestations of traumatic stress. Qualitative changes in thinking processes through maturation have been outlined by developmental psychologists. Multicultural and gender experts from numerous fields provide insight into the interaction between broad sociocultural stratification and development of personal identity. Environmental psychologists have demonstrated the multiple ways that physical environment properties, such as aesthetics, noise, and density, can influence behavior. All these disciplines—and others—help us to elaborate a truly comprehensive understanding of human behavior.

An ecological perspective is most closely related to person–environment (P-E) theory, which has been instrumental in the development of counseling and counseling psychology since the turn of the century (Herr, 2000; Martin & Swartz-Kulstad, 2000). At its heart, P-E theory is concerned with the fit of the person with his or her environment, as variously defined. The importance of P-E theory is perhaps most easily seen in career counseling with its explicit focus on understanding and enhancing the fit of an individual with the world of work (Dawis, 2000; Spokane, 1994). Other disciplines are also known for their elucidation of person–environment interactions, including social work, school psychology, and community psychology.

In recent years, references to human ecology and its implications for helping professions have become more common in the professional literature (e.g., Banning, 1989; Conoley & Haynes, 1992; Heller et al., 1984; Kelly, 1966; Lewis, Lewis, Daniels, & D'Andrea, 2003; Trickett et al., 2000). We share with these experts a focus on the interaction of persons within environments situated at multiple contextual levels. What we believe is unique to our ecological perspective, however, is integration of constructivist principles (see chapter 4). Humans not only react to the world around them, but they also create their realities through their meaning-making capacities. Environments by nature are ultimately subjective and objective, unique to each person as well as shared with others in similar situations. It is this combination of predictability and idiosyncrasy that makes the effort to understand human behavior so exhilarating and exasperating.

## Ecological Counseling Is Metatheoretical

The ecological perspective is metatheoretical in nature. A metatheoretical framework attempts to provide unifying constructs and processes that apply across diverse theories (cf. Prochaska & Norcross, 1994). It is recognized that individual theories attempt to explain a portion of the determinants and processes contributing to the totality of human behavior. Some theories are quite specific and focused, whereas others aim to explain behavior more comprehensively. Because human behavior is influenced by such a complex array of factors, ranging from biochemical processes to sociohistorical trends, at best a single theory can be valid for a minute portion of the total picture. A useful analogy is that of blind individuals trying to describe an elephant by touching one part of its anatomy. Unless they have encountered the idea of elephant before, they might be convinced that "elephantness" equals a rough hide, huge ears, or a mobile trunk. Their whole perspective would change if they understood that they have accurately described a fraction of the elephant's being. In a similar sense, counselors championing one particular theory need to remember that they might be doing a very good job of understanding a very small part of the dynamics shaping their clients' lives.

A metatheoretical perspective is an attempt to situate pieces of psychological truth into a broader picture. Subich and Taylor (1994) proposed that an integrative, coherent perspective may be valuable to explain vocational behavior. In contrast to Krumboltz's (1994) description of theories as separate maps to explain the same geography, Subich and Taylor suggested that (career) theories address different routes and/or destinations of the same terrain. The best route depends on what a person wishes to see, what resources he or she has to bring on the trip, where the trip began, what detours are present, and so on. In summary, they wrote

> different routes may be necessary to apprehend different people's vocational behavior and the obstacles they may encounter. . . . [W]hat we may need to develop is a systematic guide that informs us about what routes are available from particular points of origin to various destinations and what the advantages and disadvantages are of each. (p. 171)

To use Subich and Taylor's clever analogy, we need a metamap. The ecological perspective is basically a metamap. The issue for counselors is not necessarily what theory is correct, although the validity of each theory must be carefully evaluated in its own right. Depending on the destinations our clients are seeking to visit, their resources and detours, and the ruggedness of the terrain they must cross, certain routes are likely to be more straightforward, economical, or pain free than others. Counselors essentially serve as travel agents, helping clients plan convenient, successful, and hopefully enjoyable trips (Subich & Taylor, 1994). Good travel agents can play with alternatives based on their own professional expertise to meet the travel needs of a diverse clientele.

The ecological perspective is intended to help counselors serve as travel agents for diverse clients with diverse destinations. Within the ecological perspective, counselors are reminded that no two clients' life journeys are the same; no one destination is necessarily the only one to be pursued; and the same endpoint can be reached by adopting different strategies. The ecological perspective operating as metatheory is meant to help counselors conceptualize the diverse possibilities and, with their clients, plan interventions that will help clients reach their own goals with the resources they can command. One client may need to learn new ways of behaving; another with the same presenting problem may need to change jobs or file for divorce. The challenge for counselors is to organize the possibilities in a way that sparks creative interventions tailored to the unique confluence of factors presented in a problem situation.

## In Ecological Counseling, Individuals Are Integrated Beings

In everyday life, we are accustomed to thinking of individuals as a collection of parts: body–mind–psyche–spirit, or some subset of these parts. Wellness consists of paying attention to all these domains, so that we experience a balance, or are optimized (cf. Myers, Sweeney, & Witmer, 2000). We have all known individuals who seem to complete a mental checklist for their health: take vitamins and work out daily for the body, see a counselor when a psychic tuneup is in order, watch public television to keep the mind limber, and meditate for the good of the soul.

The counselor's version of this mental checklist is thinking-feeling-behavior (or cognition–emotion–conation). We want to be sure to address each domain that is involved in a presenting problem and worry that we are overemphasizing one domain at the cost of a client's ultimate well-being. We might choose a particular counseling approach based on which aspect the theory seems to favor, a focus that often resonates with the kind of individual we see ourselves to be: practical, emotional, mystical, and so on.

In ecological counseling, such distinctions are an illusion. Individuals operate as integrated beings. Depression can be the expression of a disordered metabolism, spiritual crisis, or troubled relationship—or all three simultaneously. Meditation enhances the body's physiological response to stress. Spiritual development can incidentally be accompanied by healing of a chronic health condition, or improvement in one's behavior on the job. Rather than be surprised when such complementary changes occur, we should expect them as common course for humans. Definitive causes for most complex behaviors will likely never be found, if indeed, such singular causes actually exist.

Ecological counselors recognize that there may be good reason to focus on one or more dimensions in a given counseling relationship. For example, an anxious child may benefit from behavioral lessons in how to make friends, or a recent widower from discussions with a member of the clergy. However, ecological counselors should also remember that there is no one single right intervention for a given client; they should consider multiple possibilities for enhancing the functioning of the complex organisms that are their clients.

## In Ecological Counseling, Individuals Are Part of an Ecosystem

As described earlier, the metaphor inspiring ecological counseling is ecology of the natural world. Humans are a part of a constantly changing dynamic with other living and nonliving things. The oxygen produced by trees is essential to human life; small temperature rises in the Earth's overall climate has repercussions throughout the planet; introduction or eradication of a species of tiny insect can influence the entire food chain.

A term commonly found in ecological discussion is *ecosystem*. We define ecosystem as the sum total of interacting influences operating in a person's life, including such diverse factors as his or her biological makeup, interpersonal relationships, the physical environment, and the broader sociocultural context. Such influences can be *proximal* (close by or direct) or *distal* (distant or less direct), and important or inconsequential. For example, the weather in an individual's home region and in a region producing a favorite food are a part of the individual's ecosystem.

From the broadest ecological point of view, literally everything is part of everyone's ecosystem. Fortunately, counselors working within an ecological perspective do not have to account for every nuance at every contextual level in order to be effective counselors. Because human behavior is determined by myriad interconnected factors, an exhaustive analysis is both impossible and unnecessary. Counselors can focus on

11

how specific contextual interactions are played out within the daily life of an individual or targeted group. That is, rather than asking about all of the conceivable contributing factors, counselors attempt to discern the most important and generally proximal ones that are potentially amenable to modification. Phrased in terms of statistics, what variables account for the greatest portion of the variance in the targeted problem?

Although counselors are typically concerned with a person's unique life, it is worth remembering that this life is situated within a broader ecosystem with features that may or may not seem relevant to the person, but probably do have some impact, however indirect. For example, a war on the other side of the world may have great or little salience to people depending on their political interests or whether they know anyone fighting in the war. Either way, the war may have some impact on their personal lives through how foreign policies influence the national economy or attention given to domestic affairs. We might ask whether and how a person feels connected to the broader environment, and whether less direct or distal events might help us understand the events of the person's own life now. A person can do little to change the course of distal events, but does have an ability to determine how he or she can understand and eventually respond to such events.

## Ecological Counseling Is Interactional

The importance of dynamic, interactional, and reciprocal processes in explaining behavior is emphasized within the ecological perspective. Rarely is behavior unidirectional, with a certain factor causing a change in a person without that person's response having an impact in return. Conversely, seldom will a person's behavior cause or influence an environment to change without the person, in turn, being affected.

People and environments are in a dynamic state of mutual interdependence. Return for a moment to the case of Jamie, introduced at the beginning of this chapter. She is both an actor in her bus environment and is acted upon in that environment. Jamie roams the bus aisle at times as she attempts to connect with others while the bus driver, recognizing the need to enforce safe riding conditions, responds with warnings for her to be seated. Jamie and the bus driver are not the only individuals affected directly in this interplay. Others impacted include fellow bus riders, Jamie's parents, and the school's assistant principal. In addition, concern for how Jamie is doing in the bus environment is not restricted to that particular environment. Rather, this concern extends to the home, other school situations, the assistant principal's office, and so on. How school personnel react to her parents' interventions (and vice versa) will influence how the situation is eventually resolved. The ongoing interactions between people and environments represent a critically important nexus for understanding and intervening in problem situations.

We have come to see humans in terms of a process rather than a collection of innate characteristics alone: each human being can be thought of as a person interacting with his or her environment, or $P \times E$. With few exceptions, all human behavior is evoked, acted upon, and/or shapes the environment in multiple ways. Our previous experiences influence the likelihood of doing something similar in the future; others respond to us on a moment-by-moment basis; we have imaginary conversations with absent significant others when we are trying to make important decisions. Whenever we look at an individual, we see a being whose history, presence, and possibilities could not exist separately from the moment-to-moment transactions with the world in which he or she is encompassed. The nature and consequences of this interpenetrating $P \times E$ unit is the central concern of ecological counseling.

The interactional emphasis in ecological counseling encourages counselors to remember that there are multiple ways to portray individuals vis-à-vis their environments. Western psychology is typically based on a view of humans as independent creatures, separate from others and with clear boundaries between self and the world around them. Numerous experts (e.g., Helms & Cook, 1999; Jordan, Kaplan, Miller, Stiver, & Surrey, 1991; Markus & Kitayama, 1991) have argued that this view of human nature does not represent the felt experience of many individuals, who conceive of themselves as primarily beings within relationships with others. In other words, what is widely acknowledged in psychology as a blueprint for healthy human functioning—the autonomous, bounded self—is only one among many possibilities for representing the nature of the individual (see Herr, 2000).

The ecological view of an individual as representing a $P \times E$ unit permits multiple speculations on the nature and importance of this person–environment interaction in determining the course of human life. Some cultures see the individual as interdependent, less than human when taken out of the cultural context defining and sustaining him or her. Others see individuals as primarily separate from others, needing others for support and important resources but whose essence as a human being is well differentiated from them. Individuals sharing a cultural context also differ from one another in how they have internalized these templates for the self through their own meaning-making processes. The nature of these processes will be discussed shortly.

13

## Ecological Counseling Considers Multiple Contexts

People interact with environments that are anchored in time and place. That is, there is a context surrounding behavior. In turn, time and place combine to yield unique contexts within which people live out their lives.

The following is a particular example. When in San Francisco, I (Bob Conyne) always make it a point to go to Glide Memorial Church, located in the city's tough Tenderloin area. It is a remarkable place, like no other church I have ever attended. There are no hymnals, no reading books, no bulletins. It is very free form. One encounters a general hubbub of activity and noisy conversation when entering the sanctuary before the service. There is laughter, hugging, movement. The place is packed, with many people sitting on folding chairs and others filling the aisles. Participants appear wildly diverse, ranging from street people to those very well off from Sausalito or across the Bay, taking in all colors and hues of skin and clothing. It is joyous, full of action, with fantastic singing and expression of emotions. And the themes of the service revolve around celebration and social justice.

Glide is a unique religious context, entirely different from my usual church experience, which is quiet, stately, worshipful, and formalized. Both of these afford contexts for spiritual and religious participation, yet in wholly unique ways.

The process of living out lives occurs in real time and in real places, in contexts such as Glide. In addition, contexts include virtual, imagined, and symbolic realities that can be just as real for people. Consider, for instance, conversing with a deceased parent, visualizing the solitude of a favorite restorative refuge, or communicating via e-mail with a person on the other side of the world. Each of these contexts can play an important role in a person's life.

Therefore, it is necessary for counselors to understand the salient contexts of clients' lives. When, for example, the client is discussing his or her experience in church, the counselor needs to understand what that particular church context is like: formal or informal, active or quiet, emotional or contemplative, and so on. These contextual uniquenesses matter. Also, when a client discloses to his counselor that he is depressed, it is important for an ecological counselor to understand the conditions surrounding his depressed state—that is, to become informed about the real time-and-place issues that may contribute to his depression, as well as the intrapersonal matters that may be influential. Clients are viewed within the relevant contexts of their lives, not in isolation. In addition, this understanding suggests that a full range of client systems might serve as appropriate targets for ecological counseling, including groups, organizations, and broader social systems.

Perhaps the most influential conceptual contribution to understanding various human contexts was provided by Urie Bronfenbrenner (1979), with creative adaptations offered by several authors (e.g., Kasambira & Edwards, 2000; Maton, 2000). Note that this model is referenced by other authors in this book, demonstrating the model's generally accepted importance.

Implicit in Bronfenbrenner's human ecology model is the concept that contexts, which he referred to as systems, could be both proximal to (near) and distal from (far away) a person. Thus, four successively broader levels of contextual systems are posited by Bronfenbrenner to exist in relationship to an individual or individuals. Figure 1.1 presents an illustration of the model (adapted from Kassambira & Edwards, 2000) focused in relation to a child–parent situation.

## Figure 1.1
## Bronfenbrenner's Levels

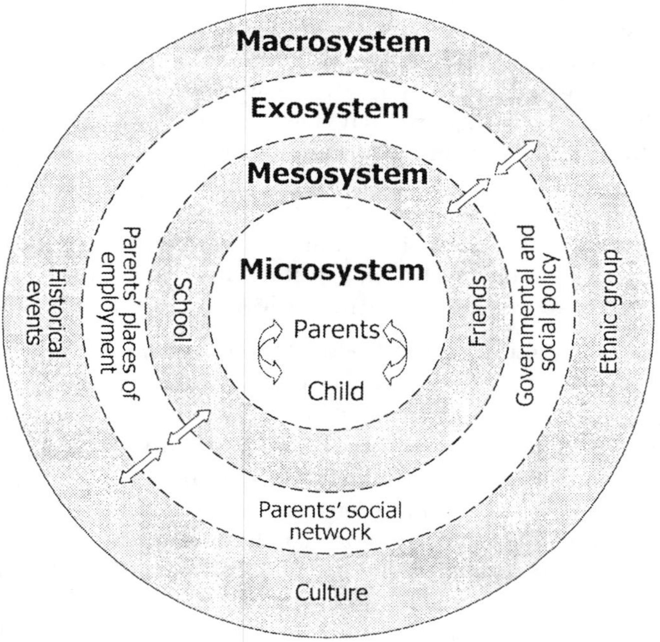

*Note.* Adapted From Kassambira & Edwards, 2000

The levels generally can be described as follows:

- *Microsystem:* Contexts or settings in which a person or persons have primary face-to-face contact with influential others, such as family, workplace, peer group, or school. By definition, microsystems are proximal influences.
- *Mesosystem:* Relationships and connections existing between microsystems, or the ways in which situations interrelate. Examples include connections between home and school, workplace and family, or peer group and parents.
- *Exosystem:* Larger systems within which a person does not directly participate but in which important decisions and actions emerge that affect the person. Bronfenbrenner (1977) noted that the exosystem encompasses major social institutions that operate at a local level, including the world of work, local government, health care system, and mass media. This level refers to distal influences.
- *Macrosystem:* The most pervasive system containing blueprints for defining and organizing social and institutional life in a society, including general values, political and social policy, and ideology. Bronfenbrenner (1979) emphasized that whereas the other three levels of systems refer to specific contexts affecting a person's life, the macrosystem determines the nature of these concrete contexts either explicitly (e.g., written laws, policies), or more often informally and implicitly in the form of ideologies influencing everyday customs and practices (op.cit., see p. 515). Macrosystem-based ideas about what is a successful life, a dutiful parent, a good American, a masculine man, or feminine woman can influence behavior at every systemic level. Although these influences are abstract and global in nature, they permeate every other level.

Bronfenbrenner (1992) emphasized that interactions of an individual within the immediate external environment, such as within a person's home or school, have the greatest direct impact on subsequent personal development. However, other systems are also important to consider. Bronfenbrenner argued that systems should be thought of as "nested," or situated within the broader systems. For example, families are nested within extended kinship networks, neighborhoods, and cities, all affected by the national economy and political system, and all levels further shaped by macrosystemic blueprints for behavior. In his words, "the power of developmental forces operating at any one systems level of the environment depends on the nature of the environmental structures at the same and at all higher systems levels" (p. 11). Thus, to fully under-

16

stand an individual's life, it is essential but not enough to analyze the nature of his or her intimate relationships, work, friendships. How these everyday dynamics are shaped by less direct systems is important to think about as well.

Kasambira and Edwards (2000) and Maton (2000) have proposed adding an outer ring to the model, referred to as world (Maton) or globalsystem (Kasambira & Edwards). The September 11 terrorist attacks exemplify how global politics reverberate throughout, intersecting private lives and public policies. Countless persons grieved the horrific deaths and suffered psychic scarring from witnessing the events of September 11. Jobs were lost and businesses wiped out in shock waves throughout the economy; airport security was transformed; heroes were raised up and new enemies named; illusions of safety were destroyed. The lives of millions of Americans were changed as a result of political movements rooted half a world away. In a very real way, the American context has been forever altered due to these attacks and their aftermath.

Bronfenbrenner's work continues to be extremely influential in psychological theory and research dedicated to unraveling complex person–environment interactions. Bronfenbrenner is not a human services practitioner, however, and has not been primarily concerned with applications to professional practice. In our ecological counseling model, we find the following terminology to be useful, as well.

Bronfenbrenner's terminology for systems refers to the interconnected nature of settings where human behavior takes place. For example, microsystems are settings where face-to-face interactions occur. Counselors are more apt to be interested in the nature of the human activity itself, at progressive levels of abstraction ranging from the individual to complex, impersonal social institutions—and in ways change can be fostered at each level.

The most salient person–environment interactions are addressed by the terms *ecological niche*, *life pattern*, and *life space*. In our model, ecological niche (adapted from Willi, 1999) refers to the portion of the ecosystem regularly influential in an individual's daily life, including both animate and inanimate objects. In its broadest sense, all aspects of the ecosystem influence an individual's life, but the ecological niche refers to more proximal influences (e.g., weather in the home region, people the individual sees regularly, physical features of his or her home). An ecological niche can be described by the person inhabiting it and observed by an outsider tracking a person throughout daily life. The concept of ecological niche answers the question, "Where does the person live?"

The concept of life pattern recognizes that much of a person's life is organized according to his or her own meaning-making processes. Human behavior tends to be purposive, and the need to derive or maintain meaning is especially motivating. All humans regularly make choices reflective of how they understand a certain situation, and to be consistent with certain preferences and values. Life pattern refers to salient, recurrent meanings generally expressed over time and across situations. These meanings can be global determinants of a person's life over time, such as a religious belief system prescribing a multitude of behavioral choices, or more subtle ones implicit in many minor, everyday choices. The life pattern describes the why of a person's life: Why does the person spend more time at the office than at home, or vice versa? Why does the person prefer shopping at locally owned stores rather than national chains?

Generally speaking, the ecological niche paints an objective view of the person's life at a point of time, and the life pattern relates to the subjective or phenomenological reality implicit in a person's daily life. It is often possible to detect elements of the life pattern in portions of the ecological niche. That is, a person might use a distant parking lot at work to get exercise, or to avoid socially discomfiting interactions with coworkers. There is not always an obvious correspondence, however, between the ecological niche and life pattern. Elements of the life pattern might be outside the person's awareness, as in the case of a person not recognizing how her extreme social anxiety determines much of her daily behavior. Elements of the ecological niche might not be particularly expressive about a person either, as when a person takes a certain bus because no other bus lines are available.

Counselors cannot work with the total ecosystem, but they do regularly address both the ecological niche and life pattern. The ecological niche describes how a person is situated within various contexts: Where does she go each day? What does he do? What other persons are part of the life context for this person? The life pattern describes what these elements mean from the person's perspective: What choices bring pleasure, dissatisfaction, or a sense of connection or alienation to the person? What broader cultural values, family rules, or past life lessons are reflected? Life events may be random—whether your house is in the path of a hurricane or not, for example—but significant events never remain outside the person's meaning-making processes. If a person cannot explain a certain event within familiar patterns of meaning, he or she will struggle to find new ways to make sense of the event and the impact it has had on his or her life.

Life space refers to the combination of life pattern and ecological niche. In the ecological perspective, a person's life can be adequately defined only when both the objective and the subjective elements are considered. Life space describes both what an external observer might describe about a life (e.g., settings, family members, tasks, group affiliations), elements not obvious to others (e.g., a rich fantasy life), and the meanings invested in them by the person (e.g., family life seen as nourishing or noxious; a seemingly superficial relationship taking little daily time but treasured by the person). The nature of a person's life space as elaborated over time is the life course. The sum total of the contexts we occupy and the meanings we express throughout them are progressively modified over time until, at the end, a unified life narrative is completed. Ecological counselors recognize that time is an essential element in understanding how this process unfolds.

## Ecological Counseling Recognizes the Importance of Time

In ecological counseling, the importance of time is recognized in two ways: (a) in situating clients within a given context, and (b) in conceptualizing change efforts.

Time is an essential although invisible part of our life context. Bronfenbrenner (1992) used the term *chronosystem* to capture the interconnected nature of persons, environment, and proximal processes over time. All of us are influenced by the state of the world around us when we grew up—compare the Great Depression survivors with baby boomers, for example. Discrete events throughout life can decisively shape our experiences. The events of September 11, 2001, demarcated a rapid shift in the political and social context. People reported feeling differently before and after this date. Many personal life events have this benchmark quality for individuals.

When an event occurs for someone may also be important to consider, as Elder's (1995) research on the Great Depression indicates. Both authors of this chapter had children when we were approaching midlife. This certainly influenced our individual career development in early adulthood, and our weekends at present are very different from those of other baby boomers who are now grandparents! In ecological counseling, we remain aware that it is important when something happens within a person's lifetime.

How change efforts in counseling are conceptualized in terms of time is also important in ecological counseling. The ecology of a person's life is ever changing. When we meet a client for counseling, we need to remember that we are viewing a freeze-frame of his or her life. Although the continuity inherent in a person's life often becomes a focus in counseling, counselors keep in mind that things continue to change as well. Our change efforts may be thought of as throwing a rock—or a lifeline?—into the ongoing stream of a client's life. The intervention will have ripple effects that we cannot see. What came before in a client's life, and what is yet to come, interacts with the counseling process at this moment. Sometimes change efforts are focused on the past (remedial) or set the stage for continued development into the future (developmental or preventive). Counselors can be pleased at the eventual impact of a subtle intervention, or dismayed at how little difference it makes in the future. To use Subich and Taylor's (1994) earlier analogy, we counselors/travel agents simply do our best to get clients to their desired destinations eventually, with a minimum of foreseeable travel glitches, and at a cost they can afford.

## Ecological Counseling Is Concerned With Meaning

Every person's life is composed of certain unique personal characteristics he or she brings to every life event; interpersonal relationships central to defining his or her ecological niche; groups and organizations at different levels of complexity of which he or she is a part; and abstract ideals, values, and ways of representing the world that are transformed by meaning-making processes at every level of system. In ecological counseling, what occurs when people interact with their environment, at whatever level, is subject to the meaning they derive from the ongoing encounter.

Human life as we know it is impossible without meaning making. In the words of Heller et al. (1984), "The environment is not perceived directly; rather, psychological processes involved in perception affect the way that individuals interpret and then act on environmental information" (p.138). Through meaning-making processes, persons define and understand what happens in their lives. Hayes and Oppenheim (1997) noted that "[h]uman development represents the course of our attempts to make sense of those changes going on around us—to understand what it means 'to be me in a world like mine at a time like this'" (p. 23).

Whether we see ourselves as primarily autonomous and goal directed, in contrast to social creatures whose well-being is inextricably connected with others, depends on our meaning making. In particular, who and what we define as part of our immediate, self-defining life circumstances—our ecological niche—is a direct reflection of meaning making. The nature of our meaning making, however, is often not apparent to others. A religious mystic may include dead persons or strangers as part of the community of saints with whom she communes regularly. A role not yet assumed by a person (e.g., future parent or corporate leader) may have very real importance in how he or she thinks about him- or herself today. A pet or an inanimate object, such as a piano, may seem intimate to one person and merely a thing to another.

The most familiar form of meaning making is language. Language serves as a symbol system representing how we understand the world (Hayes & Oppenheim, 1997, p. 25). All communication is based on a set of symbols (letters and words) implicitly agreed upon and passed down from generation to generation. Each word is a meaning unit in that a specific pattern of sounds, lines, or dots (as in Braille) is attached to sensory input that our brain learns to identify in a particular way. These meaning units form the building blocks for more complex thinking processes involving constructs: hypotheses that serve to organize and systematize events and experiences that occur, as well as the environmental context itself (Ivey, D'Andrea, Ivey, & Simek-Morgan, 2002).

Certain words can carry individualized meanings not apparent to others. For example, I (Ellen Cook) have called my daughters "bunnies" since infancy, occasionally causing confusion ("You mean you have pet rabbits attending the elementary school?"). Adolescents also delight in inventing new words or definitions for familiar words to confound their parents and create a sense of solidarity among themselves. An amusing example of how adolescent words can confound adults was provided in the recent movie *The Princess Diaries*. Upon hearing a surprising piece of news, a teenage girl exclaims, "shut up!" (meaning "you must be kidding!") to her exquisitely well-mannered grandmother. Since this was not real life, a trusted associate was, of course, available to mollify the shocked grandmother with a timely translation!

Another familiar type of meaning making is evaluative, where a person attaches an evaluative label or quality to a thing or event. As Kelly (1955) pointed out years ago, these qualities are often bipolar in nature: good/bad, loving/rejecting. Most people agree that a car accident is a bad thing, but it can also be good to the owner if no one is hurt and it disposes of a car that has been a real lemon. These evaluations can play a central role in counseling as well. Counselors working with survivors of domestic violence are all too aware that targets may interpret a partner's jealousy and suspicions as a sign of love. Meaning making of the survivors becomes a central counseling theme: What is a loving relationship? What do you deserve from others?

The naming and evaluative levels of meaning making fall into what Reker and Chamberlain (2000) identified as *implicit meaning*. In

21

implicit meaning, people are engaged in attaching understanding and personal significance to the experiences, objects, and events of daily life. That is, they try to make sense of their ongoing experience by asking what particular significance inheres in the experience itself. Does the presence of gray clouds in the sky suggest a storm is brewing? How do I make sense of the e-mail message I (Bob) received from my daughter early her freshman year in college saying, "Well, I don't know how it's all going here, we'll talk when I get home for break next week"? Is this an SOS or an offhand way of telling parents that life is basically okay?

In the most complex type of meaning making—reflexive meaning making—one looks at oneself and life in general and interprets what it means in broader terms: Do I deserve fair treatment from my family? Am I at a dead end in my life? Is life ultimately good, or as Shakespeare penned in *Macbeth*, "a tale told by an idiot, full of sound and fury, signifying nothing"? The meaning making occurring at this most abstract level can be extraordinarily complex and subtle, often implicit rather than conscious. This meaning making can have a profound impact on the shape and quality of a person's life over time. In explaining the importance of this meaning making to life satisfaction, Gordon and Efran (1997) asserted that "circumstances alone do not constitute problems, but they become problems when they appear to violate an individual's personal theory about how life should be lived" (p. 104).

Reflexive meaning making incorporates Reker and Chamberlin's (2000) discussion of existential meaning. People strive to understand how life events fit into life itself, so that issues of coherence, philosophy, and life mission are invoked. In a sense, the significance of each event is tied to broader life meanings: Who am I and where am I headed with my life? What have I accomplished over my career? What kind of intimate partner or friend am I? When I die, how might I be remembered? Am I living my life consistent with what I profess as my values? Reflexive meaning making also goes beyond the sense of Reker and Chamberlin's discussion of existential meaning, to incorporate a host of meanings attached to a person's everyday experience of self in the world (e.g., "who I am as a man/gay person/American").

How people create meaning from their life experiences is the fundamental concern of constructivism (e.g., Gergen, 1991; McAuliffe & Eriksen, 1999; Neimeyer, 1993; Sexton & Griffin, 1997; White & Epston, 1991; see also chapter 4). Existential theorists such as Frankl (1963), Maslow (1962), and Yalom (1980) also pondered the meaning of life itself within the tradition of psychotherapy. For instance, Frankl's classic book, *Man's Search for Meaning*, poignantly demonstrated how people can create a will to live in the most deplorable conditions, if they can find a "why" to live. Maslow was concerned with how humans can reach their highest potential, suggesting that existential meaning and healthy functioning were intertwined. Yalom was interested in how humans choose and create existential meaning as well as meaning that is implicitly derived from their life situations. His research on encounter groups, with colleagues Matthew Miles and Mort Lieberman, demonstrated the salience of how group leaders can help group members develop implicit meaning by translating group events and experiences into cognitive understanding that can be applied in external situations (Lieberman, Yalom, & Miles, 1973).

Thus, ecological counseling should be viewed as a contextualized, interactional, and existential endeavor. In the Lewinian formula of $B = f(P \times E)$, the dynamic $\times$ refers to both the interaction of people and environment, and to the translation of interactive experience into meaning. This meaning expresses the cognitive processing of past and present experience, and the creation of new experiences based on this framework of idiosyncratic and shared understandings.

The next principles refer more explicitly to application of ecological principles to counseling practice.

## Ecological Counseling Seeks Concordance

A key issue in ecological counseling is how well a person is able to thrive within the context of his or her life. A biologist can easily enumerate what is required for a certain species of tree to grow to full stature. Beyond a few biological givens, the answer is infinitely more complex for humans because of our adaptability and our meaning-making capacities. In ecological counseling, the central tenet revolves around the concept of a balanced, harmonious system, or what we label ecological concordance.

At the heart of P-E theory is the notion of fit between a person and the environment, and the goal of optimizing fit appears in discussions of ecological interventions (e.g., Conoley & Haynes, 1992). This notion is intuitively appealing. Each of us can probably describe a situation where we felt we did not fit within a given context—a feeling that has been romanticized in popular movies such as *Rebel Without a Cause* and *Crocodile Dundee*. The goal of fit may be appropriate in referencing fairly stable and specific features of the person–environment interaction, such as correspondence between a person's educational background and the content mastery needed for good job performance. When referring to more volatile, less objective targets such as family functioning or happiness, the concept of fit seems less satisfactory.

In ecological counseling, ecological concordance is a dynamic term referring to concepts of balance, synergy, and improvisation (see the chart). Ecological concordance implies a constantly recalibrated balancing of elements central to the person–environment interaction. The environmental context provides the nutrients essential to human survival—notable examples include food and shelter or safety and love—while catalyzing change and growth crucial to long-term development.

Human systems require a combination of challenge and support from those participating in the interaction. Too much challenge and too little support can overwhelm participants' resources; support without challenge stagnates growth. Instead, what exists—at least for the moment in a dynamic system—is a harmonious balance between challenge and support (see Blocher & Biggs, 1983). To use an analogy, ecological concordance does not imply the perfect fit between person and environment as might be sought for a dress glove. Rather, concordance is a state allowing for and encouraging growth while taking advantage of strengths and supports—an "optimal misfit." The ideal is closer to fitting a mitten on a child so that it provides warmth and protection now, while allowing for the child's hand to grow over the next year or two.

Ecological concordance also incorporates the idea in terms of synergy. Synergy generally refers to combined or connected action between related elements—or, colloquially speaking, things working together smoothly. Within an ecological framework, synergy exists when elements of an ecosystem work smoothly to sustain and enhance the connected life they share.

Further, ecological concordance includes the idea of improvisation. Concordance is approximately achieved and can flow dynamically. In a sense, people are always innovating, anticipating, and responding dynamically to changing inner and outer worlds. It is, in a sense, a dance of nature where each partner subtly shifts to accommodate the other, or the riffing of jazz musicians as they improvise entirely new sounds within a standard piece.

Ecological concordance thus refers to a mutually beneficial interaction between person and environment. No environment is perfect for an

**Ecological Concordance**

- *Goal:* An optimal misfit between people and environment
- *Qualities:*
  Balance
  Synergy
  Improvisation

individual or group. Individuals (or groups) can thrive only within the context of environments that, by necessity, contain elements both crucial and inimical to their own present level of functioning. Resources available to the person within the interaction must be adequate to meet the challenge to change. In turn, individuals help to constitute the environments of others. As in any ecosystem in the physical world, healthy development of any single organism requires interdependence. When necessary, counselors can help clients redefine, modify, or replace aspects of their own ecosystem—including personal characteristics—to maximize their ability to live happily and productively.

## Ecological Counseling Uses a Full Range of Intervention Targets

Embracing the concept of client systems allows for development of a full range of intervention targets that is consistent with the Counselor Functioning Cube developed by Morrill, Oetting, and Hurst (1974). This range of intervention targets includes (a) individual persons, including dyads; (b) primary face-to-face groups, such as families and counseling groups; (c) associational groups, such as clubs and organizations; (d) institutions, inclusive of several associational groups; and (e) community, comprised of multiple individual, primary, associational, and institutional levels. Examples of counseling interventions that an ecological counselor might deliver include

- *individual target intervention:* individual counseling, individual psychotherapy;
- *primary group target intervention:* counseling groups, psychoeducational groups, psychotherapy groups, family counseling;
- *associational group target intervention:* task groups, organizational consultation, program development and evaluation, training and development, strategic planning; and
- *institutional target intervention:* community development, social advocacy, primary prevention, system change.

Meaning-making processes can be targeted at any level. For example, an HIV-positive person can consider what constitutes a meaningful career when his or her long-term health is compromised. A family might explore how to maintain its ethnic identity after emigration to a very different culture. A business might work on a mission statement to clarify implicit values held by the organization. An activist organization can plan how to change macrosystem-based portrayals of people with disabilities on television.

It is important to emphasize that all counselors can deliver interventions that are targeted across the levels. Ecological counseling practice is especially well suited to such a broad application because of its comprehensive, holistic, and systemic characteristics. When a certain aspect of a person–environment interaction is targeted for change, neither a client nor the environment is automatically blamed for the problematic $P \times E$ interaction. Instead, the entire ecosystem is implicated, subject to additional ecological assessment.

## Ecological Counseling Implements Parsimonious Interventions

Some ecological counseling interventions are developed consistent with the principle of parsimony. That is, the smallest changes are attempted that might hold the greatest likelihood of success (Conoley & Haynes, 1992). Sources and techniques for change come, whenever possible, from within the existing ecological situation. New and often costly approaches are resisted, if possible, to take advantage of existing resources. Taking this approach of parsimony can improve implementation success in two ways: (a) what is used is familiar to the people involved, recognizes the value of local resources, and does not involve the introduction of novel or complex ideas and practices from the outside; and (b) such interventions usually are cost-effective.

A brief example follows. A counseling group is meeting and seems to be going nowhere but downhill. Maybe the members of the group are contributing to this decline. The leader may be distracted or overwhelmed. Some members may be acting out severely. But it also might be that causal factors rest within the environment.

In this case, the group is unable to progress because of boundary problems. The sessions themselves occur in a nonsecure room usually used as a nurse's station, where staff and patients are accustomed to just walking in. And that is what frequently happens, which upsets group activities and violates confidentiality. Regrettably, no understandings or procedures have been instituted to keep the room private during group time.

Discussion with the group counselor's supervisor involved a review of the group experience, focusing on the ecology of the setting in which the group was being held. This discussion led to making a change in procedures to keep the room private for the 2-hour meeting, which was done by communicating at a staff meeting and placing a sign on the door: "Private: Counseling Group in Progress." Following this change, the group's functioning began to improve.

All experienced counselors probably treasure a memory of a certain client interview where a simple statement appeared to make an enormous difference to a client. The director of the counseling center where I (Ellen) conducted my doctoral internship called this phenomenon cure at intake. Experienced counselors also know that some interventions seem to fall short but plant a seed of change that will bear fruit later. For example, supporting a client's involvement in a warm, vibrant church congregation can eventually establish enduring social relationships, raise self-esteem, help the client resolve issues related to a toxic religious upbringing, and provide a safe place to develop self-assertion and leadership skills that are also valuable in the client's job. The challenge lies in determining possibilities for change; this is where counselor–client collaboration is particularly crucial.

## Ecological Counseling Is Collaborative

The question of who determines efforts directed at client system change is important. In fact, it rises to the level of an ethical imperative. Processes of ecological counseling are intended to be horizontal and not vertical, shared and not imposed, two-way and not one-way. The ecological counselor and the client system members both possess unique competencies and sets of experiences that can contribute positively to forward movement. Both parties are considered experts in this ongoing process. For example, the ecological counselor brings conceptual knowledge, ethical principles, best practices, and intervention competencies to the endeavor, whereas members of the client system bring experiential knowledge and skills. Both realms of expertise need to be tapped in the collaboration.

Community psychologists, a group recognized for their ecological sensitivity, were once asked on an electronic mailing list, "How many community psychologists does it take to replace a light bulb?" (Society for Community Research and Action, 1999). Among the answers were the following:

- "Ecologically speaking, this question raises serious issues that must be considered BEFORE replacing the bulb. First, who determined that the bulb needs replacing? Based on whose values, whose needs, and what criteria were used?"
- "None; we empower them to change themselves."
- "A community psychologist would never replace a light bulb. Rather, he/she would work collaboratively with the bulb to strengthen its damaged filaments."

It is clear that in the eyes of these responders, ecological interventions are produced collaboratively, with the client or client group retaining responsibility for the direction and initiation of change.

Many issues abound as they relate to collaborative decision making in any particular ecological counseling situation. Following are just a few of them in an individual counseling setting, where the client describes himself as failing in college. The presenting problem here might revolve around the client attaining failing grades accompanied by feeling tremendous anxiety and pressure. What sources of the problem might be located in the college environment (e.g., are the courses appropriate for him or her)? What sources might be found within the person (e.g., how well does he or she like his or her teachers and student peers)? What sources might be found in the interaction between the client and the environment (e.g., what is his or her pattern of class attendance)? And what sources might be found in the meaning he or she draws from his or her experience in school (e.g., how important is it for him or her to do well at school)? Also, what would represent a feasible solution in this situation?

The role of the counselor in this process needs to hew closely to the ethic of collaboration: working together as coequals to reach mutually desired ends. The ecological counselor helps the client explore the ecological interactions involved in his or her problem and helps identify parsimonious change strategies emerging from these identified interactions that address realistic goals that both the client and his or her environment can support.

## Ecological Counseling Seeks Empowerment of Clients and Systems

Ecological counseling draws from the principles discussed so far in order to empower client people and systems (Conyne, 1987). Principles of collaboration, contextualizing problems, developing meaning, and others are conducted in the service of assisting members of client systems to become more empowered. From an ecological counseling perspective, empowerment means developing an increased capacity for both personal and environmental competence (Steele, 1973). People are empowered when they have become successful in creating environments that allow personal growth. A supportive environment with adequate range and accessibility of resources is important. Worell (2001) described a "healthy (person) within a healthy environment" as "competent, strong and confident, connected to a supportive community, and resilient" (p. 340). In a very real way, improved $P \times E$ interaction competencies result from ecological counseling. These P × E competencies permit the alleviation of current distress while contributing to the prevention of future problems.

How can this occur? Members of client systems who have experienced successful ecological counseling can assess themselves in relation to their life contexts more accurately. They can become more aware of how they appraise their interactions with others and within the major settings of their lives, and become better at converting meaning into action. They can recognize possibilities for change and can better use available resources in their environment. In short, they can become more competent at perceiving, drawing meaning from, and managing their life situations in ways that are productive, satisfying, and contributory.

It is important to emphasize that ecological counseling does not aim to make all persons conform better in their environment. It is certainly true that some clients, such as adolescents adjudicated as delinquent, might benefit from learning how to fit better in their environments, at least in some respects. Many other clients, however, might need to recognize their current environments as toxic, and develop strategies for either leaving or changing these environments, as in the case of domestic violence victims. Units within a broader organization might need consultation on how to reduce sexual harassment throughout the company, for example, or individuals might come to see their efforts to counter injustice one person at a time as meaningful if not always overtly successful. All these possibilities can be empowering, and ultimately life affirming.

## Ecological Counseling Is Interdependent

Running throughout ecological counseling is the principle of interdependence (see, for example, Trickett, Kelley, & Todd, 1972). One of the central tenets in all discussions of ecology is the interconnectedness or interdependence of systems, that "everything is connected to everything else" (Commoner, 1968). Because of this concept, a change in any one part of a system will ultimately affect other parts of that system and may also extend to other systems. We presently have a project introducing problem-based learning within several classrooms in another college at the University of Cincinnati. This new group-based strategy demands a number of accommodations that were anticipated (e.g., training faculty in necessary group skills) and some that were not (e.g., including discussion of this innovation in course syllabi). The ecological counselor needs to think and act interdependently, because that is the way life functions.

## A Way to View Ecological Counseling

In Figure 1.2 (modified from a figure of Kasambira & Edwards, 2000), we have sought to capture concisely the foregoing discussion of concepts that are important for ecological counseling. As the contents of this figure suggest, a person functions over time within a larger ecosystem. Ecological counseling can occur at any of four levels, as the person interacts within and across them. The counselor works collaboratively with the client to evolve meaning from these interactions, which then can lead to improved ecological concordance.

## Figure 1.2
## A View of Ecological Counseling

**Meaning ⟹ Ecological Concordance**

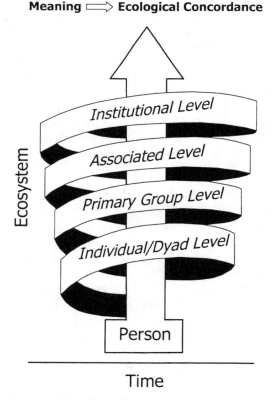

*Note.* Adapted from Kassambira & Edwards, 2000

## Conclusion

Many possible versions of ecological counseling are consistent with the features described in this chapter. Some readers may see their current counseling practice fitting comfortably within these features, even though their approach may bear another official label. Because ecological counseling as we have described it is intended to provide a place for diverse truths about human life, we recognize that concordance or synergy comes in many different forms!

We believe that at its best, ecological counseling invites counselors to leave their comfort zones, to consider new conceptualizations, goals, and ways of delivering services. Mental health counselors may be challenged to explore the features of their clients' physical environments, for example, and organizational consultants the impact of macrosystemic influences in day-to-day corporate functioning. Counselors accustomed to direct service delivery may see the value of program development or social advocacy, and vice versa. Putting into practice what we preach about meaning making, we recognize that for such a provocative invitation to work across counseling disciplines and areas of practice, we need to provide a common language we all can use to explore our own professional practice. We hope that this chapter provided the beginnings of this common language.

What follows in this book is a focus on counseling processes that accommodate diverse clientele, targets of interventions, and modes of delivering counseling services. We do not expect readers to agree with all of them, but simply to try them as a way of thinking about what we all do. We acknowledge that some aspects of this model may be uncomfortably vague. To some extent, this vagueness may be an inevitable consequence of any effort to map a route through miles of terrain—to use Subich and Taylor's (1994) metaphor. If this map gets us to our desired destination, traversing a rocky road is well worth the effort. Each counselor should consider what additional concepts and processes are needed to flesh out a more comprehensive model consistent with his or her own professional work, and whether ecological counseling as described appears to be valid and workable.

As for Jamie, whose troubles on the school bus opened this chapter, her crisis had a happy ending ecologically speaking. Ms. Jones, a behavioral specialist from a social services agency for developmentally disabled people, was called in by Jamie's distraught parents. She volunteered to ride the bus with Jamie for several days and talk to the bus driver in order to assess the situation, and then presented her recommendations at a school meeting attended by the assistant principal,

Jamie's teacher, and Jamie's parents. Ms. Jones acknowledged Jamie's limited social skills on the bus, but also pointed out that discipline on the bus in general was at best inconsistent. The assistant principal blanched upon hearing examples of other students' behavior that had gone unnoticed by the driver. Ms. Jones suspected that Jamie was doing with enthusiasm what other students were able to hide or had asked her to do. Such behaviors did relieve the tedium of a long bus ride, as well as Jamie's loneliness.

A number of interventions were implemented after the meeting. The transportation coordinator had a talk with the bus driver. All the students on the bus heard *two* of the assistant principal's fire-and-brimstone lectures on the consequences of bad behavior, which were followed by a letter to parents. Each student was given an assigned seat, per transportation policy, and the ones suspected of teaching Jamie to misbehave were placed several rows away. Ms. Jones and Jamie made a handsome chart depicting things Jamie did well on the bus (e.g., looking at a book). Jamie was proud of the chart. Ms. Jones also developed a game for Jamie to play while riding, by which she kept track of students entering or leaving the bus and systematically greeted each one by name. Students began to greet Jamie in return and were very interested in Jamie's cool bus game. Jamie's disruptive behaviors disappeared.

How might *you* have analyzed Jamie's situation? What might you have done?

## Learning Activities

1. You are asked to give a continuing education presentation of 1 hour at the state counseling association meeting. People have heard about ecological counseling and wonder about its basic principles. Develop an outline for a presentation (10 minutes) and then meet with a partner to discuss each of your outlines (20 minutes).

2. Form a panel of student presenters. Each student is assigned to make a 2-minute presentation to the rest of the class on one (or more) of the basic principles underlying ecological counseling. The audience engages in questions and answers (60 minutes total).

3. Think of a fairly concrete counseling situation. How do the basic principles underlying ecological counseling apply? (15 minutes). Note your questions, and your learning, and bring them into a group discussion of three to five other students (30 minutes).

# References

Banning, J. H. (1989). Ecotherapy: A life space application of the ecological perspective. *Campus Ecologist, 7*(3), 1-3.

Blocher, D., & Biggs, D.C. (1983). *Counseling psychology in community settings.* New York: Springer.

Bronfenbrenner, U. (1977). Toward an experimental ecology of human development. *American Psychologist, 32*, 513-531.

Bronfenbrenner, U. (1979). *The ecology of human development.* Cambridge, MA: Harvard University Press.

Bronfenbrenner, U. (1992). Ecological systems theory. In R. Vasta (Ed.), *Six theories of child development: Revised formulations and current issues* (pp. 187-250). Greenwich, CT: JAI Press.

Capra, F. (1996). *The web of life: A new scientific understanding of living systems.* New York: Anchor Books.

Commoner, B. (1968). *The closing circle.* New York: Basic Books.

Conoley, J., & Haynes, G. (1992). An ecological approach to intervention. In R. C. D'Amato & B.A. Rothlisberg (Eds.), *Psychological perspectives on intervention* (pp. 177-189). White Plains, NY: Longman.

Conyne, R. (1987). *Primary preventive counseling: Empowering people and systems.* Muncie, IN: Accelerated Development.

Dawis, R. (2000). The person-environment tradition in counseling psychology. In W. Martin, Jr., & J. Swartz-Kulstad (Eds.), *Person-environment psychology and mental health: Assessment and intervention* (pp. 91-111). Mahwah, NJ: Erlbaum.

Elder, G. H., Jr. (1995). The life course paradigm: Social change and individual development. In P. Moen, G. H. Elder, Jr., & K. Luscher (Eds.), *Examining lives in context: Perspectives on the ecology of human development* (pp. 101-139). Washington, DC: American Psychological Association.

Frankl, V. (1963). *Man's search for meaning.* New York: Washington Square Press.

Gergen, K. (1991). *The saturated self.* New York: Basic Books.

Gordon, D. E., & Efran, J. S. (1997). Therapy and the dance of language. In T. L. Sexton & B. L. Griffin (Eds.), *Constructivist thinking in counseling practice, research, and training* (pp. 101-110). New York: Teachers College Press.

Hayes, R. L., & Oppenheim, R. (1997). Constructivism: Reality is what you make it. In T. L. Sexton & B. L. Griffin (Eds.), *Constructivist thinking in counseling practice, research, and training* (pp. 19-40). New York: Teachers College Press.

Heller, K., Price, R., Reinharz, S., Riger, S., & Wandersman, A. (1984). *Psychology and community change: Challenges of the future.* Homewood, IL: Dorsey.

Helms, J., & Cook, D. A. (1999). *Using race and culture in counseling and psychotherapy: Theory and process.* Boston: Allyn & Bacon.

Herr, E. (2000). *Counseling in a dynamic society* (2nd ed.). Alexandria, VA: American Counseling Association.

Ivey, A., D'Andrea, M., Ivey, M., & Simek-Morgan, L. (2002). *Theories of counseling and psychotherapy: A multicultural perspective* (5th ed.). Boston: Allyn & Bacon.

Jordan, J., Kaplan, A. G., Miller, J. B., Stiver, I. P., & Surrey, J. L. (1991). *Women's growth in connection: Writings from the Stone Center*. New York: Guilford Press.

Kasambira, K. P. & Edwards, L. (2000). Counseling and human ecology: A conceptual framework for counselor educators. In *Proceedings of the Eighth International Counseling Conference: Counseling and Human Ecology* (pp. 43–52). San Jose, Costa Rica.

Kelly, G. (1955). *The psychology of personal constructs*. New York: Norton.

Kelly, J. (1966). Ecological constraints on mental health services. *American Psychologist, 21*, 535–539.

Krumboltz, J. D. (1994). Improving career development theory from a social learning perspective. In M. L. Savickas & R. W. Lent (Eds.), *Convergence in career development theories: Implications for science and practice* (pp. 9–31). Palo Alto, CA: CPP Books.

Lewin, K. (1936). *Principles of topological psychology*. New York: McGraw-Hill.

Lewis, J., Lewis, M., Daniels, J., & D'Andrea, M. (2003). *Community counseling: Empowerment strategies for a diverse society* (3rd ed.). Pacific Grove, CA: Brooks/Cole.

Lieberman, M., Yalom, I., & Miles, M. (1973). *Encounter groups: First facts*. New York: Basic Books.

Markus, H. R., & Kitayama, S. (1991). Culture and the self: Implications for cognition, emotion, and motivation. *Psychological Review, 98*, 224–253.

Martin, W., Jr., & Swartz-Kulstad, J. (Eds.). (2000). *Person-environment psychology and mental health: Assessment and intervention*. Mahwah, NJ: Erlbaum.

Maton, K. (2000). Making a difference: The social ecology of social transformation. *American Journal of Community Psychology, 28*, 25–57.

McAuliffe, G., & Eriksen, K. (1999). Toward a constructivist and developmental identity for the counseling profession: The Context-Phase-Stage-Style model. *Journal of Counseling & Development, 77*, 281–293.

Morrill, W., Oetting, E., & Hurst, J. (1974). Dimensions of counselor functioning. In C. Parker (Ed.), Thirty-six faces of counseling. *Personnel and Guidance Journal, 52*, 354–359.

Myers, J. E., Sweeney, T. J., & Witmer, J. M. (2000). The wheel of wellness counseling for wellness: A holistic model for treatment planning. *Journal of Counseling & Development, 78*, 251–266.

Neimeyer, R. (1993). Constructivism and the problem of psychotherapy integration. *Journal of Psychotherapy Integration, 3*, 133–157.

Prochaska, J., & Norcross, J. (1994). *Systems of psychotherapy: A transtheoretical analysis* (3rd ed.). Belmont, CA: Brooks/Cole.

Reker, G., & Chamberlain, K. (Eds.). (2000). *Exploring existential meaning: Optimizing human development across the life span*. Thousand Oaks, CA: Sage.

Society for Community Research and Action. (1999). SCRA community news. *The Community Psychologist, 32*, 38–39.

Sexton, T. L., & Griffin, B. L. (Eds.) (1997). *Constructivist thinking in counseling practice, research, and training*. New York: Teachers College Press.

Spokane, A. R. (1994). The resolution of incongruence and the dynamics of person-environment fit. In M. L. Savickas & R. W. Lent (Eds.), *Convergence in career development theories* (pp. 119–135). Palo Alto, CA: CPP Books.

Steele, F. (1973). *Physical settings and organization development*. Reading, MA: Addison-Wesley.

Subich, L.M., & Taylor, K. M. (1994). Emerging directions of social learning theory. In M. L. Savickas & R. W. Lent (Eds.), *Convergence in career development theories* (pp. 167–175). Palo Alto, CA: CPP Books.

Trickett, E., Barone, C., & Watts, R. (2000). Contextual diversity and community psychology: Still hazy after all these years. *Journal of Community Psychology, 26,* 264–279.

Trickett, E., Kelly, J., & Todd, D. (1972). The social environment of the high school. In S. Golann & C. Eisdorfer (Eds.), *Handbook of community mental health* (pp. 331–406). New York: Appleton-Century-Crofts.

White, M., & Epston, D. (1991). *Narrative means to therapeutic ends*. New York: Norton.

Willi, J. (1999). *Ecological psychotherapy: Developing by shaping the personal niche*. Seattle, WA: Hogrefe & Huber.

Worell, J. (2001). Feminist interventions: Accountability beyond symptom reduction. *Psychology of Women Quarterly, 25,* 335–343.

Yalom, I. (1980). *Existential psychotherapy*. New York: Basic Books.

# Chapter 2

# The Context of American Life Today

## *Edwin L. Herr*

---

### *Chapter Highlights*

- *The interaction of people and their environments is a critically important feature of ecological counseling.*
- *The United States is a land of multiple ecological contexts.*
- *Social transformations (i.e., economic, political, social) can create vast opportunities or upheavals in peoples' lives.*
- *Four major ecological challenges for counselors and clients are the pervasive effects in the home and workplace of advanced technology; the changing American family; pluralism and diversity; and the growing number of at-risk situations.*
- *Ecological contexts are the origins of and the conduits for pressures on people to behave in certain ways, to view themselves in particular roles, and to internalize selected values.*
- *The environments individuals experience in the United States are likely to differ depending on whether they are (a) a member of a majority or minority culture; (b) a man or a woman; (c) a person of color or a Caucasian; (d) a native-born American or an immigrant; (e) a member of a particular religious tradition or none at all; (f) well educated or illiterate; or (g) a member of a lower socioeconomic class or the middle or upper class.*

---

L ife in the United States is not a singular phenomenon. Rather, it is a vast and complex array of contexts and systems with which their inhabitants interact. Many of these contexts and systems are undergoing major transformations in response to the economic, political, and social events that shape them. In the process, new social and economic structures are being created and older institutions, behavioral metaphors, and psychological structures are being refined, replaced, or terminated. Thus, the contexts, environments, and ecologies that Americans occupy are not static; they constantly churn and change.

In this book, the term *ecological* is used to focus attention on the interaction of individuals and the environments or contexts in which they function and the counseling problems or issues that might arise from such interactions. In this chapter, we discuss a number of ecologies and the ecological–individual interactions that can be used to examine the physical and psychological environments individuals occupy and the behavior, needs, and aspirations or beliefs they may produce in relation to such interfaces or transactions.

## Ecological Contexts in Perspective

Ecological contexts are not standardized within or across nations. The environments individuals experience in the United States are likely to differ depending on whether they are a member of a majority or minority culture; a native-born American or an immigrant; a man or a woman; a person of color or a Caucasian; a member of a particular religious tradition or none at all; well educated or illiterate; or a member of a lower socioeconomic class or the middle or upper class.

Whatever ecological contexts an individual inhabits define subjectively (and often objectively) the life spaces—those crucibles in which individuals negotiate their personal identities, live out their self-concepts, interact with others, are exposed to particular forms of education, participate in family life, and aspire to and implement a work life. Within these ecological interactions, different persons are demeaned or nurtured, provided respect and dignity or taught that they are inferior, or provided access to opportunity or denied such access. The ecological contexts that individuals occupy are the sites in which racism, sexism, and ageism may serve as mediators of how individuals view themselves, their worth, their competencies, and their freedom of action. As such, these transactions between individuals and the contexts they occupy have the potential to be positive or negative, supportive and encouraging or the opposite; as such, the ecological contexts an individual occupies are the seedbeds for growth and positive development as well as for the anxieties, informational deficits, depression, and problems in living that a person may experience.

The interaction of person × environment—in a sense, the essence of ecological counseling—is an affirmation that individuals do not live in a vacuum, that they live in contexts. These contexts are multidimensional within and between them. Thus, it is accurate to say that people live in life spaces, not a life space; in contexts, not a context; in environments, not an environment. Neville and Mobley (2001) contended that

> ecological models differ in their foci and definitions of key components. However, most models operate from the assumption that human behavior is multiply determined by a system of dynamic interactions between social systems. Individuals' psychological adjustment is thus dependent on who or what he or she interacts with on a daily basis as well as those systems that structure [an] individual's day-to-day realities. (p. 472)

Depending on their age or other factors, people tend to interact daily with multiple contexts (i.e., family, school, work, community) that offer what Gibson (1982) called affordances. Affordances are the objects, events, or people that provide information, stimulation, and opportunities—or the negative converse of these—depending on what the individual's characteristics are and the types of interactions individuals have with the affordances available to them. The contexts one is likely to occupy or move among, and individual interactions within these contexts, are affected by one's gender, race, ethnicity, socioeconomic status, level of education, and other characteristics. However, the effects of contexts on individuals are often determined by chance events (e.g., meeting a particular person, hearing of the availability of a desired job by a chance remark, experiencing an accident and sustaining an injury, witnessing a particular event on television) as well as by more predictable processes. According to Cabral and Salomone (1990), how people respond to unforeseen encounters or events has to do with their locus of control (external or internal) and their self-concept (positive or negative). Such personal traits act as filters through which persons perceive events and people across the contexts they occupy. In chance and in more predictable life events, individuals are likely to act in ways that reinforce and implement their self-concepts and their perception of their locus of control, in addition to how they can affect the future or live at the hands of fate.

## Theoretical Views of Contexts

Throughout the 20th century, selected theorists have articulated the importance of individual–context or person–environment transactions. In some cases, the emphasis has been on the stimuli provided by the environment to reinforce or shape individual behavior. At other times, the emphasis has been on the reciprocal affects of individual–environment interactions. In either case, a line of distinguished American theorists has created the conceptual underpinnings of ecological counseling by articulating the importance of person–environment trans-actions or fit. Examples include Murray and Kluckhohn (1956), who advanced the notion that individual development is determined by the physical and the family environment as well as by the larger societal and cultural institutions. Stern, Stein, and Bloom (1956) contended that to understand behavior we must study both the individual and the environ-ment. They wrote that behavior

> is the resultant of the transaction between the individual and other structural units in the behavioral field. For convenience, these other units may be referred to collectively as the environment. This environment provides a continual source of actual and potential stimulus demands and consequences. (p. 35)

Lewin (1951) used the concepts of field theory to explain individual behavior. He argued that we can conceive of the person and the envi-ronment as interdependent regions of life space, his term for the total psychological field at any given time. Lewin described behavior as selec-tive and creative, motivated by psychological forces, and functioning within the psychological field existing at the time behavior occurs.

Such views of the interdependence of individual behavior and the environmental context in which it operates have led some theorists to argue that it is possible and advisable to classify an environment in terms of the kinds of benefits (facilitations, satisfactions) and the kinds of harm (obstructions, injuries, dissatisfactions) that it provides. For example, Murray (1938) differentiated the characteristics of environ-ments (reinforcements, norms, expectations), which he labeled press, from the characteristics of individuals, which he labeled needs. In this view, the assumption is that some environments provide gratification for certain needs but not for others, meaning environments provide rein-forcements, expectancies, and environmental conditions that satisfy the needs of specific individuals, to which some persons adapt. If their needs are unsatisfied and the environment is uncongenial, however, some people will leave such an environment to seek one that is more congenial and where their needs can be satisfied.

Holland (1985) extended the thinking of Murray and others and applied it, in particular, to career problems. His theory of six personality types, including the notion of the modal personal orientation, describes the hierarchy of methods by which persons of different types or per-sonal orientations respond to environments. Within such perspectives, among his basic theoretical assumptions are the view that "[p]eople search for environments that will let them exercise their skills and abili-ties, express their attitudes and values, and take on agreeable problems and roles" and that "[a] person's behavior is determined by an interaction between his [or her] personality and the characteristics of his [or her] environment" (Holland, 1973, pp. 2-4).

Explicit in Holland's (1985) theory is the perspective that environments differ in the personality types they attract because environments differ in the problems, the interpersonal relations, and the values they reflect. As such, according to Holland, both individuals and environments can be classified as realistic, investigative, artistic, social, enterprising, and conventional. Congruence between individual personality type and the type of environment the individual occupies is likely to lead to satisfaction and persistence in that environment. Lack of congruence is likely to lead to dissatisfaction with the environment and a search for other environments in which the individual can more fully express his or her personality style.

A major example of the classification of environments is the conceptual work of Bronfenbrenner (1979), which began the process of popularizing ecological models a quarter of a century ago (see chapter 1 and Figure 1.1 for an introduction to this model). This perspective is less concerned about predictions of the environments in which individuals with different needs or personal orientations will be most congruent or satisfied, and more concerned with the interdependence of four interacting systems to which each individual is exposed and by which his or her psychological growth is affected. These four systems are in a sense a continuum of environments from the most intimate and direct (the *microsystem*) to the most abstract and indirect environment to which individuals are exposed (the *macrosystem*). By definition, the microsystem, the first system, includes the interpersonal relationships, goal-directed activities, roles, and expectations that a person experiences most directly in the intimate—often dyadic—interactions with parents, siblings, and peer group members. The *mesosystem*, the second system, is a linking mechanism between two or more systems in which the person is an active participant. Such linkages between systems or settings (home, school, workplace, social network, church, community), as they spill from one system to another, are likely to reflect different demands, expectations, norms, and emotional stimuli on the individual. The demands of these various settings may be in conflict and affect each other. Thus, the demand of the school or the workplace may be different from those of the family and home and may affect the individual's performance or happiness in the latter (e.g., the failing student may act out frustration originating in the classroom by oppositional or defiant behavior toward his or her parents; the worker who feels vulnerable to unemployment or demotion may behave negatively to his or her spouse or children). Persons sometimes have difficulty in the microsystem and in the mesosystem.

The third system that Bronfenbrenner proposed is the *exosystem*. Exosystems reflect the indirect effects on children and adults of the events in a parent or spouse's system. For example, if a parent experiences sudden unemployment in the workplace, his or her child will suffer even though the child is not actively or directly involved in that workplace. In this case, the economic and psychological turmoil experienced by the parent will change the characteristics of the home and family environment of the microsystem. When such a situation occurs, a series of personal identity, economic, interpersonal, and aspirational processes may be altered for the child as an indirect effect of the parent's experience in the exosystem.

The fourth ecological system, the macrosystem, is seen as the most encompassing. The other three systems are essentially nested in the macrosystem, which is the purveyor of the major cultural beliefs, the historical traditions, and the metaphors of the society. The macrosystem is composed of the processes that sustain national images and ideologies about such matters as the opportunity structure, sex roles, achievement expectations, acceptable personality traits, and behavioral sanctions.

The important concepts presented by Bronfenbrenner have defined and stimulated the interdependence of several key concepts in ecological perspectives. They include the notion that ecology is an interdisciplinary and integrative field of inquiry that brings together the findings of such areas of study as (a) sociobiology; (b) the interaction of nature and nurture, genes and culture, and self-interest and prosocial behavior; (c) natural selection; (d) individual–environmental reciprocity; (e) individual capacity for commitment to a belief system, to rules, to expectations of others, and to creating our own social environments; and (f) cross-cultural psychology, cultural diversity, culture and ethnicity, enculturation, socialization, and acculturation (Berry, 1994; Gintis, 2001; Nesse, 2001).

In a major sense, the ecological context includes the independent variables that affect an individual's behavioral responses (e.g., the stable and relatively permanent characteristics of the environment, sociopolitical context, learning). The context also includes the situational circumstances that may account for particular behaviors at a given time and place—specific roles or social interactions, and cultural and biological adaptations made by a group or more specifically, an individual.

These independent variables may lead to such outcomes as (a) customs—the long-standing, developed, established, collective, and shared patterns of behaviors discovered in a cultural or ethnic group; (b) repertoires—the relatively stable complex of behaviors, including cognitive values and racial identity, that have been learned by an individual over time in the recurrent experiential or learning context; or (c) performances—behaviors that appear in response to immediate stimulation or experience (Berry, 1994).

## Ecological Definition

To reiterate, then, the effects of ecology can be examined through different windows: anthropological, physical, social, economic, and psychological. *Webster's Dictionary* (1983) offered two definitions of ecology. The first indicated that ecology is "the branch of biology that deals with the relations between living organisms and their environment" (p. 574). One could subsume under such a definition terrorist attacks, the greenhouse effect, industrial pollutions and smog, unbridled population growth in some parts of the world, the AIDs epidemic, and drug and alcohol abuse. Although the origins of such interactions between individuals and their environments are physical or biological, the effects of these interactions are psychological and behavioral because they spawn anxiety, information deficits or distortions, fear, stress-related diseases, posttraumatic stress disorders, and other emotional and psychological concerns that fall within the purview of ecological counseling.

It is also important to consider the second major definition of ecology, according to *Webster's* (1983): "In sociology, the relationship between the distribution of human groups with reference to material resources and the consequent social and cultural patterns" (p. 574). This definition indicates that individuals of different racial, cultural, or ethnic backgrounds are likely to experience different habitats, life spaces, environments, resource availability, and ecological conditions that vary because of one's cultural, racial, or ethnic characteristics. Thus, ecological impacts on human behavior are likely to vary in degree and in kind depending on one's status in a given society. In essence, ecological impact on individuals and their interactions with their environments differ in a complex manner in response to environmental stimuli, social metaphors, traditions, and meaning or value structures that define the psychological and physical boundaries within which various population subgroups function in their daily behavioral transactions. Ecological contexts differ among nations, and also among people living within a pluralistic nation such as the United States.

For example, as one observes even the most superficial glimpses of the ecological contexts of nations as seen by the nightly news on television, it is clear that national ecological contexts—sociopolitical and physical environments, fiscal and natural resources, homogeneity or heterogeneity of belief systems about race, gender, socioeconomic states—differ dramatically. For example, while this chapter was being written, the United States was waging war in Afghanistan against terrorism. Daily news clips revealed many facts about Afghanistan: it is a very poor country; schooling for women has been prohibited for most of the past two decades; different tribal groups have more or less power; physical resources in the country have been virtually destroyed by war and drought; the roles of men and women are rigidly differentiated and controlled; and there has been no consistent national sense of unity for much of recent history. This is in sharp contrast with other nations in North America, Europe, and parts of Asia. Although characterized by specific social and political limitations, these nations are nevertheless more open to individual mobility, have and make available more comprehensive and differentiated resources (e.g., financial, infrastructural, psychological, social) to their people, and are less definitive and restrictive in terms of, for example, gender roles and religious observances.

In essence, as one looks around the world, one finds a continuum of nations in different forms of transition in their political and economic systems, from the least developed to the most highly developed in terms of their technological, political, social, and resource systems. The ecological contexts they provide their citizens mirror in many ways their levels of development, although this does not imply that there is homogeneity of treatment of citizens and immigrants as it does in culturally diverse and pluralistic societies such as the United States. In one sense, within complex, heterogeneous, and culturally pluralistic societies, there are population subgroups that vary in status, mobility, educational access, behavioral repertoires, and reputations, and in the expectations of them held by other subpopulations. In such ecological contexts, overt or covert sets of discrimination, segregation, separation, and marginalization sometimes confound the national rhetoric of social justice and equality for all. In the United States, the latter example of ecological emphases as related to women, to African Americans, to Native Americans, to people with disabilities, and to older Americans has been responded to by civil rights movements and by legislation prohibiting specific forms of discriminatory behavior in housing, jobs, and educational access. Although such national efforts attempt to stabilize the ecological contexts for citizens in terms of equity and access, there are other elements of the ecological context that differentiate subpopulations.

As suggested previously, ecological contexts are multidimensional rather than unidimensional. The interactions among the various aspects of one's life space exert influences or limits on how gender and family roles are conceived and implemented, the achievement and economic mobility images likely to be nurtured, the resources available, and the accuracy and forms of knowledge provided. In such respects, ecological contexts can be likened to percolators of information and reinforcement, the flow and substance of which is filtered by cultural, socioeconomic, racial, and other factors. For example, a poor person is not simply a rich person without money. A poor person by definition has experienced different ecological contexts than has a rich person. The poor person's information, reinforcements, and resources are likely to be significantly different from those available to a rich person. So is the poor person's likely belief system or sense of self-efficacy about his or her personal power to gain an education or the necessary skills to improve his or her lot in life or to increase life chances. Thus, the ecological context to which a given individual is exposed is likely to affect his or her philosophy of life, sense of self-worth, feelings of power to change life circumstances or to alter ecological contexts, role expectations, and other behavioral processes.

There are other ecological phenomena functioning in pluralistic societies. For example, in most nations, cultural, racial, and ethnic diversity is related to economic and other life changes. Minorities in a predominantly Caucasian culture are likely to be poorer, less well educated, and have less access to material resources and fewer savings and other support systems that allow for planning and acting upon long-term goals. They are more likely to attribute an external locus of control to their life course rather than an internal locus of control. They are more likely to live where industrial pollution, poor sanitation, chronic physical ailments, stress, victimization, and alcohol and drug abuse are the norm than is true for Caucasians or members of the majority culture. Therefore, the psychology of choice and identity, and the interaction of physical, economic, and social or cultural ecologies, is different for individuals at different socioeconomic levels in any society. Because of the strong correlation between socioeconomic status and gender or race or culture in virtually all societies, the reinforcement of ecological contexts for personal growth, personal security, and educational and occupational opportunity vary dramatically for individuals differentially described by these characteristics.

In the second definition of ecology as a sociological perspective, social history, cultural traditions, and racial differences converge within ecological contexts. In essence, then, there is no one social, economic, or political ecology; all of these factors and others are intertwined and result in what is in reality multiple ecologies. Depending on when, where, and what the substantive content of a given set of ecological conditions represents, individuals react to these conditions and internalize the information or behavioral metaphors they provide and set upon them as they have been socialized to do. The United States is a land of multiple ecological contexts that differ by geography and setting, by historical period, and by the messages these contexts convey about idealized behaviors, achievement, sanctioned behavior. The messages that people of different cultural traditions, socioeconomic level, age, or other characteristics receive from the ecological context may vary widely.

The United States is a land of immigrants who have come with widely varying cultural traditions, beliefs, and expected behaviors. Thus, the U.S. population is composed of subsets of people whose views of the ecological contexts vary in terms of their enculturation into a specific racial or ethnic or cultural group and in terms of their acculturation into the dominant societal norms. The enculturation and acculturation of individuals is often a function of viewing ecological contexts through diverse cultural lenses. Cultures vary in information processing, worldviews, cognitive mechanisms, individual or group reference points for behavior, representations of normality, gender roles, and behavioral expectations of its members. It is not that members of diverse cultures making up the population of the United States cannot agree and act in accordance with certain universal goals for the nation, such as freedom, equality, and the right to pursue opportunity. They can and do; however, given the great complexity of the social, physical, and economic psychological structures of the United States, ecological contexts are not the same in all parts of the country nor, given the great range of human diversity in the United States, do they affect all people the same way. For cultural or racial subpopulations in a majority or adopted culture, the distinctive cultural, ethnic, or racial traditions persist for a long period in self-concepts and behavioral norms. In this sense, the cultural groups to which they belong interpret the ecological contexts at issue and provide guides to behavior within the extant ecological conditions. As such, religious, racial, or other cultural groups provide figurative maps or templates about ecological conditions. These templates are elements with which individuals are socialized. As such, these interpretations help group members organize their reality, create perceptual cues about matters to which they should attend and give meaning, and define appropriate self-perceptions and manners of expressions. Such learning reduces ambiguity and increases predictability in the behavior of members of specific cultural groupings. The socialization of individuals that is maintained informally and formally by various ethnic, racial, or cultural groupings provides structures or classification systems by which to sort out and interpret the constant stream of signals or messages from the environment every individual experiences daily. Culturally mediated interpretations and dispositions ultimately end up in the cognitions of each individual as assumptions and symbolic representations of a world that is in the last analysis unique to each individual and, in a less specific sense, unique to different cultural groups within the larger body of people we know as Americans.

From a counseling perspective, one can argue that the mechanisms which trigger most problems-in-living for individuals are their various interactions with environmental or ecological conditions. Thus, individual behavior within and across families, communities, and social and cultural groups is a continuous response to transactions within their ecological contexts. These contexts motivate them to think and feel in positive or negative ways, challenge them to create new meanings or reconstruct old meanings, affirm them or make them feel vulnerable and unworthy, guide them or confuse them, encourage them to be purposeful and productive, or limit their aspirations and vision to surviving physically and mentally each day within ecological conditions that restrict and define in negative terms who they are and what they can do. It is from these person–environment transactions that positive self-attributions and a positive repertoire of behaviors evolves or results in anxiety, depression, or information deficits. The issue then becomes one of the counselor's sensitivity to the ecological conditions that precipitated the counselee's despair, confusion, or inability to function effectively.

There are many examples of how ecological counseling might be the treatment of preference. Some examples follow.

## Ecological Counseling Examples

In the late 1970s and early 1980s, several family therapists and researchers (e.g., Aponte, 1980; Spiegel, 1982) applied the concepts of ecological counseling to their work with families, particularly African Americans. In these approaches, the major emphases were not so much on internal family dynamics as on the family's interaction with external systems and institutional contexts. Such an approach looks at the ecological dynamics that have impinged on the family and caused many of its difficulties; it also challenges counselors to help individuals to reconnect with networks such as extended families, social support systems, and friends or others who can defuse or otherwise alter family dysfunctions. In extending such points, Hines and Boyd-Franklin (1982) contended that in working effectively with African American families in the United States, counselors must be open to exploring the impact of social, political, socioeconomic, and broader environmental conditions on the families they treat. Aponte (1980) used the term *ecostructural* to describe the broader ecological treatment approach and the need to always consider a family's environment and community as relevant to the diagnostic process and planning of treatment. Citing Aponte, Hines and Boyd-Franklin observed that

> the ecostructural reality of poor, inner-city Black families is that the external systems are likely to impinge on them. These may include welfare, the courts, schools, Medicaid, food stamps, and public housing. To treat the family without considering these systems and their impact on family behavior would be a grave error. (p. 99)

In such a perspective, there are survival issues in such ecological contexts that take precedence over family conflicts or, indeed, may motivate such conflicts. So it is with poor people in many parts of the United States, necessitating counselors to view their role in ecological counseling, at least partially, as helping poor families learn how to negotiate the complexities of the bureaucracy more effectively, and to use available resources and contacts to facilitate change.

A different type of ecological problem can be identified under such terms as "grieving the loss of a cultural identity" (Sardi, 1982) or "acculturative stress" (Berry, Kim, Minde, & Mok, 1987). Such phenomena are associated with immigrant groups or, in some cases, group members who are trying to function effectively in their own ethnic neighborhoods and culture while also functioning effectively in the dominant culture as a worker, employee, or citizen. The first phenomenon, the loss of a cultural identity by immigrant populations, was first identified in Israel, where Jewish settlers came from many parts of Europe, Russia, and Africa. The point is that even when one leaves an ecological context because of economic or religious oppression, one has already formed a cultural identity (e.g., as a Russian, Ethiopian, German, Spaniard) to immigrate to a new culture is to essentially lose a cultural self and to grieve for that loss as one tries to reestablish a new cultural identity, and construct a new cultural self in a new nation with a different ecological context.

Acculturative stress is a related process where an individual is trying to be attentive and perform in terms of criteria defined by their ethnocultural group (e.g., Muslims, Native Americans, Chicana) while also attempting to manifest the behavior, dress, attitudes, and language of the dominant culture to which they are becoming acculturated. Depending on how the individual is treated (e.g., as a minority, as different, as foreign), the individual may experience significant identity confusion, feelings of marginality, depression, anxiety, and other emotions emanating from acculturative stress. Acculturation across groups always involves conflict and typically involves some form of adaptation, which may include responses such as assimilation, separation, integration, or marginalization (Berry, 1994). Each of these response sets carries with it a psychology and a subjective aspect of attachment to one or more groups, to feelings of belonging or the opposite, and to identity and other issues. Again, depending on the particular circumstances of this ecological counseling problem, the counselor has a role in affirming cultural pride, hope, and the dignity of the counselee. The counselor must help the counselee sort out the multiple demands with which he or she is coping and the alternative sets of behaviors prized by each group—not as superior or inferior sets of behaviors, but as alternative behaviors or competencies that the counselee needs to understand and be able to tailor to the different ecological conditions he or she now faces. It is quite likely that the counselor will need to help the counselee grieve for the loss of a cultural identity or to help the counselee construct or rescript his or her identity to accommodate the expectations of his or her original ethnocultural group as well as the new groups with which the counselee is now in contact.

A third example of an ecological counseling problem has to do with cognitive values. Ethnocultural groups differ in their goals and the characteristics of cognitive development. The ways individuals apply cognitive skills, like so many other aspects of human diversity, are also objects of socialization of children by a particular ethnocultural group or society. The social metaphors by which the United States is frequently described often emphasize science and technology, innovativeness and creativity, and a cognitive style that is individual, quick, analytic, and abstract (Berry, 1994). These are the methodologies taught by the school system and measured by typical school achievement measures. However, these are not the only cognitive goals to which immigrants or children in particular ethnocultural groups may be socialized. Some groups value more deliberate, reflective, holistic, or collective discussion about a problem. To the degree that a given child uses such an approach, the cognitive development of this child may be underestimated and the child penalized for performing in a manner not considered the norm in a particular ecological context. The counselor practicing ecological counseling needs to understand that different families in different ethnocultural groups, including immigrants, conceive of cognitive competency differently, identify and transmit it differently, and socialize their children with different cognitive values than do other groups or families. Their views of cognitive values are not wrong, but they are different. They may emphasize taking one's time in solving problems, being patient in learning, persevering until one gets the answer, or engaging in hard work but not hurrying (Berry & Bennett, 1992). Again, such socialization differs from quick problem-solving, skimming the top of material but not understanding the details, allocating limited time to studying, and giving up on a problem if one cannot get a quick answer.

## Trends in Ecological Contexts

These three examples of the interactions of the ecological context shaping or affecting individual behavior and, indeed, its interpretation could be multiplied many times within and among groups in the United States. However, there are other major influences on ecological contexts worth noting. These ecological conditions—manifested as social, economic, political, and technological—operate at the national level and permeate the systems with which people interact as they create and play out their self-concepts and find their personal meaning. Such trends influence the metaphors by which nations describe themselves, the public policies that are implemented, and the content that individuals internalize and, often, bring to the ecological counseling process.

In the first of these sets of trends, the Organization for Economic Cooperation and Development (OECD), of which the United States is a member, has identified four simultaneous and powerful societal transformations that will give rise to more variety and interdependence in social diversity and in encouragement of technological, economic, and social dynamism(Stevens, Miller, & Michalski, 2000). Some of these transformations are well along their road to implementation, and I will offer some brief observations about how they conform to the notion of ecological counseling. The first of these transformations is from "the uniformity and obedience of the mass era to the uniqueness and creativity of a knowledge economy and society" (Stevens et al., 2000, p. 3). As one of many forms of change to which Americans are finding cause to adapt, this transformation is likely to accent less expectation of individual conformity and uniformity to some set of collective behavioral expectations, to problem-solving techniques, or to modes of interaction, and a greater emphasis on celebrating the individual contributions of Americans, of their knowledge, their innovativeness, and their creativity to the common good. Thus, individuals who think for themselves, who are imaginative, who bring their unique knowledge to bear on social, economic, political, or technological programs are prized, not marginalized. Their knowledge and other unique contributions to the society are seen as assets to their community, workplace, and nation, not aberrations or unusual behavior.

Related to this first societal transformation, suggesting the reinforcement of psychological movement from conformity to uniqueness, is an evolving set of social metaphors that have attempted to capture the essence of citizenship in the United States. Social metaphors as used here are the images that nations create for themselves, and by which, as social psychologists argue, related personality types and other behaviors are reinforced. The use of metaphors to capture the essence of a particular time, group, or behavioral emphasis has existed through many centuries of recorded history. Terms such as *Dark Ages, Age of Enlightenment, Cold War, Iron Curtain, Baby Boomers, Generation X, Cult of Efficiency, Age of Discontinuity, Triumph of Meanness, Post-industrial*, and *Cyber Society* are efforts to identify in symbolic labels the essence of fundamental changes that have occurred or are occurring. These terms, however, are also methods of channeling the character of citizens of a nation by creating environments in which acceptable behavior is implicit and internalized by people as part of national or regional ideologies. Fromm (1962) spoke to this point by addressing the interaction of the individual and social character. He observed that societies differ in their structural elements and objectives, in their social taboos, in their national language, and in their sanctions for unacceptable behavior. He put the core of the point as follows:

> [I]t is the function of the "social character" to shape the energies of the members of society in such a way that their behavior is not a matter of conscious decision as to whether or not to follow the social pattern, but one of wanting to act as they have to act and at the same time finding gratification in acting according to the requirement of the culture. In other words, it is the social character's function to mold and channel human energy within a given society for the purpose of the continued functioning of the society. (p. 79)

However, part of the social transformations that are now underway in the United States—as they change the ecological context—exist in changing social metaphors. Some of these have been suggested previously, but the evolution of an additional metaphor can be useful here. One of the mainstays of the American image has been the concept of its role as a melting pot. This notion suggests that wherever you came from, or whatever cultural traditions you have experienced, when you come to the United States those differences are eliminated or suppressed and you become an American. In acting out such a metaphor, many immigrants to this country were essentially denied an ethnocultural identity, were encouraged to speak only English, or were expected to dress in clothing that was seen as American. Such a metaphor as sometimes practiced does not acknowledge cultural differences in citizens' origins or socialization, sometimes treats citizens from particular racial or ethnic backgrounds as inferior, relegates them to particular neighborhoods, ghettos, or barrios, and marginalizes them. A melting pot phenomenon suggests that Americans are a homogenized group of people, not a heterogeneous group of people who have migrated to the United States under many different conditions, from diverse cultures, and for multiple purposes.

Because of the potential exclusionary interpretations of the melting pot metaphor and a growing acknowledgement of the cultural pluralism embedded in the histories and lives of American citizens, new metaphors have been sought to more clearly and positively affirm the contributions of all Americans to the collective goal. As a result, new metaphors have increasingly been introduced that suggest both the uniqueness of individual contributions and the interdependence of such contributions in achieving national goals. The latter concepts are reflected in such metaphors as *salad bowl, soup*, and *mosaic*. The latter metaphors do not argue for the relinquishing of one's cultural identity to become an American, but rather that the cultural integrity of a group can be maintained while also allowing the group to become an integral part of a larger societal framework and cooperate within a larger social system. In implementing such metaphors, the contributions of the members of the distinct ethnocultural groups that comprise America are recognized and their heterogeneity is celebrated. The basic assumption is that cultural diversity among Americans enriches rather than denigrates the common good.

Obviously, the transformation of national metaphors from conformity to uniqueness, from melting pot to salad bowl or soup, carries with it differences in the psychology of identity, integration, and acculturation. But simply changing the image of the ecological context through the metaphors one uses does not instantly change individual behavior. Some individuals in any society are stuck between metaphors; they are not clear about expected behaviors or how to access the available opportunity structure, or how to adapt to the freedom to construct a social reality for themselves.

A second of the four social transformations projected by the OECD to affect the ecological context of the United States and other nations is the change from "rigid and isolated command planning to flexible, open and rule-based markets" (Stevens et al., 2000, p. 3). Briefly, such a transformation reflects decentralization of governance structures, policy making, and responsibility from central planning and governance units to local initiatives. Such decentralization of responsibility allows for greater flexibility and openness of participation by citizens. It changes the method of functioning of managers and administrators from top-down (command) planning to planning that emerges from the bottom up. Such planning is more inclusive of people with unique skills and perspectives. It also distributes planning information more widely through organizations and communities.

Such a transformation emphasizes significantly more individual participation, responsibility, and adaptation to changes than is true when all authority for decision making is invested with a central leader or unit. Such processes also require participants to be more knowledgeable and informed about issues than is true when the individual's expectation is to receive orders from those in administrative capacities and to act on those orders, without participating in their creation or challenging their content. Again, the psychology of centralized versus decentralized planning is different in its expectations of individual responsibility to carry out mandates as opposed to creating them and tailoring them to local needs. These differences are reflected (a) in the site management of each school by an administrator rather than by a superintendent who is responsible for multiple schools and uses one-size-fits-all rules that tend to ignore demographics and other critical differences; (b) in quality circles and self-governing work units in a manufacturing organization that are charged with making decisions about how best to develop a product or service; and (c) in communities or other organizations where elected councils are charged with recommending policy and monitoring its implementation rather than following the directives of a single leader. From an ecological counseling perspective, such different styles of planning and participation increase the need for individuals to work effectively in teams, to be cooperative and willing to listen to others, to respect differences of opinion, to have effective interpersonal skills, to be flexible and not resistant to change, and to be able to process information and participate in informed decisions even when all of the desired information is not available. Not all individuals are able to function this way, nor do they wish to do so. Some need structure rather than openness and central leadership rather than personal responsibility for workplace decisions. Whether apparent or not, such situations can cause anxiety, discomfort, and physiological, psychological, and behavioral problems that an individual might not understand as being triggered by external, contextual issues rather than other intrinsic issues or incompetence.

The third transformation described by OECD is the transition "from predominantly agricultural structures to industrial urbanization" (Stevens et al., 2000, p. 3). As the United States entered the 21st century, however, it had already begun the transition from industrial urbanization to an information-and-service society. Its transition from an agriculturally structured society to industrial urbanization had largely been achieved during the 20th century. Advanced technology (e.g., computer driven lathes, robots, inventory and distribution systems, transportation) has permeated the workplaces of most industries, requiring shifts in the language and organization of work, in the education required to conduct the work, and in the teachability and flexibility of workers to maintain the necessary skills. Relatively few jobs are created today that do not require basic academic skills (e.g., reading, writing, mathematics) or computer literacy and the ability to work with others. Increased pressure is being placed on workers to be prepared to manage their own careers, to assume that their careers will be less linear in time and less oriented to upward mobility. The changing occupational structure, work content and processes, pervasive effects of technology, expectations for teamwork in the workplace, and responsibility for multiple tasks are not the typical contextual variables that were present in industrialization until the last two decades of the 20th century. Because of such ecological shifts, job stress has become one of the major mental health problems in the United States (Keita & Sauter, 1992). So have the side effects of the downsizing of work organizations, the decrease in the number of permanent workers, the rise of temporary workers and the use of specialty firms for services that were once performed by permanent workers, and the increase in individual worker responsibilities for quality control and for implementing multiple tasks, including using computer technology as a major tool.

Such work situations and their unpredictability have changed the nature of career paths and the psychology of the workplace for individuals in many occupations and many settings. As such, the interaction of workers and work environments as ecological contexts are being reshaped and are often the source of anxiety, information deficits, and related behaviors. In an ecological context in which workplaces are called learning organizations and more than 50% of workers are called knowledge workers (i.e., individuals who produce or apply knowledge to work), the workplace is more complex than it has ever been, causing pressures that are unique. In addition, those with minimal training or capacity to learn are increasingly vulnerable to unemployment and to being the have-nots of society. The complexity and knowledge intensity of a society in which learning is a primary social asset creates new and information-focused ecological contexts that elevate the better educated and limits the opportunities for those who do not have strong academic skills, teachability, and personal flexibility.

The fourth transformation, according to OECD, is the movement "from a relatively fragmented world of autonomous societies and regions to the dense and indispensable interdependencies of an integrated planet" (Stevens et al., 2000, p. 3). This perspective suggests that for an increasing number of people, the important ecological context is not their local community or even their nation, but the emerging global economy and other global political and financial structures. It is clear that international economic competition as well as political collaborations across countries to deal with global problems (e.g., terrorism, AIDS) is rapidly becoming a standard for national interdependences. Political borders between states or nations have little meaning when ideas, currency exchanges, and the management of work can flow around the world via the Internet, satellites, and telecommunications without being controlled by national political entities. It has been said that 5 of the 10 largest economies in the world are those of multinational corporations. The global reach and influence of these entities is, in many instances, more powerful than that of many nations. However, in terms of ecological context, as individual nations lose their economic and political sovereignty to coalitions of nations (e.g., the European Union, the North American Free Trade Agreement), the perspectives of many citizens of these nations also changes. Financial markets, export-import trade, transportation, manufacturing, and communications require national interdependency. However economically or militarily competitive a nation may be, it also must be interdependent with other nations in its communications, diplomacy, sharing of knowledge. Such realities accent the need for individuals in the United States who are multilingual and knowledgeable about the legal and economic systems, cultural and religious traditions, and histories of nations that are our competitors, adversaries, or allies. Over the course of their work lives, more people will have transnational experiences on a short- or long-term basis, and they will need to be able to function in societies that are unfamiliar to them and their families. During this process, they may experience identity confusion, conflict, loneliness, and feelings of incompetence.

The characteristics of the global ecological context within which these individuals will function will require new forms of orientation, information, support, stress, and anxiety management in ecological counseling.

In the future, the unfolding of the global economy will create other pressures that will affect more Americans and become much more of an issue. In essence, the world now has a large global labor surplus, many of whom are highly skilled and talented people for whom there is insufficient job creation in their own nations. The governments of these nations and the individuals who are underemployed or unemployed are finding new ways to compete for American jobs. The most obvious of these mechanisms is the decision by American or multinational corporations to move particular industries and their accompanying jobs offshore (i.e., to other countries), where they can find cheaper labor and other expenses. Textiles, steel production, and electronics are examples of such situations. Less discussed, however, are other mechanisms by which nations can compete for American jobs. Among them are the decisions of select nations to change their tax structures to welcome American companies and to create technologically enriched facilities by which their indigenous work forces can process American data and other information via telecommunications. For example, Ireland, India, and some Caribbean nations now contract with American companies to download information from satellites, process it, and upload it back to the originating company in the United States. The result of such global pressures on American jobs means that workers in the United States in many industries are no longer competing for jobs with other individuals in their communities; they are competing for their jobs with individuals in other nations.

Such pressures on the U.S. work force and the occupational structure available to it from international competition is reflected in the following observations related to the sweeping impact of the global economy and the international competition among nations (Stevens et al., 2000):

> [T]he integration of national markets did (and still does) give rise to fiercer competition in all markets (goods, services, labour, finance); to increases in economic specialization; a more elaborate division of labour; and to changes in the geographical redistribution of economic activities on the basis of locational differences such as the quality of the local labour force, the weight of local transaction costs, specific regulatory burdens, local environmental conditions, etc. (p. 17)

These four social transformations identified by the OECD are seedbeds for social upheavals, crises, and individual confusion in many nations, as well as in the United States, as individuals are required to abandon their models of employment and career paths, the importance of experience rather than knowledge, the utility of hard-earned skills that are rapidly becoming obsolescent, expectations about family patterns and child rearing, familiar values and institutions, and the physical location in which their families have lived for generations. Such changes in the ecological context of the nation undoubtedly will create new opportunities in work styles, learnings, family structures, policies, and communications, but such changes will also result in uncertainty, choice overload, conflicts, differences in people's capacity or willingness to change, and, perhaps, the speed of change itself. The triggering mechanisms and pressures that cause new problems in living for many people may not be adequately reflected in extant counseling theories and stimulate serious dissonance between current approaches to mental health and the new tasks required of counselors as they shape and implement the interventions of ecological counseling.

As suggested by the application of the four social transformations identified by the OECD to the United States, the context of American life today is multilayered. Its complexity affects different Americans in different ways depending on where they are in their own personal development, their racial or ethnic identity, their age and gender, their socioeconomic status, their physical and mental capacities, and other characteristics. The latter mediate or position individuals' interaction with the ecological contexts and the variety of systems of which they are composed. Within such complexity of individual status in interacting with ecological conditions, there are other perspectives on ecological influences that can affect the focus and content of ecological counseling. Herr (1999) has suggested four of these, which are both products of changing, transformative ecological conditions and the drivers (i.e., the motivators) of new ecological conditions. Although these four classes of influences overlap somewhat with the OECD framework, they also differ in some of their emphases.

To be brief, the four ecological challenges that have been identified as exerting significant pressure on different populations include (a) the career, economic, educational, and psychological effects of the pervasiveness of advanced technology in the society, (b) the changing American family, (c) pluralism and diversity in the American population, and (d) the growing number of children, youth, and adults who are classified as at risk of academic, social, or work failure. These pressures exert physical, psychological, and intellectual demands on those experiencing them, and they represent substantial demands for new interventions and paradigms of counseling. As in any forms of transformation, these four factors are stimuli generating a psychology of uncertainty and anxiety for some people and an environment of opportunity and growth for others. The status of some groups in the society is elevated (e.g., knowledge workers, intact families); other groups (e.g., the poorly educated, single parents) are increasingly put at risk of economic or social marginalization, or worse. As such, each of these four ecological conditions represents a setting or category of influences for which counselor intervention is important. In a sense, each of these four categories of pressures is at the root of many existing individual behavioral problems, or in some cases the products of ecological contexts.

To reiterate: To understand human behavior and the potential of counseling—and especially approaches to ecological counseling—is to understand that individuals live in diverse social, cultural, political, and economic environments or ecological contexts. These contexts exert influence on or apply limits to gender and family roles, the achievement images likely to be nurtured, the cognitive and interpersonal styles employed, the resources available, the forms and comprehensiveness of information provided, and one's feelings of competence and worth or the reverse. The mixes of ecological contexts through which people move and negotiate their identity are affected by birth order, place of origin, socioeconomic status, and history, among other factors. Ecological contexts, however, are not static; elements of them are constantly transforming or in transition as new knowledge, social metaphors, and political and economic structures emerge and recede in influence. As ecological contexts constantly change, individuals are under constant pressure to receive, interpret, and act upon messages directly or indirectly related to personal behavior that emanate from the ecological contexts and systems with which the individual interacts. Each of the factors cited here is a dominant influence on ecological contexts, reflects major pressure on changes in human behavior, and also is a potential target for counseling intervention. The four major aspects in the context of American life are discussed in the next sections.

## The Impact of Advanced Technology

The pervasive impact of advanced technology in the workplaces and homes of the United States has been a major transformative force in the nation for several decades. The implementation of advanced technology is now a central factor in international economic competition and in participation in the global economy, politics, and trade. It is stimulated and undergirded by the dramatic linkages between scientific breakthroughs and their rapid adaptations into technologies that are incorporated in commercial, medical, governmental, industrial, and military systems. Advanced technology has rearranged the occupational structures of the United States and other countries. It has also changed teaching and learning processes and has created new styles of entertainment and social discourse. Advanced technology has replaced experience as a primary requirement of employability along with basic academic skills, teachability, and flexibility. Advanced technology, computers, and the Internet have increased the academic and technical skills required in many jobs and have redefined human–machine interactions. Advanced technology has reduced the number of people required to operate, maintain, and troubleshoot workplaces in manufacturing, financial services, information production and dissemination, agriculture, and other industries. Advanced technology has changed the organization of work from hierarchical, pyramidal structures to flatter, more participatory structures. It also accents the need in such organizations for workers who have skills in conflict resolution, interpersonal facilitation, collective decision making, problem solving, personal responsibility, and self-management. Advanced technology changes the roles of managers and employers and the way they interact, and it increases the need for constant worker retraining and information about personnel development, mobility, career ladders, and lattices. Advanced technology changes the social psychology of work, as computers become integral tools in work stations at all levels, and it changes the flow of information workers need for their jobs. Advanced technology changes the stresses and strains that workers experience from those that are physical to those that are mental and emotional. Advanced technology places many workers at risk of underemployment, unemployment, or even temporary employment, since they may be unable to acquire the skills and work habits necessary to use such technologies.

The challenges for ecological counseling from the comprehensive implementation of advanced technology are many. How can counselors help young people explore, choose, and prepare for jobs and occupations that are often located behind large fences and in skyscrapers, in computer files and software applications, and are themselves in dynamic flux? If basic academic skills, computer literacy, teachability, flexibility, commitment to lifelong learning, and interpersonal competencies are fundamental employability skills, how do counselors interpret those requirements and facilitate their acquisition by counselees? If retraining of workers is the norm in technologically rich environments, how do counselors ensure that workers understand the elasticity of their current skills, the options for retraining, and the career paths likely to emerge from such training? Since fewer workers will have permanent and long-term employment and a growing number of workers will have temporary and part-time employment, how should counselors assist with associated issues of new models of career paths, career self-management, underemployment, reduced quality of life, and feelings of uncertainty and vulnerability?

## The Changing American Family

Because of many factors, both economic and social, American family structures have changed, as have their reasons for existing. Many of the historical roles that gave family units cohesion and purpose have been diluted or changed. Economic survival and the propagation and raising of children have been modified or eliminated in favor of views of marriage as units that provide personal and social relationships. Family patterns have become more diverse. The historical idealized role of an intact family—mother as homemaker, father as financial provider, and two children—has now become the exception. Single parents, usually headed by the mother, blended families, and same-sex families have rapidly grown in numbers. The majority of married couples now have both parents working, with a large proportion of such parents paying someone for child care (Farley, 1996).

In many communities, schools are becoming child-rearing institutions offering free breakfasts and lunches and are the one predictable environment in many children's lives. About half of all women with children under age 18 are now in the labor force. Child poverty has become a persistent problem in the United States. In 1993, 15.7 million children lived in households with incomes below the poverty line (Farley, 1996). There is an increasing incidence of dysfunctional parents who are unable or unwilling to take responsibility for raising their children. Whether because of substance abuse, violence in the home, or incarceration, physical or emotional illnesses render them incapable of parenting. In the past decade or so, there has been a 40% increase in the number of households in which a grandparent has assumed parental responsibilities (Pinson-Millburn, Fabian, Schlossberg, & Pyle, 1996).

Within the context of changing family structures, the frustrations, stresses, and strains of family living have changed. Societal confusion about expectations for families has created new tensions and discomforts for people within families and for those considering creating a family. Within many family units, the patterns of intimacy, relationships, and communication are sources of stress. In some instances, stressors are economic; in others, psychological. Within ecological contexts that have witnessed changing family structures and roles of family members, the norms of childhood and the circumstances in which children are being raised have changed. Counselors are being challenged by the new and insistent needs of latchkey children, children of alcoholics, children of disintegrating or blended families, children and other family members experiencing codependency, and children in single-parent households. These challenges stimulated many ecological counseling roles on behalf of both children and their parents (e.g., advocacy roles for social policies supporting effective day care; interventions in child abuse and spouse battery; flextime and parental-leave provisions in the workplace; coordination of community resources to provide greater continuity and nurturing for children).

## Cultural Diversity and Pluralism

America is increasingly conscious of the extent and comprehensiveness of its cultural diversity. Statistics portraying the demographics of the United States indicate that legal and illegal immigration to the United States remains essentially as high as it was during the great waves of immigration in the early 1900s. However, the countries of origin of immigrants have shifted from Europe to Asia and the Spanish-speaking nations of Mexico, Central America, and South America. African American populations are now the majority populations in several of the major cities of the United States, such as Atlanta, Detroit, and Washington, D.C. As suggested previously in this chapter, cultural diversity and pluralism can be treated in several ways. On one hand, these differences can be ignored, and all can be treated as though they have the same experiences, learning, and traditions. In such cases, the assumption is that people from all cultural traditions will be absorbed into the dominant culture, denied their feelings of cultural identity, and the American population will be homogenized. On the other hand, cultural diversity and pluralism can be celebrated, and the contributions of people from diverse cultural traditions to the common American good can be acknowledged and valued. Although these two approaches to cultural diversity and pluralism are caricatures of reality, they nevertheless frame some of the issues that are part of the ecological context of the United States, for which ecological counseling is important.

But, how can historic enmities and religious or cultural disagreements among American subpopulations, ethnocultural and racial groups, and other elements of social pluralism be addressed most effectively in services provided, public policies, and legislation? How can the counseling profession most effectively move from theoretical counseling approaches that are primarily intracultural to counseling approaches that are cross-cultural and culturally sensitive? How do counselors learn about the worldviews and perceptual windows to which persons of different cultural groups are socialized and which guide their behavior? What are the primary roles in ecological counseling with individuals whose work ethics, personal identities, achievement motives, and other characteristics come from traditions and histories that are not

Western? How are predominant views of culture as racial and ethnic in origin influenced by information that suggests that poverty and socioeconomic states are also cultural mechanisms that, in turn, regulate interpersonal behavior?

Although poverty and socioeconomic status may interact with racial and ethnic variables, they can also stand alone as powerful influences in ecological contexts.

## Children, Youth, and Adults at Risk

Partly because of the factors just discussed, there are increasing numbers of children, youth, and adults who are at risk of academic, social, and economic failure. Problems of living that put people at psychological, social, or economic risk are typically multidimensional, and their effects ripple through the social systems with which those at risk interact. For example, when a family member becomes alcoholic, mentally ill, or unemployed, his or her behavior affects other people inside and outside the family and workplace. These individuals may be caught up in or a codependent of the network of problems, dysfunctions, or negativism in which the primary person at risk is embedded.

The questions for ecological counseling relative to populations of people at risk take many forms, including, for example, advocacy for these individuals' needs and for multidimensional delivery systems that offer early identification and treatment, support systems, stress management, and outreach services (e.g., relapse prevention programs, employee assistance programs, family consultation). A major role for ecological counseling is in the influencing of major institutions—schools, churches, employers—to consider carefully the ingredients of their environments to affirm those who nurture mental health and individual responsibility; the diagnosis, treatment, and support of at-risk individuals and groups; and the promotion of wellness and behavioral health.

## Conclusion

Much more can be said about the ecological context of American life today or, perhaps more precisely, the array of subcontexts that exist in various parts of the United States. Suffice it to say the examples offered here accent the interaction of individuals with their environments and suggest some of the behaviors that result from such interactions. Ecological contexts are the origins of and the conduits for pressures on individuals to behave in certain ways, to view themselves in particular roles, and to subscribe to selected values. Frequently, however, the fit of individuals and their ecological contexts is not a congenial relationship. The results may be marginalization, segregation, or separation—if not physically, then surely in psychological or behavioral terms.

Ecological contexts are in some aspects always changing, always dynamic in their influences. The unfolding of social, political, and economic events may create new opportunities for choice and opportunity or new and different stressors for different population groups. Such contextual factors may be reflected in the anxieties, uncertainties, confusions, information needs, and perceptions of self-worth or competence that people experience. As the chapter has continuously reinforced, external psychosocial events shape behavior as they are filtered through perceptions, information-processing mechanisms, feelings of self-efficacy, and other intrapsychic processes by which possibilities are translated into activities. The success or failure of such mechanisms and how the client interprets and acts upon these external pressures and events frequently become the content of counseling.

The range and scope of ecological contexts and ecological counseling requires counselors to function within wide lenses of understanding and analysis. They need more than a psychological window by which to interpret and understand the ecological pressures on their counselees; they also need interdisciplinary insights from the behavioral, economic, and political sciences. As such, to engage in ecological counseling, counselors cannot be insular or encapsulated within limited models of individual/environment transactions. Instead, counselors must develop a metalanguage of the substance and the changes in the environments their counselees occupy (e.g., the occupational structure and work organizations, the family, leisure contexts, educational and training opportunities). They must examine how these environments affect counselee behavior, how individuals understand the circumstances and events of their lives, and the multiple intervention strategies that can be implemented to address such individual/environmental interactions.

## Learning Activities

1. In this chapter, three ecological counseling examples are discussed. One deals with the potential impact of external systems (e.g., welfare, courts, public housing) on inner-city Black families; a second deals with immigrants experiencing the loss of a cultural identity; a third deals with cultural differences in learn-

ing and cognitive styles. Review each of these counseling problems and (a) identify as specifically as possible how the external environment affected individual behavior; (b) discuss with a colleague what ecological counseling processes might be employed to address each problem; and (c) describe three additional counseling challenges that you have experienced with ecological factors that affect individual behavior.

2. Write down all of the systems of which you are now a part (e.g., employment, politics, religion, education, family). How have these individual systems affected your behavior and your feelings about yourself? Are these affects the same from system to system? Are the systems with which you now interact the same as those you would have identified 5 years ago? How do you anticipate your environments will change in the next 5 years?

3. Read the newspaper each day for a week, and each day list the types of ecological challenges to individuals that you find. Such challenges may occur in financial or other economic terms, work stoppages, violence, interpersonal issues, educational requirements, family or community concerns, or other emphases. At the end of the week, discuss your list and its implications for you as a counselor with a colleague.

4. You have read in this chapter about behavioral metaphors that nations or scholars use to describe national characteristics (e.g., Triumph of Meanness). As you watch television or listen to the radio, jot down any behavioral metaphor that you identify as a description of contemporary environments. Compare what you find with the metaphors listed or discussed in this chapter.

## References

Aponte, H. (1980). Family therapy and the community. In M. S. Gibbs, J. R. Lachenmyer, & J. Sigel (Eds.), *Community psychology: Theoretical and empirical approaches* (pp. 311–333). New York: Garner Press.

Berry, J. W. (1994). An ecological perspective on cultural and ethnic psychology. In E. J. Trickett, R.J. Watts, & D. Birman (Eds.), *Human diversity: Perspectives on people in context* (pp. 115–141). San Francisco: Jossey-Bass.

Berry, J. W., & Bennett, J. A. (1992). Ecological conceptions of cognitive competence. *International Journal of Psychology, 27*, 73–88.

Berry, J. W., Kim, U., Minde, T., & Mok, D. (1987). Comparative studies of acculturative stress. *International Migration Review, 21*, 491–511.

Bronfenbrenner, U. (1979). *The ecology of human development*. Cambridge, MA: Harvard University Press.

Cabral, A. C., & Salomone, P. R. (1990). Chance and careers: Normative versus contextual development. *The Career Development Quarterly, 39*, 5-17.

Farley, R. (1996). *The new American reality. Who we are, how we got here, where are we going*. New York: Russell Sage.

Fromm, E. (1962). *Beyond the chains of illusion*. New York: Simon & Schuster.

Gibson, E. J. (1982). The concept of affordances in development: The renascence of functionalism. In A. Collins (Ed.), *The concept of development: Vol. 15. The Minnesota Symposium of Child Psychology* (pp. 55-81). Hillsdale, NJ: Erlbaum.

Gintis, H. (2001). Foreword: Beyond selfishness in modeling human behavior. In R. M. Nesse (Ed.), *Evolution and the capacity for commitment* (pp. xiii-xviii). New York: Russell Sage Foundation.

Herr, E. L. (1999). *Counseling in a dynamic society. Contexts and practices for the 21st century* (2nd ed.). Alexandria, VA: American Counseling Association.

Hines, P., & Boyd-Franklin, N. (1982). Black families. In M. McGoldrick, J. K. Pearce, & J. Giordano (Eds.), *Ethnicity and family therapy* (pp. 84-107). New York: Guilford Press.

Holland, J. L. (1973). *Making vocational choices: A theory of careers*. Englewood Cliffs, NJ: Prentice-Hall.

Holland, J. L. (1985). *Making vocational choices: A theory of vocational personalities and work environments* (2nd ed.). Englewood Cliffs, NJ: Prentice-Hall.

Keita, T. P., & Sauter, S. (1992). *Work and well-being: An agenda for the 1990s*. Washington, DC: American Psychological Association.

Lewin, K. (1951). *Field theory and social science: Selected theoretical papers*. New York: Harper.

Murray, H. A. (1938). *Explorations in personality*. New York: Oxford University Press.

Murray, H. A., & Kluckhohn, C. (1956). Outline of a conception of personality. In C. Kluckhohn (Ed.), *Personality, nature, and society* (2nd ed., pp. 1-26). New York: Knopf.

Nesse, R. M. (2001). Natural selection and the capacity for selective commitment. In R. M. Nesse (Ed.), *Evolution and the capacity for commitment* (pp. 1-44). New York: Russell Sage Foundation.

Neville, H. A., & Mobley, M. (2001). Social identities in contexts: An ecological model of multicultural counseling psychology processes. *The Counseling Psychologist, 29*, 4, 471-486.

Pinson-Millburn, N. M., & Fabian, E. S., Schlossberg, N. K., & Pyle, M. (1996). Grandparents raising grandchildren. *Journal of Counseling & Development, 74*(6), 548-554.

Sardi, Z. (1982). *The psychological aspects of immigration to Israel*. Paper presented to the International Round Table for the Advancement of Counselling. University of Lausanne, Switzerland.

Spiegel, J. (1982). An ecological model of ethnic families. In M. McGoldrick, J. K. Pearce, & J. Giordano (Eds.), *Ethnicity and family therapy* (pp. 31–54). New York: Guilford Press.

Stern, G. G., Stein, M., & Bloom, B. J. (1956). *Methods in personality assessment.* Glencoe, IL: Free Press.

Stevens, B., Miller, R., & Michalski, W. (2000). *Social diversity and the creative society of the 21st century.* Paris: Organization of Economic Cooperation and Development.

*Webster's New Universal Unabridged Dictionary* (2nd ed.). (1983). New York: Dorset & Baber.

## Chapter 3

# The Perspective of Ecological Counseling: Beyond Subject/Object

### *Joseph A. Stewart-Sicking*

---

*Chapter Highlights*
- *The ecological approach to counseling begs one central question: namely, how can counselors conceptualize the interaction of people and their environments without privileging one perspective over the other?*
- *Models that equate person-environment interaction to natural systems are inadequate for expressing an ecological perspective.*
- *The ecological perspective corresponds well to sociological theories of agency-structure integration.*
- *An ecological perspective implies that people and their environments are inseparable from one another.*
- *An ecological approach suggests that relationships, and not people or environments alone, are the primary reality of the social world.*

---

The ecological approach to counseling might appear straight-forward: effective counseling should consider the interaction of person and environment. Perhaps this seems to be nothing more than a reminder to place the client in the context of larger social systems. That seems like a good idea, but not an especially revolutionary one.

This chapter suggests that an ecological approach to human behavior is more challenging. In fact, following the logic of an ecological approach necessitates changing the conventional ways counseling has understood people and their environments. By exploring the theoretical implications of the ecological approach, it proposes a new way of conceptualizing clients and interventions that focuses on relationships and interactions rather than objects and subjects.

## Objects or Subjects

In simultaneously asking counselors to consider the person *and* the environment, the ecological approach begs one central question: How can counselors conceptualize the interaction of people and their environments without privileging one perspective over the other?

Most of the conceptual tools that counselors typically use tend to focus on *either* the person *or* the environment. Although it seems that the ecological counselor need simply add the two perspectives together, they are not entirely compatible.

For instance, a great many conceptual tools can roughly be categorized as environmental: examining the distribution of stimuli for maladaptive behavior, considering how the client has been affected by societal discrimination, considering how the client is wearing the symptom of his or her family system, and so on. Despite their obvious differences, these perspectives share a common feature: their primary concern is for what is objectively occurring outside the client. Certainly these perspectives contain some truth—the client is impacted by the environmental structures he or she identifies. However, to the extent to which these perspectives see the client as an object, obeying inviolable laws of the social world, these perspectives are difficult to integrate with perspectives that focus on the client's unique characteristics.

Likewise, there are also a great many personal counseling tools that focus on what is happening inside the client as a subject, such as examining the transference relationship, restructuring belief systems, helping the client renarrate his or her life experiences, and so forth. Again, there is no question as to the efficacy of these techniques. However, to the extent the techniques isolate the subjective reality of the client from its dependence on its physical and social context, these approaches tend to interface poorly with views that focus on how the environment determines behavior.

Given these incompatibilities, it seems that a more subtle approach needs to be taken toward integrating personal and environmental perspectives than merely superimposing them. How, then, can an ecological perspective encompass a person and his or her environment without privileging either perspective and succumbing to these difficulties?

## Counseling on the Shores of Walden Pond?

To move forward in answering this question, it is necessary to step aside for a moment to avoid a potential trap: the term *ecological* seems to be everywhere in contemporary society. Thus, to use it for a specific purpose in counseling, *ecological* must first be freed from some of its more common connotations. Briefly put, *ecological* in counseling is not the same as *ecological* in natural science or popular culture.

Indeed, the term *ecological counseling* may at first conjure up idyllic scenes of a counselor and client seated in Adirondack chairs on the wooded shores of a still lake, drawing healing from the rising mist; or perhaps it suggests using counseling advocacy to fight global warming or promote recycling. Neither vision is entirely objectionable, but the roots of this approach lie much deeper. At its core, ecological counseling is concerned with the interaction between people and their environments, both physical and social, and the implications of this interactive reality for healing.

The term *ecological* was first used in this sense by Bronfenbrenner (1979), who conceived of the person as embedded in a multilayered, complex web of environmental relationships. Bronfenbrenner suggested that human development is most accurately portrayed as a function of proximal processes relating people and their environments through recurrent and increasingly complex reciprocal interaction (Bronfenbrenner, 1999). Consistent with his usage, the ecological perspective seeks to apprehend people within the context of their relations to their environment.

These person–environment interactions can be modeled in various ways. Traditionally, social scientists tend to borrow models of ecosystems from natural science without much modification. The limitations of this practice are seen in the two most common of these naturalistic models: general systems theory and organic functionalism (see Ritzer, 2000, and Turner, 1998, for specific examples of these models in sociology).

General systems theory considers social systems (e.g., societies, families, groups, organizations) to be analogous to physical systems. It assumes that social systems are homeostatic. Through processing feedback, the system takes action to maintain equilibrium, just as a thermostat controls temperature or a scale stays balanced.

By analogy, this thermostat model is applied to social systems by a wide variety of social scientists (e.g., family systems theories, Gale & Long, 1996; reality therapy, Glasser, 1986; and general systems theory, Turner, 1998). To use it, one must identify the inputs and outputs of the system as well as its feedback loops and regulative functions. For example, a family will resist therapeutic change because it disrupts the equilibrium established in the roles and actions of its members.

Similarly, organic functionalism likens social systems to an organism, which possesses differentiated parts, each functioning for the good of the entire organism (Parsons, 1953; Turner, 1998). For instance, the human body is an organism that possesses a variety of internal systems, none of which may stand alone, but each of which provides a vital function for the remainder of the body. Each component of a system is identified by what function it plays for the organic whole. In the human organism, the heart is that organ whose function is to pump blood and thus oxygen and nutrients to the rest of the body. To understand any part of a system, one must understand how it is integrated into the whole.

By assuming that social behavior is analogously for the good of the entire society, organic functionalism can explain any social phenomenon through identifying its function vis-à-vis the whole (Turner, 1998). For example, we may consider the function of a scapegoat in a group as an outlet for aggression that minimizes the threat of aggression toward each member. Every action is made for the good and stability of the entire system.

Although these examples may appear straightforward, they mask a weakness. As in popular use, Bronfenbrenner's term *ecological* does imply an interconnected system, but unlike ecology in natural science, ecology in counseling deals with human beings whose lives are filled with meaning and unpredictability in ways that plants and clouds are not. Thus, while physical or biological models of ecosystems may seem appropriate (and, indeed, many counseling theories already use natural systems theory), their fundamental assumptions can be incompatible with counseling.

## Critiques of Natural Ecology as Human Ecology

Both general systems theory and organic functionalism are appealing, but they illustrate how human ecology cannot simply borrow directly from the ecology of the physical world. Although naturalistic models can be useful metaphorically in conceptualizing social systems, they are driven by assumptions that often are not tenable. Specifically, these approaches assume that social systems operate according to unbreakable laws of systemic action or organic unity, ignoring that social systems are composed of conscious human beings, not mindless objects. An ecological approach to counseling must avoid this trap.

70

In sociology, some theorists have begun to argue more vehemently against the uncritical use of systems and functional theories. For instance, one prominent social theorist objected to such models outright: "[This model] excludes functionalism and organicism: the products of a given field may be systematic without being products of a system . . . characterized by common functions, internal cohesion and self-regulation" (Bourdieu & Wacquant, 1992, p. 103). Social systems cannot be equivalent to natural systems because they are produced by human beings. Unlike computers, plants, or planets, human beings are self-aware. It is problematic to maintain that human systems automatically reach some collective and coordinated decision and course of action to maintain equilibrium or optimum functionality.

Another sociological theorist, Giddens (1984), provided a more detailed attack on the depiction of human beings in functional and systems theories. Although members of a social system may choose to act in accordance with feedback, this reflexivity is not equivalent to the thermostat model of homeostatic theories. Unlike a thermostat, individuals do not necessarily perceive all inputs to the system accurately, nor do they necessarily stay fixed upon a stable goal. Moreover, human beings change their own goals; there is not some external entity turning up the heat.

Giddens also argued that the homeostatic systems metaphor of interdependence does not take into account the problem of unintended consequences. As opposed to a mechanical system whose equilibrium is guaranteed by unbreakable physical laws, a social system maintains its equilibrium only because its members desire to maintain routine and use social rules and resources to do so. Moreover, even when they are attempting to maintain equilibrium, human beings act in ways that produce unintended consequences. Since people make decisions based on their own thinking, social systems do not necessarily behave according to natural laws.

As this discussion indicates, an ecological perspective to counseling cannot rely on naturalistic models of ecosystems to integrate person and environment. Instead, it must focus on the interactions between conscious human beings and their physical and social environments. Accordingly, the most fertile basis for outlining this approach comes from philosophical and sociological approaches that have expressly considered these problems, rather than from naturalistic analogies that tend to obscure them.

The explorations that follow examine the work of four thinkers who have formed their ideas in response to the bifurcation in

Western thought between personal and environmental perspectives. From their insights, the basis for an ecological perspective to counseling emerges.

## Philosophy and Ecology

### There Are No God's-Eye Views of the World: Quantum Epistemology

One of the most problematic consequences of privileging the environmental perspective over the personal is that it assumes that counselors can acquire a God's-eye view of the world as it actually is. Ironically, while American social scientists were attempting for most of the 20th century to study humanity through this naturalistic model of science, natural scientists were altering its very foundations.

The breakthrough came in physics. When physicists began to examine phenomena on successively smaller scales, the model governing that field began to break down. Classic physics was replaced by a quantum physics that required a radical revision of scientific epistemology (i.e., the theory of how knowledge is acquired).

This new epistemology is exemplified in Werner Heisenberg's uncertainty principle (Goswami, 1992). Heisenberg realized that a system cannot be observed except through physical means that interact with it. Every act of observation makes the observer and his or her apparatus part of the observed system. Consequently, there is no clear boundary between observer and observed (Goswami, 1992). Heisenberg's conclusions issue a direct challenge to the basic assumption of a purely objective/environmental perspective.

The Heisenberg uncertainty principle shows that even in natural science, investigators cannot remove themselves from what they are studying. Investigators into social phenomena have also reached the same conclusion. The Hawthorne effect is precisely the social scientific analogue to this physical principle: observing people alters their behavior; the investigator is not separable from the social reality being investigated. No amount of controlling for investigator artifacts can change this situation. The interaction between observer and observed is a fundamental aspect of science.

This philosophy of science challenges the commonly held principle that one can acquire a view of reality as it is as if one were not a part of it. There is no objective perspective from which to view reality separate from one's relationships to it. A counselor cannot have an entirely objective view of a client apart from a relationship; there is no place from which a counselor can formulate such a view of the client's environment. Thus, an ecological perspective must recognize that the environmental perspective is in some sense irrevocably tied up with the personal perspective.

## There Is No Private Language: The Philosophy of Ludwig Wittgenstein

Another important perspective on the relationship between objective and subjective realities comes from the German-British philosopher, Ludwig Wittgenstein (1889–1951). By exploring the nature of mind and language, Wittgenstein was able to show the problems of a hard dividing line between external and internal realities.

Wittgenstein took up this issue in his *Philosophical Investigations* (1953/1958), which centered on the nature of language and the criteria for its use in ordinary life. In them, he confronted a common way of thinking about language: namely, that it consists of assigning words to language-independent realities. For example, it seems reasonable that the word "anger" is simply the sound assigned by English speakers to a specific set of internal sensations. Wittgenstein's investigations into how people acquire and use language showed that it is not so simple.

One of the most important concepts Wittgenstein developed is the *language game*. Wittgenstein deliberately chose a metaphor for language that argues against the existence of eternal, unequivocal, and explicit rules for language use. The notion of a language game draws attention to the role of nonlinguistic surroundings and learning in language acquisition and use (Schulte, 1992).

As in any other game, one learns to play a language game not by having the rules explained, but rather through training and practicing within a specific context. The "teaching of language is not an explaining but a training" (Wittgenstein, 1953/1958, §5). Instead of presenting a language user with a set of language-independent phenomena and their designations, the training of an individual in language use necessarily entails unquestioned entry into a communal understanding of use.

Moreover, language necessarily shapes life into its categories. Thus, to imagine a language is to imagine the world produced through its use, which Wittgenstein defined as a *form of life*. Forms of life emerge through the practices of a linguistic community (Schulte, 1992). Through their patterns of language use, communities make judgments: "communication by means of language requires not only agreement in definitions, but also (strange as it may sound) agreement in judgments" (Wittgenstein, 1953/1958, §242). Communities cannot simply agree to assign the word "book" to a bound collection of organized pages. Any designation is meaningless unless it also endows an object with a significance, position, and use within a community.

Language is not reducible to a system of assigning signs to language-independent thoughts. It is in the end a dynamic, learned system that does not exist apart from use. The notion of language-independent realities awaiting codification in language is deceptive. In fact, the converse is true: language constitutes the thoughts and judgments one has about the world.

Even in the subjective realm of personal experiences, one is part of a community of use. "The essential thing about private experience is really not that each person possesses his own exemplar, but that nobody knows whether other people also have *this* or something else," Wittgenstein wrote. "The assumption would thus be possible—though unverifiable—that one section of mankind had one sensation of red and another section another" (Wittgenstein, 1953/1958, §272). No one can have a private language for expressing subjective experiences, since such a language does not possess the basic elements of language in general: public criteria, intersubjective evaluation, and confirmation (Schulte, 1992). Language, and hence thought, is tied to community. No one is an island.

Wittgenstein's linking of objective/communal and subjective/personal realities provides a powerful philosophical argument for an ecological approach to social science, for in the very place that is seemingly most mine, most separate, most interior, most independent of others—in sum, most personal—in this place, the very substance of my thoughts is inescapably intertwined with my environment. I cannot come up with my own language, and I cannot help but be shaped by the form of life in which I participate, even in my description of my own internal states. Even my emotions are not simply names for internal sensations. They locate my sensations within a form of life. My form of life influences my emotions—both as internal sensations (which in reality are never unaccompanied by their construction as emotions in the form of life) and as attributions. Wittgenstein's theory leads to the inevitable conclusion that my life as a person is inseparable from the life of my environment.

An exploration of the philosophies of Wittgenstein and Heisenberg has shown the difficulties inherent in postulating a firm dividing line between person and environment, fact and opinion, and subjectivity and objectivity. To move forward in constructing an ecological perspective, we therefore must consider theoretical links across these boundaries. Because its subject matter explicitly considers persons in the context of their environments, sociology proves to be a key resource in this project.

## Agency/Structure Integration: Sociological Theory and the Ecological Perspective

Sociologists have been at the forefront of the theoretical effort to integrate the personal and environmental perspectives. In contemporary European sociological theory, this concern has led to an important strain of thought exploring the nature of the relationship between social agency and social structure (Ritzer, 2000)—i.e., how the actions of self-conscious social entities are related to abiding social realities of all types: symbolic, physical, economic, power. Agency–structure integration theories begin by recognizing that these two are intimately related, and that neither one can be considered without the other. Thus, this group of theories constitutes a concerted effort to avoid the either/or problems of the person–environment split in Western thought.

### Renouncing the False Dichotomies of Social Science: Pierre Bourdieu

One of the most prominent agency–structure theorists is the French thinker Pierre Bourdieu. Bourdieu's work is unified by its attempt to overcome the false dichotomies of subject and object, research and practice, and agency and structure. As Wacquant (1992) wrote,

> [B]ased upon a non-Cartesian social ontology that refuses to split object and subject, intention and cause, materiality and symbolic representation, Bourdieu seeks to overcome the debilitating reduction of sociology to either an objectivist physics of material structures or a constructivist phenomenology of cognitive forms. (p. 5)

With the ecological approach, Bourdieu sought to avoid the false choices forced by isolating personal and environmental perspectives from one another.

Bourdieu based his work on three crucial assumptions (Wacquant, 1992). First, he focused on the practice of social interaction rather than social structures or individual perceptions. Secondly, following the classic account of Durkheim (1912/1995), he asserted that mental structures correspond to social structures, since repeated exposures to the structures of society lead one to internalize its symbols and ways of structuring reality. Finally, Bourdieu believed that social reality lies in relationships, not in objects or subjects, since only relationships have the potential to be dynamic.

For Bourdieu, the dynamic, relational character of society was best conceived as simultaneously a set of objective positions in society and subjective dispositions toward society, known as *field* and *habitus* (Bourdieu, 1977; Bourdieu & Wacquant, 1992; Wacquant, 1992). In his theory of habitus and field, Bourdieu attempted to implement the fundamental insight of the ecological perspective, the interpenetration of person and environment: "The notion of habitus accounts for the fact that social agents are neither particles of matter determined by external causes, nor little monads guided solely by internal reasons, executing a sort of perfectly rational internal program of action" (Bourdieu & Wacquant, 1992, p. 136). Bourdieu envisioned social action and structure as constantly developing through the interplay of objective positions (fields) and subjective predilections for action (habitus).

*Field* designates a set of structured relationships between positions in the social world that are historically embodied and maintained through forms of social power and capital. It exists through relationships: "[T]o think of a field is to think relationally" (Bourdieu & Wacquant, 1992, p. 97). Like a gravitational field, Bourdieu's field is a relational configuration with a specific pull on all who enter it. It is an objective given to those who enter it and imposes a distribution of capital, power, and status.

Within any field, actors compete for different types of capital, which allows them to influence the further development of the field (Bourdieu & Wacquant, 1992; Turner, 1998). Economic capital consists of monetary and material resources to create goods and services. Cultural/informational capital is composed of manners, credentials, tastes, and general information, which confer influence in one's culture. Social capital is the sum of the resources accompanying one's network of relationships. These three are monitored by symbolic capital, which is the use of symbols to legitimate the distribution of other types of capital. By amassing and using capital, actors can influence their position in the field.

For instance, in the field of professional counseling, individuals strive to obtain a good salary (economic capital), appropriate credentials and the latest popular training (cultural capital), and a good referral network (social capital). All of these are shaped by the counseling literature and training standards (symbolic capital). In gaining these forms of capital, the counselor is able to influence his or her place in the field.

Societies are composed of many such fields of action: "In highly differentiated societies, the social cosmos is made up of a number of such relatively autonomous social microcosms . . . that are *specific and irreducible* to those that regulate other fields" (Bourdieu & Wacquant, 1992,

p. 97). Although all fields impose their logics on actors, each ends up operating according to quite different rules, since each is continually produced by practical actors who make their own rules. Thus, there is no grand systemic logic uniting all fields; for instance, academe is an inherently different field than professional soccer. To succeed in academe, one needs to publish, obtain appointments, and gain the respect of one's peers. Success in professional soccer comes with playing time, salaries, and endorsements. The capital and skills needed in each field are quite independent.

The complement to field is the *habitus*, which is the internalization of a field's structures in individuals' perceptions, beliefs, and actions. It is a "system of lasting and transposable dispositions which, integrating past experiences, functions at every moment as a matrix of perceptions, appreciations, and actions and makes possible the achievement of infinitely diversified tasks" (Bourdieu, 1977, p. 95). A habitus is triggered by an encounter with a specific field and structured by it through conditioning. In short, "habitus is socialized subjectivity" (Bourdieu & Wacquant, 1992, p. 126). Habitus is ideally suited to participate in the field from whence it has arisen: "When habitus encounters a social world of which it is the product, it is like a 'fish in the water'" (Bourdieu & Wacquant, 1992, p. 127). However, when a habitus is activated, its actions are below the level of consciousness. They are automatic and strategic, not necessarily rational or consciously self-interested. Nonetheless, habitus is not a rigid law of conduct: it is vague, improvisational, and, above all, pragmatic.

Neither habitus nor field makes sense without the other; a configuration of social positions makes no sense without practical actors willing to live out this structure, and constructs of social reality make no sense other than being triggered by a social system in which these are the rules of participation. Moreover, habitus and field are not a static pair; they subtly shape one another as in a game. As with any game, it is possible that players may improvise (Bourdieu & Wacquant, 1992). Thus, fields evolve over time. For instance, in academe, individuals and groups lobby for funding and prestige, changing the value of different skill sets and the influence of different departments and positions. In this way, a social field is *not* equivalent to a gravitational field because actors struggle to change its configuration. Bourdieu saw the relationship between habitus and field above all as fluid, responsive, and practical.

By adopting an ecological perspective that focuses on the relationships between objective and subjective reality, Bourdieu opened a wide range of new ideas about how people interact with their environments. Most important, Bourdieu's work suggested that counselors focus primarily on the interconnectedness and fluidity that links environments and individuals.

## Escaping the Dualism of Objectivism and Subjectivism: Anthony Giddens

The British sociologist, Anthony Giddens, provided another important account of society that seeks to overcome the opposition of agency and structure. Like Bourdieu, Giddens saw the dominant streams of social theory as too dualistic, and he formulated a new account of the nature and constitution of society to overcome this problem: structuration theory. In *The Constitution of Society*, Giddens (1984) introduced his structuration theory by asserting, "In formulating structuration theory I wish to escape from the dualism associated with objectivism and subjectivism" (p. xxvii). Giddens assumed an ecological perspective at the very core of his theory.

Structuration theory seeks to study social practices ordered in space and time through the actions of reflexive (i.e., self-monitoring) human agents. Giddens' key insight was that social structures and social agents are not separate, but two sides of the same coin:

> The constitution of agents and structures are not two independently given sets of phenomena, a dualism, but represent a duality. According to the notion of the duality of structure, the structural properties of social systems are both [the] medium and outcome of the practices they recursively organize. (p. 25)

Social structures such as institutions, languages, and economies are both the result of human practices and the media through which human beings act. Through our social practices, human beings create a society that endures beyond any particular one of us. Yet, society cannot exist apart from the individuals and groups reproducing it.

Giddens' account of social agency centered on the concepts of routine, purposefulness, and reflexivity. Day-to-day life is shaped by the need for "*ontological security* expressing an *autonomy of bodily control* within *predictable routines*" (p. 50). Thus, the routinization of daily life is an essential bulwark against insecurity, providing trust in the continuity of the social world. In everyday life, individuals ensure security through the purposeful use of routine, though their actions are not always at the level of rational thought.

Though routine, human action is not automatic. Rather, it is reflexive and purposeful. Social agents achieve their purposes by reflexively monitoring their social contexts and using their knowledge to attain their purposes in that context. Unlike feedback loops in machines, however, human reflexivity is limited by unintended consequences and the unconscious. These two bounds upon human self-monitoring add unpredictability and newness to human social behavior. In Giddens' structuration theory, human beings act routinely and reflexively, but not mechanically.

In structuration theory, the flip side of social agency is social structure. Giddens defined structure as "the properties [of social systems] that make it possible for discernibly similar social practices to exist across varying spans of time and space and which lend them systemic form" (p. 17). These properties consist of rules and resources. Rules are procedures of social interaction that either constitute meaning or sanction conduct. Resources are the media of exercising power in routinized situations through allocation and authority. Neither can be conceived apart from the other. Together, they constitute the enduring features of society.

Agency and structure are linked through the process Giddens referred to as structuration: "[T]he structurating of social relations across time and space, in virtue of the duality of structure" (p. 376). Structuration takes place through specific modalities that relate "the knowledgeable capacities of agents to structural features" (p. 28). Because social structure is both the medium and outcome of social interaction, "actors draw upon the modalities of structuration in the reproduction of systems of interaction, by the same token reconstituting their structural properties" (p. 28). Thus, the modality linking the structure of signification with the interactive world of communication is the interpretive scheme. For example, when someone uses gender-stereotyped language (interpretive scheme) to understand a friend and then formulates a response in those terms, that person perpetuates the existence of those ways of looking at the world (structure) in the realm of communication (interaction). The worlds of social interaction and social structure are flip sides of one another. Using the modalities in interaction produces structure. The modalities also realize structure in the world of interaction.

In structuration theory, structure is seen to order action, but not necessarily constrain it, as most social theory tends to convey: "Structure is not to be equated with constraint but is always both constraining and enabling" (p. 25). Why is this the case? Giddens argued that the duality of agency and structure means that while structures can constrain the options of some actors (e.g., allocating resources inequitably so that some individuals do not have the power to accomplish certain goals), they are also the medium of any purposeful social action. Moreover, structural constraints are not equivalent to natural laws of the social world. Although some social forces cannot be resisted, this is only the case because of the goals the actors have that cannot be accomplished. Changing the goals eliminates the force. As Giddens wrote, "Structural constraints do not operate independently of the motives and reasons that agents have for what they do. They cannot be compared with the effect of, say, an earthquake which destroys a town and its inhabitants without their in any way being able to do anything about it" (p. 181). The more institutionalized (i.e., stretched out over time and space) a structure is, the more powerful the perception of constraint, but a social force can never be equivalent to a natural one.

Giddens' structuration theory provides an example of how an ecological perspective can theoretically link macroscopic with microscopic social perspectives. Specifically, Giddens' theory is able to account for both psychologically motivated individuals as well as abiding social realities. Since ecological counseling must also be able to account for people and environments in the same theory, structuration theory is a strong candidate for informing ecological counseling theory.

Many ideas from structuration theory can be of particular interest to counselors: that agency and structure are two sides of the same coin; that natural systems are imperfect analogues for human behavior; that structure is both enabling and constraining; and that structure is something participatory and dynamic rather than external and static. All of these insights flow from Giddens' fundamental critique of the dualism of subject and object.

## Discussion: An Ecological Ontology

From this interdisciplinary exploration of authors who have examined the relationship between person and environment, several recurring themes emerge, suggesting the following principles of an ecological ontology (i.e., an account of what exists) of the social world:

1. The subjective reality of people and the objective reality of environments are inseparable and irreducible to one another.
2. Relationships between people and their environments are the primary reality of the social world.

Some corollaries follow from these two assertions, first about counseling practice, then about counseling itself.

   a. *Every analytical description of a social situation inevitably must reference both the subjective reality of the conscious per-*

80

*son and the objective reality of the physical and social environment.* This statement follows directly from the ecological perspective's avoidance of the subject/object dichotomy. Although conceptualizing a situation primarily from one or the other lens can be helpful, any such perspective is incomplete and will eventually require input from the other. Consider, for example, the case of a client diagnosed with depression. From the perspective of the person, the counselor notices the client's description of depressed emotion and might identify beliefs associated with this depression: "I'm worthless" or "I'm in a horrible situation" or "It'll never get better." In considering this client further, the counselor inevitably will need to consider environmental factors, such as the support systems available to the client and the client's cultural systems. Moreover, the counselor will need to consider the links between the two, such as the sources of these beliefs, the situations of their activation and reinforcement, and the client's sources of capital. Because person and environment are interrelated, either perspective will lead to consideration of the other, and neither will allow for effective intervention if considered alone. Moreover, the complete picture does not result from a simple addition of the person and environment perspectives: the two must be linked and their relationships conceptualized.

b. *Interventions are necessarily at both the personal and environmental levels.* Because counseling interventions are essentially social, they will necessarily change the person and the environment as well as their relationship. In considering the personal impact of environmental interventions, or vice versa, counseling can approach therapy with a much broader palette. For instance, a can of paint can be just as much an intervention as talk therapy (cf. Conyne, 1975).

It is with this realization that many of the constructs of sociological theory can be put to practical use in counseling. Specifically, agency–structure theories such as those of Bourdieu and Giddens identify the mechanisms through which personal and environmental realities interact. Thus, the counselor may look to these theories for conceptualizations and interventions.

For instance, Giddens' account of social constraints offers suggestions for those who seek to examine how social structure impacts mental health and client behavior. Because of the duality of social structure, counselors should consider how the rules and resources clients use both enable and constrain their actions.

Additional examples come from the work of Bourdieu. For instance, Bourdieu's delineation of different types of capital is quite useful for ecological counseling. In an ecological assessment of the client (see chapter 5), an analysis of the types and amounts of capital the client possesses is integral to formulating ecological interventions for that client (e.g., augmenting a client's capital, identifying deficiencies and resources, using the types of capital the client possesses).

Further, both Bourdieu's and Giddens' accounts of the production and reproduction of social structure are important in unveiling the ways that individuals interact with their societies. For counselors interested in social justice and advocacy issues, both theories provide ways to conceptualize the interaction of social processes with individuals. For instance, one might explore the effects of participating in different fields, dominant ideologies, popular culture, and mass media on clients' construction of themselves and their problems as well as the solutions to those problems.

Because counseling itself is also embedded in a social ecosystem, the ecological principles also apply to it, leading to some interesting results.

c. *Social science conditions and shapes what it studies.* As shown in the discussion of Heisenberg's uncertainty principle, social scientists and society are linked. Social scientists cannot remove themselves or their theories from their contexts in society; they have no privileged vantage point. Thus, social scientific constructs do not unveil some esoteric and mysterious reality different from the social reality everyone experiences. Rather, they highlight and name facets of this reality.

Moreover, the descriptions of social reality that are uncovered by social science are used as a knowledge resource by the very people they attempt to describe. Social scientists tell people who they are and give them words to shape and describe their lives. Because people use the constructs of social science, social science cannot help but alter society. Social science is not detached and disinterested: by its nature, it changes what it studies. Thus, social science implies social criticism.

d. *Social science is value laden.* By definition, social science creates narratives about how individuals and societies operate. However, as Wittgenstein indicated, these narratives are not simply an uncovering of some prelinguistic reality. The narratives of social science create a worldview with certain values. Thus, the ecological perspective leads to conclusions similar to those of Wittgenstein, for whom psychological research was not a scientific process—one decontextualized and ahistorical—but rather a moral and political problem with important public consequences (Shotter, 1991). Those who use psychology must be aware of the form of life it establishes regarding what is good, normal, or desirable for individuals and society.

Likewise, the use of language in the counseling process establishes nonobjective values and behavior as normative. Every construction of the client's world and every counseling intervention include a subjective value judgment. For instance, counselors assume that prosocial behaviors are preferable to antisocial ones. When they choose to intervene, counselors are judging the client's thoughts and behaviors as undesirable and providing new thoughts and behaviors suggested by their theoretical orientation and its worldview.

## Conclusion

As this exploration shows, the ecological perspective provides counseling with important new heuristic venues. In integrating subject and object, it suggests that counseling focus on relationships. In highlighting the interpenetration of person and environment, it suggests that the counseling endeavor must attend to and critically consider forms of life, physical environments, social rules, and social resources. Yet, it also warns against the wholesale import of natural science models into social science.

The theoretical approach proposed in this chapter is a relatively new one. Thus, though there is little extant research in the counseling literature on the topic, the ecological approach suggests that counselors examine the relationship between variables expressing person–environment relationships (e.g., capital) and mental health, as well as how interventions in these relationships are related to counseling outcomes.

By exploring thinkers who have moved beyond thinking in terms of person or environment, this chapter offers an ecological approach that provides important new ways of approaching the counseling relationship. However, this is only one example of how thinkers from other fields may provide valuable insights into ecological counseling. Since it is a perspective and not a particular theory, the ecological approach is open to insights from a variety of sources that will enable counseling to address the challenges of a rapidly changing, pluralistic society. It is likely that as the field matures, it will generate other such explorations into related fields. And perhaps this is its greatest strength.

## Learning Activities

1. Consider your own position within the field of counseling using the concepts of Bourdieu's theory: What kinds of capital do you possess? How much of each? How does this distribution of capital affect your behavior and ability to participate in the field? How might another distribution (e.g., cultural capital without social capital, more social capital than economic capital) change this? Does Bourdieu's concept of habitus as socialized subjectivity make sense of your experience in the counseling field? For instance, do you find that when you are participating in counseling activities, the way you approach the world changes (e.g., different language, different perceptions, different ways of behaving)? How have you noticed the counseling field evolving? Does it behave similarly or differently from other fields in which you are engaged? Discuss your observations with a partner for 15 minutes.
2. Giddens stated that social structure consists of rules and resources. What are the rules and resources of the environments in which you find yourself (e.g., the classroom, the counseling relationship, your work setting)? What do they enable? What do they constrain? How do you perpetuate them by using them?
3. The ecological approach contends that counseling both conditions and shapes what it studies. Identify how popular culture uses the output of counseling. What worldview does this imply? What cultural rules and resources does it generate? What values does it uphold?

## References

Bourdieu, P. (1977). *Outline of a theory of practice*. Cambridge, United Kingdom: Cambridge University Press.

Bourdieu, P., & Wacquant, L. J. D. (1992). *An invitation to reflexive sociology*. Chicago: University of Chicago Press.

Bronfenbrenner, U. (1979). *The ecology of human development: Experiments by nature and design*. Cambridge, MA: Harvard University Press.

Bronfenbrenner, U. (1999). Environments in developmental perspective: Theoretical and operational models. In S. Friedman & T. Wachs (Eds.), *Measuring environment across the life span: Emerging methods and concepts.* Washington, DC: American Psychological Association.

Conyne, R. K. (1975). Environmental assessment: Mapping for counselor action. *Personnel and Guidance Journal, 54*, 150-155.

Durkheim, E. (1995). *The elementary forms of religious life* (K. E. Fields, Trans.). New York: Free Press. (Original work published 1912)

Gale, J. E., & Long, J. A. (1996). Theoretical foundations of family therapy. In F. Piercy, D. H. Sprenkle, J. L. Wetchler, et al. (Eds.), *Family therapy sourcebook* (2nd ed). New York: Guilford Press.

Giddens, A. (1984). *The constitution of society.* Berkeley: University of California Press.

Glasser, W. (1986). *Control theory.* New York: Harper and Row.

Goswami, A. (1992). *Quantum mechanics.* Dubuque, IA: William C. Brown.

Parsons, T. (1953). *Working papers in the theory of action.* Glencoe, IL: Free Press.

Ritzer, G. (2000). *Sociological theory* (5th ed.). New York: McGraw Hill.

Schulte, J. (1992). *Wittgenstein: An introduction* (W. H. Brenner & J. F. Holley, Trans.). Albany: State University of New York Press.

Shotter, J. (1991). Wittgenstein and psychology. In *Wittgenstein centenary essays.* Cambridge, United Kingdom: Cambridge University Press.

Turner, J. H. (1998). *The structure of sociological theory* (6th ed.). Boston: Wadsworth.

Wacquant, L. J. D. (1992). The structure and logic of Bourdieu's sociology. In P. Bourdieu & L. J. D. Wacquant, *An invitation to reflexive sociology.* Chicago: University of Chicago Press.

Wittgenstein, L. (1958). *Philosophical investigations* (G. E. M. Anscombe, Trans.). Oxford, United Kingdom: Blackwell. (Original work published 1953)

Chapter 4

# Ecological Counseling: Constructivist and Postmodern Perspectives

*Susan Allstetter Neufeldt and Mary Lee Nelson*

---

*Chapter Highlights*

- *Each form of knowledge in Western thought has developed to fill deficits in the previous method. The scientific method, highly valued today among social scientists, developed over centuries in response to the received knowledge that was based on the religion and customs of the medieval era. In turn, as contemporary populations more frequently encounter others from a variety of cultures and places, many thinkers now note that people construct knowledge—even scientific knowledge—within a cultural and geographical context.*

- *The pioneers of psychology and counseling in the late 19th and early 20th centuries, Freud and his followers, believed that psychological problems were based within the individual. Logically, then, they believed that the counselor's job was simply to help clients resolve their specific problems. However, in the latter part of the 20th century, ecological counselors, along with multicultural counselors, began to recognize that problems and their resolution occur within a cultural context. Solving the problem involved the whole system in which the client lived and worked.*

- *Psychologists, counselors, and medical practitioners treated people's minds separately from their bodies in the first half of the 20th century. More recently, however, as scientists studied biochemistry, physiology, and psychology, they discovered that each influenced the other. The body was often integral to the emotional problem and its solution, as was the mind to the physiological problem.*

- *By examining a number of the contexts in which people constructed meaning and experienced life events, ecological counselors learned to incorporate context into their understanding of client problems. No longer, for instance, could counselors consider that the self entirely determined a client's ability to function, nor could they focus solely on the self to resolve problems. Consequently, ecological counselors now strive to change not only their clients' behavior but also the environments in which they live.*

---

Ecological counseling and its theoretical root, constructivism, examine historical events, philosophical and scientific knowledge, and the human experience through a contextual lens. To understand any of these from a constructivist perspective requires knowledge of the settings in which events occurred and perceptions developed. In order to discuss ecological counseling and constructivism in a manner consistent with its approach to truth, it is necessary to establish the context in which it has developed in Western thinking. A brief history of constructivism's Western cognitive and social roots follows.

## Historical Background of Social Constructivism

For several millennia, human beings have examined their lives and the world, defined it based on their understanding of its animate and inanimate characteristics, and determined meaning and moral action within an associated belief system and social structure. Social structures provide the constraints within which humans live, think, and feel. In fact, it is very difficult to live without them.

People within Western culture developed their own belief systems, values, and social structures through a series of cognitive and philosophical revolutions related to the events and human activity of the period in which they lived. Although the history of Western thought properly begins with the Greeks, we start the discussion in this chapter with Western Europe in the Middle Ages, in which religious perspectives of reality dominated human life. These perspectives included the lack of scholarly knowledge (termed darkness) and a belief in superstition as well as the reign of apparently arbitrary political power, often justified in religious terms (Saul, 1992).

The ignorance, suspicion, and ecclesiastical power and warring political factions within medieval Christendom precipitated a powerful reaction: the Reformation and Renaissance, and eventually the Enlightenment. Martin Luther symbolically initiated the revolution known as the Reformation in the 16th century by publicly criticizing the practices of the Pope and those within the church hierarchy (Dillenberger, 1961). New theologians arose who believed not in the biblical interpretations of the Pope or other experts but in the ability of common people to read and interpret the scriptures themselves, which led, of course, to Protestantism. This led, in turn, to the belief in the ability of human beings to understand the world directly, through their own experiences. The blossoming of human knowledge led inevitably to what is called the Enlightenment.

To counter the various and often quarrelsome forms of religious authority still extant, the philosophers of the Enlightenment, such as Voltaire, championed the use of reason by individual humans—and not church and political authority—to understand the world (Saul, 1992). Use of the mind to observe the world and use of human reason to interpret the world developed eventually into a formally structured scientific method. The scientific discoveries that followed led to a remarkable explosion of scientific knowledge and to industrialization of economic endeavor.

The scientific and social ecosystem of that era has evolved—some say too far—and continues to hold sway today in the United States and Europe. The overriding philosophy of science became the basis of objective truth (i.e., truth held to be untainted by human perspectives, truth discovered through the carefully defined scientific method, now described as empirical research). Like prior philosophies, the Western scientific method developed its own rules, structures, and appropriate approach to knowing. At its most extreme, this positivist approach led to specialization, where the valued medical scholar might be one of the few who understands the causes and mechanisms of a particular disease. However, as Saul (1992) asked, "Is this an educated person?"

In an era where knowledge is shared among humans from all regions of the world, the scientific method, as applied to natural sciences, translates rather well across cultures. Water boils at the same temperature, whether it is called 212 degrees Fahrenheit or 100 degrees Celsius, and variables such as temperature, mass, and motion can be isolated so that one can be manipulated while the others are held constant.

In an attempt to apply the scientific method across the behavioral sciences, however, cultural differences have complicated the interpretation of objective observations. How, for instance, does one hold the belief systems of cultural groups constant when examining their behavior across cultures? Can scientific, Western psychotherapy and counseling always relieve a set of symptoms across cultural groups? Can the behavior of men toward women in every situation in every culture be explained in terms of biological imperatives? Is facilitating autonomous behavior for all people an appropriate goal?

As just illustrated, all people live within cultures (i.e., social organizations originating from and often continuously located within a particular geographical environment); establish their own social environments, or social ecosystems, in which people develop their sense of self and their sense of the true, the good, and the right and view reality and behave accordingly. Yet, for a very long time, Western psychologists and coun-

89

selors believed that people had universal attributes, no matter where or with whom they lived. Consequently, they assumed counseling and therapy approaches could be used scientifically in a similar fashion with all people.

## Postmodern and Constructivist Psychology

Postmodernism might be considered a movement, or Zeitgeist, in intellectual inquiry that questions accepted truths, laws, theories, and practices. A response to modernism, or the practice of accepting preexisting theoretical and scientific foundations and basing new intellectual developments upon the old, postmodernism is seen as the rebellious child of classic philosophy and science. Postmodern thinkers actively challenge scientific assumptions because they view all observations in a cultural context and seek not to apply them universally (White & Epston, 1990).

Foucault, one of postmodernism's heroes, recognized that when one searches for truths at the root of commonly accepted theories, one cannot find them (Foucault, 1997). Instead, one finds a spiral of constructions, emerging through time and the space of human discourse, and influenced by the contexts in which they developed. As a highly sensitive and aspiring young philosopher growing up in the repressive and cut throat French intellectual climate of the 1950s, Foucault experienced firsthand the hegemony of accepted paradigms and practices and felt profoundly confined by them (Eribon, 1991). As his philosophy developed, he viewed his intellectual mission as being unwilling to accept common understandings without rigorous examination of the bases on which they were formed. The necessity of analyzing accepted assumptions and their foundations is central to the postmodern endeavor.

Embedded within the postmodern movement is social constructivist thought, which views human knowledge not as truth, but as a product of social and cultural influences. From a social constructivist perspective, human experience is a reflection of a person's interaction with a constantly mutating environment, where values and definitions change over time according to the culture's prevalent discourses (Foucault, 1997; Merleau-Ponty, 1962).

Education, research, and counseling practices that are informed by social constructivist thought emphasize the importance of allowing participants to examine the meanings of their experiences in light of their relation to their own contexts (Sexton & Griffin, 1997). In a constructivist approach, counselors initially assess clients, not strictly by using the diagnostic system of the *Diagnostic and Statistical Manual of Mental Disorders* (American Psychiatric Association, 2000), but instead by examining the client's concerns within the cultural context, including race, ethnicity, gender, historical moment, and community and institutional location. Moreover, from a postmodern standpoint, the counselor does not claim to possess a thorough understanding of the client's dilemma. Rather, counselor and client together construct a narrative, or life story, that is informed by the client's context and that is meaningful for the client. Together they select an approach that constantly evolves as the sessions proceed and events within and outside the sessions alter the counselor and client's perspectives of the problem and its resolution. Within the counseling sessions, the counselor assists the client in constructing a developing and evolving sense of self within the world in which the client lives. The healing narrative constructed in counseling is a product of both counselor and client working together to craft meaning and arrive at solutions that seem to help the client.

Postmodern and social constructivist thought are influenced by existential phenomenologists such as Husserl and Merleau-Ponty, who emphasized the importance of becoming aware of one's own lived experience (Polkinghorne, 1988). Both viewed personal experiences as subjective—not representations of reality, but creations of an individual's perceptual system. Whereas Husserl viewed human perception as independent from the perceived, Merleau-Ponty viewed perception as the product of a dialogue between the perceiver, who is an embodied expression of nature in a natural context, and other objects and aspects of the same natural context. He viewed bodily experiences as important aspects of the natural context and saw them as having a profound influence on individual perception. He also argued that experience is constrained by the culturally influenced linguistic context, the meaning structure that frames an individual's experience. French, for instance, has no word for "achievement" as understood in English, and some cultural anthropologists have argued that it has no cultural equivalent either (Hofstede, 2001). Thus, Merleau-Ponty provided a rich vision of the individual as a physical being in communication with other aspects of nature and in dialogue with his or her culture about the meaning of his or her physical, social, and internal experiences.

The commonalities between the concepts of ecological counseling and counseling from a constructivist or postmodern perspective are obvious. Like postmodern thought, the approach to ecological counseling rejects traditional assumptions about human motivation. Rather than viewing anxiety as a product of unreleased tensions or unmet interpersonal needs, the ecological therapist seeks to understand clients' perceptions about the sources of their stress. Rather than relying on extant psychological constructs about personality or mental health, an ecological therapist views clients as partners in the examination of contextual factors that seem to be contributing the most to clients' difficulties. Like Merleau-Ponty and other postmodern thinkers who view the mind as embodied, or inextricable from body experience, ecological counseling views the body as an aspect of context; thus, experience is a product not only of culturally influenced perceptions but also of perceptions that are influenced by physical events.

Understanding the multiple influences of one's context on one's current sense of malaise can empower clients to assume greater authorship of their lives. This chapter addresses what postmodern and constructivist positions have to offer a model of ecological counseling. We provide a constructivist understanding of ecological factors in counseling: that is, we delineate the contextual factors that frame the counseling endeavor and the way these factors offer change through environmental and socially constructed events within the relationship not only of counselors and clients but also of clients and the social and physical environments in which they live.

## Contextual Factors in Psychology and Counseling

Steenbarger (1993) suggested that Western cultural discourses have *decontextualized* the individual. Western ideas that prize individualism, separation, and competition over community and family well-being disconnect people from their social roots and deprive them of opportunities to understand how their experiences are influenced by cultural and familial meanings. According to Steenbarger, counseling can be a process of *recontextualizing* individual experiences—helping people to understand how the meaning they place on their experience derives from cultural and family influences. The process of recontextualization can involve an examination of the multiple contexts that shape individuals, including race, language, world region, religion, country, community, school, workplace, family, and the body of the individual. To understand contextualization and recontextualization, we have to examine the historical context of positivist thinking.

We talk as though Western psychology has always operated according to positivist and individualistic perspectives; however, psychologists have incorporated context into psychological concepts of development from the beginning. Freud initially described basic drives, or instincts for life, which he couched in sexual terms, or death, which he associated with aggression. He said, however, that one's personality, sense of meaning, and behavioral patterns developed out of the interaction of those drives within a given person's family. Rejecting nonobservable concepts such as the unconscious, learning theorists based their ideas on learning. Pavlov's classic learning involved, again, basic drives such as hunger and thirst and his animal subjects' learning to pair them with certain environmental stimuli (e.g., the ringing of a bell) that could trigger a physiological response. Operational learning, however, involved deliberate rewards (often still food) for specific emitted behaviors selected by the reward manager for reinforcement. Although both relied on the basic drive of hunger, both also described the interaction of hunger, its satisfaction, and the context in which it was satisfied as essential to learning and human development (Zimbardo & Gerrig, 1999). Family systems theorists enlarged the context of interdependent behavior with the idea that each person within a family influenced the functioning of the entire system, in a way that assured its continued functioning.

How, then, to change human behavior depended on manipulating certain contextual variables. Significant expansion of the contexts from European and Euro-American families occurred as (a) the United States and Western Europe increasingly incorporated individuals who originated in different cultural groups; (b) globalization increased exposure to cultures outside the West not just for anthropologists but also for large numbers of ordinary European and American people (e.g., travelers, businessmen, students, families of intermarrying cultural groups, and families that included nonheterosexual members); and (c) socially, economically, and politically oppressed groups expressed dissatisfaction with their lives. It is in this changing economic and political context that European and American psychologists have developed new, more ecological ways of understanding human lives. Because we are talking about the evolution in Western thinking from superstitious prediction to positivist empiricism to social constructivism, we speak here of the evolution of European and American psychological constructs. Ideas of the self, causes of a problem, the relationship between counselor and client, and the healing processes are now seen by social constructivists and ecological counselors as situated within the culture in which a client operates. Further, the relationship between client and counselor, a significant focus in most therapeutic endeavors, is certainly affected by the worldviews both have and the ways in which the counselor can display respect for the client's worldview and values.

In order to understand the evolution of the psychological constructs within the ecological counseling model, it is necessary to examine the ways in which culture has been treated as unimportant within counseling. For instance, within the context of countries where Western thought has developed (and, indeed, in many other countries), there are people whose ancestors originated in other countries or continents, and people whose skin color and facial features differ from those of Europeans and Euro-Americans. Although some of these people are indigenous (e.g., Native Americans), many of them or their ancestors came to the countries where they now live under pressure, either from the societies they entered (e.g., African slave immigrants) or from the societies they left either from political pressure, (e.g., many Vietnamese immigrants), or economic pressure (e.g., many Irish immigrants). Or they migrated simply from a desire to be educated in a system they perceived to be better than their own. In many cases, those immigrants were perceived to be inferior to the Europeans and Euro-Americans at the top of the socioeconomic and political systems within Europe and the United States. In the United States, for instance, Euro-Americans are usually considered to have unearned privileges by virtue of their color or colorlessness (McIntosh, 1998). If White, many of the descendants of immigrants were treated as members of the dominant population; however, persons of color, whether indigenous or immigrant, continued to be oppressed socially, politically, and economically both overtly and covertly. Their values were shaped by their original cultures, the cultures in which they now lived, and their status as oppressed people. Yet counselors and therapists treated them with approaches based on studies of those in the dominant culture.

## Psychological Approaches to Culture

Since Europeans and Americans live less and less within enclaves where their values and behaviors are unchallenged and considered superior (Ponterotto, Casas, Suzuki, & Alexander, 1995), psychology—and particularly psychotherapy—must be reconstructed. In general, we assume that counseling is a way of understanding the meanings people make of their lives and working with the client to modify those internal meanings along with any external changes. Postmodernism contributes a view of ecological factors to this meaning-making process. It adds to the analysis of the individual's internal self the contexts in which the self is formed. In particular, the constructivists say, ecological counselors work to understand and treat people in a way consistent with the values, attitudes, and behaviors of the client's own cultural group and the client's own physical experience. Understanding the client in context, or the person–environment interaction, begins the process of case conceptualization.

## Case Conceptualization: Understanding the Client

Initially, therapists seek to understand how clients experience problems. They look at how clients have developed, their cultural history and experiences, their emotions, and their behavior. As one aspect of that culturally influenced process, constructivists point out that development occurs in a context that affects the way people develop and the meaning they make of developmental milestones.

Child development is a primary focus of current studies (Super & Harkness, 1997), rather than the invariant sequence of universal experiences of people initially described by Erikson (1950, 1968, 1976). Super and Harkness suggested that "not only does the *content* of cultural routines vary, but also the *nature* of children's participation in them" (p. 9). Children acquire their cultures as they acquire language, in a series of practices designed to establish a social and moral order and provide the method by which children participate in a culture (and therefore subsequently transmit it) (Miller & Goodnow, 1995). Further, Valsiner and Lawrence (1997) suggested that development occurs throughout the lifespan. In essence, people learn the signs and symbols of a culture which mediate interactions between a person and either the self or other individuals. "The world of human beings," they wrote, "is a *personally meaningful* world, where that meaningfulness is a result of joint construction by the person and the social world" (p. 71). In addition, each person's development is unique because each makes different choices at different points from culturally sanctioned or unsanctioned pathways and then operates by the social constraints of that pathway. So when counselors and therapists seek to understand their clients, as a part of the case conceptualization process, they must understand each client's original cultural constraints (e.g., family, community, national, ethnic) and those within which the person is now operating. Otherwise, counselors may misunderstand the client's concerns.

As just shown and in what follows, we argue that constructivists understand that clients' experiences and behavior, and the meanings they make of those experiences, are based on their cultural environments. Further, the counselor's understanding of the meaning of what a client presents is a function of the counselor's own culturally influenced experiences and derived meanings.

95

In addition, counselors and therapists understand their clients by trying to recognize a client's display of emotions and the emotions that underlie that expression. Emotions and their expressions develop within a cultural context (Markus & Kitayama, 1994a, 1994b; Mesquita, Frijda, & Scherer, 1997). This again supports the constructivist idea of shared meaning in an area that gets significant attention in counseling, and the shared meanings of emotional display are part of the ecological context of counseling.

From an understanding of development and emotions, counselors seek to understand how clients see themselves. The self is constructed within a social culture. As Markus and Kitayama (1994b) wrote,

> The self of any given individual is some organization of all the various influences of his or her individual social and developmental history. This organization, in which some sociocultural influences are elaborated and emphasized and others are resisted or ignored, affords the person considerable agency and idiosyncrasy. (p. 92)

Markus and Kitayama added that the person who feels a particular emotion incorporates a "unique construction of experience. However, there are still ways of feeling that can be linked systematically to particular cultural frameworks, even though a given emotional state cannot be completely explained from these perspectives" (p. 92).

A third element in understanding clients—their behavior—generally is influenced by their values (Hofstede, 2001). "Values are invisible," Hofstede wrote, "until they become evident in behavior" (p. 10). Individualism, for instance, is a value that is reflected in both the self-construal and the behavior of Euro-Americans and Europeans, whereas collectivism is a value and self-construal reflected in the behavior of Asians, Latin Americans, and many of the world's other populations (Kagitçibasi, 1997; Triandis, 1990). Recently, in an initial practicum supervised by one of the authors in a PhD program known for its multicultural training, a student therapist reported that she had an Asian client she would have understood inaccurately without an understanding of collectivist cultures. In her first session, the client described working hard to graduate with the ability to support not only herself after graduation but also her parents and younger siblings. Because of her training, the Euro-American counselor avoided labeling the client as dependent or enmeshed and instead recognized the culturally normative values of her culture that encouraged this behavior.

Nonverbal behaviors, particularly facial expressions, influence counselor and therapist understanding of clients' emotions. Yet these, too, are culturally influenced. A study cited by Markus and Kitayama (1994b) found that Darwin's belief that facial expressions were consistently linked to emotions across cultures was not supported in terms of people's felt experiences. Levenson, Ekman, Heider, and Friesen (1992) compared the facial expressions and emotional experiences of the Minangkabau people of West Sumatra with those of North Americans. When the Minangkabau people in the study were asked to assume facial expressions consistent with both Darwin's description and the North Americans' physical manifestations of particular emotions, they evidenced physiological responses similar to the North Americans, who described negative and positive emotions associated with those physiological responses. The Minangkabau, however, did not report the same subjective experience of feelings. This phenomenon suggests that there is a strong cultural influence on the experience of emotion. A counselor from North America, then, could misread a Minangkabau client (should one unexpectedly appear in the North American's counseling office) without knowing this.

In other words, what appears critical in understanding clients' nonverbal behaviors is not physiology but rather appraisal—another person–environment interaction. How people appraise situations, particularly as threats or nonthreats, determines their emotional reactions (Mesquita et al., 1997). The appraisal of a given situation differs from culture to culture. Interpersonal conflict, for instance, may be experienced by an Asian client from a collectivist culture as a threatening situation, while a North American might experience it as an opportunity to convince another of a particular point of view. Similarly, Sue and Sue (1999) described a university faculty meeting where the assertive and expressive conflictual style of an African American faculty member appeared to unnerve the other, more restrained Caucasian males at the meeting. The latter considered the former to be unnecessarily emotional and aggressive, while the former just wanted to speak and hear the underlying truths in the situation. In other words, the observer or recipient of nonverbal behaviors constructs a meaning from what he or she observes. The counselor then needs to understand cultural nuances reflected in nonverbal behaviors in order to construct meaning from what the client displays.

## Case Conceptualization: Planning Interventions

Constructivist and ecological counselors and therapists now recognize that they need to consider a client's culture; they also recognize that their therapeutic approaches need to be matched to their clients' cultural beliefs and values. In the United States, considerable research has been aimed at skills and interventions appropriate for different populations. Research by cultural and cross-cultural psychologists form the basis for much of multicultural counseling methodology as developed by counseling psychologists and counselor educators (e.g., Arredondo, 1998, 1999; Arredondo et al., 1996; Atkinson, Bui, & Mori, 2001; Constantine, 1997; Neimeyer, 1995; Pedersen, 1994; Steenbarger, 1993). Although some mainstream psychotherapy researchers (Beutler & Clarkin, 1990) have studied the best matches of treatments for individuals with particular personality styles, multicultural counseling researchers have added cultural components to the match (Ponterotto et al., 1995; Ponterotto, Casas, Suzuki, & Alexander, 2001).

It has been a challenge for well-intended counselors and therapists to use that research to formulate their work with clients in North America. As Martinez and Holloway (1997) wrote,

> Developing the ability to apply cultural knowledge in a relationship with a person from another culture is part of the domain of skill development in multicultural training. Integrating information about a particular culture into applied interactions becomes a real challenge to most helpers. (p. 337)

In particular, understanding clients and devising appropriate interventions has required the recognition that each client is a unique product of his or her personal and family history, cultural background, cultural identity development, personality characteristics, and genetic characteristics. Although some approaches may fit with the average person from a given culture, there is no guarantee that with this particular client that approach will be appropriate (Atkinson & Lowe, 1995). Whereas Asians, for instance, are often described as preferring directive approaches in counseling, that might not be true for a particular Asian client with a particular personal and cultural history. Interpersonal therapy may be desirable instead in some more industrialized and urban areas such as Taipei or Kaohsiung in Taiwan (Klerman, Weissman, Rounsaville, & Chevron, 1984). Those in these industrialized regions are more accustomed to the complexities of modern life and to the self-direction that is integral to the corporate and media worlds to which they are regularly exposed.

Some counselors in the recent past, as cited by Atkinson and Lowe (1995), have suggested that clients who are matched with counselors of the same ethnic background form the best working alliance, since a person of the same culture can provide counseling and therapy that is effective and consistent with cultural beliefs, particularly about healing. However, some clients function at different levels of ethnic identity development (Helms, 1995), and assigning clients to therapists of the same ethnicity may be effective only if a client is beyond believing that everything White is superior, for instance, and everything Black is inferior. Further, in recent studies, clients reported a good working alliance most consistently if counselors appeared to them as people who held similar values and worldviews (Atkinson, Morten, & Sue, 1998).

Clearly, a high level of knowledge about a given client's cultural background can only assist the therapist who seeks to understand this particular client, build a good working alliance, and provide appropriate therapy. All of these elements provide the context within which ecological counseling operates. In addition, a therapist must understand how clients experience and understand their own bodies. Many clients from a variety of cultures may only experience their emotional distress as physical distress. Others may experience physical illness and imagine they have psychosomatic pain. Still others may experience physiological disturbance but may have been taught to ignore it.

### Body as Context

Like culture, body is a context for thinking about oneself. Clients who present with physical symptoms, such as difficulty sleeping, incessant crying, cognitive confusion, or panic attacks, are clearly experiencing physical discomfort. In Western cultures, however, we have embraced the Cartesian idea that body and mind are separate entities. Thus, doctors treat the body and counselors treat the mind. In *The Embodied Mind*, Varela, Thompson, and Rosch (1991) addressed the futility of regarding human experience as either purely physical or purely rational. As constructivists argue, such splits do not work, whether one is talking about individual vs. context or body vs. mind. They contend that experience is not complete without both rational and biological inputs. Indeed, Saul (1992) argued that Western culture's overdependence on rationality as a guiding strategy for decision making has led modern intellectual thought into an evolutionary eddy. By disregarding the body experience, modern culture has prevented itself from integrating an enormous amount of data that could inform major educational, political, economic, and diplomatic policies and practices.

In *Descartes' Error*, Damasio (1994) illustrated how the brain cannot make sound, rational decisions without input from the right prefrontal cortex, which is the seat of a variety of emotional states. Many of the difficulties humans experience can be attributed to the meanings they make of their body experiences, and those meanings are attributable to prevalent cultural discourses about body experience. Thus, from an ecological counseling perspective, the body should be considered a highly important aspect of an individual's experienced context, and clients should be helped to understand how their experiences are influenced by their body states. For some clients, however, it is profoundly difficult—in fact, it may seem impossible—to access, acknowledge, and work with negative feelings.

Understanding, accepting, and working with one's body experience is a challenge for several reasons. For centuries, philosophy and religion have framed unpleasant or negative biological experiences in terms of bad faith. Early Christian clerics identified seven common emotions as cardinal sins: (a) pride, (b) covetousness, (c) lust, (d) envy, (e) gluttony, (f) anger, and (g) sloth (Aquinas, 1273/1989). The framing of the seven common emotions in terms of cardinal or deadly sins has undoubtedly affected the experience of cultures for centuries. Likewise, Buddhism regards the six basic unwholesome emotions as attachment, anger, arrogance, ignorance, indecision, and opinionatedness (Varela et al., 1991). Other emotions regarded as unwholesome include resentment, jealousy, gloominess or dullness, restlessness, lack of trust, laziness, forgetfulness, and inattentiveness. At the foundation of two major philosophical/religious forces on Earth, therefore, is a rejection of negative human feeling states and a pronouncement (particularly in Christianity) that such states are sinful (and therefore punishable). Thus, in both Eastern and Western cultures, the individual is asked to deny and attempt to suppress significant portions of his or her experience. Undoubtedly this pressure had a profound civilizing effect on humankind. It may, however, have outlived its purpose in that individuals are now constrained in the process of making sense of their reactions and actions.

The body is the most immediate container of the experiencing self, and its messages are the most immediate of influences. Since the advent of Reich's (1945) ideas, early 20th century views evolved and encouraged acceptance and celebration of one's animal nature to achieve psychological health. In emphasizing access to one's authentic emotional experiences, as shown by Amen and Carmichael (1997) and Perls (1969), Western psychology has acknowledged the importance of more holistic views of the individual, including body awareness and healing practices. Many modern therapeutic practices involve some type of body work, such as meditation or relaxation training. However, the emphasis of most types of modern body work is to free an individual from stress or bound-up energy. Little emphasis has been placed on the need of individuals to make meaning of their physiological experiences or to understand how their biology may interact with other contextual factors to affect their perceptions of the world. Body experience may be considered as important a contextual influence on one's sense of self and well-being as any other contextual influence.

Until recently, the concept of health psychology was distinguished from other areas of psychology because of its emphasis on assisting clients to manage physical challenges. Physical challenges have traditionally been defined as observable physical disabilities and illnesses. With the advent of studies in neuroscience, it is becoming clear that many emotional and behavioral difficulties such as depression, anxiety, obsessions and compulsions, and attention problems have strong biological components (Amen & Carmichael, 1997; Krystal, D'Souza, Sanacora, Goddard, & Charney, 2001; Martin, Martin, Rai, Richardson, & Royall, 2001; Thase, 2001).

Thus, helping a client with depression, anxiety, or attention deficit disorder may entail assisting the client to recognize biological symptoms, referring the client for medication, and helping the client to manage not only the symptoms but also the changes brought about by pharmacological agents. For instance, clients who have suffered from chronic cyclical depression may have developed perceptual sets from which they regard life's challenges as overwhelming. Although their medical treatment may involve a lightening of mood and increase in energy, most clients need help learning problem-solving skills that were never developed during years of debilitating depressive episodes. Counseling may involve helping a client to recognize that absolute truths are not independent of context, and that one's life context no longer involves the constant depression and inability to concentrate that previously framed the experience of the world, and that the client therefore is able to learn and apply new life skills with much greater ease. Getting a client to this happy outcome, however, can sometimes be profoundly difficult.

Since Reich (1945) and Perls (1969), counselors and therapists have emphasized the importance of emotion in therapeutic change, and most professionals are trained to help their clients develop awareness of their emotional states. Less clear, however, is the degree to which the field of counseling and therapy has helped clients to identify how cultures have influenced their experiences of bodily states and the values they place on bodily experiences. Although we are beginning to learn just how profoundly biology affects experience, we still have difficulty believing it. The cultural taboos against having negative feelings make it difficult to frame negative affect in a desirable light. Because we live in a culture that regards most negative affects as either sinful or inappropriate, we need help to overcome the shame associated with admitting to these affects before we can move forward. We are also constrained by the value that Western culture places on individuality and independence. The virtuous person, therefore, feels bound to deny negativity, and if one does experience it, one must take responsibility for expelling it or disposing of it in some way. The recognition that one might be having a negative experience because of a neurological imbalance, or that it is important to access negative affect in order to understand one's experience thoroughly, contravenes Western definitions of virtue, which dictate that it is shameful to have a negative affect, and it is shameful to do anything other than overcome it through the power of virtue and will. Thus, assisting clients to deconstruct the forces that have shaped their beliefs about anger, depression, anxiety, and other negative feeling states, and the ways in which those feelings interact with and influence life's challenges, may be an important goal of ecological counseling.

### Recontextualization

Steenbarger's (1993) term *recontextualization* is appropriate to describe the process of dismantling the myriad influences that come to bear on a client's experience. This process can be liberating in that a client comes to see his or her experience as an understandable natural outcome of many meaning-laden forces rather than as a set of symptoms, character flaws, or bad habits. From this position of understanding, a client is empowered to make alterations to his or her worldview and to select methods of change that are in accord with the standpoint that makes the most sense to him or her.

## Conclusion

A constructivist perspective is consistent with theoretical developments within the counseling profession and helps to distinguish ecological counseling from ecological perspectives as practiced by other professions. The power of meaning-making processes has been largely neglected in other discussions of person–environment transactions.

Understanding how people make sense of their contextualized experience is a central tenet of ecological counseling. Individuals do not simply react passively to externally determined circumstances; they are active cocreators of their life realities through how they perceive and interpret what happens to them. How meanings are shaped by social, cultural, spiritual, intellectual, environmental, and physiological contexts is the focus of this chapter. The goals of ecological counseling from this perspective involve assisting the client to understand these contextual influences on his or her mind–body experience and to develop viewpoints and behaviors that are informed by that understanding.

## Learning Activities

1. This exercise can be done alone or with a partner. Imagine that a friend describes a religious experience he or she had while meditating in a beautiful natural environment. Explain it from each of the following perspectives: (a) received knowledge, (b) objective, scientific knowledge, and (c) constructed knowledge. (5 to 7 minutes)

2. Join with a partner. Consider a client who complains of stress in the workplace because of a difficult job under a demanding boss. One of you should represent the strand of psychology in which the problem is viewed as lying within the individual and that it is up to the individual to address it. The other should take the position that this is a problem within a context and needs to be understood and addressed both in terms of the individual and the environment within which the problem apparently occurs.

3. Join with a partner. One person should assume the role of a counselor. The other should play the role of a client who complains of an inability to get out of bed in the morning; a loss of interest in eating, sex, or any other previously pleasurable activity; and difficulty concentrating. The counselor should treat the problem strictly as an emotional problem and use the counselor's chosen counseling approach. After about 5 minutes, switch roles. This time, the client should present the same symptoms, but the counselor will address the client and the problem from a stance that incorporates the mind–body interaction. After another 5 minutes, stop and discuss both individuals' experiences with each approach.

4. This exercise may be done alone or with one or more partners. Consider a client who volunteered to serve in the military reserve, wound up fighting in an unpopular war, and has now returned home. The client suffers from nightmares about the experience and is hesitant to share them with family members

who might not understand. Further, the client is unhappy and lonely at work because most coworkers opposed the war, opposed the client's decision to go to war, and no longer readily accept the client into their group. The work group had previously been the client's primary social group. As an ecological counselor, how might you approach this problem?

# References

Amen, D. G., & Carmichael, B. D. (1997). High-resolution brain SPECT imaging in ADHD. *Annals of Clinical Psychiatry, 9*, 81-86.

American Psychiatric Association. (2000). *Diagnostic and statistical manual of mental disorders* (text revision). Washington, DC: Author.

Aquinas, T. (1989). *Summa theologica.* (T. S. McDermott, Trans.). London: Eyre and Spottiswoode. (Original work published 1273)

Arredondo, P. (1998). Integrating multicultural counseling competencies and universal helping conditions in culture-specific contexts. *The Counseling Psychologist, 26*(4), 592-601.

Arredondo, P. (1999). Multicultural counseling competencies as tools to address oppression and racism. *Journal of Counseling & Development, 77*(1), 102-108.

Arredondo, P., Toporek, R., Brown, S. P., Jones, J., Locke, D., Sanchez, J., & Stadler, H. (1996). Operationalization of the multicultural counseling competencies. *Journal of Multicultural Counseling and Development, 24*(1), 42-78.

Atkinson, D. R., Bui, U., & Mori, S. (2001). Multiculturally sensitive empirically treatments—An oxymoron? In C. M. Alexander (Ed.), *Handbook of multicultural counseling* (2nd ed., pp. 542-574). Thousand Oaks, CA: Sage.

Atkinson, D. R., & Lowe, S. (1995). The role of ethnicity, cultural knowledge, and conventional techniques in counseling and psychotherapy. In C. M. Alexander (Ed.), *Handbook of multicultural counseling* (pp. 387-414). Thousand Oaks, CA: Sage.

Atkinson, D. R., Morten, G., & Sue, D. W. (1998). Current issues and future directions in minority group/cross-cultural counseling. In *Counseling American minorities* (pp. 303-359). Boston: McGraw-Hill.

Beutler, L. E., & Clarkin, J. F. (1990). *Systematic treatment selection: Toward targeted therapeutic interventions.* New York: Brunner/Mazel.

Constantine, M. G. (1997). Facilitating multicultural competency in counseling supervision: Operationalizing a practical framework. In D. B. Pope-Davis & H. L. K. Coleman (Eds.), *Multicultural counseling competencies: Assessment, education and training, and supervision* (pp. 310-324). Thousand Oaks, CA: Sage.

Damasio, A. R. (1994). *Descartes' error: Emotion, reason, and the human brain.* New York: Putnam.

Dillenberger, J. (Ed.). (1961). *Martin Luther: Selections from his writing*. Garden City, NY: Doubleday.

Eribon, D. (1991). *Michel Foucault*. Cambridge, MA: Harvard University Press.

Erikson, E. H. (1950). *Childhood and society*. New York: Norton.

Erikson, E. H. (1968). *Identity: Youth and crisis*. New York: Norton.

Erikson, E. H. (1976). Reflections on Dr. Borg's life cycle. *Daedalus, 105*, 1-28.

Foucault, M. (1997). *The archaeology of knowledge*. London: Routledge.

Helms, J. E. (1995). An update of Helms's White and people of color racial identity models. In C. M. Alexander (Ed.), *Handbook of multicultural counseling* (pp. 181-198). Thousand Oaks, CA: Sage.

Hofstede, G. (2001). *Culture's consequences: Comparing values, behaviors, institutions, and organizations across nations* (2nd ed.). Thousand Oaks, CA: Sage.

Kagitçibasi, C. (1997). Individualism and collectivism. In J. W. Berry, M. H. Segall, & Y. H. Poortinga (Eds.), *Handbook of cross-cultural psychology: Vol. 3. Social behavior and applications*, pp. 1-49). Needham Heights, MA: Allyn & Bacon.

Klerman, G. L., Weissman, M. M., Rounsaville, B. J., & Chevron, E. S. (1984). *Interpersonal psychotherapy of depression*. Northvale, NJ: Jason Aronson.

Krystal, J. H., D'Souza, D. C., Sanacora, G., Goddard, A. W., & Charney, D. S. (2001). Current perspectives on the pathophysiology of schizophrenia, depression, and anxiety disorders. *Medical Clinics of North America, 85*, 559-577.

Levenson, R. W., Ekman, P., Heider, K., & Friesen, W. V. (1992). Emotion and autonomic nervous system activity in the Minangkabau of West Sumatra. *Journal of Personality and Social Psychology, 62*, 972-988.

Markus, H. R., & Kitayama, S. (1994a). The cultural shaping of emotion: A conceptual framework. In S. Kitayama & M. R. Markus (Eds.), *Emotion and culture. Empirical studies of mutual influence* (pp. 339-351). Washington, DC: American Psychological Association.

Markus, H. R., & Kitayama, S. (1994b). The cultural construction of self and emotion: Implications for social behavior. In S. Kitayama & H. R. Markus (Eds.), *Emotion and culture: Empirical studies of mutual influence* (pp. 89-130). Washington, DC: American Psychological Association.

Martin, S. D., Martin, E., Rai, S. S., Richardson, M. A., & Royall, R. (2001). Brain blood flow changes in depressed patients treated with interpersonal psychotherapy or venlafaxine hydrochloride: Preliminary findings. *Archives of General Psychiatry, 58*, 641-648.

Martinez, R. P., & Holloway, E. L. (1997). The supervision relationship in multicultural training. In D. B. Pope-Davis & H. L. K. Coleman (Eds.), *Multicultural counseling competencies: Assessment, education and training, and supervision*. (pp. 325-349). Thousand Oaks, CA: Sage.

McIntosh, P. (1998). White privilege: Unpacking the invisible knapsack. In M. McGoldrick (Ed.), *Re-visioning family therapy: Race, culture, and gender in clinical practice* (pp. 147-155). New York: Guilford Press.

Merleau-Ponty, M. (1962). *Phenomenology of perception* (L. Smith, Trans.). New York: Humanities Press.

Mesquita, B., Frijda, N., & Scherer, K. (1997). Culture and emotion. In J. W. Berry, P. R. Dasen, & T. S. Saraswathi (Eds.), *Handbook of cross-cultural psychology: Vol. 2. Basic processes and human development* (2nd ed., pp. 255-297). Needham Heights, MA: Allyn & Bacon.

Miller, P. J., & Goodnow, D. M. (1995). Cultural practices: Toward an integration of culture and development. In F. Kessel (Ed.), *Cultural practices as contexts for development: Vol. 67. New directions for child development* (pp. 83-101). San Francisco: Jossey-Bass.

Neimeyer, R. A. (1995). Constructivist psychotherapies: Features, foundations, and future directions. In R. A. Neimeyer & M. J. Mahoney (Eds.), *Constructivism in psychotherapy* (pp. 11-38). Washington, DC: American Psychological Association.

Pedersen, P. (1994). *A handbook for developing multicultural awareness* (2nd ed.). Alexandria, VA: American Counseling Association.

Perls, F. S. (1969). *Ego, hunger, and aggression: The beginning of gestalt therapy*. New York: Random House.

Polkinghorne, D. E. (1988). *Narrative knowing and the human sciences*. Albany: State University of New York Press.

Ponterotto, J. G., Casas, J. M., Suzuki, L. A., & Alexander, C. M. (Eds.). (1995). *Handbook of multicultural counseling*. Thousand Oaks, CA: Sage.

Ponterotto, J. G., Casas, J. M., Suzuki, L. A., & Alexander, C. M. (Eds.). (2001). *Handbook of multicultural counseling* (2nd ed.). Thousand Oaks, CA: Sage.

Reich, W. (1945). *Character analysis* (V. R. Carfagno, Trans.). New York: Simon & Schuster.

Saul, J. R. (1992). *Voltaire's bastards*. New York: Vintage.

Sexton, T. L., & Griffin, B. L. (1997). The social and political nature of psychological science: The challenges, potentials, and future of constructivist thinking. In T. L. Sexton & B. L. Griffin (Eds.), *Constructivist thinking in counseling practice, research, and training* (pp. 249-261). New York: Teachers College Press.

Steenbarger, B. N. (1993). A multicontextual model of counseling: Bridging brevity and diversity. *Journal of Counseling & Development, 72*, 8-15.

Sue, D. W., & Sue, D. (1999). *Counseling the culturally different: Theory and practice*. New York: Wiley.

Super, C., & Harkness, S. (1997). The cultural structuring of child development. In J. W. Berry, P. R. Dasen, & T. S. Saraswathi (Eds.), *Handbook of cross-cultural psychology: Vol. 2. Basic processes and human development* (2nd ed., pp. 1-39). Needham Heights, MA: Allyn & Bacon.

Thase, M. E. (2001). Neuroimaging profiles and the differential therapies of depression. *Archives of General Psychiatry, 58*, 631-640.

Triandis, H. C. (1990). Values, attitudes, and interpersonal behavior. *Nebraska Symposium on Motivation, 27*, 195-259.

Valsiner, J., & Lawrence, J. (1997). Human development in culture across the life span. In J. W. Berry, P. R. Dasen, & T. S. Saraswathi (Eds.), *Handbook of cross-cultural psychology: Vol. 2. Basic processes and human development* (2nd ed., pp. 69–106). Needham Heights, MA: Allyn & Bacon.

Varela, F. J., Thompson, E., & Rosch, E. (1991). *The embodied mind*. Cambridge, MA: MIT Press.

White, M., & Epston, D. (1990). *Narrative means to therapeutic ends*. New York: Norton.

Zimbardo, P. G., & Gerrig, R. J. (1999). *Psychology and life*. New York: Longman.

## Chapter 5

# The Process of Ecological Counseling

### *Ellen P. Cook, Robert K. Conyne, Cheryl Savageau, and Mei Tang*

---

*Chapter Highlights*

- *Ecological counseling recognizes the complex, circular causality intrinsic to human problems and a client's presenting problem as an expression of dynamic, interdependent forces.*
- *The ecological assessment process typically involves (a) situating the problem within the client's life space, (b) elaborating the web of person-environment interactions characterizing this unique problem, and (c) identifying resources and challenges important in this ecosystem change.*
- *The goal of the data collection process is to compile a comprehensive description of a client's life space.*
- *Working together, the client and counselor set goals for action steps that appropriately take into account not only the assessment data and the meaning made from these data by the client, but also such matters as client values, setting characteristics, feasibility, plausibility to the client, and available resources and barriers to the change process.*
- *A broad range of interventions can be used to enhance ecological concordance at the individual, group, organizational, or community contextual levels. Counselors are encouraged to expand their repertoires to address aspects or levels of the person-environment interaction not typically emphasized in their practice.*
- *Evaluation is both a final stage and an ongoing process in ecological counseling (outcome and process evaluation). Ecological counselors must determine what assessment plans provide adequate data about the relevant person-environment interactions explored in counseling, in addition to addressing the exigencies of their institutions and fitting the nature of the counselor-client interactions that form the substance of their practice.*

---

In chapter 1, we defined ecological counseling and then discussed its basic principles. The example of Jamie illustrated in a general way how ecological counseling might occur. In this chapter, we focus on how assessment, goal setting, intervention, and evaluation can be understood from an ecological perspective.

Counseling from an ecological perspective follows familiar steps observed by counselors implementing other perspectives. Clients ask counselors for professional help with a life problem (or, in some cases, counselors may initiate social action or advocacy approaches). The problems can be as simple as choosing an academic major or as complex as working through a lifetime of abuse by others. Counseling flows through a set of more or less explicit, progressive phases: assessment, goal setting, implementation, and evaluation. Counselors can choose from a set of strategies that are consistent with their own expertise and the client's needs. Ideally, counseling is discontinued when the client and counselor both agree that the problem has been satisfactorily resolved.

What fundamentally distinguishes ecological counseling from other perspectives is the recognition of the complex, circular causality intrinsic to human problems. Little in human life can be adequately explained by a simple cause-effect connection; rarely is there only one good solution to a problem. Ecological counselors understand that a client's presenting problem is an expression of dynamic, interdependent forces. Such an understanding carries both freedom and a unique challenge: counselors are relieved of the onus of finding the single right intervention, but in turn must carefully weigh many possibilities for therapeutic success.

Is it possible that an ordinary counselor has the breadth of understanding and expertise needed for this challenge? We believe so, although many competent counselors might not consider themselves ecologically oriented. Most counselors understand, for example, that having the right type of shoes may help an adolescent adjust to a new school; the decade in which a person was born may shape his or her political views; the state of the national economy may influence an individual's comfort with the aging process; or the presence of green space within a neighborhood may prove to be a resource in battling drugs. Ecological counseling invites counselors to consider the power of such factors more explicitly, and to explore how these factors may be used deliberately in the healing process.

In this chapter, we consider how ecological principles can enrich our professional practice. We humbly acknowledge that we are not proposing to abandon tried and true counseling strategies in favor of our own version, but we *are* proposing a different way of examining what many of us already do as counselors, and in so doing we hope to open your eyes to new possibilities.

This chapter is organized according to four major phases of counseling: assessment, goal setting, implementation, and evaluation. Our discussion incorporates the principles of ecological counseling discussed in chapter 1.

## Phase 1: Assessment in Ecological Counseling

Assessment is crucial in ecological counseling as a guide to action. Counselors can intervene in many ways, ranging from individual counseling to organizational consultation and social advocacy. Assessment helps a counselor determine the most feasible, parsimonious, and potentially effective ways to initiate changes in the client's ecosystem.

All counseling begins when a client first describes his or her concerns or troubles to a counselor, or when a counselor identifies a system level concern and seeks to address it proactively. Ecological counselors understand that most problems are situated within the broader ecosystem. A client describes his or her life space as he or she experiences it. Each description contains important clues to the client's experience of the problem: the central individuals and/or processes involved (proximal processes), the impact of time (Why now? How will this impact the past, present, future?), and any triggering events prompting the need for change now.

Although counselors are usually introduced to a problem by an individual, the actual client may ultimately be on a different contextual level than the individual (e.g., a family, work setting, a community). Ecological counseling can occur in context with an individual, a primary group, an organization, or a community. In turn, the targeted contextual level is influenced by the other levels. If, for example, the targeted contextual level for ecological counseling is an organization—a mental health center, for example—that center needs to be examined as both affecting and being affected by people and primary groups within it and by the larger community of which it is a part. Moreover, all contextual levels are part of, and influenced by, the larger surrounding ecosystem. Clients within the targeted contextual level are viewed in ecological counseling as being engaged in the ongoing process of making meaning from events and experiences.

This meaning making of contextualized experience is central to ecological counseling. In fact, the client's problem description is inseparable from the meaning-making process. Each description reflects the client's attempts to understand and evaluate his or her life experiences. In recognizing this, the counselor respects the client's description as essential and valid from his or her point of view, although counseling may beget changes in its comprehensiveness and clarity.

Ecological assessment is intended to elaborate this problem introduction into a fuller picture of the existing person–environment (P $\times$ E) interaction, and to identify the meaning of this situation to clients. The first step in ecological assessment is formulation of a clear problem statement. When a client seeks counseling for issues that are only vaguely defined, the ecological counselor begins the counseling process by helping the client clarify his or her reasons for seeking help. A vague problem statement, such as "I am concerned about how well my child is doing in school," might be reformulated to specify the type, frequency, and context of the problem, and the client's derived meaning from the situation. For example, a clear statement of the problem might be "I am seeking counseling because I am feeling worried that since November my child's classwork does not seem to match his potential, and nearly every week he says that he hates school."

A clear problem statement is crucial in helping the counselor and client know what information to seek when they begin the data collection phase of the assessment process. The problem statement assists in narrowing the universe of data potentially implicated in an ecological assessment. For a simple example, consider the following client statement: "I need help in finding a job." Career counselors know that it makes a significant difference to the counseling process whether the client really means

- I'm a single mother of two preschool children, and my welfare benefits run out in a few months;
- My parents say I have to earn some money if I want to have a car, and I don't know how to go about getting a decent after-school job; or
- I'm having problems finding a use for my oceanography degree here in the Midwest.

Each client needs relevant information not only about job possibilities but also about his or her personality. Just what information is needed, however, and how this information represents the unique resources and challenges facing the client in his or her life space, probably differs dramatically in each situation. That is why the problem statement provides a useful starting point in the data collection process.

The second step in ecological assessment involves data collection, the goal of which is to compile a comprehensive analysis of a client's life space. During this phase, the counselor and client explore together the various facets of a client's ecosystem and gather descriptive information relevant to the problem statement, including environmental conditions, person variables (e.g., personality, coping skills), meaning-making patterns, and the interactions among these factors. A special effort should be made to describe client and environmental strengths and resources that may be used constructively in the counseling process.

The steps in an ecological assessment process typically involve (a) situating the problem within the client's life space, (b) elaborating the web of person–environment interactions characterizing this unique problem, and (c) identifying resources and challenges important in this ecosystem change. The counselor attempts to determine *what* is the presenting concern; *who* is involved; *when* and *where* this happens; *why* the client believes it happens; and *what this problem means* to her or him.

It is important to get as detailed and specific information as possible. For example, in Jamie's situation, the counselor easily identified that the problem occurred on the bus but involved complex interrelationships between Jamie's parents, the bus driver and Jamie, Jamie and other children, and the school and Jamie's parents. The problem behavior happened maybe only once a week, but the bus driver was alert to possible problems daily. Jamie could not account for why the problem occurred, but the school and bus driver attributed it to Jamie's developmental disabilities and learned ways of interacting with others. The counselor recognized this attribution as an important part of Jamie's life space, but not as the only way the situation could be explored.

Counselors operating from an ecological perspective also gather information about the client's *resources* and *barriers*, or *challenges*, to the change process. A partial picture of Jamie's resources includes support from her family, her interest in having satisfying interactions on the bus, and her outgoing disposition. Barriers might include her limited ability to understand reasons for her behavior and to generate alternatives, her school's labeling of her as a problem child, and stereotypes other children hold about developmental disabilities.

A counselor and client could conceivably generate voluminous amounts of data that are in some way relevant to the problem statement and P × E concordance. Conoley and Haynes (1992) have suggested, in fact, that all data collected can be potentially useful. As in any counseling interaction, counselors must determine which data to assess and which to ignore at every contextual level. These judgments are largely shaped by counselor expertise and theoretical point of view (i.e., professional meaning making). A constructivist counselor might emphasize meaning-making processes, a family systems counselor the nature of family relationships, and a community counselor the interaction of systems external to the client. What makes the process ecological is the willingness of each expert to place this emphasis in the framework of P × E interactions. The constructivist understands, for example, how individual meaning making is influenced by peer relationships; the family expert, how family systems are shaped by macrosystemic factors; the community counselor, how individual characteristics help determine a person's vulnerability to environmental influences.

Data collection in an ecological assessment can be facilitated by using assessment tools already familiar to counselors, as amply illustrated by the authors in later chapters of this book. For example, a counselor might make use of a career interest inventory, an assessment of racial identity (chapter 9), or psychological diagnostic measures commonly used in mental health counseling (chapter 6). These tools provide valuable information about personal characteristics shaping the manner in which clients interact within the world around them.

Ecological counselors understand, however, that individual assessment provides only part of the information needed in assessment of person–environment interaction. Counselors need to gain a clear understanding of the human and physical contexts composing a client's life. Recognizing that individuals may behave differently across different settings (Linney, 2000), counselors look for patterns of concordance or discordance in various interactional settings within the client's life space.

Munger (2000) argued that "every underlying environmental structure merits observation and consideration, because each fills an important place in the individual's life space" (p. 20)—a statement that may be more ideal than practical considering the time limitations placed on many counseling relationships today. Nevertheless, counselors ought to consider features of their clients' person–environment interactions that might otherwise be overlooked. For example, consider the following:

- *Family:* What is the size and structure of the family (e.g., extended or nuclear; who serves as head of the family)? What are the daily routines and activities? What is the nature of the physical space affecting family interaction (e.g., where do people sleep)?
- *Work setting:* What are the policies for leave of absence, sick leave, or child care? How available are beverages and lunch facilities? What is the layout and attractiveness of the physical workspace (e.g., private or shared offices)?

- *Neighborhood:* What is the nature of interaction patterns among neighbors? Is the neighborhood attractive and/or safe? Does the client feel integrated within the neighborhood (e.g., feels he or she belongs)?

Much of this information can be gathered by interviewing the client, as described earlier. The ecological counselor also must recognize that other members of the client system have expertise that can be helpful in the assessment process, both as participants in and observers of the client's life space. Whenever possible, ecological counselors should actively seek input from other members of the client system, with the client's cooperation. Ecological school counselors or psychologists commonly consult with parents, school personnel, and perhaps even a physician or recreation program staff member about a child's difficulties. For older clients, others can also provide valuable information, with the client's permission: a dining room supervisor in a nursing home, for example, or a sibling when there is a parent/adolescent conflict. The client's descriptions of the involvement of others can also be informative, even if the other people interpret the client's situation differently. For Jamie, understanding how the adults perceived her possibilities and limitations was crucial to understanding the situation she faced daily on the bus.

Counselors can also explore varied methods of environmental assessment (Conyne & Clack, 1981). For example, the Multiphasic Environmental Assessment Procedure (Lemke, Moos, Mehren, & Gauvain, 1979) focuses on features of the physical environment as well as organizational features and perceptions of individuals in the setting. The family of social climate scales (Moos, 1974) helps collect self-perceptual data in relation to a range of settings (e.g., classrooms, correction facilities, families, groups) as well as the dimensions of these settings (Moos, 1973). Construction of an ecomap (Horton, 2000) through interviews provides a graphic representation of the structure and nature of important interactions with others. Many other assessment strategies are available (e.g., see Martin & Swartz-Kulstad, 2000, and Friedman & Wachs, 1999).

The most important tool in this assessment process is what we call *ecological empathy.* The counselor is able to understand the client's life space from his or her own perspective, and is able to intuit less obvious connections that offer promising possibilities for change. In the case of Jamie, for example, the counselor readily acknowledged the importance of her dispositional impulsivity and her limited ability to understand the reasons for rules as contributors to her misbehavior. The counselor, however, also wondered about how Jamie felt as a special child with no friends on the bus, and about the other children's willingness to break the boredom of a tiring bus ride home by stimulating Jamie's own special brand of behavioral mayhem.

By now it should be clear that formal diagnostic assessment, as commonly occurs in mental health counseling, certainly has its place in ecological counseling. Counselors, however, need to be aware of the limitations and meaning-making issues inherent in the very nature of this assessment. Because of the importance of these issues, we discuss them at some length in the following section.

## Traditional Assessment of the Individual: The *DSM-IV*

For many counselors, individual assessment means developing a multiaxial diagnosis using the *Diagnostic and Statistical Manual of Mental Disorders (DSM-IV)* (American Psychiatric Association, 1994). For agencies that require such diagnoses as a part of their insurance reimbursement, it can be argued that this approach to assessment is ecologically warranted. Using the *DSM-IV* is not the only or necessarily the best way to assess clients' functioning, however. Ecologically oriented counselors need to be aware of some limitations to traditional diagnostic systems in assessing individuals.

The *DSM-IV* is a system of labels—a consensus among mental health experts on what constitutes psychological problems. The labels provide an elegant shortcut for conveying complex patterns of behaviors to other professionals. For example, describing someone as borderline implies a host of intrapersonal and interpersonal behavioral tendencies and associated implications for the counseling process. Training in the use of the *DSM-IV* is an enculturation process where the novice learns how to apply the language and its implicit meanings accurately and rapidly.

In effect, the *DSM-IV* is a system of meanings. In the meaning-making process used to develop and revise it, decisions were made about what constitutes disorder (see the discussion in Brown, 2000). These decisions inevitably reflected broad cultural values concerning normal and desirable personal characteristics. Some disorders were added or dropped over time as experts' judgments about certain disorders changed (e.g., elimination of homosexuality as a disorder). Other disorders were the target of considerable controversy about whether they should be included (e.g., self-defeating personality disorder; Brown, 2000). As experts changed their ideas about what is disordered behavior, the corresponding labels as codified within the *DSM-IV* also changed.

The *DSM-IV* is also culture bound, as is any system of meanings. The simple fact that the *DSM-IV* uses terminology from medicine reflects our culturally based consensus about the link between psychological distress and physical illness. There is little doubt that psychological distress can cause physical illness and vice versa, but our diagnostic classification practices go beyond this recognition of circular causality to frame psychological distress as disease. (See Kleinman, 1988, for a fascinating discussion of meaning making associated with illnesses.) Whether this assumption is defensible is beyond the point here; we simply want to emphasize that this view of psychological distress as disease is commonly taken for granted, but it is not the only way to conceptualize it.

The specifics of disorders included within the *DSM-IV* are clearly dictated by meaning-making processes. In addition, certain disorders prevalent in other cultures were not included, and some disorders were packaged differently than they are elsewhere in the world (e.g., Kleinman, 1988). Feminists (e.g., Brown, 2000; Caplan, 1995) have roundly criticized various revisions of the *DSM* for gender bias in how disordered behavior is conceptualized, labeled, and identified within the general population. Ecological counselors agree that cultural and gender bias should be eliminated whenever possible, but they also recognize that such bias is common in any human endeavor to comprehend complex patterns of behavior. A classification system inevitably embodies implicit worldviews of those who develop and implement it. We need to understand such worldviews if we hope to appreciate the wisdom and the shortcomings of how we commonly conceptualize distress. Again, we remind counselors that the *DSM-IV* in its present form is not the only way that psychological distress can be understood.

Many counselors fully cognizant of the *DSM-IV*'s limitations continue to find it useful because of the common language it provides for their professional work. Unfortunately, as with many meaning systems, it is all too easy to overlook its limitations. Consider, for example, its emphasis on individual causation of problems. The *DSM-IV* has been criticized (e.g., Brown, 2000) for how exclusively individual traits and deficiencies are implicated as causes of various disorders. It is a small step to blaming the individual for his or her diagnosis, and stigmatizing him or her as defective (Gergen & McNamee, 2000). Unfortunately, the very act of assigning a diagnosis may make it less likely that the counselor considers contributions to the problem other than the client (Gergen & McNamee, 2000). Ecological counselors certainly agree that an individual's idiosyncratic characteristics shape significant behavior patterns, but they also ask, Where is the environment in this P $\times$ E interaction?

The *DSM-IV*'s underplaying of environmental determinants of behavior has been significantly implicated in many of its critiques. Environmental circumstances are taken into account in a comprehensive multiaxial assessment, and certain diagnoses explicitly note environmental causes (e.g., posttraumatic stress disorder). Yet there is no diagnosis for expectable and normal reactions for horrific life circumstances, or for trauma common to a population. The impact on one's life of living through insidious trauma (Root, 1992), such as racism or sexism, or indirect trauma, such as witnessing domestic violence among family members, is also not recognized.

The challenge for counselors using the *DSM-IV* is to become fully aware of the meaning system in which it is situated. For example, how and by whom was the *DSM-IV* developed and revised? What criteria were used for developing symptom patterns? How and why might it be culture bound, and how will this affect my understanding of my clients? What assumptions about the nature of psychological distress are coded within the *DSM-IV*, perhaps underplaying or ignoring other essential determinants? To what extent is the *DSM-IV* prescriptive as well as descriptive (i.e., carrying implications for prognosis and professional interventions)? Are the implications for treatment warranted by research and professional experience? Perhaps most fundamentally, how might usage of the *DSM-IV* blind a counselor to other possibilities of understanding and working with clients?

In our view, traditional diagnostic processes can be used with discretion, but they are rarely sufficient. The goal of traditional assessment is to fit the individual into a standardized diagnostic category defined by research conducted with other people in other times and places. Traditional assessment is often reductionistic in flavor, boiling down the uniqueness of the person into a summary paragraph or two. Does this summary paragraph elegantly represent the essence of the person, as diagnostic experts might argue, or constitute an overly terse, even myopic view of the person's life? How much does it help the counselor to know Jamie's IQ scores and her levels of emotional maturity? Such information is very helpful indeed in describing her uniqueness, but it says little about why Jamie is having problems *this* year but not *last* year on the bus.

Ecological assessment is not exclusively person focused, but is concerned with the web of life that makes up an individual ecosystem. Rather than being reductionistic, ecological assessment is expansive. A counselor must consider the meaningfulness of a behavior within its context; any behaviors are reflective of a person interacting within context. Ecological assessment attempts to recognize numerous salient variables that contribute to or detract from ecological concordance while also paying attention to client-derived meanings. Diagnostic conclusions involve complex descriptive data in place of labels, and are always original and unique to each case rather than copied from a standardized manual. This detailed, idiosyncratic assessment provides counselors invaluable guidance in designing a change process that fits the ecosystem under consideration.

## Phase 2: Goal Setting in Ecological Counseling

The overriding goal of ecological counseling is to improve ecological concordance. Because every individual and every environment is unique, the nature of improved P $\times$ E fit will be uniquely defined in every case. The ecological counselor cannot open a standardized manual to find a definition or a set of treatment goals that are relevant to improved P $\times$ E interaction in a particular client system.

*Collaboration* is critically important in ecological goal setting. Ecological counselors certainly bring their own expertise to the goal-setting process, but they do not see themselves as the only experts in the room, as often happens in more traditional contexts. Ecological counselors are not determiners or arbiters of poor P $\times$ E interaction and do not take sole responsibility for designing goals to alter any mismatch.

Working together, clients and counselors set goals for action steps that appropriately take into account not only the assessment data and the meaning made from these data by the client, but also such matters as client values, setting characteristics, feasibility, and available resources and barriers to the change process. This analysis results in goals that are well thought out and carefully fitted to the unique situation at hand.

In addition, goal setting and then strategy selection need to consider the concept of *plausibility*. Goals that exceed the client's perceptions of what is possible may not seem inspirational to the client; they may even seem unreasonable or ludicrous. (Of course, counseling may help a client reach a series of goals over time, including any previously considered impossible ones.) Goals that are incompatible with an individual's values or the culture of an organization or community likewise are discrepant with what the client may easily consider possible. For example, a community with a long history of racial insensitivity may not be expected quickly to develop and implement by itself an integrated housing program. Faculty members hired 25 years ago to engage in research, teaching, and service are unlikely overnight to assume the role of entrepreneur. Particularly for counselors engaged in social change or advo-

119

cacy, the change process may require careful planning of a series of changes over time. Goals need to harmonize with a client's resources, values, and environmental situation. Solutions work best if they use component building blocks already familiar to the client (Steenbarger & Pels, 1997, p. 114).

Levels of *challenge* and *support* are two especially important factors in setting goals for ecological counseling. On the one hand, clients need to be appropriately challenged, meaning that a moderate state of tension should exist between available resources and the demands being faced. These demands can be understood in terms of such variables as complexity, ambiguity, novelty, intensity, and abstraction (Blocher, 2000). On the other hand, and at the same time, clients need an appropriate level of support to address these challenges. Sources of support can be experienced in an environment consisting of a network of personal relationships that is caring, empathic, and honest. Counselors become part of this environment for the client.

In the case of Jamie's behavior on the bus, the consultant quickly learned that all parties involved, including Jamie, agreed she should continue riding the bus if possible. Jamie thought it was fun; the adults perceived the bus ride as important for Jamie to socialize with her peers outside special education, and for her to learn how to behave in settings where she was expected to follow the same rules as everyone else. Helping Jamie to ride the bus more successfully became the official goal for the interventions. From the consultant's perspective, this goal involved restructuring the Jamie–bus interaction so that she could fit more comfortably and happily in the bus environment. Jamie and the riders (including the driver) each contributed to the interaction, and each could contribute to increasing the ecological concordance for Jamie.

## Values Issues in Goal Setting and Related Interventions

Counselors today are commonly taught that imposition of the counselor's values on a client is unethical. In ecological counseling, because of the complex conceptualization of the nature of human behavior, we recognize that the issues are more complicated than simply avoiding telling a client what to do. In particular, the issues related to the ripple effect of ecological changes and value differences between counselor and client deserve special consideration.

It is well known that changes implemented on one level of an ecosystem will influence other levels because of their interdependence.

Experienced counselors understand, for example, that changes in a child's behavior initiated at school may influence family dynamics for better or worse, or that a client's recovery from alcoholism can be threatened by friends who miss their old drinking buddy. This ripple effect occurs across other levels of the ecosystem as well. Consider the recent welfare reforms requiring mothers to enter the paid labor force. True, these initiatives did succeed in prompting women who otherwise might have remained at home to go to work; however, for a variety of reasons, the initiatives also meant that these women often assumed minimum wage, entry level positions with little flexibility and poor benefits. Plus, their children lost daytime supervision by a parent, and schools and community programs faced new challenges. The issue is not whether welfare reform is good or bad, but that politically inspired policy changes reverberate throughout the ecosystems of those targeted by them.

Doherty (1995) has argued that we are ethically bound to consider the far-reaching implications of the changes we help clients to implement. He cites the example of a divorced parent considering a career change requiring a move many miles away from his children. Should the counselor encourage the client to consider the potential negative impact of this tempting career opportunity on his children's lives? There is also the case of a woman we know who is beginning to explore her spiritual values, questioning her preoccupation with material things. Until now, along with her husband and children, she has enjoyed a beautiful home and many possessions. Should she consider what her spiritual development might do to her husband and children, even if she is convinced that a less materialistic life is morally better for them all?

Ecological counselors cannot take responsibility for the occurrence of every consequence initiated through counseling. To do so claims far more power over people's lives than we possess. Whenever possible, however, we do have the obligation to encourage clients to consider the spectrum of possible outcomes. We *can* reasonably anticipate, for example, that the children of Doherty's client will be affected by his decision; we can help him consider whether the job change is worth the cost to his relationship with them, or whether the change might be the impetus for an enhanced relationship (e.g., he could gain custody of the children, which would have its own ripple effect). In addition, we can—and should—help women who are entering nontraditional jobs to be prepared for possible sexual harassment (Cook, Heppner, & O'Brien, 2002).

These examples also implicate possible value conflicts between counselors and clients. Value conflicts discussed in counselor training programs typically concern emotionally charged, easily discernible values such as abortion rights or religious group affiliations. These conflicts are probably the easiest to handle, since counselors and clients are readily aware of them. The question becomes what to do about them: Refer? Confront? Explore together?

Implicit, pervasive value issues are more difficult to handle, since they are ingrained in the important meaning-making processes of the counselor and client. Multicultural experts (e.g., Helms & Cook, 1999) have drawn to our attention how many culturally specific attitudes, expectations, and behaviors associated with the counseling process can sabotage development of a good working relationship between the client and counselor. In particular, those in an individualistic culture may find the perceptions of someone in a collectivist culture to be virtually incomprehensible. A collectivist individual who views career decisions as a way to enhance family welfare might find Doherty's client to be morally suspect; another might consider the career move a reasonable sacrifice to provide for the children financially. In contrast, a person espousing individualistic values for success and self-realization might view the career move as an expected next step in the divorced person's new life, with the family stresses an unfortunate but common side effect.

Such cultural differences become so problematic not only because of their complexity, but also because the participants commonly assume that their way of understanding the nature of life is universal. Multicultural experts also remind us that there is considerable variability among members of an identified group. We cannot assume, for instance, that an African American client espouses Afrocentric worldviews; one of the individuals most loyal to Native American culture I (Ellen Cook) have ever met has only a tiny fraction of Native American blood. As we have repeatedly stated, there is more than one way to view things. Counselors are obligated to learn as much as they can about these implicit—and explicit—differences in how people view the world and their place within it.

Counselors working for social change are also acutely aware that the changes they (and often their clients) champion are not likely to be welcomed by the broader social context. For example, corporations enacting race or gender discriminatory practices are not likely to embrace challenges to their status quo, particularly if such changes are costly in terms of time, energy, financial rewards, and personnel demands. Schools whose classroom practices fail to meet the needs of certain categories of pupils may be convinced that innovation will threaten their educational philosophy or personnel. Professional responsibility requires counselors to articulate as clearly as possible the alternative reality they are striving to realize with and on behalf of their clientele. Counselors contemplating social action must be willing to consider carefully what they are asking, and to be successful must become skillful in working with—and despite—resistance.

## Phase 3: Interventions in Ecological Counseling

As already stated, ecological counseling does not require counselors to abandon particular interventions, or to start from scratch in learning again how to counsel. Ecological counseling is a way of thinking about human behavior in terms of person–environment interaction that ideally expands the counselor's range of action. The learning that occurs as a consequence of exploring ecological ideas only adds to a counselor's repertoire, increasing his or her flexibility. In ecological counseling, we recognize that there are many causes of human problems and equally many strategies for a person to make desired changes in his or her life. Our professional code of ethics specifies the values we vow to live by in helping our clients, but beyond those limits, we can still do many things to help our clients.

For example, an ecological counselor might do any or all of the following:

- explore early childhood trauma in a client to understand current behavior patterns;
- with a client who has lost a beloved companion, develop new reasons to live through constructivist or existential philosophies;
- change maladaptive, absolutistic thinking patterns with the help of rational–emotive exercises;
- practice assertive behavior skills with a client whose shyness has interfered with career success;
- provide expert legislative testimony regarding needed substance abuse prevention policy; and
- consult on the design of a research project investigating positive mental health.

The ecological counselor shares with other counselors an appreciation for how these popular interventions can change people's lives by developing personal readiness to change, creating or capitalizing on personal resources, interacting more skillfully with others, and so on. The only difference between an ecological and nonecological counselor who uses these interventions may be in why they are chosen. An ecological counselor sees a client as a being-within-context, both idiosyncratic and shared with others, and the interventions as tools to improve the client's ecological concordance.

We also encourage counselors to see how such popular interventions might not promote the full spectrum of changes possible through counseling. Counselors frequently overlook ways of changing the client's environment to effect changes in the client–environment interaction. In addition, counselors often restrict their practice to individual direct service. This form of counseling has been literally life-giving for countless clients. Nevertheless, by considering other types of interventions and with other targets than the individual, counselors may dramatically expand their potential scope of effectiveness.

## Environmental Interventions

We are accustomed to thinking of counseling interventions as changing only the person, not the environment. If the idea of person–environment interactions is true, then any personal interventions by necessity also change the environment. For example, a couple successfully completing marriage counseling probably creates a more harmonious home climate for their children. A boss who has completed anger management training can encourage subordinates to be more creative and productive. After completing chemical dependency treatment, a newly sober person may unwittingly challenge former family and peer relationships.

Ecological counselors also consider ways to change the environment more directly in addition to doing so indirectly. The following list of intervention strategies in ecological counseling, amended from earlier work (Banning, 1987; Conoley & Haynes, 1992; Conyne, 1985; Conyne & Rogers, 1977; Kaiser, 1974; Sarason, 1972; Western Interstate Commission for Higher Education, 1976), is meant to be heuristic rather than exhaustive. The fictional case of Heidi illustrates some possibilities. Heidi is a pretty and intelligent undergraduate psychology student who is very respectful and compliant around authority figures. She has recently become unnerved by the inappropriate, intimidating, and emotionally intrusive behaviors directed at her by her highly placed and powerful psychology professor.

- *Strategy 1: Expand awareness of the range of choices.* Often people become stuck because they are unable to generate choices or find it difficult to choose among competing alternatives. Help-

124

ing individuals to consider and weigh choices from a person–environment perspective broadens the available repertoire. In Heidi's case, a counselor could help her recognize her options of being more assertive with her professor and/or working with the campus ombuds officer, who is specifically qualified to help with this kind of problem.

- *Strategy 2: Exit the environment.* Escaping an oppressive context that seems to afford no other feasible alternative sometimes may be the best, or the only, choice available. If assertive responses and the ombuds' office fail to solve her problem, Heidi could exit the psychology program and select a new major, or drop out of school entirely.
- *Strategy 3: Encapsulate within the environment.* Sometimes people need to find an island of safety, a place where—at least as a temporary measure—they can find protection and security. Heidi could begin to select only those courses that are taught by professors she knows to be safe.
- *Strategy 4: Reconstrue the existing context.* Cognitively restructuring an existing unsatisfactory situation without any other direct changes in it may be an acceptable way to cope. Heidi might be much less unnerved by her professor's behavior if she were able to view the problem as being more about him and all-too-common gender dynamics than about her.
- *Strategy 5: Develop a niche.* People can learn to select or create for themselves positive places where they feel not only a sense of comfort, protection, and security but also opportunities for growth and development. What makes a good ecological niche for a person is idiosyncratic. A campus support group that deals with women's issues might help Heidi have more confidence in dealing with aggressive males.
- *Strategy 6: Modify aspects of the present environment.* People can learn to change aspects of their environment to better fit their needs and values. For many, this idea is an empowering revelation. Heidi can immediately change the present environment in her classroom by arriving only in time for class and leaving promptly with a friend when class is over. With support from a counselor or university personnel, Heidi may also file an official grievance against the faculty member or consult a lawyer about taking possible legal action against him.
- *Strategy 7: Select a new setting.* Intentional and planful selection of a different setting or context may be possible for some. This action is different from exiting, discussed in Strategy 2, which is an

125

escaping strategy. Heidi could drop out of the current class and take it with a different faculty member or at a neighboring university, or perhaps over the Internet.

- *Strategy 8: Create a new context or setting.* In some circumstances, people may choose to innovate by developing a brand new context that seems to fit them better. This strategy, however, sometimes involves considerable risk and resources. Heidi could complete her course requirement by getting approval to study independently using her own set of selected readings under the supervision of another faculty member.

## Contextual Levels of Intervention

Ecological counseling can be conducted at the individual, group, organizational, or community contextual levels. The intervention strategies described in the previous section apply within each of these levels. In fact, it is entirely possible to consider a strategy of creating a new context or setting from either the individual, group, organizational, or community levels. In ecological counseling, any intervention is developed collaboratively with clients, is associated with ecological counseling strategies, and is implemented within the person–environment contextual perspective.

Following are brief descriptions of the interventions that are associated with each contextual level of ecological counseling. More detailed information about each of these interventions can be found in available texts dealing with change interventions.

### Individual Contextual Level Interventions

The dominant individual level interventions in ecological counseling include counseling and therapy, advising, mentoring, supporting, coaching, consultation, assessment, and testing. Because an ecological counselor views an individual client within context, potential interventions always need to be considered in relation to other levels of influence.

### Group Contextual Level Interventions

The dominant group level interventions in ecological counseling include therapeutic group leading and facilitation, task group facilitation, process observation and feedback, and process group consultation. In all cases, from an ecological perspective, a group is considered to be an open, complex, and interactive social system that is embedded within physical, temporal, sociocultural, and organizational contexts (Arrow,

McGrath, & Berdahl, 2000). Typical ecological counseling interventions at the group level, therefore, address organizational context (mission, supportive culture, rewards, technology, physical environment, nested placement); group structure (goals, tasks, membership, roles, time, group culture); group processes (problem solving, decision making, communication, boundary management, norms, participation, influence, task maintenance); group expectancies (performance standards and outcomes, group maintenance, member needs); and smaller and larger environments (Conyne, Rapin, & Rand, 1997; Schwarz, 1994).

## Organization Contextual Level Interventions

The dominant organizational level interventions in ecological counseling include assessment, training, facilitation, process consultation, organizational consultation, and research. An organization is conceived of as a dynamic social system that influences and is influenced by surrounding elements and processes. In working with organizations from an ecological counseling perspective, it is important to be aware a number of interrelated factors: surrounding context, available resources, structure, processes, products, social climate, leadership, physical elements, technology, and how all these elements are being coordinated (Weisbord, 1978).

## Community Contextual Level Interventions

The dominant community level interventions in ecological counseling include assessment, community development, community consultation, social advocacy, and research. In ecological counseling, community is the largest feasible level at which interventions can be mounted. Community, as all intervention levels, both influences and is influenced by proximal and distal factors. Community itself can be understood in various ways. It can be defined as a place (e.g., block, neighborhood, larger community); in terms of demographics, census tracks, or catchment areas; as being comprised of institutions and organizations; as a network of relationships and resources; or in relation to a perceived sense of community—that is, the feeling of the community in regard to membership, influence, value sharing, meeting of needs, and shared emotional connection (Heller, Price, Reinharz, Riger, & Wandersman, 1984).

In ecological counseling, interventions can occur for a variety of reasons and at a number of contextual levels. Most counselors adopting an ecological approach find themselves needing to learn about interventions that had never before been a part of their practice. Continuing education gains a new sense of urgency and appropriateness in professional

127

counseling as it becomes clear how expanding one's professional repertoire can lead to rewarding new vistas for the practice.

Other counselors adopting an ecological perspective may find their practice changing little in terms of what they do, but how they consider what they do may change. A counselor who has spent many productive years in psychodynamic counseling may have a renewed appreciation of how the client creates interpersonal environments through his or her behavior patterns. Another counselor may have a better sense of how his or her professional work has a place within the client's ecosystem, and may try to forge new collaborative relationships with other professions within the community. In ecological counseling, a change in one's meaning making, whether personal or professional, can constitute a major shift in one's life space.

## Phase 4: Evaluation in Ecological Counseling

In ecological counseling, evaluation is both a final stage and an ongoing process. Interventions need to be evaluated as they are being implemented (i.e., process or formative evaluation) and for their capacity to meet goals (i.e., outcome or summative evaluation). The guiding criterion for any ecological evaluation is whether ecological concordance was enhanced.

Changes in the client's life space begin the moment the counselor and the client agree to work together. When a productive working relationship is established, the counselor becomes a valued source of both support and challenge within the client's life space. The quality of the ongoing counselor–client interaction determines the eventual outcome. In contrast to other relationships within the client's life, this relationship is explicit in its mutual expectations, roles, and desired outcome. Ecological counselors are acutely aware of how everyone's life space, with its network of interactions and meanings, is unique. The counselor elicits and communicates respect for the client's perceptions throughout the process. Without an understanding of the client's meaning making, any evaluation will become irrelevant. As the Chinese proverb goes, "Only feet know whether shoes fit or not." Within the ecological counseling ethic of collaboration, counselors and clients review together whether the interaction is comfortable, whether the client's goals are plausible and reasonable, whether the strategies are within the client's capability, and whether the criteria for effectiveness is meaningful to the client.

Ecological counselors also understand that even simple interventions can have reverberating changes throughout the client's ecosystem.

For example, one client noted that when his counselor labeled him "effective in problem solving" it relieved much of his self-imposed guilt about past problems and enabled him to face present stresses with more equanimity. Evaluation throughout counseling allows the counselor and client to adjust their work to changes that gradually emerge over time.

Counselors might consider a number of questions as they work with their clients to improve the interlocking person–environment interactions characterizing the client's life:

- Do intervention goals and strategies acknowledge the interdependence of individuals within the client's life space?
- Is the partnership between counselor and client nurtured through the counseling process?
- Do counseling goals and strategies fit the clients' relevant life context?
- Do clients learn how to anticipate and manage changing environmental circumstances?
- Do clients know the consequences of changes to themselves and others, and know how to deal with the changes?
- Can clients maintain changes over time? What might support this maintenance?
- Are counseling strategies parsimonious, cost-effective, and focused on existing strengths and resources?
- How have clients' meaning-making processes been confirmed or altered in the counseling process? What long-term implications might such meaning-making changes have for the client's life?
- Was concordance furthered? In what ways?

For many counselors, process and outcome evaluations tend to be informal and seamlessly integrated within counseling interviews. In certain professional contexts, the agency's ecology may mandate specific models of goal setting and evaluation to meet agencywide accountability standards (see chapter 10). The philosophy of ecological counseling also supports more formalized, systematic assessment of person–environment characteristics. Although more time consuming and demanding for the counselor, such assessments have the advantage of recognizing the inherent limitations of any single source of data about the complex person–environment interaction at multiple levels characterizing a client's life. Ecological counselors must decide for themselves what assessment plans provide adequate data. They must also address the exigencies of their institutions, and fit the nature of the counselor-client interactions that form the substance of their practice.

## The Case of Cassie

The fictitious case of Cassie illustrates the process of ecological counseling. Cassie is a 29-year-old full-time homemaker with three children. She is married to a man who occasionally gets drunk and hits her. A concerned neighbor recently called the police, whose only intervention was to give Cassie the phone number of a counseling agency. After the next violent episode, Cassie began talking with a counselor about her situation. She indicated that her husband did not know she was seeking help and that she only came because she was concerned that her vocal and assertive 12-year-old daughter might soon become the next target of her husband's violence. Cassie assured the counselor that her husband "wasn't that bad" since he was a good provider and his violence was never severe enough to send her to the hospital. She also emphasized that she did not want to leave the marriage because she loved her husband, had no money of her own, and was convinced that the children needed their father.

Cassie began working with a counselor, but she attended intermittently following additional violent incidents. The counselor described Cassie as "tough to work with" and "not serious" about therapy. He also labeled her as a little "schizy" because of her poor eye contact and low speaking voice. His efforts to get her to leave her violent partner caused her to "no show" for weeks. Unable to connect with Cassie, he diagnosed a personality disorder (borderline, dependent) and recommended medication to control her symptoms. Eventually, Cassie stopped coming altogether.

The reactions and conclusions of this counselor are typical of a traditional, person-centered approach to working with cases involving domestic violence. The hallmark of this approach is the belief that the problem is located solely within the person. When Cassie failed to comply with the counselor's prescriptions to get serious about therapy and leave her violent partner, the frustrated counselor, unable to make a personal connection, diagnosed personal pathology and suggested medication.

Fortunately, Cassie's neighbor convinced her to try a second counselor who was better equipped to understand the complexities of Cassie's situation. When Cassie first arrived for counseling, the new counselor wisely postponed all diagnostic conclusions until Cassie's life space was thoroughly understood.

Because of Cassie's interpersonal demeanor and her painful living conditions, the counselor was concerned about the possibility of severe anxiety and/or depression. The counselor carefully questioned Cassie about possible symptom patterns, and determined that she was coping very well thus far. She did not appear to need medication or an immediate focus on the emotional consequences of her life space. Because Cassie's previous counselor communicated to her that he thought she was disturbed, she was a little surprised and pleased with her new counselor's assessment of her. The counselor and Cassie agreed to check in about these possible problems on a regular basis as counseling proceeded.

In a collaborative manner, Cassie and the ecological counselor set out to clarify the *what* of Cassie's problem as she saw it. With some help, Cassie was able to state that her problem involved coping with the violence and protecting her children from it. It was clear to the counselor that Cassie wanted to stay married, for reasons that were currently unknown to the counselor and perhaps to Cassie herself. At this point, Cassie also did not consider the violence against her as a focus of counseling. The counselor noted to herself that this minimization of violence is common among persons like Cassie, and that Cassie's right to have a safe, mutually supportive relationship would need to be explored. She decided to raise this as an issue to explore later in counseling.

With the problem statement in mind, Cassie and her counselor proceeded to identify who was involved in Cassie's problem. Although to date, the violence only directly involved Cassie and her husband, their 12-year-old daughter was becoming increasingly involved by challenging her father and attempting to intervene during violent episodes. The counselor helped Cassie appreciate that *all* of her children were involved in this situation, since they were witnesses who were learning some very negative life lessons. Cassie's parents, who she saw nearly every day, were also involved in Cassie's problem, because they felt it was her duty to tolerate the violence for the sake of the family.

Cassie and her ecological counselor also clarified *when* and *where* the problem occurred. Cassie was able to recognize that her husband's violence typically erupted during the months when he was working third shift, which disrupted his body clock, and after he came home from drinking with his friends on Saturday nights. She also determined that the violence most often followed their arguments about his drinking; he knew that she considered his drinking a problem, but he viewed it as a harmless way to blow off steam. She reported that he was very remorseful the day after he hit her, though, and typically blamed the violence on drinking too much.

In a collaborative manner, Cassie and her counselor also sought to understand from her perspective *why* the violence happened.

Cassie considered her husband's violence to be a result of the frustration he felt being trapped in a job. Despite the job's high pay, her husband often strained his back and suffered with chronic pain. She agreed with her husband that he had a right to party with his buddies, but she nevertheless believed that he was a problem drinker. In addition, she explained that her husband's friends at work believed that occasional roughness with women is needed to show them who's boss. The counselor also learned that Cassie and her husband both grew up in homes where violence against women was tolerated as long as it didn't get too severe.

Cassie's way of making meaning around the problem is a key point for the ecological counselor. Cassie essentially regarded the violence as something she had to tolerate in order to enjoy the benefits of an intact marriage—a lesson she learned from her family while growing up. She valued the financial security marriage provided, feared experiencing the stigma of divorce in her church community, and believed there is great value in keeping her children with their father. Because she and her husband had dated since high school, Cassie also believed they were "meant to be together." In describing her marriage, Cassie vacillated between romanticizing the relationship and expressing anger and frustration because she felt afraid and trapped in the marriage. She repeatedly engaged in either/or thinking: either her marriage was a great romance or it was a failure. She also refused to believe that her husband was an alcoholic. She thought he could stop drinking whenever he chose, but he needed an outlet for his stress. However, she did tell the counselor that "his outlet doesn't have to be me or the kids." The counselor supported Cassie's tentative shift in meaning making without pushing her to take action at this point.

Finally, the counselor and Cassie assessed the available *resources* and *barriers* to change across the various levels of her life space. Cassie's personal resources included her health, intelligence, early job experience as a secretary, love for her children, and motivation to solve her problem. Her personal relationship resources included a caring neighbor, friends at church who expressed shock and concern about her "secret marriage problems," and a sister who had successfully resolved a similar problem of her own. Some time ago, Cassie had seen on Oprah Winfrey's television show a woman whose husband had beaten her. This woman made a big impression on Cassie. She admitted that she thought about this woman as a secret sister and admired her courage in changing her life. The counselor recognized this woman as part of Cassie's life space, and a potential symbolic ally for her.

In addition, a number of organizations in the community were able to provide ongoing counseling, education, and support for Cassie, and a new statewide campaign raised awareness about the costs of domestic violence.

However, Cassie also faced formidable barriers to change. Her personal pattern of devaluing her needs and right to safety (originating in her childhood), her parents' acceptance of the status quo, and her husband's refusal to quit drinking or change jobs all made it hard for Cassie to realize her goals. Also, the nonchalant attitude of police responding to the neighbor's calls communicated to Cassie that she shouldn't bother them with her problem.

The ecological assessment process focused on Cassie and her environment in an effort to fully understand her problem. The counselor could readily understand why Cassie felt stuck in her life situation, yet also saw resources Cassie could use to make changes in her life. She considered Cassie courageous in tolerating an awful situation for what she perceived as necessity, and serious about wanting a better life. Cassie cried when the counselor communicated this to her.

## Goal Setting

Working collaboratively, Cassie and her counselor set out to identify goals that would increase the P $\times$ E concordance between Cassie and her environment. The counselor realized that appropriate goals for Cassie would be unique to her situation and determined by her values, her meaning-making processes, and her acumen about her own life space.

This presented a real dilemma for the counselor. She knew that domestic violence frequently became worse over time, and that Cassie (and perhaps her children) were in real danger of becoming seriously hurt during one of these episodes. She also knew that Cassie would resist any external directives to leave her husband. The counselor recognized within Cassie a determination to do what she felt was necessary (a trait Cassie labeled stubbornness). This determination could be used as a real strength in making some difficult changes in her life, and deserved respect.

From Cassie's perspective, staying with her husband represented a desirable goal because it would provide continued financial security and a father for her children, and it allowed her to stay with someone she regarded as basically a good man. She also believed that her church opposed divorce except in cases where the partner was an unrepentant sinner. The counselor shared her concern about the situation with

Cassie, and her faith in Cassie's ability to choose what felt right to her if given the resources and support. After exploration with her counselor, Cassie admitted that she did not want violence and fear to be part of her children's or her life anymore. The counselor and Cassie agreed that appropriate goals for counseling were (a) keeping the family together, and (b) protecting herself and her children from further violence. Cassie also agreed to be honest with the counselor about the severity and frequency of any violent episodes in the future, and to discuss options for leaving the marriage just in case it ever seemed desirable to do so.

During this goal-setting process, the counselor helped Cassie identify goals that presented a reasonable level of challenge. Seeking to take her children and leave her marriage would have been too great an ordeal for Cassie for many reasons, and was not one she was willing to undertake at this point. However, finding less drastic ways to increase safety while keeping her family together presented a reasonable challenge for Cassie, one both she and her counselor thought she could manage because of the available resources and barriers to change that were present in her life space.

The counselor knew that Cassie would need support as she attempted to achieve change. Using metaphors with which Cassie was comfortable, they discussed how she might draw on a "community of saints" to give her strength, and then contribute to them in return. The counselor recognized how such relationships could lend Cassie support for a long period of time as her life changes solidified, and would immediately relieve the isolation Cassie reported feeling. She agreed to add a local women's advocacy group to her network of support. This group would also provide understanding and referrals for social services if the violence recurred or worsened.

The relationship between Cassie and her counselor solidified during the goal-setting process because the counselor showed respect for Cassie. The counselor had assisted her in formulating reasonable goals that fit her personal values and her way of making meaning. Unlike the traditional counselor/expert who previously prescribed medication, diagnosed pathology, and finally lost his opportunity to help Cassie, the ecological counselor and Cassie became a team ready to move onto the next phase of the counseling process.

## Selecting Strategies and Interventions

The process of selecting strategies and interventions for realizing Cassie's goals involved evaluating every strategy in light of Cassie's values, meaning-making resources, and existing barriers to goal attainment. Selected strategies should always be comprehensible, accessible, and manageable. For example, Cassie's counselor knew of a wonderful women's retreat center 300 miles away, but Cassie lacked the financial backing, child care, or support from her husband to attend. Nevertheless, Cassie had the chance to successfully learn new ways to request help from others. Cassie's ecologically oriented counselor helped her select strategies that were uniquely suited to her personal life space and that helped her reach her goal.

Cassie's broadened awareness included recognition of the nature of her husband's drinking problem and an increased awareness of available community resources. She found an escape for her children and herself by going to her sister's house overnight when her husband left to go drinking. (She recounted with some pleasure how her husband spent the night in jail after pounding on her sister's door and yelling for her to come home.) At one point, she went on a weekend church retreat with her sister to gain some thinking time and deepen their relationship. Cognitive restructuring occurred when Cassie began to recognize that domestic violence represents abuse instead of normal male behavior, and that "blowing off steam" might be a euphemism for alcoholism. She enhanced her ecological niche by finding a job and by joining a local battered women's support group. Her decision to become employed altered her husband's life through a ripple effect: Cassie's new income made it possible for her husband eventually to accept a lower paying job with regular hours that was less stressful for his back. She also impacted her broader environment by informing local officials about the ineffective help she had received from the police who came to her home when she was in trouble.

The counselor and Cassie recognized how the abuse problem originated with her husband and not herself. She could learn to cope with the situation and to change their interactions pertinent to this problem, but he had the responsibility of changing his own behavior. With the supportive presence of some church elders, she confronted her husband about his drinking. He agreed to enter a treatment program, and a popular church program for men designed to help them fulfill their roles as husbands and fathers. The counselor gently reminded Cassie that alcohol abuse and domestic violence were very difficult problems to change, in part because attitudes condoning violence are so entrenched. In counseling, Cassie and the counselor considered what she might expect from his efforts to change (e.g., relapse, verbal instead of physical abuse), what she was willing to tolerate in the interest of maintaining the marriage, and what she might do if these things reoccurred. Cassie came to see the change process as a gradual one. She might need support from counseling over time not because she was weak, but because these were such difficult problems (change in meaning making). She began to ask herself what the role model she observed on television might do. This strategy represented a shift in Cassie's valuing of herself as a resourceful and strong person.

These strategies include a combination of those that emphasize personal change (**P** $\times$ E) and those that primarily target the environment for change (P $\times$ **E**). Cassie's broadened awareness helped her change the way she perceived herself and her husband's violence as well as the way she interacted with her husband. Her environment changed significantly when she enhanced her ecological niche, developed her relationship with others, found a safe place to be when her husband was drinking, and gained a healthier, happier husband to live with in a new lower stress home environment. As expected, Cassie's husband continued to engage in drinking and abuse from time to time, although the patterns changed in frequency and severity. Cassie made it clear that their marriage depended on him continuing to work on these issues. She implemented an escape plan several times, and reported that she felt she could handle such incidents better in the future.

## Conclusion

The process of ecological counseling is both similar and different from other counseling approaches. Certainly, its phases of assessment, goal setting, implementation, and evaluation resonate with other approaches. It is within those phases that qualitative differences can be found. These differences revolve around perspective and intervention levels.

In terms of perspective, ecological counseling is centered within the concept of context. In a very real sense, ecological counseling is contextualized help giving. From this framework, people are always situated within context, both proximal and distal, and are not considered independent parties. It is within such contexts that reciprocal person–environment interactions occur. Ecological counselors employ ecological empathy as they work collaboratively with clients to help them understand the meaning that emerges from these P $\times$ E contextualized interactions. This evolving meaning provides the substrata for growth and change.

A second hallmark of ecological counseling is that it can occur at multiple levels. The range of intervention levels includes individual, group, organizational, and/or community. The ongoing case example of

Cassie developed in this chapter demonstrates how the contextual perspective can be applied across varying intervention levels.

Intervention strategies within ecological counseling are freed from being focused on either the person *or* the environment. Ecological counseling intervention choices, at whatever level of implementation, are aimed at the meaning that is created by clients from their contextualized $P \times E$ interactions. Unique counseling strategies emerge, including exiting, reconstruing the existing context, developing a niche, and creating a new context or setting—to name only a few that were discussed in this chapter.

Finally, we considered (all too briefly due to space) some issues related to process and outcome evaluation. Attention needs to be given to whether concordance was promoted, the degree to which the changes initiated will be sustainable, and how collaboration was employed in seeking improved concordance.

Illustrations of several ecological counseling interventions are presented in detail in Section II. These interventions more substantially demonstrate the variety of ways that ecological counseling can be applied.

## Learning Activities

1. In the beginning of this chapter, we note that what "fundamentally distinguishes ecological counseling from other perspectives is the recognition of the complex, circular causality intrinsic to human problems." Think of an example of a human problem and explain how it might be rooted in complex, circular causes.

2. Identify ways the assessment process in ecological counseling is the same as in traditional approaches, and also how it is different.

3. Using your example of a human problem from Learning Activity 1, complete the following assessment steps:
   a. Situate the problem within the life space.
   b. Elaborate the ecological web.
   c. Identify resources and barriers.

4. Give an example of how three individuals having the same experience might make meaning of that experience in three different ways. Why is it so important for a counselor to have *ecological empathy?*

5. What are the hazards of basing treatment plans solely on a *DSM-IV* diagnostic label? What other information might an ecological counselor want before engaging in treatment planning?

6. What differences in interaction style and method would you expect between a traditional counselor and an ecological counselor who recognizes a client's own strengths and the strengths of others in the client's life space?

7. Why could it be a mistake to set good grades as the simple treatment goal for a bright junior high student who is self-conscious about acne, whose parents are divorcing and only providing fast food at home, and whose best friend is the class troublemaker? What other treatment goals might an ecological counselor discuss with this student and/or his or her family? What other professionals or individuals might be able to help with this case? How?

8. Explain how taking a well-paying corporate job could be an appropriate ecological goal for one woman and inappropriate for another who is equally credentialed and identical in all other observable demographics, such as income, marital status, number of children, health, and age.

9. Using the list of eight ecological counseling intervention strategies described in this chapter and the example from Learning Activity 1, design two ecological intervention strategies for each contextual life space level (i.e., individual, group, organization, and community) that might improve $P \times E$ concordance. Be sure to include strategies that emphasize both person (P) and environment (E).

10. How might the intervention strategies planned in Learning Activity 9 be evaluated? When? What role should the client play in the process of ecological evaluation? Why?

## References

American Psychiatric Association. (1994) *Diagnostic and statistical manual of mental disorders* (4th ed.). Washington, DC: Author.

Arrow, H., McGrath, J., & Berdahl, J. (2000). *Small groups in complex systems: Formation, coordination, development, and adaptation.* Thousand Oaks, CA: Sage.

Banning, J. (1987). Environmental change: A seven question process. *The Campus Ecologist, 5,* 1–3.

Blocher, D. (2000). *Counseling: A developmental approach.* New York: Wiley.

Brown, L. S. (2000). Discomforts of the powerless: Feminist constructions of distress. In R. A. Neimeyer & J. D. Raskin (Eds.), *Constructions of disorder: Meaning-making frameworks for psychotherapy* (pp. 287–308). Washington, DC: American Psychological Association.

Caplan, P. J. (1995). *They say you're crazy: How the world's most powerful psychiatrists decide who's normal*. Reading, MA: Addison-Wesley.

Conoley, J., & Haynes, G. (1992). An ecological approach to intervention. In R. D'Amato & B. Rothlisberg (Eds.), *Psychological perspectives on interaction* (pp. 177–189). White Plains, NY: Longman.

Conyne, R. (1985). The counseling ecologist: Helping people and environments. *Counseling and Human Development, 18*, 1–12.

Conyne, R. K., & Clack, R. J. (1981). *Environmental assessment and design: A new tool for the applied behavioral scientist*. New York: Praeger.

Conyne, R., Rapin, L., & Rand, J. (1997). A model for leading task groups. In H. Forrester-Miller & J. Kottler (Eds.), *Issues and challenges for group practitioners* (pp. 117–131). Denver: Love.

Conyne, R., & Rogers, R. (1977). Psychotherapy as ecological problem solving. *Psychotherapy: Theory, Research, and Practice, 14*, 298–305.

Doherty, W. (1995). *Soul searching: Why psychotherapy must promote moral responsibility*. New York: Basic Books.

Friedman, S., & Wachs, T. (Eds.). (1999). *Measuring environment across the life span: Emerging methods and concepts*. Washington, DC: American Psychological Association.

Gergen, K. J., & McNamee, S. (2000). From disordering discourse to transformative dialogue. In R. A. Neimeyer & J. D. Raskin (Eds.), *Constructions of disorder: Meaning-making frameworks for psychotherapy* (pp. 333–349). Washington, DC: American Psychological Association.

Heller, K., Price, R., Reinharz, S., Riger, S., & Wandersman, A. (1984). *Psychology and community change: Challenges of the future*. Homewood, IL: Dorsey.

Helms, J., & Cook, D. A. (1999). *Using race and culture in counseling and psychotherapy: Theory and process*. Boston: Allyn & Bacon.

Horton, C. B. (2000). Assessing adolescents: Ecological and person-environment fit perspectives. In W. E. Martin, Jr., & J. L. Swartz-Kulstad (Eds.), *Person–environment psychology and mental health* (pp. 647–668). Mahwah, NJ: Erlbaum.

Ivey, A. E., & Ivey, M. B. (1998). Reframing *DSM-IV*: Positive strategies from developmental counseling and therapy. *Journal of Counseling & Development, 76*, 334–350.

Kaiser, L. (1974). Designing campus environments. *NASPA Journal*, 34-39.

Kleinman, A. (1988). *The illness narratives: Suffering, healing, and the human condition*. New York: Basic Books.

Lemke, S., Moos, R., Mehren, B., & Gauvain, M. (1979). *Multiphasic Environmental Assessment Procedure (MEAP): Handbook for users*. Palo Alto, CA: Social Ecology Laboratory and Stanford University School of Medicine.

Linney, J. A. (2000). Assessing ecological constructs and community context. In J. Rappaport & E. Seidman (Eds.), *Handbook of community psychology* (pp. 647-668). New York: Kluwer Academic/Plenum Press.

Moos, R. (1973, August). Conceptualizations of human environments. *American Psychologist*, pp. 652-664.

Moos, R. (1974). *The Social Climate Scales: An overview*. Palo Alto, CA: Consulting Psychologists Press.

Munger, R. L. (2000). Comprehensive needs-based assessment with adolescents. In W. E. Martin, Jr., & J. L. Swartz-Kulstad (Eds.), *Person–environment psychology and mental health* (pp. 647–668). Mahwah, NJ: Erlbaum.

Root, M. P. P. (1992). Reconstructing the impact of trauma on personality. In L. S. Brown & M. Ballou (Eds.), *Personality and psychothopathology: Feminist reappraisals* (pp. 229–265). New York: Guilford Press.

Sarason, S. (1972). *The creation of settings and the future societies*. San Francisco: Jossey-Bass.

Schwarz, R. (1994). *The skilled facilitator: Practical wisdom for developing effective groups*. San Francisco: Jossey-Bass.

Steenbarger, B., & Pels, L. (1997). Constructivist foundations for multicultural counseling: Assessment and intervention. In T. Sexton & B. Griffin (Eds.), *Constructivist thinking in counseling practice, research, and training* (pp. 111–121). New York: Teachers College Press.

Weisbord, M. (1978). *Organizational diagnosis: A workbook of theory and practice*. Reading, MA: Addison-Wesley.

Western Interstate Commission for Higher Education (WICHE). (1976). *Training manual for an ecosystem model: Assessing and designing campus environments*. Boulder, CO: Author.

# Section II

## *Ecological Counseling Interventions*

Chapter 6

# Ecological Psychotherapy

## F. Robert Wilson

---

### Chapter Highlights

- *Ecological psychotherapy is a model for assessment, problem formulation, and treatment planning that focuses on development of the personal niche in which the individual can experience interpersonal effectiveness.*
- *Ecological assessment examines the person in his or her niche, gathering data on the client's characteristics, the qualities of the niche environment, and the client's pattern of interactive, coevolutionary, niche development strategies.*
- *Ecological treatment, selected to fit the level of impairment experienced by the client, uses client strength and niche resources to achieve a better fit for the client within the client's ecological niche.*

---

Ecological psychotherapy is a model for assessment, problem formulation, and treatment planning that strives to facilitate the development of the personal niche in which the individual can experience interpersonal effectiveness (Dawis, 2000; Willi, 1999). Grounded in the tradition of person–environment theorists, ecological psychotherapy seeks to understand behavior not only as a function of the person or of environmental conditions but also as a function of their reciprocal interaction. This approach has general utility in mental health counseling practice and may be particularly useful with traditionally underserved populations (Martin & Schwartz-Kulstad, 2000). This chapter presents the guiding principles of ecological psychotherapy and the processes and competencies needed to engage in this work, and provides an extended case study to illustrate the ecological orientation to psychotherapy. Methods for assessment, problem formulation, and treatment planning are detailed.

## Theoretical Underpinnings

### Conceptual Linkages

Psychotherapeutic tradition (e.g., Allport, 1937; Freud, 1949; Murray, 1938) has focused on the study of organismic, personological variables such as traits, dispositions, attitudes, and needs. Consistent with this view, the focus of assessment, problem formulation summarized by a multiaxial diagnosis (American Psychiatric Association, *Diagnostic and Statistical Manual of Mental Disorders*, 2000), and intervention rests on the intrapsychic process of the individual. In fact, human problems (especially personality problems) are considered relatively context insensitive, manifesting themselves regardless of the environmental context in which an individual is placed. The *DSM-IV-TR* has reified the personological view by defining the term *mental disorder* as a

> clinically significant behavioral or psychological syndrome or pattern that occurs *in an individual* [emphasis added] and that is associated with present distress (a painful symptom) or disability (impairment in one or more important areas of functioning) or with a significantly increased risk of suffering, death, pain, disability, or an important loss of freedom. (p. xxxi)

Though claiming to separate the description of the disorder from etiological explanations, the *DSM-IV-TR* clearly chooses sides in the debate about whether behavior is more a function of within-person factors or whether it is more a function of environmental forces.

Although ignored in traditional literature on psychotherapy, environmental press (i.e., environmental forces that exert pressure on individuals, affecting them positively or negatively) has held the attention of social theorists for decades. Inadequate and inaccessible health care facilities, inadequate educational facilities, the disappearance of jobs for individuals with limited education, erosion of civil rights, discrimination, architectural barriers, inadequate and overcrowded housing, and the toxic qualities of life in neighborhoods fraught with violence and predation create barriers to effectiveness, happiness, and peace. However, environments rich in nutrients—timely access to competent health care, access to competent educational facilities, availability of employment opportunities, secure civil rights, accessible architecture, and adequate housing in safe neighborhoods—allow individuals the opportunity to succeed (DuBois & Miley, 2002).

Articulation of the synthesis that behavior is a function of the interaction between the person and his or her environment also first appeared in the early 20th century (e.g., Parsons, 1909). It was Lewin (1936) who crystallized the concept in the now familiar mathematical formula, $B = f(P \times E)$. Extension to the realm of psychotherapy was foreshadowed by Sullivan's (1953) interpersonal theory of psychiatry and formally articulated by Willi (1999). This was supported by the work of modern interpersonal theorists such as Weissman and Markowitz (1994), Weissman, Markowitz, and Klerman (2000), and Wilfley, MacKenzie, Welch, Ayres, and Weissman (2000), in addition to advocates of multi-systemic therapy such as Henggeler and Schoenwald (Henggeler & Schoenwald, 1998; Schoenwald, 2000a, 2000b). In sum, the ecosystemic epistemology shifts the focus of counseling and psychotherapy from an exclusive focus on intrapsychic phenomena to an appreciation of the embeddedness of individuals within an ecological relationship system (Banning, 1989).

## Principles Guiding Ecological Psychotherapy

In ecologically oriented psychotherapy, the focus is on the person in his or her environment (Conoley & Haynes, 1992), the manner in which individuals assimilate and accommodate to their ecosystem (Banning, 1989; Bronfenbrenner, 1979; Conoley & Haynes, 1992), and their effectiveness in creating a satisfactory personal niche or working space within their surrounding ecosystem (Willi, 1999). The individual's created niche contains "the objects of real and current interactions, against which individuals assess their own reality and receive responses to their effectiveness" (Willi, 1999, p. 26). Each person engages in constant and intense interactions with the environment in order to create and maintain this personal niche (assimilation) in which his or her developmental potential can be reached (Willi, 1999). In reciprocal fashion, the personal niche shapes the niche dweller's perception and impels and guides action while simultaneously constraining one's freedom to act (accommodation).

Ecologically oriented psychotherapy views personal health as a function of interactive effectiveness. As Wachtel (1993) noted, "[P]eople live in contexts and our behavior, both adaptive and maladaptive, is always in relation to someone or something" (p. 24). *Interactive effectiveness* is defined as a reciprocal process involving a person and an object in which a person acts toward an object with the hope of gaining a desired end (an attempt to accommodate or assimilate) and becomes the recipient of the object's reaction, which serves as feedback and informs the person's plans for new action (to accommodate or assimilate). This process progresses in spiral fashion throughout time (Willi, 1999).

In person-to-person interactions, each strives to influence the other and each seeks interactive effectiveness. Relationships between humans cannot be viewed as simple action–reaction sequences, as is the case when the object of assimilative activity is inanimate, but rather as recip-rocally causal (Banning, 1989).To support individuals in their participa-tion in coevolutionary cocreation of their personal niches, ecologically oriented psychotherapy strives to improve the client's capacity and capability to form and manage relationships. In this, ecological psy-chotherapy echoes the interpersonal focus of Sullivan (1953) and joins modern interpersonally oriented theorists such as Weissman et al., (2000), Wilfley et al. (2000), and Villeneuve (2001).

## Processes Involved and Competencies Needed

The ecological view of counseling and psychotherapy shapes the initial and ongoing assessments of a client, the subsequent diagnoses and formulations of the client's problems, and the course of therapeutic intervention.The processes involved and the competencies needed for each of these facets of the therapeutic encounter are discussed in turn.

### Assessment

Ecological psychotherapy is grounded in the notion that mental health is best studied by assessing person–environment fit (Banning, 1989). Willi (1999) advocate assessment based on the ecological cycle, a cycle featuring three themes: (a) the client's intrapersonal spheres—the con-structs (schemata, beliefs, and internal objects) that form the basis of his or her intentions, plans, and actions; (b) the elements of the client's niche, particularly the intrapersonal spheres of the people with whom he or she interacts and their constructs as the basis of their intentions, plans, and actions; and (c) the interactional sphere which features the interactions between clients and the people in their niches, the real effects the clients produce, and the real responses these effects provoke from their partners.

*Intrapersonal assessment.* Historically, assessment with psy-chotherapy clients has focused on intrapersonal traits and attributes (Conoley & Haynes, 1992; Conyne, 1975; Conyne & Clack, 1981; Delworth & Piel, 1978).A host of encyclopedic works have documented the variety of methods and instruments invented for this purpose (Anastasi & Urbina, 1996; Impara & Plake, 2001; Maruish, 1999). Intra-personal assessment, in fact, has been judged so central to diagnosis in psychotherapeutic settings that the *DSM-IV-TR* established a separate axis (Axis V) for recording an intrapersonally oriented Global Assessment of Functioning (GAF). The ecological view of counseling does not turn its back on the intrapsychic–intrapersonal tradition, but rather views intrapersonal variables as an important part of the interactive pattern.

***Environmental assessment.*** Across the years, environmental assessment has not kept pace. To correct this deficiency, ecologically grounded assessment strives to obtain an in-depth description of the daily contexts that make up an individual's life, including evaluation of both the objective qualities of the individual's environmental niche and his or her subjective perception of those qualities (Munger, 2000). To guide qualitative assessment of the ecological niche, Munger suggested examining several core niche elements: (a) residence-shelter, (b) family, (c) social contact, (d) education-vocation, (e) medical care, (f) psychological-emotional care, (g) legal involvement, (h) safety, (i) cultural-ethnic considerations, and (j) community characteristics. A problem-focused list of environmental components has been provided on Axis IV of the multiaxial formulation of the *DSM-IV-TR* consisting of (a) problems with primary support group; (b) problems related to the social environment; (c) educational problems; (d) occupational problems; (e) housing problems; (f) economic problems; (g) problems with access to health care services; and (h) problems related to interaction with the legal system. Both lists highlight key elements of environmental nutrition that warrant assessment. Qualitative environmental assessment is assisted by the *DSM-IV-TR* Axis IV problem-focused list, and a quantitative rating of environmental quality can be obtained through use of the Ancillary Impairment Scale (Kennedy, 2001).

A time-honored tool for describing the evolution of a client's ecological niche is through construction of a lifeline, a mapping of life events over the span of one's life (Goldman, 1992). Graphic portrayal of family composition and multigenerational problems may be accomplished through the genogram, a tool commonly used in family therapy (Marlin, 1989; McGoldrick & Gerson, 1985). Niche content may be directly described and analyzed with an ecomap, which diagrams an individual's relationships with others and with social institutions within his or her environmental niche (Hartman, 1995). In addition to identifying the cast of people and institutions that constitute an individual's family or niche, and the order in which key events have occurred through the individual's life flow, the lifelines, genograms, and ecomaps can be enriched by noting the degree and manner in which each time period, person, and institution exhibits nutritive or nonnutritive qualities. WonderWare (1995) has published computer software to facilitate creation of genograms and ecomaps.

A final approach to gathering information about environmental quality, known as environmental assessment, collects perceptions of multiple inhabitants of a single environment. In their work in this area, Conyne and Clack (1981) reviewed several instruments for assessing the person–environment relationship. Such contextual data could be particularly valuable to counselors whose clients come from a relatively homogeneous environment, as may be the case with employee assistance program therapists or therapists working with clients from inner-city neighborhoods.

*Interpersonal assessment.* In the ecological view of psychotherapy, the interaction of the person with the elements and systems of the environment is paramount (Bondurant-Utz, 1994; Horton & Bucy, 2000). A variety of assessment tools have been developed for this process, including quantitative self-report instruments, guides for qualitative assessment, and clinician rating scales (e.g., Bondurant-Utz, 1994; O'Hanlon & Beadle, 1997). The best practice for ecological assessment of interactional patterns might be nonintrusive, naturalistic observation and documentation of patterns and sequences of behavior in naturalistic, simulated, or role-play situations.

One notable attempt to assess goodness of fit in the interpersonal arena was Leary's (1957) circumplex method for the interpersonal diagnosis of personality, later adapted by Lorr and McNair (1966), Wiggins (1979, 1982), and Kiesler (1983). Other memorable attempts were instrumentation developed to assess the Schutz (1958) FIRO model of interpersonal compatibility; the Horowitz, Rosenberg, Baer, Ureno, and Villasenor (1988) Inventory of Interpersonal Problems for assessing distress associated with client-identified interpersonal problems; and Hudson's (1997a, 1997b, 1997c) series of instruments to assess peer, family, and sibling relationships. VanDenburg, Schmidt, and Kiesler (1992) recommended routine inclusion of a brief interpersonal assessment battery to determine how clients experience their own interpersonal functioning and how others, in turn, experience the client's interpersonal functioning.

A rich description of the quality of clients' interactions within their ecosystem can be captured in genograms, ecomaps, and lifelines by coding connections among individuals and institutions according to what Lee (1985) referred to as life-space patterns, the individual's "characteristic ways of negotiating time, space, people, and activity in their day-to-day lives" (p. 624). Qualitative questions such as "What is a typical day like for you?" or "Who do you interact with on a regular basis?" or "What is it like living in your home and in your neighborhood?" help flesh out the nature of life in the individual's niche and contribute to the development of a thick description of life within the client's ecological niche (Csikszentmihalyi & Larson, 1984). Willi's (1999) six-level schema for categorizing client relationship activities—(a) simple forms of interactions, participating without interaction; (b) nonreciprocal interaction; (c) brief contacts without commitment; (d) reciprocal relationships without responsibility; (e) relationships with minimal personal closeness; and (f) dyadic relationships with binding commitments—can also be used as a guide for analysis of qualitative interview data. Although not studied empirically, this hierarchy of relationships has intuitive appeal.

Quantitative ratings of interpersonal functioning may be obtained through use of the *DSM-IV-TR* Global Assessment of Relational Functioning Scale (GARF). Like the GAF, this scale guides clinician rating of the quality of relational functioning in a family or other ongoing relationship within an individual's niche, as evidenced in client self-report data. The GARF focuses on such relational phenomena as the quality of agreed-upon patterns or routines that support meeting the needs of relationship members, the shared understandings and agreements about roles, tasks, and behavior, and the freedom of expression of ideas and feelings present in the relationship (Yingling, Miller, McDonald, & Galewaler, 1998).

***Competencies needed for ecologically grounded assessment.***
Ecological assessment, then, involves complete assessment of intrapsychic, environmental, and interpersonal dimensions taking place within an ecological niche. Besides being familiar with a broad spectrum of assessment measures and methods (cf. Kennedy, 2001; Maruish, 1999; Schutte & Malouff, 1995), the ecologically oriented assessor must understand the social and cultural realities and circumstances of the client's ecological niche (Paniagua, 1994, 2001). To foster a collaborative assessment relationship, the assessor must join with the client in mutually developing a comprehensive picture of the client's ecological niche as it is and as the client hopes it could be (Paniagua, 2001; Tyler, Brome, & Williams, 1991). Clients may need to engage in ongoing assessment outside the therapy hour.

### Problem Formulation

From the ecological perspective, mental health is achieved through active, effective interaction with the coinhabitants of the individual's personal, ecological niche. As a corollary, mental illness results from disruptions in the correspondence between the individual and the niche— i.e., a failure of fit (Willi, 1999). Problem formulation, therefore, is a process of parsing the portion of the individual's problem presentation that is a function of the individual's inadequate behavior (intrapersonal factors), the portion that is a function of inadequacy or toxicity on the part of the niche and its objects (environmental factors), and the portion deriving from interactive ineffectiveness (interpersonal factors). Symptoms, impairments, and risk of grave loss—the hallmark indicators of mental and emotional illness (*DSM-IV-TR*)—are judged relative to the ecosystem in which they occur (Banning, 1989).

*Considering intrapersonal factors in problem formulation.* Disruptions in the correspondence between the person and niche certainly may be due to inadequate behavior on the individual's part (Willi, 1999), as represented on the first three axes of the *DSM-IV-TR*. Structural and functional impairment through brain disease, disruption of the rhythms of drive satisfaction and motivation and associated behavior disregulation, and the enduring effects of cognitive capacity and character structure have well-documented impact on physical health and interactive effectiveness (McHugh, 2002; Millon, 1981; Willi, 1999). The reciprocal interactions between the personological factors of cognitive capacity, personality, clinical syndromes, and general medical conditions, and the ecological niche factors of environmental nutrients and stressors have also been extensively documented and lucidly described (Millon, 1981; Millon & Davis, 1999; Preston, O'Neal, & Talaga, 1997).

Among the first three axes of the *DSM-IV-TR*, Axis II is pivotal. It is, after all, through one's capacity for thought and one's habitual beliefs, perceptions, and behavioral reactions that one knows, selects, and influences the environment, thereby creating one's niche (Millon, 1981; Millon & Davis, 1999; Willi, 1999). As Willi (1999) observed, psychological and physical symptom formation may develop in the service of shoring up failing interactive effectiveness under stress and obliquely communicating distress to others in the ecological niche.

*Considering environmental factors in problem formulation.* It is also possible that disruptions in the correspondence between individual and niche may be caused because of environmental inadequacy (Willi, 1999). Environments vary in availability of physical and psychological nutrients and the presence of physical and psychological stressors and toxins, thus facilitating or frustrating the individual as he she strives for self-actualization. The *DSM-IV-TR* does permit recording psychosocial and environmental problems on Axis IV, but it attends exclusively to deficits in critical nutrients and presence of toxic elements while ignoring by omission the nutritious, supportive elements that may be available within the niche.

Because no widely agreed-upon list of environmental nutrients and stressors, or any well-accepted taxonomy of environments, has been produced, evaluating the role of the client's environment in facilitating or hindering healthy development is somewhat a matter of subjective judgment. Various sources suggest that key diagnostic considerations might include

- primary family support, including current primary relationship;
- social environment, including friendships and peer support;
- healthfulness and safety of neighborhood and housing;
- educational supports and problems, including environmental barriers to learning;
- satisfactoriness of employment, including environmental barriers to employment and advancement;
- sufficiency of monetary resources;
- health care supports, including environmental barriers to obtaining satisfactory health care;
- legal supports and difficulties;
- satisfaction and support derived from daily activities; and
- support derived from spirituality and religious activity.

Failure to attend to the potent effects of impoverished or toxic environmental conditions can defeat even the most well-meaning intrapsychically or interpersonally oriented interventions, and failure to recognize the niche resources to which the client has or could have access reduces the potency of the therapeutic effort.

***Considering interpersonal effectiveness in problem formulation.*** Intrapersonal and environmental factors are, however, backdrop for examination of the cocreative activity that takes place within the personal niche. The ecological view of mental health and mental illness holds that mental health is not a condition, but a process. People create their mental health through active, effective interaction with their environment and the individuals who coinhabit their personal niche. The Lewininan ecological formulation, $B = f(P \times E)$, may arguably be rewritten as $B = f(\text{Axis II} \times \text{Axis IV})$, highlighting the key role of cognitive capacity and personality as receiver and interpreter of stimuli arising from within the ecological niche, and as actor, negotiating with the environment to secure physical and psychological nutrients and minimize stress and toxicity (Smead, 1982; Willi, 1999). According to Willi (1999), "every form of psychological disorder involves a disruption in the formation of the personal niche" (p. 25). That means an individual's effectiveness in interacting with people within the ecological niche is crucial to the development of a healthy ego, one well grounded in accurate reality appraisal, and to a self-esteem undergirded by a solid sense of identity.

Interactive effectiveness is a reciprocal process involving action and reaction, attempts to influence others in one's niche, and the receipt of feedback from them (Willi, 1999). To be successful, this reciprocal process requires three elements: (a) intentional correspondence—whether the individual wants to and has niche mates who are interested in forming healthy, mutually supportive, nonmanipulative relationships; (b) compatibility of construct systems—whether the person and the niche mates have an adequate range of linguistic tools and compatible systems of attitudes, norms, values, and social rules to enable them to develop interlocking patterns of interrelatedness; and (c) free license to interact—whether the individual and the niche mates are free to pursue and engage in such a relationship. Leigh and Reiser (1982) and Willi (1999) extended these criteria with discussion of defense mechanisms operating in situations of relationship failure. Such theoretical speculations have not yet been translated into clear diagnostic criteria.

*A tripartite view of problem formulation.* From the ecological perspective, then, problem formulation must be based on a multifaceted assessment including strengths and problems that originate within the person [B = f(P), or in *DSM–IV–TR* axial terms, B = f(I × II × III)], nutrients and stressors that arise from the ecological niche [B = f(E), or in axial terms, B = f(IV)], and the patterns of relatedness that arise from the interaction between them [B = f(P × E), or in axial terms, B = f(II × IV)]. An expanded version of the *DSM–IV–TR* axes, illustrated by the ecological problem formulation worksheet (presented in Figure 6.1), encourages a more comprehensive examination of intrapersonal, environmental, and interactive factors by encouraging enumeration of strengths, problems, and disorders.

1. *Problem formulation for intrapersonal concerns [B = f(P)].* The first step in gaining a comprehensive ecological diagnostic formulation is to complete the traditional axis-by-axis description of the client's assets and strengths, deficits and excesses, and diagnosable disorders (as advocated by Lazarus, 1976) on the first three of the DSM–IV–TR diagnostic axes. Following this axis-by-axis diagnostic exercise, a systematic review of interactive processes should be conducted, noting how the client's psychological and physical assets, deficits, excesses, and disorders might interact to exacerbate or ameliorate one another. For example, for a client diagnosed with essential hypertension (Axis III), prominent personality characteristics (Axis II), which may be causal or contributory, may be noted to highlight their significance. Circular areas on the worksheet (see Figure 6.1)—

# Figure 6.1
# Ecological Problem Formulation Worksheet

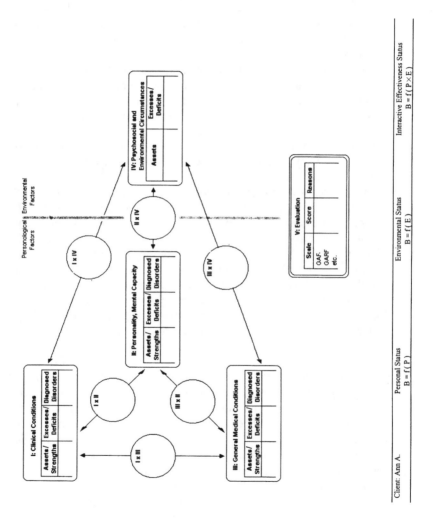

denoted "I × II," "I × III," and "II × III"—prompt the clinician to perform this integrative diagnostic work.

2. *Problem formulation for environmental concerns [B = f(E)].* In the second step, the quality of the client's niche contents (Axis IV) is described. Consistent with the philosophy of Lazarus

(1976), the worksheet again guides the assessor to attend to environmental assets, deficits, and excesses to ensure that the availability of nutrients is examined in addition to the presence of stressors and toxic elements. In the previous step, the formulation of the client's intrapersonal concerns was partly a summary of unsatisfied need and the client's part in a failed effort to gain need satisfaction. In assessing the environmental niche, the ecologically oriented psychotherapist should describe the capacity of the environment to fulfill the need. Does the environment hold the right sorts of nutrients—e.g., jobs, housing, food sources, health care facilities, education and training facilities, social services, recreation sites, and people? To what extent is it free from debilitating toxins—e.g., poor air, dangerous housing, dangerous work sites, predatory people, neighborhood strife, and civil unrest?

3. *Problem formulation for interpersonal concerns [B = f(P × E)].* In the third step, to ensure that attention is paid to interactive dynamics between the individual and the environment, the worksheet provides circular areas denoted "I 3 IV" and "III 3 IV." These prompt the clinician to give diagnostic attention to the ways in which the environment may contribute directly to an individual's intrapsychic functioning and general medical health. For example, living within a dangerous neighborhood (Axis IV) can certainly exacerbate the symptoms of generalized anxiety disorder (Axis I). Most critical to evaluating the role of the person's interactions within the environmental niche is an analysis of the person's interactive effectiveness and coevolutionary activity heralded by the circle denoted "II 3 IV." Wachtel (1993) has eloquently described how in trying to prevent a feared outcome, one can manage to do exactly what it takes to produce it. Clients with amplified narcissism (Axis II) might find that their bragging and overbearing manner may drive off niche mates (Axis IV), thereby further depriving the client of the interest, admiration, and engagement of others that he or she desperately craves. In this analysis, the ecologically oriented problem formulation borrows from the work of family and systems therapy and theorists from the school of interpersonal psychotherapy.

***Competencies needed for ecologically grounded problem formulation.*** Ecological problem formulation creates a comprehensive view of the person, the person's niche, and the interactive life that transpires within the niche. To create meaning from such diverse assessment data, the ecologically oriented psychotherapist must adopt a more sweeping view than is typically required in traditional intrapsychic work. Integrative problem formulation addresses all levels of human systems—individual, family, neighborhood, and broader social and cultural systems (Bronfenbrenner, 1979; James & Gilliland, 2002; Willi, 1999)—including not only the client's culture but the cultures present within the client's environment (Paniagua, 1994, 2001; Tyler, 1991). Discovering the interrelatedness of how one creates one's niche, and is reciprocally created by it, requires thoughtful reflection (James & Gilliland, 2002; Willi, 1999), an activity unfortunately not recorded in productivity unit accounting.

### Treatment Planning and Treatment Delivery

From the ecological perspective, treatment involves more than symptom reduction, the goal endorsed by third-party reimbursers and pursued by traditional mental health professionals (Banning, 1989). Ecological psychotherapy involves developing goals and selecting interventions that are consistent with the tripartite problem formulation just described. The aim should be to improve the client's goodness of fit within his or her ecological niche, graded according to the client's overall level of functioning (Willi, 1999).

Ecologically oriented psychotherapy can be appropriate for clients classified along a continuum of impairment using scaling techniques described earlier (e.g., GAF, Ancillary Impairment Scale) and specific treatment approaches selected according to the assessed locus of the client's difficulties. Specific treatment selection varies with whether the client's problems arise primarily from disruptions in biological processes (e.g., schizophrenia, bipolar disorder), from disruption of the rhythms of drive expression (e.g., sexual, eating, and sleep disorders; chemical addictions; impulse control disorders), from personality structure (e.g., immaturity, lack of conscience, high emotional reactivity), or from self-reflection on experiences and actions that constitute a lived life (e.g., dissociation, unwanted reexperiencing of life events, overvalued ideas, unrelenting shame) (McHugh, 2002).

*Treating intrapersonal problems.* Candidates for ecological psychotherapy are assumed to evidence some degree of ineffectiveness in niche creation, partly because of intrapsychic problems. Typical intrapsychic goals include helping the client to reduce painful symptoms and to develop the knowledge, skills, attitudes, and values necessary to adjust him- or herself to the demands of the environment (Smead, 1982). Although for problems that originate in biological processes, where psychotherapeutic intervention is often coupled with psychopharmacological intervention, those involving drive regulation, personality structure, and making meaning from a lived life are appropriately addressed by both brief and longer term psychoeducational and psychotherapeutic work (McHugh, 2002; Willi, 1999).

*Treating environmental problems.* When examination of the environmental status reveals nutrient deficits or excess of stressors, focused effort on niche improvement may be required. Environmentally oriented goals may include either (a) promoting change in the environment or ecosystem to increase nutrients or reduce stressors and toxins or (b) increasing the individual's awareness of and access to nutrients already present in the environment and sources of protection from stressors and toxins (Smead, 1982). Although ecologically oriented psychotherapists typically work with individuals and their relationships with families, friends, neighbors, and coworkers, interventions with larger systems are in keeping with the spirit of this approach. As much as it is important to help clients identify available sources of need satisfaction, it is also clearly in keeping with the ecological therapeutic perspective to engage in community resource development—working to increase the availability of affordable housing, transportation, employment, and health care facilities—and to foster community safety—working to decrease environmental pollution and neighborhood predation and violence.

*Treating interpersonal problems.* Of paramount interest are goals related to interactive effectiveness (Segrin, 2001; Villeneuve, 2001). With clients who are sufficiently intact to be able to establish a personal niche autonomously, a focus on improving interactive effectiveness is warranted and might include such goals as (a) developing knowledge, skills, attitudes, and values necessary to negotiate with and influence the environment to change (typical of family therapy and other therapies that focus on relationship management), and (b) helping the client find an ecosystem that would produce a healthier fit, a variant of the relationship management approach (Smead, 1982). Creativity is especially required for relationship-oriented treatment plans when the parties are not family members (e.g., neighbors, coworkers, building managers, social services employees, law enforcement personnel). To increase therapeutic effectiveness, the ecologically oriented therapist must think beyond the confines of the office setting, perhaps meeting with the client and individuals with whom the client has difficulty in settings within the client's niche.

*Planning for treatment.* At a theoretical level, the ecological problem formulation worksheet presented in Figure 6.1 helps in grasping the overall complexity of the diagnostic process, but actual treatment planning may be facilitated by a more simplified planning form. One basic planning tool consists of a grid with columns representing the three foci of the ecological view of psychotherapy (i.e., the person, the environment, and their interaction) and rows for noting the assessment data, problem formulation, treatment goals, and treatment strategies. In keeping with the overarching philosophy of ecological psychotherapy, one's record of intrapersonal, environmental, and interpersonal assessment data should chart assets and strengths as well as excesses, deficits, or disorders for which the therapy is being designed. (Note: Table 6.1, which accompanies the case study at the end of this chapter, illustrates this simplified grid.)

*Competencies needed for ecologically grounded treatment planning.* Ecological treatment planning requires the counselor to actively collaborate with the client in developing the plan for treatment. Willi (1999) recommended the development of a *focus formulation*, his term for a counseling contract, which describes the ends to which the counselor and client will work. Therefore, for ecologically grounded treatment planning to be successful, it is important that the counselor develop several competencies:

- Ecological psychotherapy is not performed on a client, but is a collaborative relationship in which the counselor and client work together to design a plan by which the client becomes increasingly effective in niche creation. Therefore, the counselor must be open to and skillful in collaborative planning.
- To meet the goal of holistic treatment, practitioners of ecological psychotherapy must be well grounded in multiple service systems and function as counselor, consultant, collaborator, and coordinator (James & Gilliland, 2002; Willi, 1999). The ecologically oriented psychotherapist strives to become a partner in the client's total care.
- Because ecologically grounded therapy includes direct environmental work, ecological psychotherapists must also be willing to get out of the office and walk the client's streets—to join with clients as they deal with environmental systems, such as the courts, social services, housing, and child care.
- Because a common characteristic of mental health clients is the loss of a hopeful future perspective, a counselor must have enlightened optimism—a reasoned belief that a better fit between client and niche is possible (O'Hanlon & Beadle, 1994, 1997).
- Much of the work in mental health counseling requires vigilance to avoid replicating in the therapy relationship the same destruc-

tive patterns as those in the client's key niche relationships. Ecologically grounded treatment planning includes personal preparation and the use of professional collaboration and supervision to maintain vigilance and to take self-corrective measures when necessary.

## Case Study

To illustrate the work of ecological psychotherapy, introduced here is a hypothetical composite client, Ms. Ann A., who might request services at a mental health center. First, a description of Ann's personal and intrapsychic characteristics is presented: her *mental status examination*. Next, a description is provided of Ann's environment, its nutrients and its toxins: an *environmental status examination*. The coevolutive process that permeates Ann's interaction with the people in her ecological niche is then described, with an explicit focus on her relationship with her son. Also described, and displayed in Table 6.1, are assessment data and treatment options from each of the three views.

As is often the case in a public mental health facility, the counselor's introduction to a client may be through a mental status examination, such as the following report prepared for this hypothetical client:

Ms. Ann A. is a 60-year-old Caucasian woman who presented with fear and anxiety, which she reported stemmed from her dependent, adult son's escalating verbal and physical abusiveness toward her and others. Ann was neatly groomed in clean but faded, worn clothing. Her attitude was attentive and cooperative, and she evidenced no abnormalities of motor activity but appeared tired and worn, as might a woman 10 years greater in age. Her speech was measured but normal in rate, tone, and volume. Her mood was depressed, which she said dated from her teenage years, and her affect had normal range, intensity, stability, and connectedness to her verbal presentations. She was coherent and logical—no evidence was found of disturbance in thought process, nor was evidence found for hallucinations or delusional thought. Although she appeared preoccupied with her denunciations of the health care system for failing to provide adequate treatment for her son, no evidence of disturbance in thought content was found. She seemed deliberate rather than impulsive and did not appear to be at risk for harming self or others behavior; however, she expressed worry about her health status. She admitted using prescribed psychoactive medication, but denied use of alcohol or recreational psychoactive drugs. She was alert, fully oriented, and attentive with intact immediate and remote memory. She appeared to be of above average intelligence and had a good fund of general knowledge, was accurate in describing similarities and differences, provided accurate, though humorous, interpretation of proverbs, and showed considerable knowledge of treatment literature regarding her son's condition. Her gross judgment seemed intact, but she appeared to have circumscribed lapses in judgment with regard to her relationship with her son and lack of insight with regard to her depressed mood, her son's needs, and her limited ability to make changes in his life course. Ann reported physical complaints, including diabetes and arthritis, for which she receives treatment from a physician. Her sleep is fitful, and she reports her typical sleep pattern is 6 hours of interrupted sleep. She is insulin dependent but is unable to maintain a diet consistent with her physician's recommendations. She met criteria for dysthymia, complaining that she experienced a chronic depressed mood during most of her teenage years and again for the past 7 years. Over the past 3 years, she reported weight gain, sleep disruption, loss of energy, tenseness and agitation, loss of interest in formerly pleasurable activities, diminished concentration, and hopelessness about the future (though, as noted, she denied suicidal ideation or intent). She says her depression has interfered with her ability to attend to home upkeep, and her fitful sleep has resulted in her not having the energy to pursue friendships. As a teenager, her family expressed worry about her depressed moods. She has received both psychosocial treatment and medication for this condition (current prescription: Celexa 20 mg/day). She blames her circumstances for her depressed feelings. GAF: 55 (current).

Ann's problem, formulated from an intrapersonal perspective, is one of dysthymia.

Because Ann was an intelligent, verbal, psychologically minded individual whose GAF suggested moderate symptom severity, and because dysthymia has many features in common with depressive personality disorder (Klein & Vocisano, 1999), Willi (1999) would suggest ecologically grounded, supportive therapy. Supported by continuation of her antidepressant, Celexa, selected in part because it is not known to accelerate weight gain, therapy would consist of low frequency, long duration interventions focused on enhancing her relationships and her interactive effectiveness within them. Psychoeducational techniques might be employed to educate Ann on the importance of physical and psychological self-care. Working on her depression using the thought modification techniques of cognitive therapy (Beck, 1976) and working to increase her sphere of positive social contacts using tools drawn from interpersonal therapy (Weissman & Markowitz, 1994; Weissman et al., 2000) would be consistent with ecologically oriented supportive psychotherapy. To respond to her concerns about failing health, a medical evaluation should be sought, and exploratory work might be used to guide Ann through a life review process to help her assess her accomplishments and failings through life (McHugh, 2002; Willi, 1999). During her life review, the therapist would encourage and support recognition of her positive qualities and help her resist her tendency to interpret the ongoing hardships associated with caring for an adult man with a major mental illness as personal failures.

However, Ann lives within an ecological niche that she has been instrumental in creating. One's understanding of Ann can be dramatically enriched by conducting an *environmental status examination* (à la Moos, 1976) that illuminates the niche in which she lives, its nutrients, and its stressors.

> Ann is estranged from her husband and from three of her four sons. She lives with her fourth and youngest son, Bill, a 40-year-old man with developmental disabilities and mental illness who has relied on her for food, housing, spending money, and psychological support since childhood. Bill has been dually diagnosed as having borderline intellectual functioning and schizoaffective disorder. In addition to the periods of mixed manic and depressive episodes, he has paranoid delusions with command hallucinations instructing him to retaliate against those he believes mean to harm him. Ambivalent toward treatment, Bill has refused to take prescribed antipsychotic medication for more than a year, and in recent months has experienced amplification of his paranoia and escalating rage. He has threatened retaliation against the postman and various neighbors who he believes keep him from receiving letters from a son he fathered with a woman from whom he is estranged. In addition, he has threatened to go to his former girlfriend's house and "settle things with her and her damned boyfriend." Recently, during a rageful episode, he brandished a hunting knife, threatened to cut his mother's throat, and stormed out of their house. A loud argument with a prostitute on the street attracted police attention, and he was arrested for carrying the hunting knife as a concealed weapon. Ann has worked as an office worker, but for the past 11 years she has been unemployed due to her deteriorating physical condition and due to the amount of energy she expends in the care of her son. Twice in this 11-year period, Ann has been homeless and has relied on public shelters and soup kitchens for sustenance. The neighborhood in which they now live is run down and fraught with danger. Her son works occasional jobs, but is very poor at resisting the drug dealers, prostitutes, and other predatory individuals patrolling the streets near their dwelling who talk or bully him out of his money. The family's resources are scant, and they rely on support from social security disability assistance, subsidized housing, and public transportation. Because of Bill's violent threats and Ann's low level of energy for social contact, the family lives somewhat in isolation; however, she has one friend in whom she confides. Because of her and her son's physical and emotional problems, Ann has frequent

contact with a variety of health care providers, including her case manager, her physician, and her mental health counselor. On behalf of her son, she also makes frequent contacts with his case manager, the city client's rights officer, and a pro bono service lawyer.

Ann's niche has been impoverished for a period of 30 or more years due to stress associated with caring for her emotionally disturbed son and due to her deteriorating health. Immediate goals for enriching Ann's environment and reducing the level of dangerousness she experiences might include (a) reducing the drain on her resources and the threats to her safety by finding placement for her son; (b) finding subsidized housing in a neighborhood with better policing, populated with age mates who have not yet learned to be afraid of her son; and (c) identifying and encouraging her to join social groups to support autonomous niche creation.

From the perspective of ecological psychotherapy, examination of Ann's mental and environmental status is necessary, but not sufficient for full understanding of her fit within her ecological niche. To complete the picture, one must examine the dynamic flow of her life, her interactive effectiveness. With individuals such as Ann who have been engaged in long-term, intense interaction with another person, a key focus will be the coevolutionary process by which she and her son reciprocally influence each other's personal development (Willi, 1999).

From the time Ann first entered the office, she talked only of her son, Bill. Her presenting questions were about what the clinic could do for her son. Questions about the state of her own life were quickly deflected. Over the years, she has made repeated, unsuccessful visits to agencies to enlist their help for her uncooperative son. Despite Bill's escalating suspiciousness, anger, verbal abuse, and threats to cause her physical harm, she has remained his stalwart advocate, defender, and protector. She admitted that she wants Bill to be on his own, but only if his welfare and safety is secure. She appeared to be caught in a vicious cycle. When Bill's suspiciousness and rage escalate, Ann begins to consider evicting her son. When his abusive treatment becomes high and she feels frightened, she has him removed from her home, sometimes to emergency care, sometimes to police custody. When his temper cools or he gains release from custody, he is released to the streets. Having no home of his own, he then returns to his mother, requesting food and shelter. Faced by a contrite and needful Bill, Ann feels guilt for not having taken good care of him, and so she readmits him to her house. Once again, Ann begins her search for a public agency that will accept responsibility for providing for Bill's long-term welfare despite the fact that Bill does not seek or cooperate with treatment. After a period of unsuccessful search in which the sought-after treatment fails to materialize, she becomes aware of her increasing sense of helplessness and hopelessness. Sometimes in her frustration and despair, she picks fights with agency staff, which she reports has made them less sympathetic to her plight. When Bill's symptoms once again start to escalate, Ann becomes aware anew that she is depressed, angry, and scared for her safety. This repeating cycle consumes her time and resources, leaving her with little energy to attend to her own physical and psychological health.

Willi's (1999) ecologically oriented supportive family therapy and Weissman and colleagues' interpersonal therapy (Weissman & Markowitz, 1994; Weissman et al., 2000) would seek to modify the inability of the mother and son to promote the son's emancipation as a key family developmental step. Certainly, the coevolution of this family rests on cooperation between mother and son—the mother in developing tolerance for her son's faltering steps toward emancipation and becoming more invested in enhancing her own personal niche, and the son in developing a personal sense of responsibility for self-care and becoming more tolerant of separation from his mother.

As a further step in making this relationship work, Bill and his mother should also be encouraged to make specific changes in their lives. To help Bill cooperate with the joint need for emancipation, Bill may require more intensive, environmentally oriented intervention. The therapist, in the role of collaborator with the mother, may help in negotiating for effective case management, secure housing, supported work conditions, and protection for the son's earnings. The son's lack of cooperativeness with treatment planning may be circumvented by the appointment of a guardian, who would have power to make decisions for him. To assuage the loss Ann may feel as Bill transfers his dependence to a case manager and various social institutions, Ann must also grow.

Fortunately, Ann is intelligent, informed, and interpersonally attractive. Though expanding her interest beyond the advocacy role she has played for her son may be difficult, as her son gains more independence, she may be encouraged to use her interpersonal assets to develop friendships and engage in social activities in which she can develop new forms of interactive effectiveness. To help Ann increase awareness of their coevolutionary relationship patterns, the ecological therapist may encourage her to list the things over which she has or does not have control. Written criteria to help her assess her son's level of dangerousness may help her make more wise decisions regarding whether she allows Bill to visit or stay in her house. In family sessions, Ann may also be encouraged to speak forthrightly about her own failing health and her concerns about Bill's safety were she to become incapacitated or succumb to her illnesses. Such forthrightness might stimulate Bill to place less reliance on her for protection. Further, though her preoccupation with her son has led to impoverishment in her own life, she has gained considerable knowledge and skill in advocacy that might be channeled into service as a volunteer client rights advocate within the local human services system.

Supported by individual growth and environmental enrichment, Ann and Bill may be able to change what has been a chronically dysfunctional relationship into a more positive relationship that allows for the emerging development of both. Ecologically oriented supportive family work may help Ann and Bill become more tolerant of their mutual need for emancipation—Ann's need to have greater safety, security, and quiet so she can attend to her own failing health and need for psychological nurturance, and Bill's need to develop a new safe harbor in preparation for his mother's increasing inability to care for him.

## Conclusion

Ecological psychotherapy is a viewpoint rather than a technique, "a way of noticing, of using professional vision to encompass the client's complex reality" (Meyer, 1987, p. 414). Ecological psychotherapy strives to understand behavior not only as a function of the person, as have a host of intrapersonal schools (including the psychoanalytic, person-centered, and cognitive-behavioral schools), or of environmental conditions, as have behavioral theorists, but as a function of their reciprocal interaction within nested social systems. The goal of ecological psychotherapy is facilitating the development of a personal niche in which the individual can experience interpersonal effectiveness. In addition to the traditional role of psychotherapist, therapists with ecological grounding also may take the roles of consultant, collaborator, and coordinator. All aspects of the therapeutic encounter (e.g., assessment, problem formulation, and treatment planning) fall within its purview.

The ecological view of assessment suggests that systematic and formal assessment be made of environmental and interactive factors as well as historically valued intrapersonal factors. It notices deficits and excesses, but values assets and strengths; thus, assessors are urged to identify what is going well for the client and that which is problematic. In problem formulation, it recognizes the necessity of accurate diagnosis of intrapersonal disorders, but urges broader problem formulation to for-

Table 6.1

Ecological Treatment Planning Worksheet

| Client: Ann A. | Personal Status<br>$B = f(P)$ | Environmental Status<br>$B = f(E)$ | Interactive Effectiveness Status<br>$B = f(P \times E)$ |
|---|---|---|---|
| Multifaceted Assessment | Assets/Strengths:<br>• *Attitude*: open, self-disclosing, cooperative, help-seeking, persistent<br>• *Mood*: affect has normal range, intensity, lability, connectedness<br>• *Anxiety*: does not appear overly fearful of anything except the direct threats made by her son<br>• *Substance Use*: does not use mood-altering substances<br>• *Perception, Cognition, Memory, Thought*: all normal<br>• *Intelligence*: above average<br>• *Education*: post-high-school education in secretarial skills<br>• *Impulse Control*: no evidence of impulse control problems<br><br>Excesses/Deficits:<br>• *Sleep*: sleeps fitfully<br>• *Eating*: has poor diet<br>• *Thought*: preoccupied with advocacy and caretaking for 40-year-old son<br><br>Disorders:<br>• Axis I: dysthymic disorder; chronic depressed mood plus low self-esteem and difficulty making decisions<br>• Axis III: arthritis, diabetes | Assets:<br>• *Educational Assets*: post-high-school training in secretarial skills<br>• *Assets in the Social Environment*: one woman friend<br>• *Economic Problems*: SSDI<br>• *Access to Health Care*: can obtain health care (medical, mental health) for herself<br><br>Excesses/Deficits:<br>• *Problems With Primary Support Group*: estranged from her husband, three of her four children, and her grandson<br>• *Problems With Social Environment*: neighbors are fearful of Ann's son and so tend to avoid her<br>• *Occupational Problems*: unemployed (due to poor physical health and due to her preoccupation with caring for her son)<br>• *Housing*: subsidized housing in a rough neighborhood (prostitution and drug dealers work nearby)<br>• *Problems With Access to Health Care*: ongoing advocacy efforts on the part of her son<br>• *Problems With Legal System*: ongoing involvement with police and courts on behalf of her son | Assets/Strengths:<br>• *Relationship Assets*: Bill has a source of food, clothing, and shelter and a loyal advocate when he gets in trouble; Ann feels pride in her staunch advocacy for her son.<br><br>Excesses/Deficits/Problems<br>• *Problems With Role Transition*: Ann and her son are engaged in a mutually destructive, coevolutionary pattern in which Ann's preoccupation with Bill's safety and security prevents her from caring for her own, and Bill's reliance on Ann as his sole source of support prevents him from developing the freedom of emancipation. |

*continues*

Table 6.1 continued

| Client: Ann A. | Personal Status $B = f(P)$ | Environmental Status $B = f(E)$ | Interactive Effectiveness Status $B = f(P \times E)$ |
|---|---|---|---|
| Problem Formulation | • Ann feels depressed and discouraged most of the day most days of the week as evidenced by low self-esteem, overeating, loss of energy, and fitful sleep, which has resulted in her losing interest in previously valued activities; being unable to find, get, and keep a job; and having insufficient energy to pursue friendships. | • Ann's environment is impoverished as evidenced by the lack of family contact, the lack of suitable people with whom Ann could form friendships, and the lack of safety in her neighborhood, which has resulted in Ann having insufficient positive social contact to support self-esteem.<br>• Ann's home life is chaotic and frightening because of the erratic, threatening behavior of her son. | • Ann has experienced role transition difficulties for the last 20 years as evidenced by her preoccupation with providing shelter, care, support, and intervention on behalf of her adult son with mental illness whose behavior is uncooperative, erratic, and threatening even though she, herself, has extremely limited personal resources. |
| Goals for Treatment | • Increase self-esteem<br>• Increase socialization (knitting, chatting with friends)<br>• Reduce overeating at dinner and snacking between meals<br>• Increase physical activity to improve muscle tone and to lose weight | • Find alternative placement with supportive services for son (e.g., residential program, case manager, payee)<br>• Raise awareness of niche contents<br>• Obtain housing in a less dangerous neighborhood | • Clarify the boundary between Ann and her son (listing areas of control, listing criteria for safety, openly discussing Ann's health status)<br>• Increase Ann's and Bill's socialization and development of friendships<br>• Encourage Ann to volunteer as client advocate in a social service agency |
| Treatment Interventions | • *Psychiatrist:* monitor dysthymia, treat with pharmacological agents<br>• *Counselor:* conduct a life review of accomplishments and failings (exploratory); management of dysthymic symptoms (cognitive-behavioral); physical and psychological self-care education (psychoeducation)<br>• *Physician:* monitor health status, treat problems | • *Counselor:* develop a personal ecomap of Ann's niche; assist with applying for housing in a safer neighborhood | • *Counselor:* increase role differentiation and interpersonal competence (ecological supportive therapy; interpersonal therapy)<br>• *Counselor:* develop agreements between Ann and Bill that will facilitate each emancipating from the other (ecological supportive therapy; interpersonal therapy) |

mally recognize the separate and interwoven contributions of intrapersonal, environmental, and systemic interactive factors. Finally, ecological treatment planning entails crafting an ecologically valid plan for facilitating the client's use of personal strength to achieve a better fit within his or her ecological niche.

## Learning Activities

1. Traditional psychotherapy focused exclusively on intrapsychic or intrapersonal phenomena. In fact, as the *DSM–IV–TR* points out, *DSM–IV*, published only a few years ago, defined mental disorder as "a clinically significant behavioral or psychological syndrome or pattern that occurs in an individual and that is associated with present distress. . . . or disability. . . . or with a significantly increased risk of suffering [grave consequences]" (p. xxxi). To what extent and in what manner does ecological psychotherapy depart from this view?
2. Examine your current therapy orientation. In what ways might adopting the viewpoint of ecological psychotherapy enhance your effectiveness? Prepare a chart with two columns. In the right-hand column, list five attractors—features of ecological psychotherapy to which you feel affinity. In the left-hand column, list five unattractive features. Consider how you could benefit from adopting an ecological orientation in your work while minimizing the consequences of its unattractive features.
3. Select a client with whom you can conduct a thorough ecological assessment, problem formulation, and treatment plan.
4. Prepare a complete ecological assessment that details the client's mental and environmental status and describes the client's coevolutionary patterns of interpersonal relatedness with key niche mates.
5. Prepare a problem formulation statement that describes the client's intrapsychic, environmental, and interpersonal problems.
6. Prepare an ecologically valid treatment plan to increase client interactive effectiveness in niche creation.

## References

Allport, G. W. (1937). *Personality: A psychological interpretation*. New York: Holt.
American Psychiatric Association. (2000). *Diagnostic and statistical manual of mental disorders* (text revision). Washington, DC: Author.

Anastasi, A., & Urbina, S. (1996). *Psychological testing* (7th ed.). New York: Prentice Hall.

Banning, J. H. (1989). *Ecotherapy: A life space application of the ecological perspective.* Retrieved October 8, 2001, from http:\\isu.indstate.edu/wbarratt/dragon/ce/v7n3.htm

Beck, A. (1976). *Cognitive therapy and emotional disorders.* New York: International Universities Press.

Bondurant-Utz, J. A. (1994). *A practical guide to infant and preschool assessment in special education.* Boston: Allyn & Bacon.

Bronfenbrenner, U. (1979). *The ecology of human development.* Cambridge, MA: Harvard University Press.

Conoley, J. C., & Haynes, G. (1992). An ecological approach to intervention. In R. C. D'Amato & B. A. Rothisberg (Eds.), *Psychological perspective on intervention: A case study approach for prescription to change* (pp. 177–189). New York: Longman.

Conyne, R. K. (1975). Environmental assessment: Mapping for counselor action. *Personnel and Guidance Journal, 54,* 151–154.

Conyne, R. K., & Clack, R. J. (1981). *Environmental assessment and design: A new tool for the applied behavioral scientist.* New York: Praeger.

Csikszentmihalyi, M., & Larson, R. (1984). *Being adolescent: Conflict and growth in the teenage years.* New York: Basic Books.

Dawis, R. V. (Ed.). (2000). *The person-environment tradition in counseling psychology.* Mahwah, NJ: Erlbaum.

Delworth, U., & Piel, E. (1978). Students and their institutions: An interactive perspective. In C. A. Parker (Ed.), *Encouraging development in college students* (pp. 235–249). Minneapolis: University of Minnesota Press.

DuBois, B., & Miley, K. K. (2002). *Social work: An empowering profession* (4th ed.). Boston: Allyn & Bacon.

Freud, S. (1949). *An outline of psychoanalysis.* New York: Norton.

Goldman, L. (1992). Qualitative assessment: An approach for counselors. *Journal of Counseling & Development, 70,* 616–621.

Hartman, A. (1995). Diagrammatic assessment of family relationships. *Families in Society, 76,* 111–122.

Henggeler, S. W., & Schoenwald, S. K. (1998). *The multisystemic therapy supervision manual: Promoting quality assurance at the clinical level.* Charleston, SC: MST Institute.

Horowitz, L. M., Rosenberg, S. E., Baer, B. A., Ureno, G., & Villasenor, V. S. (1988). The Inventory of Interpersonal Problems: Psychometric properties and clinical applications. *Journal of Consulting and Clinical Psychology, 56,* 885–892.

Horton, C. B., & Bucy, J. E. (2000). Assessing adolescents: Ecological and person-environment fit perspectives. In W. E. Martin & J. L. Swartz-Kulstad (Eds.), *Person-environment psychology and mental health: Assessment and intervention* (pp. 39–57). Mahwah NJ: Erlbaum.

Hudson, W. W. (1997a). *Index of brother (sister) relations*. Retrieved September 19, 2001.

Hudson, W. W. (1997b,). *Index of family relations*. Retrieved September 19, 2001.

Hudson, W. W. (1997c). *Index of peer relations*. Retrieved September 19, 2001.

Impara, J. C., & Plake, B. S. (Eds.). (2001). *The 14th mental measurements yearbook* (14th ed.). Lincoln, NE: Buros Institute.

James, R. K., & Gilliland, B. E. (2002). *Theories and strategies in counseling and psychotherapy* (5th ed.). New York: Allyn & Bacon.

Kennedy, J. A. (2001). *Kennedy axis V: Subscales for axis V*. Retrieved May 16, 2001.

Kiesler, D. J. (1983). The 1982 interpersonal circle: A taxonomy for complementarity in human transactions. *Psychological Review, 90*, 185–214.

Klein, D. N., & Vocisano, C. (1999). Depressive and self-defeating (masochistic) personality disorders. In T. Millon, P. H. Blaney, & R. D. Davis (Eds.), *Oxford textbook of psychopathology* (pp. 653–673). New York: Oxford University Press.

Lazarus, A. (1976). *Multimodal behavior therapy*. New York: Springer.

Leary, T. (1957). *Interpersonal diagnosis of personality: A functional theory and methodology for personality evaluation*. New York: Ronald Press.

Lee, M. (1985). Life space structure: Explorations and speculations. *Human Relations, 38*, 623–642.

Leigh, H., & Reiser, M. F. (1982). A general systems taxonomy for psychological defense mechanisms. *International Psychosomatic Research, 26*, 77–81.

Lewin, K. (1936). *Principles of topological psychology*. New York: McGraw-Hill.

Lorr, M., & McNair, D. M. (1966). Expansion of the interpersonal behavior circle. *Journal of Personality and Social Psychology, 2*, 823–830.

Marlin, E. (1989). *Genograms: A new tool for exploring the personality, career, and love patterns you inherit*. Chicago: Contemporary Books.

Martin, W. E., & Schwartz-Kulstad, J. L. (Eds.). (2000). *Person-environment psychology and mental health*. Mahwah, NJ: Erlbaum.

Maruish, M. E. (Ed.). (1999). *The use of psychological testing for treatment planning and outcome assessment* (2nd ed.). Hillsdale, NJ: Erlbaum.

McGoldrick, M., & Gerson, R. (1985). *Genograms in family assessment*. New York: Norton.

McHugh, P. (2002). Classifying psychiatric disorders: An alternative approach. *Harvard Mental Health Letter, 19*, 7–8.

Meyer, C. H. (1987). Direct practice in social work: Overview. In A. Minahan (Ed.), *Encyclopedia of social work: Vol I* (18th ed.) (pp. 409–422). Silver Spring, MD: National Association of Social Workers.

Millon, T. (1981). *Disorders of personality: DSM-III, axis II*. New York: Wiley.

Millon, T., & Davis, R. D. (Eds.). (1999). *Developmental pathogenesis*. New York: Oxford University Press.

Moos, R. (1976). *The human context*. New York: Wiley.

Munger, R. L. (Ed.). (2000). *Comprehensive needs-based assessment with adolescents*. Mahwah, NJ: Erlbaum.

Murray, H. A. (1938). *Explorations in personality*. New York: Oxford University Press.

O'Hanlon, B., & Beadle, S. (1994). *A field guide to possibility-land: Possibility therapy methods*. Omaha, NE: Possibility Press.

O'Hanlon, B., & Beadle, S. (1997). *Guide to possibility land*. New York: Norton.

Paniagua, F. A. (1994). *Assessing and treating culturally diverse clients: A practical guide*. Thousand Oaks, CA: Sage.

Paniagua, F. A. (2001). *Diagnosis in a multicultural context: A casebook for mental health professionals*. Thousand Oaks, CA: Sage.

Parsons, F. (1909). *Choosing a vocation*. Boston: Houghton Mifflin.

Preston, J. D., O'Neal, J. H., & Talaga, M. C. (1997). *Handbook of clinical psychopharmacology for therapists* (2nd ed.). Oakland, CA: New Harbinger.

Schoenwald, S. K. (2000a, Summer). *Inside multisystemic therapy: Therapist, supervisory, and program practices*. Retrieved January 8, 2002, from http://www.findarticles.com/cf_0/m0FCB/2_8/62804299/print.jhtml.

Schoenwald, S. K. (2000b, Spring). *Multisystemic therapy: Monitoring treatment fidelity*. Retrieved January 8, 2002, from http://www.findarticles.com/cf_0/m0AZV/1_39/61522928/print.jhtml

Schutte, N. S., & Malouff, J. M. (1995). *Sourcebook of adult assessment strategies*. New York: Plenum Press.

Schutz, W. (1958). *FIRO-B: A three-variable theory of interpersonal relations*. New York: Rinehart.

Segrin, C. (2001). *Interpersonal processes in psychological problems*. New York: Guilford Press.

Smead, V. (1982). "I hurt, but I am not sick": Individual psychotherapy provided within an ecological/environmental framework. *Psychotherapy: Theory, Research, and Practice, 19*(3), 307-316.

Sullivan, H. S. (1953). *The interpersonal theory of psychiatry*. New York: Norton.

Tyler, F. B., Brome, D. R., & Williams, J. E. (1991). *Ethnic validity, ecology, and psychotherapy: A psychosocial competence model*. New York: Plenum Press.

VanDenburg, T. F., Schmidt, J. A., & Kiesler, D. J. (1992). Interpersonal assessment in counseling and psychotherapy. *Journal of Counseling & Development, 71*, 84-90.

Villeneuve, C. (2001). *Emphasizing the interpersonal in psychotherapy: Families and groups in the era of cost containment*. Philadelphia: Brunner-Routledge.

Wachtel, P. L. (1993). *Therapeutic communication: Principles and effective practice*. New York: Guilford Press.

Weissman, M. M., & Markowitz, J. C. (1994). Interpersonal psychotherapy: Current status. *Archives of General Psychiatry, 51*, 599-606.

Weissman, M. M., Markowitz, J. C., & Klerman, G. L. (2000). *Comprehensive guide to interpersonal psychotherapy*. New York: Basic Books.

Wiggins, J. S. (1979). A psychological taxonomy of trait-description terms: The interpersonal domain. *Journal of Personality and Social Psychology, 37*, 395-412.

Wiggins, J. S. (1982). Circumplex models of interpersonal behavior in clinical psychology. In P. C. Kendall & J. N. Butcher (Eds.), *Handbook of research methods in clinical psychology* (pp. 183–221). New York: Wiley.

Wilfley, D. E., MacKenzie, K. R., Welch, R. R., Ayres, V. E., & Weissman, M. M. (2000). *Interpersonal psychotherapy for group.* New York: Basic Books.

Willi, J. (1999). *Ecological psychotherapy.* Seattle, WA: Hogrefe & Huber.

WonderWare, I. (1995). *Ecotivity.* Silver Spring, MD: WonderWare.

Yingling, L. C., Miller, W. E., McDonald, A. L., & Galewaler, S. T. (1998). *GARF assessment sourcebook: Using the DSM-IV Global Assessment of Relational Functioning.* New York: Brunner/Mazel.

Chapter 7

# Training and Supervision

*Geoffrey G. Yager*

---

*Chapter Highlights*
- *Ecological counseling allows us to look at those issues that have always been important to counseling.*
- *Ecological counseling education needs to be implemented in various ways because of the diversity of counseling trainees. There is no one set way to create an effective ecological counselor.*
- *Concrete suggestions to enhance student learning are reviewed in 10 specific areas: openness, teaching in small skill steps, use of role plays, structured case presentations, trust, acceptance, creating diverse competencies and frames of reference, client and professional advocacy, personal growth as part of counseling training, and using the professor as a model.*

---

The implementation of an ecological approach to counseling training and supervision involves helping our students develop counseling and clinical skills that will ensure, relatively automatically, that they examine clients within the ecological context of those clients' lives. To do that, counseling training, as well as the subject matter of that training, must be ecological in nature.

This chapter on training and supervision is organized according to three main topics: (a) a conceptual discussion of the importance of training and supervision to the implementation of ecological counseling; (b) a brief examination of the diversity typical in counselor trainees; and (c) an extended discussion of specific training methods.

## Importance of Training and Supervision

Most of the text in this book has been, by necessity, theoretical in presentation, but this chapter is designed to be just the opposite. It is my intent to address concrete and specific suggestions on methods to help beginning counseling students learn to approach clients from an ecological perspective.

Although the purpose of this book is to introduce the ecological approach to counseling, it should be clear to the insightful reader that incorporating the client's ecology into one's ongoing counseling is not an idea previously unknown to effective counselors. In fact, the clearest illustrations of the importance of an ecological perspective are those that any well-trained counselor would have identified even 20 to 30 years ago. For example, it is reasonable to assume that an effective mental health counselor in the mid-1970s would have addressed the living environment of the African American client whose depressive symptoms were exacerbated by the racist behavior of her Caucasian neighbors. Similarly, in the 1980s, a capable counselor would have explored and discussed the physical health of a male client with multiple sclerosis in addition to any social anxiety he might have felt.

So what's new in an ecological counseling perspective? It is the systematic, intentional effort to remind ourselves to check continually all of the influences on a client's life. This ongoing ecological assessment effort, of course, is a skill of crucial importance to the counselor educator and supervisor. We can insist that the beginning counselor perform ecological assessments regularly during training and while under our supervision; however, for real success, he or she must learn to adopt this approach nearly automatically, without external prompting. This chapter addresses how this can best be accomplished.

How important are training and supervision to the successful implementation of ecological counseling? More than 50 years of tradition lends weight to the crucial nature of training in the development of a professional counselor. Nonetheless, the exact nature of this crucial training has evolved over time. In the mid-1950s, school counselors in most states became certified with a master's degree in any field plus three or four counseling-focused courses. By 2001, the Council for Accreditation of Counseling and Related Educational Programs (CACREP) required at least 48 semester hours (72 quarter hours) of course work (CACREP, 2001). Training, obviously, has been increasingly seen as a critical piece in the development of a competent counselor. Perhaps even more significantly over the past 50 years, there has been a major increase in recognizing the importance of the supervisor function, which is the second focus of this chapter. When the American Counseling Association was first formed in 1952 as the American Personnel and Guidance Association, supervision of counseling experiences during training was not considered essential. Many counseling preparation programs graduated (or certified) students without any hands-on experience. Current CACREP standards require at least 700 hours of *supervised* counseling experience in practica and internships (CACREP, 2001). When the additional supervised experience requirements for state licensure as a professional counselor are added to the academic requirements, a student's involvement with required supervision is likely to top 4,000 hours (i.e., approximately 3 years experience). Is training and supervision important to the process of developing a counselor (i.e., an ecological counselor or any other type of counselor)? Clearly, the broad response from counseling professionals and from counseling organizations is a uniform "Absolutely!"

## An Examination of the Diversity in Beginning Counselors

At the start of a new school year, incoming graduate students in counseling usually are a diverse set of individuals. Although certainly not illustrative of all potential diversity in a beginning group of students, the following three descriptions of new scholars illustrate some of the likely differences in such a group. Phillip, Maria, and Brenda are representative of a typical collection of new students.

- Phillip is a 37-year-old Caucasian male. He lives in quiet subdivision in the suburbs of a large city. He has a bachelor's degree in chemistry and for the past 13 years has worked locally as a laboratory researcher for a cosmetics firm. Although he initially enjoyed doing bench research, he reported increasing dissatisfaction as he approached the age of 40 in that he had relatively little interaction with coworkers. His involvement as a Sunday school teacher with a Methodist church made him realize how enjoyable everyday contact with children could be. After considerable thought and discussion with his wife and four children, Phillip decided to cut back his hours at work by half and start full time on a master's program in school counseling.
- Maria is a 23-year-old Roman Catholic woman who graduated with a sociology degree from a nearby state university in June of last year. Although born in Mexico, Maria has spent most of her life in the United States. Her parents had originally entered the country as migrant workers when Maria was very young. Over time, with a large number of moves, the family eventually settled down in a small community, opening a grocery store that did well enough to cover the family's expenses. When Maria received a scholarship for college, she felt she had achieved more than she ever dreamed she

could accomplish. As she completed her senior year, however, she was shocked to find relatively few positions open that were targeted to sociology majors. Since she was actively involved in the university's Hispanic Culture Club, she had become interested in the line of professional work of the club's adviser. The adviser, who became a mentor for Maria, was a woman with a master's degree in counseling, presently working in a student affairs position. Without much reflection on this career decision, Maria applied to the community counseling program and was admitted to begin full time in the fall after her college graduation. Although she remains unsure, Maria thinks she might like to work eventually in a college or university setting in a job similar to that of her college mentor. Maria currently lives in the residence halls, partially supported by her 10-hour-a-week job as a graduate residence assistant.

- Brenda is a 52-year-old African American woman. Although Brenda had lived in the inner city of a large metropolitan area nearly all her life, she recently bought a house and moved to a more suburban part of the city. She has worked with the state's Department of Child Services since she completed her bachelor's degree in education 10 years ago. She raised two children to high school age before returning to school to seek her undergraduate degree. Brenda is a motivated individual who has been promoted twice in 10 years. Although she feels somewhat burned out in her present job as a supervisor, she wants to stay in the helping professions. Having done a great deal of work with a wide variety of counseling agencies in the community, the thought of working as a counselor was one that had run repeatedly through Brenda's mind. With house payments, car payments, and a variety of other expenses, Brenda realized she was not quite ready to leave her job and begin full-time study in a community counseling master's program. As a result, she has enrolled as a part-time student, and she plans to take two courses per term for at least the first year.

Given the various differences among these entering students, will there be an existing commonality in their understanding of a client's ecology? These individuals, all realistic representations of actual students, are illustrative of differences in at least gender, race, age, cultural background, academic background, family history, enrollment status (i.e., full time or part time), counseling program pursued (e.g., school or community), and commitments outside the counseling program (e.g., family, church, friends). Phillip may instantaneously have an understanding of the difficult life choices of a businessperson; Maria may sense the discomfort of the non-English speaking client with a unilingual English-speaking counselor; and Brenda may identify with a single parent raising teenage children. Will any of these three prospective counselors have an equal understanding of these same clients if their assignments were switched? The simple answer, of course, is that it's not likely at the start of training! Nonetheless, we certainly hope that by the end of training each counselor will be able to get to a comparable understanding of each of these clients.

How does the counseling program faculty successfully manage to get these diverse students to come together to understand a client problem using ecological empathy (see chapter 5), a perspective that includes the full complexity of the client's environmental context? Clearly, accomplishing such a goal could be difficult even *without* the unavoidable diversity of our students. Given the complexity of the differences among individual students (and, for that matter, between faculty members as well), this task becomes a greater challenge.

In fact, the nature of this challenge increases further by the realization that counselor educators and supervisors are also part of the students' ecosystems! The background and experience of each educator and supervisor will influence the student in his or her learning. When each instructor is willing to address directly the diversity within the supervisor/supervisee dyad *and* within the counselor/client dyad, ecological learning is maximized. Such a discussion might be avoided for several reasons, including (a) lack of knowledge that such diversity issues could be important influences in a supervisory relationship; (b) fear of potential discomfort in addressing personal issues; or (c) insufficient personal self-awareness that would prevent a supervisor from recognizing diversity issues when they are present. Whenever these issues are overlooked in counseling or in supervision, maximal learning is impossible.

## Specific Training Methods

The remainder of this chapter provides a variety of specific ideas that hopefully will ensure that diversity issues will *not* go unaddressed and that ecological counseling skills will be directly practiced and included in the developing counselor's repertoire. The individualized nature of these approaches allows them to be effective with a diverse population of students. Although the list of suggestions may be extended well beyond those mentioned here, I am making 10 training and supervision suggestions for counselor educators. With each suggestion, I include a concrete illustration of a method to address that suggestion. The 10 suggestions are

1. be open to new approaches;
2. break down training efforts into small skill steps;
3. use multidimensional role plays for practice;
4. implement productive case presentations to guarantee needed feedback;
5. always keep in mind the importance of trust;
6. supervise with positive acceptance;
7. use training and supervision to develop counselors with diverse competencies and frames of reference;
8. embrace the necessity to be political and advocate for clients and the profession;
9. expect ongoing personal growth and change as part of counseling training; and
10. model appropriate counseling behaviors, skills, and ecological awareness as supervisors.

## Be Open to New Approaches

Two recent publications by McAuliffe, Eriksen, and Associates (2000) and by Eriksen & McAuliffe (2001) addressed the preparation of counselors and therapists through constructivist and developmental programs. Although the constructivist and developmental model may not be the same as an ecological counseling model, it is clear in reading this edited text that there is a great deal of overlap between the two ideas. Essentially, the constructivist and developmental emphasis focuses on including students in the creation of the eventual learning of counseling and therapy. Rather than a top-down set of instructions on how to do counseling, the constructivist educator encourages attention to the experience of the learner with ongoing dialogue that eventually leads to counseling competence. This teaching style fits directly with the ecological counseling approach because any set of expert instructions on the specifics of a client's life always comes up short: the only way to understand the full impact of the client's multiple levels of environment is to listen intently to the client's descriptions of his or her life. In the preface to the McAuliffe, Eriksen, and Associates (2000) text, McAuliffe wrote

> The teacher as "talking head" seems still to be alive and well, as a walk down a college corridor will testify. Whether behind or in front of the lectern, or even informally sitting on the desk, we can hear teachers pronouncing, "Here is the most

effective counseling approach" or "Listen to my accurate diagnosis." . . . This teacher-as-expert and student-as-receiver model has been increasingly challenged as ineffective, particularly in our field which is ostensibly dedicated to bringing forth professionals who themselves might create knowledge through interior conversation and open public discourse. (p. 6)

As an ecological counselor, I find myself enthusiastically endorsing this idea. Counselor educators must be continuously looking for ways to encourage our students' involvement in their education and their investment in continuing to develop as effective counselors well beyond completion of their formal training.

In sum, this first suggested method for counselor educators is to push our teaching well beyond the methods that we might have been taught. Question the traditional, be open to what our students understand, and continue to address a wide variety of ways to get our points across with students, even as we learn new ideas from them and with them.

## Break Down Training Efforts Into Small Skill Steps

Forty years ago, it was common in mental health training to ask students to read a textbook or two and then, without further preparation, begin to work with clients. Tape recordings of sessions were made and reviewed, often very critically, by supervisors and peers in practicum classes. Although such training may have produced many effective counselors and therapists, it also may have scared to death a whole generation of mental health trainees. Today, virtually no counseling training program approaches learning in this manner. In fact, one of the primary strengths of the counseling profession has been its emphasis on reducing undue anxiety by focusing on skills training (e.g., Cormier & Cormier, 2003; Egan, 2002; Ivey & Ivey, 2003; Okun, 2002). Although social work and clinical psychology have, to some extent, included such training in their preparatory programs, the focus on skills originally came from counseling.

How is a step-by-step skills training related to ecological counseling? Essentially, the most immediate tie is that such an approach directly addresses the personal ecology of the beginning counseling student. By using a focus on small steps in the learning process, the ecological counselor educator implicitly recognizes that the internal ecology of the new counselor is one of insecurity and anxiety. If the educational process can serve to reduce this anxiety, the environment will allow greater integration of the intending learning.

*Cognitive self-instructional training* is a method for implementing small steps into the training/supervision of new counselors that reduces potential anxieties about role-playing and skill demonstrations. It is a structured method in which skills are broken down one step further than normal by teaching the counselor the process of talking to him- or herself about counseling skills. It is derived from the assumption that one's internal dialogue has an important influence on emotions and actions (Ellis, 1962; Meichenbaum, 1977).

A number of studies have related the self-instructional method to counseling training (e.g., Beck, 1980; Hector, Elson, & Yager, 1977; Ochiltree, Yager, & Brekke, 1975; Yager & Beck, 1981). These studies have indicated that empathy, confrontation, and self-management skills can be taught to counseling students by combining academic knowledge of the skill area with direct practice of the cognitive thoughts that most likely lead to the desired counseling response.

An example of a trainee's internal dialogue that might interfere with counseling performance can be seen in the response to a client who expresses hostility toward the counselor for not helping quickly enough. A threatened or anxious counselor might think, "What am I doing wrong?" or "How have I let this person down?" and "What will my supervisor think of this?" A beginning counselor might respond in this situation in various ways, from attempting to placate the client to a strong and righteous defensiveness. If, however, the counselor has learned to refocus attention to the underlying client feelings (e.g., disappointment, frustration, discouragement, disillusionment, or lack of trust), the anxiety generated by the interaction can be substantially reduced (but, quite honestly, not eliminated). In a sense, the counselor's anxiety may provide a valuable stimulus to direct the counselor's thinking in a more productive direction.

The specifics of a self-instructional approach can certainly vary greatly. For more than 25 years at the University of Cincinnati, we have taught prepracticum students six basic questions that are helpful for developing empathy or understanding responses to clients. These understanding responses are, of course, also the essential first steps necessary to gain a perspective on the client's ecology! If a counselor wishes to understand the client from the client's total life perspective, the understanding requires knowledge of that client's ecological experience of life.

The following questions are practiced out loud initially, and eventually become silent thoughts that the counselor can use to formulate a response to a client during the pause between the client's statement and the counselor's response:

1. How can I pat myself on the back for something I've actually said or for something I may have learned about the client?
2. What has the client expressed verbally about his or her emotions?
3. What has the client indicated nonverbally about his or her emotions?
4. How do I feel right now?
5. How would I feel if I had experienced the same situation that the client has just described to me? (If I were this client, with the same background and life experiences, how might I feel in the situation that has just been discussed?—*Not* "How would *I* feel?" but "How would I feel if I were this person?")
6. How can I combine the emotions that I have identified in the preceding questions with the content that I heard to make a response that clarifies what I have understood? I will say this response to myself once before I speak to the client: "You feel (an appropriate emotional word to describe the client's feelings) because (summary of the content of the client's communication)."

The first question provides an element of self-reinforcement for the trainees as they continue to help clients to explore, understand, and change behavior. The next four questions teach beginning counselors to structure their internal dialogue so as to influence what is understood about the clients' underlying emotions (a) from direct statements about feelings; (b) from nonverbal indications/cues; (c) from awareness of the role of the counselors' feelings in understanding others; and (d) from a creative process of putting ourselves into our client's perspective. The final question is merely a silent practice of the chosen response.

Knowing the specifics of the type of thinking that is expected immediately during the learning process makes development of counseling skills much less stressful. Students do not need to focus on wondering and on guessing, "What am I expected to do now?" Instead, early *out loud* practices using the cognitive self-instructional method provide a comparatively painless way to initiate counseling contacts: "If I can't think of an appropriate answer to one of these six questions, I can ask the rest of my training group for their input and ideas." Over repeated practices, the students not only need fewer ideas from student colleagues, but they also no longer need to do their thinking aloud.

Bernard and Goodyear (1998) have suggested that supervisory strategies should be geared to specific situations through multiple instructional modalities. If certain trainees learn more effectively in one modality than another, they are much more likely to encounter their best way to learn if they are exposed to many methods of teaching. The teaching strategy of cognitive self-instruction is skill-oriented and active. It involves direct supervision and facilitation through live and videotaped demonstrations of each step of the self-instructional training. It is a method that virtually ensures a student's first attempts at communicating empathy and understanding will be successful. The first try occurs in a group setting during class with the facilitation of an advanced student supervisor. The questions are asked aloud and responses to each question are discussed by the small group of four or five students. As each class member is more comfortable, it may be that the questions are asked aloud by another student, and one person—with the aid of the group, if needed—answers each question. Eventually, with appropriate fading, the demonstrations of thinking aloud continue with the presentation of relatively easy client concerns. A later practice may involve the students in role-playing as counselor and client, with the client expressing more difficult concerns while the thinking occurs silently, often with long pauses. Finally, of course, the students practice their empathy skills by thinking silently in a realistic session.

Cognitive self-instruction can be used as a primary teaching method with several counseling skills (e.g., we have used it regularly with both empathy and challenge), or it can be used in conjunction with numerous other teaching strategies. The central importance of such a method, however, is not the thinking process itself. It is that by using such a series of successive approximations, we have established an effective way to help beginning counselors reduce their performance anxiety and minimize the likely negative impact of inevitable concerns for immediate counseling competency (all too often interpreted by beginning students as "perfect counseling"). We have found this approach to be valuable in developing the skills that prevent anxiety from interfering with the counselor's ability to maintain appropriate focus on the client. The lower the anxiety in working with a client, the more counselor attention is available to determine the client's issues and to identify the contributing factors to those issues stemming from the client's social, cultural, economic, political, and religious ecological factors.

## Use Multidimensional Role Plays for Practice

If our intent as counselor educators is to help trainees develop a sense of the impact of all parts of the client's ecology, we certainly must give them the opportunity to experience as wide a variety of potential multicultural and ecological practices as possible. Counselor educators also must encourage students to become exposed to as many clients and client backgrounds as possible in their supervised experience. Nonetheless, we know that we can guarantee that the actual clients a counselor sees in a field practicum or internship will never address *all* of the potentially relevant ecological issues. Because of this awareness, we are likely to want to include as many dimensions of a client's ecology as possible in those role plays the student experiences early in training.

Although there are an endless number of possible role plays, I include here as a method of achieving this teaching/supervising suggestion several role plays that demonstrate a good deal of diversity and give our students an opportunity to come to grips with important ecological issues. The following role plays may be included in class meetings for prepractica or other on-campus skills classes. The descriptions in the scenarios apply to one gender, but each can easily be modified to accommodate a role-playing client of the other sex.

- *Terry*. You are a gay man who has been in an ongoing, committed relationship for the past 4 years. You live in a small, conservative, farming community about 50 miles from the nearest large city. You and your partner are beginning to think seriously about adopting a child. Although your partner is totally convinced that you both need the opportunity to raise a child, you have some reservations. These reservations are *not* related to your relationship with your partner; they are more tied to your concerns about personal independence, freedom, and flexibility. You are seeking help from a counselor to begin to explore (and, perhaps, work through) the reservations you have about adopting and raising a child. Clearly, you have mixed feelings about this situation, and you are willing to talk openly about your feelings as you explore where you stand.
- *Cary*. You are a woman greatly in love with a person of another race. You feel a clear and strong personal, emotional, spiritual, and physical attraction toward this person. Happily enough, these feelings are mutual. Nonetheless, when you bring up the possibility of marriage, your partner indicates significant reservations. He describes how difficult it would be to be in a biracial marriage. In addition, he has pointed out the major problems encountered, on a daily basis, by biracial children. Although you both are very religious and were raised as Baptists, your partner has been hesitant to attend your church because it seems to be racially segregated. Thus, the issue of a church home has been continuing for several years. With this issue unsettled, your partner is reluctant to agree to a marriage. Not only is your partner expressing hesitation (despite his expressed

love for you), both your parents and his have made it *very clear* they do not support a marriage. Interestingly, neither set of parents has raised major issues about your dating. It is the marriage issue that seems most important to them. Clearly, you have mixed feelings about this situation, and you are very willing to talk openly about your feelings as you explore where you stand.

- *Sally.* You are a feminist woman who has been very active in the local Democratic Party in the medium-sized city in which you live. You have come to the counselor to discuss your anger and revulsion surrounding the behavior of one of your fellow employees. Your job is as a legal assistant in a law office in a large, conservative city. One of your bosses (a lawyer in the firm) began by making uncomfortable comments about the clothing you wear and the perfume you use. Now it appears that he has escalated to comments about the size of your breasts, the shape of your rear, and the kind of underwear you wear. You have asked this person to stop making such comments immediately, but nothing has happened. At this point, you are seriously thinking about filing a sexual harassment charge against this man. As an employee in a law office, you feel that you should not have any difficulty in filing this charge. Yet, despite this, you have found yourself hesitating— and in the process, you are embarrassed that you are not taking action. Many thoughts and questions run through your head: "I know the legal system, and it won't necessarily yield a just resolution to this situation." "At best, a legal action is going to take so much time that I'll lose money at least temporarily." "Could my charge against him lose me my job?" "How can I even have any questions about this situation; what is it that is making me hesitate?" Clearly, you have mixed feelings about this situation, and you are very willing to talk openly about your feelings as you explore where you stand.
- *Bobby.* You are a client with a relatively limited intellectual capacity. Although you talk openly and readily, it becomes clear with the simplicity of your choice of words and the concreteness of your statements that you are likely to miss any subtleties within the counselor's statements. You live in a group residential facility for low-functioning adults (you refer to it as "Bootstrap House"). The reason you have come to a counselor is that Pat, another group home resident "doesn't love me like I love her. I told her that I loved her, and that made things worse." It seems that for some time Pat had been your "honey," but suddenly another resident came to the home, and it is clear that Pat seems to like this new person a

lot. Now, Pat only seems to be "your best buddy" when the new resident (Sam) is not around. When Sam is nearby, however, Pat acts as though you were "just one of the residents." You are unsure of what to do. The extent of your exploration of feelings will probably not include much more than *good*, *bad*, *happy*, *sad*, *mad*, and *I don't know*. All in all, you are eager to please and eager to "be a good client," but you will not understand much of what a counselor typically does with a client. [Talk very slowly and carefully, but use very simple sentence structure and wording. Nonetheless, don't be silly or comical; be serious, but not deep.]

- *Suzy.* You are an 9-year-old girl in the fourth grade of a large elementary school in a major city. Your parents, both busy full-time professionals, have just told you that they are planning to break up. Although she doesn't know what's wrong, your teacher has sent you to the counseling office because you seem very distracted in class. You don't want to be affected by your parents' decision to separate, but you cannot deny the accuracy of the teacher's perception. You speak in clear but simple language. You are likely to get distracted during your session, perhaps sometimes distracted when the counselor asks you to think about something difficult for you (i.e., your parents' divorce). When pushed a little by the counselor's empathy, you talk about your feelings, but it is very clear that you would rather be discussing your Barbie dolls, your favorite Disney movies, or virtually anything else.

Although the role plays described may provide a starting place to expose your students to ecological diversity, they certainly are no better than the multitude of examples you might generate based on your own experience as a counselor and supervisor. In implementing these role plays, my personal tendency has been to continue creating a teaching and learning environment that minimizes stress and anxiety. As a result, all such role plays tend to be presented to the class as a whole. One class member is selected to serve as the "spokes-counselor" for the group. The client begins to present his or her concerns in a realistic fashion, but when it is time for the counselor to respond the entire class wrestles with the issues aloud. The discussion also allows the educator to interject thoughts that aid the class in addressing any parts of the client's ecological space that may have been overlooked, such as:

- Does the client's race have any impact on the concerns expressed?
- Do you suppose that finances will influence this client's eventual counseling direction?

- Would you look differently at this client's issue if she were a man?
- If the local environment were a small town, would your thinking be different?
- What implications do religion and spirituality have on your understanding of the client's concerns?
- Is there any potential community-level intervention that might help with the concern experienced by this client?

As the group comes to some resolution regarding what the issues presented involve, the spokes-counselor responds and the interview continues. It is likely with the group's discussion that each of the role plays may take about 1 hour of class time. From an ecological perspective, it is time well spent.

## Implement Productive Case Presentations to Guarantee Needed Feedback

Case presentations are another place in the training and supervision of a counseling student where learning can be maximized. Despite this potential for learning, however, many times the use of case presentations has been unproductive in counseling classes. When case presentations are unproductive, it typically happens because attendees strive to impress one another with their knowledge and expertise rather than simply try to learn. It is not productive for the students' education to have instructors and fellow students argue with one another about the best conceptualization of this client's problems or the right way to proceed with additional counseling contacts. Instead, the case conference should always be focused on giving the student presenter as many as possible (even conflicting) ideas about the nature of the client, the source of the concern, and the ecological context from which the troublesome issues have arisen.

The following brainstorming-based case conference model is one way to deal effectively with client material during classes, and it has provided a very valuable resource for our students' learning for many years.

1. The counselor/presenter develops a case presentation description of no more than two pages (typed, single-spaced). This description is read by each member of the class in the first 10 minutes. Class membership includes the enrolled students, the instructor, and the advanced-level master's or doctoral student supervisors. The case description addresses the following areas, using each area as a subheading: (a) client's presenting con-

cerns; (b) client history of family relationships, with a review of important events during childhood; (c) counselor conceptualization on how the client's concern developed; (d) counseling approaches and strategies employed to this point; and (e) plans for the future.

2.  After the class has read the handout, the counselor is asked to add anything that may have been learned about the client subsequent to writing the case presentation, followed by a 15-minute period of questions and answers. Class members may ask any question they want about the client, but the counselor is not expected to have the information to answer all questions. Presenters need to be repeatedly reminded that asking the questions is not an indication this was information crucially important to the ongoing counseling. However, some questions—perhaps relating to the client's ecological background—might well be pursued by the counselor later as sessions continue.

3.  Following the questions and answers, there is a 15-minute period of brainstormed conceptualizations. Everyone is encouraged to add at least one conceptualization that might explain how the client developed the concerns that he or she has expressed. Of course, the brainstorming process is carried out without evaluation or reaction. All conceptualizations *cannot* be consistent, and there is no need for them to be particularly reasonable or likely. In order to allow the student presenter to listen fully to the ideas being generated, the instructor writes down the conceptualizations as they are conveyed. The course instructor's conceptualization (usually about 5 minutes) is the last given so as to (a) avoid inhibiting the class members in their conceptualizing, and (b) allow the instructor to address ecological issues that have been overlooked or misrepresented.

4.  After the conceptualization, a 15-minute period of brainstormed suggestions occurs. As earlier, the class members generate brainstormed ideas that are not evaluated. Specific suggestions on what the counselor might want to do with the client in their next session are the topics addressed in this subsection of the case conference. As with the conceptualizations, the course instructor writes down the suggestions (usually at least 20 to 25 ideas).

5.  The counselor is given 5 minutes to ask the class questions or to react to the conceptualizations and suggestions. At the end of the 1-hour case presentation, the presenter has a list of between 12 and 20 conceptualizations related to his or her client and

another list of 25 to 30 concrete, specific strategies and approaches that may be used in continued work with this client. Fortunately, hearing the variety of ideas generated in the brainstorming sections of the case presentation is nearly of equal value to the students who are not presenting as it is to the presenter. Because critiques and evaluations are so directly discouraged, it is also likely that the counselor has some sense of validation for the work that has already been accomplished with this client.

Following completion of the case presentation, there is, of course, one more crucial step in the student's learning: the discussion of all these brainstormed ideas in the supervisee's weekly supervision meeting. Sorting through the variety of potential conceptualizations and strategies requires an open and honest discussion with a colleague (i.e., the supervisor in the case of a present student) addressing the merits of each possible idea. If the supervision discussion, purposefully or by lack of awareness, totally ignores and rejects certain possible interpretations and suggestions, the maximal benefit of the case presentation will have been lost. Thus, supervisors must always be aware to give full attention to all possibilities, considering all possible environmental influences.

## Always Keep in Mind the Importance of Trust

As counselor educators, we recognize from experience that trust in the supervisor may well be the most important aspect of the supervisory relationship. Effective supervisors (as well as poor supervisors) can be found in any given model or approach to supervision, and trust remains a central feature for all.

Trust, of course, is many faceted, and it includes elements from at least the seven important classifications in the list that follows. Each of these types of trust is likely engendered by different supervisor behaviors and, therefore, may well be independent of one another. Each form of trust, however, makes a definite contribution to the relationship:

- *credibility* trust: a supervisee's belief that the supervisor is a competent counselor with appropriate skills;
- *good faith* trust: a supervisee's assurance that the supervisor will not "put down" the supervisee for a lack of knowledge, for a poor performance, or for an unusual value or attitude;
- *personal* respect trust: a supervisee recognizing that feedback from the supervisor will be communicated with understanding and caring;

186

- *honesty* trust: a supervisee's confidence that issues related to counseling performance will be raised by the supervisor despite possible discomfort on the part of either participant in the supervision;
- *constancy* trust: a supervisee's certainty that the supervisor will behave consistently from one session to another;
- *confidentiality* trust: a supervisee's knowledge that the feelings, thoughts, and concerns mentioned during supervision will not be discussed outside the supervisory relationship; and
- *flexibility* trust: a supervisee's assurance that, no matter what his or her counseling orientation or academic background, the supervisor will avoid rigidity in approaching the supervisee's learning, thereby creating an open and ecological mind set for the supervisory discussion.

All of these aspects of supervisee trust are tied directly to the supervisor's basic trust in the supervisee. Supervisors need to believe that their supervisees *can* and *will* learn appropriate helping behaviors. Trust is a two-way communication. In an openly trusting relationship, the supervisee will be able to disagree openly with the supervisor. Although the supervisory relationship might not be strong on all of the possible dimensions of trust, a supervisor and supervisee may expect a relationship that emphasizes trust.

## Supervise With Positive Acceptance

During training, virtually every program provides ongoing supervisory contact with each trainee. Although there are many models of supervision and many more supervisory techniques and methods, one basic core element needed in the supervisor's repertoire is the ability to give honest and direct feedback to the counselor in a positive and accepting manner. We must make this feedback positive so the developing counselor will stay with us long enough to learn all of the methods needed to gather crucial understanding of the client's situation and begin to generate appropriate ideas for aid in that client's actual situation. It is much too easy to turn off a new counselor to the field by being overly critical of an early effort with a real client.

Yager and Littrell (1978) defined counseling supervision as "the process by which counselor trainees or practicing counselors receive information, feedback, and support relative to maximizing their effectiveness with clients" (p. 1). Nonetheless, there is little evidence in the literature that counselors, after they have graduated and left university training, actually receive supervisory services. Despite the need for continued professional updating, typical counselor supervision (i.e., beyond that received as part graduate work) may often be more accurately labeled administration or paperwork tracking and management. In many cases, the counselor is expected to report periodically to the supervisor to discuss the particulars of the job, but *not* to discuss specific difficulties encountered in dealing with clients. From the ecological perspective, the client is not being most effectively served, and in fact, the counselor's support is undermined in such a scenario.

Although most counselors may be on their own in arranging methods to ensure their own personal and professional growth, this does not mean that they need to proceed without supervision. If counseling supervisors are not available, counselors must learn to pursue continued self-assessment and self-directed growth throughout their work lives as counselors. Thus, one focus of the training program needs to be on the counselor's personal methods of self-renewal and self-directed supervisory contacts. Self-supervisory methods are critical to the overall development of a counselor who wishes to maintain competence and professional autonomy within posttraining settings.

## Use Training and Supervision to Develop Counselors With Diverse Competencies and Frames of Reference

Although constructivist and developmental programs (cf. Eriksen & McAuliffe, 2001; McAuliffe et al., 2000) would be totally horrified at the mere thought of counseling clones, the hard truth has been that too many counseling training programs have unthinkingly slipped into just such a pattern. Given the brief descriptions of the three beginning trainees reported earlier in this chapter, a counselor educator has more than enough responsibility to get each person to a flexibly defined level of counseling competence. It would be a much more overwhelming (and, frankly, impossible) task if the objective was to help each student behave toward clients "the same way I would behave with clients."

Yes, counselor educators must make certain that all students are at least minimally competent, that (a) they can communicate an active interest in the client without imposing their own values; (b) they can help the client explore concerns through empathy, challenge, and probing; (c) they can evaluate the client's background, family situation, physical health, socioeconomic background, ethnicity, and spirituality in order to understand the complete context of the client's concerns; (d) they have a variety of ideas for helping the client make life changes that can be presented as potential, but *not* required, choices; and (e) they can effectively evaluate, on both a formative and summative basis, the progress of counseling and its outcomes. Nonetheless, the demonstration of such counseling abilities will never be exactly the same as the way the counselor educator demonstrates these skills. Clearly, we never want to be in the position of holding our personal performance as a gold standard for all our students!

## Embrace the Necessity to Be Political and Advocate for Clients and for the Profession

Over the years, the counseling profession has not been actively involved in identifying and promoting areas of needed societal and political change. This has been true even when such change might have been potentially beneficial to clients and to the profession. Counseling theories and counseling techniques first addressed an understanding of the individual client (or group) and, then, strategies to aid that client (or group) to change in ways that were consistent with personal goals. Yes, counselors were always aware that societal expectations, housing, social environment, economics, and religious upbringing all served to impact the client's likelihood of successful change, but such factors were perceived to be beyond our control.

From an ecological perspective, however, we must not only recognize these various spheres of influence, but we must also become more knowledgeable and experienced in directly advocating for changes that will benefit clients. We need to address extrapersonal, not just intrapersonal, factors as we work with our clients. Political action to increase the level of funding for education in the inner city, a letter-writing campaign to encourage legislators to provide funding for a community health clinic, or telephone calls to the city bus service to add a stop nearer to the local mental health center: all are relatively small actions that, if successful, can make life (and change) easier for our clients.

When counselors take on the task of advocacy, we are actively arguing in favor of a particular cause or outcome that will favorably impact our own clients and, most likely, many others with whom we may have no contact. Myers, Sweeney, and White (2002) found it crucial to extend the call for counselor advocacy to the counseling profession as well as to the clients themselves. Chi Sigma Iota's Counselor Advocacy and Leadership conferences summarized the need for advocacy for the profession

> Counselors must not only believe in their profession's preparation standards, graduate programs, credentialing requirements, and scope of services, but they must educate, inform, and promote them to legislators, employers, third-party payers, and the public at large. (1999, p. 1)

To avoid doing so, it is argued, will eventually threaten the profession's viability, creating the possibility of the eventual demise of the entire field of counseling. The dire nature of this warning is more than sufficient to alert us to the need to address advocacy issues and skills directly in our counseling training and supervision.

Although action in the area of advocacy may take many creative directions, five simple suggestions include (a) discussing advocacy in each of the courses in the counseling curriculum; (b) sponsoring workshops directly addressing such issues as counselor licensure, counselor identity compared to the professions of psychology or social work, and legislative updates; (c) organizing students in a letter-writing campaign in support of a state or national counseling initiative; (d) encouraging graduates to seek publicity (e.g., newspaper or television coverage) for projects of importance in their schools or agencies; and (e) sponsoring various activities to encourage counselors to maintain their own self-awareness and wellness.

## Expect Ongoing Personal Growth and Change as Part of Counseling Training

As counseling graduate students approach completion of their studies, it is certain that they can reflect training experience as an academically rewarding opportunity. Students clearly leave with much knowledge about many academic areas that were not previously studied: counseling theories, measurement, statistics and research, career development, social and cultural diversity, professional identity, human growth and development, group work, helping relationships, and, in many programs, diagnosis and treatment. Nonetheless, what this list of academic growth areas does not include is a substantial area of learning that seems to come along as a bonus to all who are studying interpersonal skills: personal growth and personal change. Although we may know that such growth is unavoidable for anyone approaching the emotional and intimate contacts that are inherent in counseling, it is important we communicate this knowledge openly and directly to each new group of counseling students:

> Dear students, you really must know that the undertaking you are about to begin is one that will change you forever! As you work with clients, you will be repeatedly confronted with yourself and your own personal issues. Although you will successfully deal with these issues by self-examination, by consultation with your peers, and by working openly with your supervisors, you will unavoidably learn about yourself in this process such that you will no longer be exactly the same person. Although in the long run, all of these changes are likely to be welcome

190

and fully desirable, your initial reaction to many may be one of increased discomfort and lack of balance. Hang in there with us in this process, and you'll find that you will come out in a good place on the other end!

In translating this information to ecological terminology, we are saying that the counseling program will focus on creating behavioral and conceptual differences in new counselors that will have a personally meaningful impact on the counselor trainee's microsystem. Personally meaningful changes in any of a trainee's important life systems will reverberate with similarly important changes in related ecosystems. If we are influenced to change in one important area of our lives, that change will impact us in every other area.

## Model Appropriate Counseling Behaviors, Skills, and Ecological Awareness as Supervisors

Holloway (1995) described one of the core functions of a supervisor as modeling. She stated that "the supervisor acts as a model of professional behavior and practice, both implicitly in the supervisory relationship and explicitly by role-playing for the supervisee or client" (p. 36). It has been my experience as a counselor educator that many of the more subtle counseling skills are *primarily* learned through modeling. Thus, within an ecological training perspective, a structured, almost programmed, ecological assessment may be taught effectively within a unit of a specific counseling class (e.g., tests and measurement in counseling) However, the more subtle skill of knowing when and where to initiate a series of ecologically related questions with a client may be most effectively learned by repeatedly seeing the instructor ask just such questions at crucial moments in a case presentation, a role play, or during supervision. If we were to make one or two presentations a year on the role of ecological ideas to counseling and not continue to demonstrate a respect for and understanding of the client's ecology (or, quite honestly, a student's ecology as well), our students would leave the program without ever fully integrating the approach in their own work.

The specific method to accompany this suggestion involves nothing more than the counselor educator's ongoing self-reminders to think about and discuss all of the potential factors influencing not only the client's life but also our own. If we do not remind ourselves to be aware of our own ecological issues as well as those in our teaching and supervision, it will be impossible for us to model such attention for our students.

## Conclusion

Training and supervision of ecological counseling is likely to be perceived as very similar to the training and supervision conducted in most counselor education programs. Nonetheless, there are subtle differences in emphasis that, over time, will have a major impact on the long-term practice of graduates. If we as counselor educators are truly able to do more than merely talk the talk and are able to aid our students, little by little, to try out traditional counseling skills within the context of the client's actual ecology, we will find graduates 10 and 20 years later who are effectively walking the walk and living the walk of ecological counseling in their everyday work and daily lives.

## Learning Activities

1. Review the 10 training suggestions discussed in this chapter. As you think through each suggestion, ask yourself, "How would implementation of this idea impact the ecological awareness of my students and supervisees?" Would the increased ecological awareness affect these students' clients?
2. Although our counseling student classes are typically very diverse on many demographic measures, what would be the impact of a training program that was extremely homogeneous? For example, if all students were women, approximately 24 years old, recent college graduates with a psychology major and no work experience, would encouraging an ecological approach to counseling be more or less difficult?
3. Which of the 10 training suggestions described in this chapter would be most difficult to implement in your setting? Which would be most easily added to your present method of teaching and supervision? What do the answers to the above questions tell you about yourself and your job?

## References

Beck, T. F. (1980). *The effect of cognitive self-instructional training on the response of beginning counselors.* Unpublished manuscript, University of Cincinnati.

Bernard, J. M., & Goodyear, R. K. (1998). *Fundamentals of clinical supervision* (2nd ed.). Boston: Allyn & Bacon.

Chi Sigma Iota. (1999). *Counselor advocacy and leadership conferences report.* Greensboro, NC: Author. Retrieved October 7, 2002, from http://www. csi-net.org/htmls/advfocus.htm

Cormier, W. H., & Cormier, L. S. (2003). *Interviewing strategies for helpers* (5th ed.). Pacific Grove, CA: Brooks/Cole.

Council for Accreditation of Counseling and Related Educational Programs (CACREP). (2001). *CACREP Accreditation Manual: 2001 Standards.* Alexandria, VA: Author.

Egan, G. (2002). *The skilled helper* (7th ed.). Pacific Grove, CA: Brooks/Cole.

Eriksen, K. P., & McAuliffe, G. J. (Eds.). (2001). *Teaching counselors and therapists: Constructivist and developmental course design.* Westport, CT: Bergin & Garvey.

Ellis, A. (1962). *Reason and emotion in psychotherapy.* New York: Lyle Stuart Press.

Hector, M. A., Elson, S. E., & Yager, G. G. (1977). Teaching counseling skills through self-management procedures. *Counselor Education and Supervision, 17,* 12–22.

Holloway, E. L. (1995). *Clinical supervision: A systems approach.* Thousand Oaks, CA: Sage.

Ivey, A. E., & Ivey, M. B. (2003). *Intentional interviewing and counseling* (5th ed.). Pacific Grove, CA: Brooks/Cole.

McAuliffe, G. J., Eriksen, K. P., & Associates. (2000). *Preparing counselors and therapists: Creating constructivist and developmental programs.* Alexandria, VA: Association for Counselor Education and Supervision.

Meichenbaum, D. (1977). *Cognitive behavior modification.* New York: Plenum Press.

Myers, J. E., Sweeney, T. J., & White, V. E. (2002). Advocacy for counseling and counselors: A professional imperative. *Journal of Counseling & Development, 80,* 394–402.

Ochiltree, J. K., Yager, G. G., & Brekke, D. (1975, April). *A cognitive self-instructional modeling approach vs. the Carkhuff model for training empathy.* Paper presented at the annual meeting of the American Educational Research Association, Washington, DC (ERIC Document Reproduction Service No. 106 706)

Okun, B. F. (2002). *Effective helping: Interviewing and counseling techniques* (6th ed.). Pacific Grove, CA: Brooks/Cole.

Yager, G. G., & Beck, T. F. (1981, April). *Cognitive self-instructional training in counseling prepracticum.* Paper presented at the annual meeting of the American Educational Research Association, Los Angeles, CA. (ERIC Document Reproduction Service No. 204 689)

Yager, G. G., & Littrell, J. M. (1978, October). *Counselor supervision: A consumer's guide.* Paper presented at the annual meeting of the North Central Association for Counselor Education and Supervision, Chicago, IL. (ERIC Document Reproduction Service No. ED 166 586)

## Chapter 8

# Ecological Group Work

## Fred Bemak and Robert K. Conyne

---

*Chapter Highlights*
- *Group counseling must be reviewed within an ecological context.*
- *Group counseling is an independent form of mental health practice.*
- *The ecological context for group counseling closely corresponds to socio-economic, political, cultural, and demographic trends.*
- *Group counseling must undergo a paradigm shift.*
- *Groups are contextualized, living open complex social systems through which information is produced.*

---

G roup work is an essential method for counselors and other human service personnel. It is recognized as a core training and service delivery area by all mental-health-oriented credentialing associations, such as accreditation bodies (e.g., Council for the Accreditation of Counseling and Related Educational Programs), licensing groups (e.g., professional counselors), and certification boards (e.g., Board for National Certified Counselors; Certified Group Psychotherapist Board). Other professional associations, such as the Association for Specialists in Group Work and the Division of Group Psychology and Group Psychotherapy (APA Division 49), are dedicated solely to selective aspects of group work, as are specialized scholarly journals such as the *Journal for Specialists in Group Work* and *Group Dynamics*. Research over the past 35 years supports the efficacy of group work (e.g., Barlow, Burlingame, & Fuhriman, 2000; Horne & Rosenthal, 1997). Therefore, it is accurate to acknowledge that, after decades of occupying an uncertain status in the counseling and mental health enterprises, group work is finally earning deserved recognition.

Despite its acceptance as a major method for counseling and mental health practice, it is our view that group work arguably enjoys no overarching conceptual framework. A review of most major textbooks in group counseling and psychotherapy, for instance, reveals that group work tends to be described and presented as a special application of preexisting theories of *individual* counseling and psychotherapy (e.g., see otherwise excellent texts by Corey, 2000; Gazda, Ginter, & Horne, 2001; Gladding, 1999; we point out that Trotzer, 1999, and Yalom, 1995, are exceptions). Person-centered group counseling, Gestalt group counseling, rational emotive behavioral therapy group counseling, reality therapy group counseling, and Adlerian therapy group counseling are examples of this approach. Attention to group properties and processes, such as to group dynamics and therapeutic forces in groups, tends to be grafted onto the basic tree trunk of individual theories that are then applied to the group setting.

A premise of this chapter is that group work stands independently as a major theory and type of mental health practice. It is not an extension of individual work, no more than it is a reduction of organizational or community work.

The individual perspective to group work is a reflection of the individualistic model that characterizes Western culture and society and lays the foundation for Western psychology. Within this framework, emphasis is placed on the individual, the self, and independence as a self-contained unit (Bemak, 1989; Conyne, Tang, & Watson, 2001; Draguns, 1988; Hofstede, 1983; Triandis, 1990), which is sometimes at the expense of the group, family, or clan (Bemak & Hanna, 1998). This worldview has served us well in promoting Western values of independence, autonomy, and self-sufficiency, yet it has limited our reach and narrowed our focus. In terms of group work, which is derived from collectivistic principles that emphasize social and family relationships and interdependence, the limitations outweigh the value. Rather than being based on an individual frame of reference, we suggest that group work can be viewed more accurately from a collectivist worldview, where the group is the primary unit and interdependence is the key. This perspective, which accommodates 70% of the world's population (Bell, 1987), needs to be given far greater attention when conceptualizing group work, particularly since almost all the psychological data come from individualistic cultures (Triandis, 1980, 1990).

## Contextualizing Group Work

Considering the contemporary trends that face society provides insight, direction, and significant impact for group facilitators. It is our belief that the work that occurs within groups closely corresponds to socioeconomic, political, and demographic trends. Thus, in this chapter we propose that it is essential to consider group work within an ecological context. To not do so is to continue to foster the precepts of group work within the construction of traditional Western psychology that is underscored by individualism and independence. To discuss group work in this frame of reference not only diminishes the importance and tremendous value of group work, but also perpetuates it as a theoretical discipline that is dependent on individual theory and practice. Therefore, to maintain consistency with the fundamental principles of group work, it is critical to view the field from an ecological perspective.

Maintaining this perspective requires an awareness of our rapidly growing and changing world. We face changes in technology that provide faster and more efficient communication. These changes have the potential to depersonalize human relationships. Social, political, and economic ties create a faster paced and more closely linked world around us, while challenging the very fabric of interpersonal relationships. The global village that McLuhan (1968, 1989) envisioned now has tremendous complexity and affects how people relate to one another and the world around them. Simultaneously, there is tremendous population growth with expectations that the world will reach about 8.35 billion people in 2020, coupled with the fact that 20% of the world's population lives in absolute poverty (Marsella, 1998). These kinds of overarching concerns provide a framework from which to consider the types of issues that influence group work, including a changing workforce, growing poverty, changing family structures, substance abuse, a drug culture with a strong economic base, high rates of sexual and physical abuse, and the high rates of migration (Bemak & Hanna, 1998).

## Counseling and Ecology

As we previously discussed, we believe firmly that group counseling is a stand-alone field in mental health practice. By its very nature and emphasis on interdependence, it is naturally linked to the surrounding world and related issues (Capra, 1996) and is founded on collectivistic precepts. Thus, the clear association between group work and collectivism becomes an interwoven basis for providing counseling within group settings.

This orientation provides a unique underlying focus for performing group work, serving to diminish our nearly exclusive attachment to Western psychology. Western psychology and counseling is wholly based on individualism and independence, emphasizing such concepts as self-actualization, self-realization, self-fulfillment, and self-development. This focus on the independent self contradicts what is an important aspect of group work (i.e., fostering human relationships that promote and clarify self within a broader context and place great importance on others, whether it be a counseling or task-oriented group).

In this chapter, therefore, we suggest that there needs to be a paradigm shift in group work that requires full and in-depth modification in thinking and practice. Group work principles and practices need to be contextualized, both incorporating and influencing socioecological issues. For example, facilitating a dropout prevention group for failing teenage girls in a middle school must consider not only their grades but also numerous other factors such as the family and community supports in their lives, the perceptions and reactions of their peers to dropping out, or the family history with education. The interplay of issues such as these with dropping out is closely linked and must be considered when performing group counseling. In summary, the purpose of this chapter is to present a conceptual foundation for group work that is grounded in a group-oriented, interdependent perspective that is both overarching and metatheoretical, while rooted in ecological constructs.

## Conceptual Foundation

### Locating Groups Within Ecological Counseling

Ecological counseling can be applied at any of four contextual level targets (see chapter 1): personal, primary group, organization, and community. By definition, *group* is centrally involved in the primary group level. Primary groups (Cooley, 1965) are those small factions that involve ongoing, face-to-face interaction and that are personally significant to people. Family and peer groups are naturally occurring examples of primary groups, as are groups created to further task or personal growth issues (Conyne, 1989).

Group also runs through the organization and community levels. Both levels comprise various collections of organized and naturally occurring small group interactions. Therefore, group is an extremely important method for ecological counseling.

### Groups and Ecology

From an ecological perspective, a group is a complex, living, open, and interactive social system (Arrow, McGrath, & Berdahl, 2000; Capra, 1996;

198

Fujishin, 2001). It involves ongoing, active two-way interactions among members, with the embedded context, and the processing of this information (Wilson, 1996). The embedded context surrounding a group includes physical (e.g., the built environment), temporal (e.g., time, development), sociocultural (e.g., values, politics, culture, economics), and organizational characteristics (e.g., size, resources, policies, procedures). Simply put, a group is a contextualized, living social system through which information is produced and processed. A group never stands alone. It always is set within and subject to a multitude of changing forces. It is influenced by its context, and in turn, it influences the context.

Imagine you are a counselor in a high school. The principal has appointed you to chair a 10-member committee that must revise the school disciplinary code. This 10-member committee is composed of four teachers, a school psychologist, an assistant principal, two parents, a central office secretary, and one student. You have 8 weeks to produce a draft of the revised code. The principal has encouraged you to seek input from others in the school and community and to review codes from other schools. Your weekly meetings are in the library meeting room, for 2 hours immediately after school on Thursdays. What, however, makes this committee a complex, open, and interactive social system that is embedded in a context?

We want to make a comment here about context that may help you as the reader begin thinking about what makes this committee conform to the characteristics of a group that we have just described. Note that the committee membership comes from varying constituencies, that the committee meets once a week and has 8 weeks to deliver a product, that the committee is encouraged to interact with others outside the committee, and so on. These points all illustrate particular contextual factors, and they influence the committee in certain ways that would be quite different if, for example, the committee comprised just teachers, that it met on four Saturdays, and the deadline was only 5 weeks. All groups exist in a particular context, therefore, with reciprocal influence occurring dynamically.

## Group Work

We consider all groups complex open systems that are embedded in context. In this chapter, however, we limit our attention to the primary group contextual level. We give exclusive attention to group work, the professional delivery method of help giving that occurs in groups of different types.

We accept the definition of group work developed by the Association for Specialists in Group Work (ASGW, 2000). Conyne, Wilson, and Ward (1997) have provided an extended discussion of this definition:

> [Group work is] a broad professional practice that refers to the giving of help or the accomplishment of tasks in a group setting. It involves the application of group theory and process by a capable professional practitioner to assist an interdependent collection of people to reach their mutual goals, which may be personal, interpersonal, or task-related in nature. (p. 14)

From an ecological perspective, the phrase "an *interdependent* collection of people to reach their *mutual* goals" (italics added) in this definition is particularly salient. The concepts of interdependence and mutuality both suggest that the group work leader should place practice priority upon the interactions occurring among group members as they pursue their interconnected goals. This orientation is fully consistent with the collectivistic worldview with which we began this chapter.

*Group work* is an umbrella term. It spans four types of groups, as described in the *Training Standards for Group Workers* (ASGW, 2000): (a) task groups, (b) psychoeducation groups, (c) counseling groups, and (d) psychotherapy groups. A brief discussion of each follows.

*Task groups* are what Arrow, McGrath, and Berdahl (2000) referred to as concocted groups. They often appear in work organizations, established by a manager by fiat who assigns members, tasks, and tools. Walton and Hackman (1986) called these groups work teams. Examples include task forces, committees, and planning groups. Some other forms of task groups conform to Arrow et al.'s (2000) definition of founded groups, whose members assemble deliberately into a new group by linking with others to accomplish task or personal goals. Examples of founded groups are discussion groups, study circles, book clubs, and learning groups.

Whether formed by external mandate (concocted) or by internal choice (founded), the purpose of task groups is to accomplish identified work tasks and goals. Conyne, Rapin, and Rand (1997) have presented a task group intervention choice model that can be helpful for task group leaders.

*Psychoeducation groups* are founded groups that use group dynamics to deliver psychoeducational content and skills to members. Examples of psychoeducational content and skills include stress management, substance abuse prevention, and problem-solving. Careful planning and balance of structured exercises and open processing are important. Conyne and Wilson (1999) presented a full model of how to plan, perform, and process psychoeducation groups in their training video.

*Counseling groups* are founded groups that help participants resolve the usual, yet frequently challenging, difficulties and problems of living through interpersonal support and problem solving. The process of group counseling is generally open and unstructured, and the members do not experience more serious levels of dysfunction. The counseling group leader seeks to generate a network of interpersonal relations and then attends closely to the ensuing interpersonal dynamics that occur.

*Psychotherapy groups* are founded groups that help members become aware of and remediate their in-depth psychological and emotional dysfunction. These disturbances are substantial enough to warrant a clinical diagnosis. It is the level of dysfunction that most clearly distinguishes psychotherapy groups from the other personal change groups.

## Important Ecological Domains Affecting Group Work

### Political Domain

One aspect of influence on group work is the political arena within which we live. This can be defined in three general spheres. The first sphere is our immediate surroundings and the prominent political perspectives that are present in that environment. For example, if we are in a workplace task group and find that underpinning our decisions is sensitivity and attention to cultural diversity and differences, it will have potentially great impact on how the group thinks and what the group decides. Or, if we work in a highly authoritarian setting where disagreement or differing opinions are discouraged, then groups will likely be autocratically governed given the politics of our work environment.

Another part of our immediate surroundings is our community. This includes our families, the physical and social dimensions of our surroundings, places of worship, schools that we might attend, and so on. Within these places closest to us are numerous political factors that impact our role and participation in groups. An example is the inner-city middle school surrounded by crack houses and drug addicts. Each morning, the principal of that school starts her day by cleaning the used needles from the school parking lot and front and side doors. Given the community environment of the school, highly restrictive policies are in force to address entry into the school and student access to the outside schoolyard during the school day. Group work coordinated within this environment gives significant attention to these matters, given that every student is highly aware of the neighborhood, has concern about walking through this area, and has reactions to school policies and enforcement of those policies within the school and by police.

A third area to be considered in the political sphere is composed of the broader policies that constitute and govern what is allowed outside one's immediate environment. These considerations include county, state, and federal laws that influence and frequently dictate what is permissible and allowed. After the September 11 attacks on the World Trade Center and Pentagon, the U.S. Government established a policy that the detention of foreign nationals under suspicion was permissible. Subsequently, in counseling a group of recently arrived foreign students, it was evident members felt significant paranoia, fear, and mistrust of civil authorities. These issues were not pathological in nature, but would have been considered as more dysfunctional behavior prior to the new policies. After September 11, however, they were understandable responses to a real event that had significant impact on this group of students.

It should be noted that this political sphere is not only governed by formal laws, but also dictated by more informal collective values that result in presenting and projecting acceptable mainstream values and attitudes regarding cultural and community norms. This constitutes another significant dimension for the political domain, one associated with political correctness. One of the outcomes of political correctness in ecological terms is that it causes group members to respond in ways they believe are appropriate given current political parameters, but it does not necessarily elicit authentic reactions and beliefs. Thus, as one emphasizes groups with an ecological focus, it is important to be aware of the impact of political correctness on members and the group process.

An important consideration regardless of the political sphere is the nature of political realities that impacts various populations and subsequently negatively affects their growth, development, and mental health. This consideration results in redefining the traditional view that clinical interventions are sufficient to address political, social, and economic discrimination to the exclusion of the very impact of politics on groups of people. Historically, politics has contributed to social, political, and economic injustice that cannot be solely attended to by limited perspectives on group work. Rather, group interventions must address the root of these injustices by focusing on the political structures that create and perpetuate these inequities. To effectively work with these political problems necessitates comprehension of the client's contextual world (Bemak & Hanna, 1998; Segall, Lonner, & Berry, 1998). Group work is in a unique position to tackle these societal and political ills, with the potential to promote the values of justice, equity, and rights far more effectively than many other mental health perspectives.

## Cultural Domain

The ethnic profile of the United States is significantly changing. It is projected that by 2050 one half of the U.S. population will be members of ethnic minority groups (Aponte & Crouch, 1995; U.S. Bureau of Census, 1996). This shift is greatly influenced by changing birth rates among various ethnic groups (U.S. Bureau of Census, 1996) and significant changes in migration and immigration patterns (Bemak, Chung, & Pedersen, 2003), with 10% of the current U.S. population coming from migrant backgrounds (U.S. Bureau of Census, 1997). Underscoring these issues are the core issues of acculturation and ethnic identity (Lee, 1997), which both manifest and greatly impact the workings of groups.

Closely related to the ethnic and cultural shifts in society is the relationship with and adaptation to the majority society. Groups can play an instrumental role in attending to these issues, particularly with greater needs to understand and appreciate cultural differences as well as sociopolitical realities faced by diverse ethnic groups. Of particular importance in group work across cultures is the attention to unique cultural needs and variations (Boyd-Franklin, 1991), underrepresentation and devaluation, and oppression and unequal power (Fenster, 1996; Sutton, 1996). We suggest that groups that are founded on principles of cultural diversity, and honestly and clearly focus on issues that affect people of all cultures, are invaluable during these times of rich cultural shifts and enhanced cultural diversity (Conyne, Tang, & Watson, 2001).

## Economic Domain

The economic domain significantly impacts group work. More than 30 years ago, Kunkel (1970) examined the interrelationship of social change and economic development. He concluded that a major problem with economic development was the ensuing change of the social environment that, in turn, affected the development of new ways of behaving within a society. During the same period, Adelman and Morris (1967) also analyzed economics as related to societal development and found a correlation with social development, particularly in developing or poorer countries, that may be associated with socioeconomic status. More recently, in defining a global community psychology, Marsella (1998) cited economics as one of 25 major global events and forces, as a contributing factor. We extend this work from more than 30 years ago and suggest that economics is an essential component with substantial impact on group work, influencing dynamics, content, and the process of all types of groups.

## Processes of Ecologically Centered Group Work

Ecologically centered group work hews closely to the domains just discussed. How does this occur? A starting point may be to examine the work of physics. The physicist, Capra (1982, 1996), has described deep ecology. From the perspective of deep ecology, life is conceived as a web where everything is holistically interconnected with the cosmos. In its deepest essence, Capra suggested that deep ecology is synonymous with spiritual awareness. These concepts in physics, which are beginning to wend their way into counseling (e.g., Gregory, 1994), provide a basis from which to examine the tenets of group work that we describe here as a major independent field, one rooted in an ecological context. In order to work on the levels Capra described, a major paradigm shift is required.

It was suggested previously (e.g., Conyne, 1985) that adoption of an ecological orientation to counseling, including group work, essentially involves a change in perspective about life and counseling. For example, it requires conceptualizing people within a larger context rather than as isolated units. We concur with Capra's suggestion that more than a change in perspective is required. In his view, it is necessary to adopt a change in values. Therefore, the paradigm shift involved with deep ecology requires a change both in thinking and in values that counterbalance the present domination placed on self-assertive tendencies, moving the emphasis to integrative tendencies.

The paradigm shift needed for deep ecology (Capra, 1996; Devall & Sessions, 1985) seeks a dynamic balance in thoughts and values across the self and other directed tendencies that are more integrative. In this discussion, the *integrative* tendencies in thinking and values are those most commonly associated with the collectivist, group-centered worldview with which we began this chapter (see Table 8.1).

Capra's discussion of deep ecology suggests the critical role of thoughts and values in applying an ecological orientation to group work. The question of how the process of ecologically centered group work occurs, then, is a direct function of the thoughts and values held by the group work leader(s).

More specifically, let us consider the process of ecologically centered group work, drawing from the description of ecological counseling con-

**Table 8.1**

**Deep Ecology Paradigm Shift: Tendencies**

| Self-Assertive Integrative Thinking | | Self-Assertive Integrative Values | |
|---|---|---|---|
| rational | intuitive | expansion | conservation |
| analysis | synthesis | competition | cooperation |
| reductionist | holistic | quantity | quality |
| linear | nonlinear | domination | partnership |

tained in chapter 5. In addition, we integrate material for best practices in group work (ASGW, 1998; Rapin & Conyne, 1999), including the steps of planning, performing, and processing. Further, we suggest an associated ecological imperative for each step, along with brief examples. Each of these ecological imperatives is rooted in the ecological principles we have discussed and maintains the need for a balance between self-assertive and integrative tendencies as advocated by Capra.

## Steps in Ecologically Centered Group Work

### Step 1. Assessment and Goal Setting: Planning Ecologically Centered Group Work

The group leader needs to conceptualize and design all aspects of the group prior to the first session. Although assessment and goal setting are critically important aspects of planning, the group leader also needs to design other elements, including group structure, location, strategies, activities, leadership responsibilities, member recruitment and screening, and the evaluation of both process and outcome.

During this step, the leader can be considered an architect who partners with others to create a design that fits needs and terrain. To ensure they are contextually grounded, plans for the structure and processes of the group are determined and set within the existing landscape and conditions that surround and influence prospective members. Assessment and goal setting serve to guide the creation of all other plan components, which must be assessed according to a number of ecological dimensions. Besides the more typical personal factors, such as level of member functioning and interpersonal assets and deficits, an ecological assessment should address the needs of the group and its location, the resources and constraints in the setting, and demographic variables such as culture, race, ethnicity, gender, and socioeconomic status. All of these factors, and more, are important for creating group goals that generally will lead to improved cohesion.

*Ecological imperative.* The overall plan for the group and each of its sessions must be contextually valid, emerge from collaborative processes, and yield closer knit and more cohesive groups. By being contextually valid, we mean that the plan for the group should reflect accurately the needs, culture, and values of prospective members and be located at an appropriate time and place. To help assure these contextual criteria are met, group leaders need to find ways to collaborate with representatives of the target population during planning. For example, planning groups with parents of students at risk of failing school may present numerous situations where the parents feel alienated and uncomfortable in the school environment. Collaborating with parents to find a location to meet that makes prospective group participants feel comfortable, such as in the local community center or a place of worship, may also be critical in the initial planning stages.

The ecological assessment of this step allows for specifying the overall group plan, including the setting of goals. These goals are typically intended to produce better person–environment matches or to yield concordance between group products and external expectations or demands.

### Step 2. Intervention: Performing Ecologically Centered Group Work

Performing group work is where "the rubber meets the road." It involves group work intervention (i.e., the ongoing delivery of services by the leader or leaders during the group sessions). Manifestation of core competencies, strategies, functions, and interventions are important aspects of performance, as is the leader being able to meld these effectively and appropriately with personal style.

Another way to think of this step is that it is the adaptive implementation of the plan created in Step 1. Note that a leader does not by rote implement a plan created earlier, no matter how comprehensive and ecologically valid. Rather—and most important to ecologically centered group work—the leader adapts that plan to best fit the ongoing circumstances and dynamics of the group as it evolves, and of larger contextual events as they might affect the group and its members. For instance, coleaders were conducting a psychoeducation group with inner-city middle school students on violence prevention. Halfway through the group sessions, a week-long race relations riot broke out in a neighborhood nearby. Tensions were high and safety was a concern. The coleaders faced a set of decisions. Should the group meet as scheduled? If so, should the plan for that week be implemented? Should the plan be modified or completely shelved to address the real-life contextual events surrounding the group? After deliberation and discussion with

206

school officials, the coleaders decided to meet, but to alter the planned activities to allow for open time so members could vent and hear from each other about their experiences during the riot and what these events meant.

Because the group is an interpersonal social system in context, the nature of the interpersonal interactions, group-level dynamics, and effects of external influences on members and the group itself are all especially important. Within the group, therefore, it is very important for ecologically centered group leaders to attend to group process and system-level variables. The leader needs to function as a participant-observer who is constantly aware of process dynamics, and who converts these observations effectively and appropriately to valid ecological interventions. For example, a long silence occurring during Session 9 of a 10-session group may mean something much different from a long silence occurring in Session 2. Knowledge of group development, tied to process observations, assists the leader in choosing the appropriate intervention. In another example, a group in which members talk to and through the leader (switchboard model) varies markedly in interaction style from a group in which members talk directly to each other (network model). Group leaders holding an ecological orientation are particularly sensitive to this kind of social system analysis and, in fact, generally strive to foster the creation of network models.

***Ecological imperative.*** The group leader must be concerned primarily with creating a dynamic, contextualized social system that is productive (task groups), educational and skill building (psychoeducation groups), and adept at interpersonal problem solving (counseling groups) or psychological reconstruction (psychotherapy groups). That is, the key performance issue for an ecologically centered group leader is to foster a web of interconnectedness among members that allows for desired goal accomplishment. Values of interdependence and cooperation must be predominant. The leader should always look for how the thoughts, feelings, and actions of members relate to one another, and he or she should continually search for ways to facilitate intermember involvement. The related ecological goal is to help members view themselves in relation to their larger world. That is, members need to give primacy to their place both in the group and to their place in their world. Both contexts are important. For example, in July 2001, eight individuals began a weekly psychotherapy group. During the course of the sessions, the September 11 attacks occurred on the World Trade Center and Pentagon. Three of the group members were personally affected by the attack: two knew someone who had died in the attacks and one anticipated being called to active duty since she was in the Army reserves. Personal issues such as their role and place in the group, their relationships with other members, and interpersonal support were all essential aspects of their psychotherapy. Concurrently, there were other broader issues that questioned their responsibility and reaction within their families and communities, their reactions toward the attackers and supportive countries, and how and what they would do at their work sites. It is for those reasons that the group exists: to help its members accomplish the personal, interpersonal, or task goals relevant to their lives outside the group. Issues of generalizability, transferability, and applicability are important considerations.

### Step 3. Evaluation: Processing Ecologically Centered Group Work

Evaluation includes the processing of group events and experiences (formative evaluation) and determining whether the goals of the group and its members were met (summative evaluation). Both are tied to the creation of meaning and improved concordance. Because of their complexity, groups can be quite bewildering. Events and experiences can pile up. It is necessary for group leaders to help sort out the complexity and to help members draw meaning from experience.

Processing in group work that is concerned with formative evaluation takes two forms. Within group sessions, the group leader(s) help members focus intentionally on what their experience in the group means personally as well as on the efficacy of the group experience. They also help members attribute meaning to group events and activities (Lieberman, Yalom, & Miles, 1973). In a second manner of formative evaluation processing, group leaders intentionally seek to foster their own creation of meaning through between-session examination. Both within-session and between-session processing develop important information to keep the group on track and moving in relation to its goals.

Deep processing (Conyne, 1999) affords a method for leaders to use during between-session processing, or it can be used within supervision. Its overarching purpose is to facilitate the creation of meaning from experience. Deep processing includes the following steps: (a) transposing, where leaders accurately describe their observations of a session without interpretation; (b) reflecting, where leaders seek to connect their subjective awareness, feelings, thoughts, and sensations with these observations; (c) discovery, where leaders link observations and reflections with relevant external sources of knowledge, such as theory or life experience; (d) application, where leaders convert this deepened understanding into action steps for the next and/or subsequent sessions; and (e) evolving, where leaders over time are actively involved with creating sustaining principles that can serve to ground and guide their leadership in the long-term future. Deep processing conducted within an ecologically centered approach to group work must be grounded contextually. Doing so results in single group sessions or meetings that are considered in relation to the type of group, its developmental history, its goals, its members' capacities and culture, the setting in which the group is held, and ongoing life events.

Take, for instance, just the issue of group type in relation to deep processing. A task group, such as a faculty or staff meeting, provides for an ecology that obviously is different from a psychotherapy group. Consider feeling expression in relation to these two group types. Relatively little expression of affect might be expected during a university faculty meeting or a community agency or school staff meeting where there is a higher emphasis on task accomplishment. In contrast, in a therapy group, members are expected to exhibit substantial affect as they work on personal and interpersonal issues. What does it mean, though, when exactly the reverse occurs in each of these instances? When the faculty or staff meeting is replete with affect, when the therapy group finds little or no expressed emotion? Leaders engaged in deep processing of sessions from either of these two group types must derive meaning that respects contextual elements, such as group type.

Summative, or outcome, evaluation also is important in ecologically oriented group work. As with formative evaluation, summative evaluation is connected with meaning derivation, but it is focused on the end point of the group experience. In summative evaluation, the leaders process whether group goals were attained and whether members accomplished their personal goals within the context of group interaction. As with all applications of ecological counseling, group ecological counseling seeks to improve the fit between group members and their environment—that is, to help members reach a state of improved concordance or, in task groups, that the products generated by the group are suited to the external environment. Therefore, leaders need to be sure that ongoing group development and individual member progress is in accord with translations and generalizations outside the group. Members of counseling groups, for instance, learn how to apply interpersonal problem-solving strategies to their own concerns while in the group, while giving simultaneous attention to their application to real contexts in their ongoing, everyday lives outside the group. In addition, they may take steps to act on their outside environment (e.g., work unit) to yield a more supportive work climate.

***Ecological imperative.*** A vital aspect of ecological counseling is the creation of meaning, as emphasized throughout this book. Capra (1996) discussed the connection between the deepest levels of deep ecology with a spiritual awareness. The ecologically centered group leaders must assist members in transposing events and their thoughts and reactions to these events to a broader context of existential meaning. These leaders encourage processing and evaluation within each session. To foster meaning-making, group leaders may ask members questions such as, "What does that mean for you?" "How do you connect what happened here?" "How do your values fit in with what happened here today?" "What does the statement you just made have to say about the kind of person you are, or are becoming?" or "Are there parallels between how you are in the group and how you are with your family and other loved ones?" Concurrently, leaders spend time processing their work between sessions. They should spend as much time in processing their work as they do in delivering it. Further, leaders evaluate group work in terms of its promotion of an improved concordance, or fit, among the group, its members, and the environment.

## Case Studies

To illustrate ecological group work, we provide case studies of group work in two different settings. The first group is composed of seven early adolescents from an inner-city middle school located in an impoverished neighborhood. The neighborhood is plagued by drug dealers, gangs, prostitution, and crime despite community attempts to combat these difficulties. The adolescents were referred to the group by teachers and identified as aggressive and unruly in the classroom and school. The school counselor, who has a strong background in group counseling, facilitates the group. The aim is to decrease the aggressive behavior. The second group is a countywide human services committee made up of 12 middle- and upper-level managers to discuss establishing policies and procedures that would be more culturally sensitive to the high number of ethnically diverse clientele within the county.

## Middle School Group for Aggressive Adolescents

This group, run by the school counselor, is aimed at reducing the aggressive behavior of seven middle school boys. The group combines a psychoeducational group with social skills training and a counseling group with an emphasis on dealing with the challenges and difficulties the boys face. The time in the group is equally devoted to the psychoeducational training and counseling. The group was created for a 10-week period, with member referrals from the teachers in the school. Each of the boys has been prescreened and is eager to join the group.

When considering ecological group counseling, several factors must be accounted for in facilitating this group. First, there is a need to consider the ethnic and gender composition of the group within an ecological context. The group consists of early adolescent boys from three ethnic groups. Two are of African American descent, two of Hispanic descent, and three of European American descent. Therefore, the context of interethnic relations must be considered both within the school and in community environments, and important questions must be asked in this regard: Is there tolerance and acceptance among various ethnic groups within the school? If not, how is tension manifested and how might this become apparent within the group context? What is the level of openness to address these issues within the school and subsequently the group context? Answers to these questions provide an important context for the group.

Another consideration in facilitating a group with these boys is the relationship they have with their families and communities related to aggression and their values. What messages do their families and communities convey about their aggressive behavior? Is it expected that they shouldn't let anyone push them around? Should they stand up to individuals in positions of authority in order not to feel disempowered or discriminated against? According to family and community values, is standing their ground equivalent to maintaining a position of integrity and self-pride? If these boys stopped being aggressive and tough, do their families and communities believe they might be taken advantage of in the environment where they reside? These are essential questions to ask about the broader context of these boys' lives. They strongly influence how to understand and approach work within the group context. For example, if becoming less aggressive would result in the boys being devalued by peers and unable to maintain the defenses necessary to successfully navigate their environment, then these factors must be considered in a group aimed at reducing aggressive behaviors.

Another important factor in working with an ecological group is the broader political environment. What policies govern behavior within the school and community? What are the funding sources to address the problems being discussed within the group context, and are they a priority for the school administrators and associated agencies that may be involved with these youths? If the problems being addressed by the youths are not prioritized within the context of the world in which these boys live, a different emphasis, support, and attention will be given to both the problem and the individual group members. If the informal policies of the neighborhood and region are being neglected regarding prostitution, drugs, poverty, and crime, then the attitudes of the boys in the group will reflect these values and may be contrary to values the group counselor is trying to promote and support.

Another ecological consideration in working with this group is the pressure of the school. The teachers have identified the boys as the most seriously aggressive in the school. They may have expectations and demands that may well have been initiated by the school administration, which may cause expectations for the group counselor to produce immediate results. The design of the school environment and the pressing needs of the teachers and administrators to control behavior and eliminate disruptions may be the cause of this undue pressure.

## Countywide Human Services Diversity Committee

There have been recent accusations in a large county that human services programs and policies are insensitive and unresponsive to ethnic minority clients. This claim has gotten the attention of the County Board, whose membership is ethnically heterogeneous and has a history of being divided, especially on issues related to diversity. While disagreeing about the nature of the problem and subsequent strategies for addressing it, by a slight majority the board voted to reexamine the policies and practices of the human services programs and instructed the human services agencies to develop a proposal for becoming more responsive.

Numerous ecological factors need to be considered in facilitating the Diversity Committee. First, this group is a task group given a clearly defined mission by the board, the body with authority over the group's work. Therefore, the approved directive reflecting countywide concerns defines the group's mission. Second, from a meta perspective, there is dissension on the board regarding not only this mandate but also the direction for the human services agencies. It may well be that this dissonance will be manifested within the task group itself, a dynamic that must be carefully assessed and attended to should there be a need to address it at any point in the group's work.

Consideration should be given to the pressure on each board member from the community and representative communities. Lobbying groups to this agency, input from their direct supervisors and colleagues, family and personal values and beliefs, and broader community values will all contribute to the group's functioning and dynamics. In addition, there may be disparity among the various human services agencies represented on the committee that will also provide an ecological basis for group relationships.

Community history also impacts the Diversity Committee. Typically, communities have longstanding histories where values, issues, resources, conflicts, and alliances are etched within the community's construct. These issues will once again be reenacted to various degrees within this task group, serving to influence both the process and outcome of the committee's work. Also available are funds to implement the committee's recommendations. Knowledge of available resources may influence recommendations made by the committee and guide discussion and participation of group members. In addition, there are already clearly established policies regarding diversity within the county. The committee must take into account the existing policies as a foundation for its work and investigate whether to expand, discard, or maintain the already established guidelines. The committee will consider significant ecological factors in constituting and working in this type of group.

## Conclusion

Group work needs to be regarded as an intervention major theory that stands independently from other interventions and is based on a unique theoretical platform that strongly integrates ecology. We strongly suggest that groups are ineffective without paying attention to socioeconomic, political, cultural, and demographic trends in addition to the multifarious factors in the world around us. There is an ecological underpinning to planning, performing, and processing in groups that is not only important but also essential when considering task, psychoeducational, counseling, or therapy groups.

## Learning Activities

1. Group work is founded on principles of Western psychology that emphasize individualism and autonomy. Discuss with a partner ways or ideas to embed principles from a collectivistic perspective within group work given its origins in individually oriented work.
2. Imagine and discuss a contextualized counseling group that you are facilitating. Specifically consider the impact of current socioeconomic, political, cultural, and/or demographic trends on clients or students in the group.
3. Take 15 minutes to consider the following questions: How do you feel about ecological counseling? What attracts you to it? What is unattractive about it? How might you be able to apply it

more effectively in your work? Discuss your reactions with the rest of the class.

4. Target populations for groups that come from different socioeconomic groups. Discuss any differences you might foresee in working with groups from different socioeconomic backgrounds in relationship to ecological group counseling. Include in this discussion differences in background of the group facilitator from the group (e.g., a group leader who came from an impoverished background working with group members from a wealthy school community or a group leader coming from an upper-middle-class background working with group members from an impoverished background). How might this impact ecological group interventions?

5. Describe to members of your class the various steps in ecologically centered group work. What are some of the qualities required in a group leader working within this framework that are different from traditional group work skills?

## References

Adelman, I., & Morris, C.T. (1967). *Society, politics, and economic development: A quantitative approach.* Baltimore, MD: Johns Hopkins University Press.

Aponte, J. F., & Crouch, R.T. (1995). The changing ethnic profile of the United States. In J. F. Aponte, R. Young Rivers, & J. Wohl (Eds.), *Psychological interventions and cultural diversity* (pp. 1–18). Boston: Allyn & Bacon.

Arrow, H., McGrath, J., & Berdahl, J. (2000). *Small groups as complex systems: Formation, coordination, development, and adaptation.* Thousand Oaks, CA: Sage.

Association for Specialists in Group Work. (1998). Best practice guidelines for group work. In G. Gazda, G. Gitner, & A. Horne (Eds.), *Group counseling and group psychotherapy: Theory and application* (pp. 376–381). Boston: Allyn & Bacon.

Association for Specialists in Group Work. (2000). Professional standards for the training of group workers. In G. Gazda, G. Gitner, & A. Horne (Eds.), *Group counseling and group psychotherapy: Theory and application* (pp. 363–375). Boston: Allyn & Bacon.

Barlow, S., Burlingame, G., & Fuhriman, A. (2000). Therapeutic application of groups: From Pratt's "Thought Control Classes" to modern group psychotherapy. *Group Dynamics: Theory, Research, and Practice, 4,* 115–134.

Bell, D. (1987). The world and the United States in 2013. *Daedalus, 116,* 1–31.

Bemak, F. (1989). Cross-cultural family therapy with Southeast Asian refugees. *Journal of Strategic and Systemic Therapies, 8,* 22–27.

214

Bemak, F., Chung, R. C.-Y., & Pedersen, P. B. (2003). *Counseling refugees: A psychosocial cultural approach to innovative multicultural interventions.* Westport, CT: Greenwood Press.

Bemak, F., & Hanna, F. J. (1998). The 21st century counselor: An emerging role in changing times. *International Journal for the Advancement of Counseling, 20,* 209–218.

Boyd-Franklin, N. (1991). Recurrent themes in the treatment of African-American women in group psychotherapy. *Women and Therapy, 11,* 25–40.

Capra, F. (1982). *The turning point.* New York: Simon & Schuster.

Capra, F. (1996). *The web of life.* New York: Anchor Books.

Conyne, R. (1985). The counseling ecologist: Helping people and environments. *Counseling and Human Development, 18,* 1–12.

Conyne, R. (1989). *How personal growth and task groups work.* Newbury Park, CA: Sage.

Conyne, R. (1999). *Failures in group work: How we can learn from our mistakes.* Thousand Oaks, CA: Sage.

Conyne, R., Rapin, L., & Rand J. (1997). A model for leading task groups. In H. Forester-Miller & J. Kottler (Eds.), *Issues and challenges for group practitioners* (pp. 117–132). Denver, CO: Love.

Conyne, R., Tang, M., & Watson, A. (2001). Exploring diversity in therapeutic groups. In E. Welfel & R. E. Ingersoll (Eds.), *The mental health desk reference* (pp. 358–364). New York: Wiley.

Conyne, R., & Wilson, F. R. (1999). *Psychoeducation group demonstration: A career development group for international students (Parts 1 and 2)* [Videotape 14Z1812]. (Cosponsored by the University of Cincinnati and the Association for Specialists in Group Work.) New York: Insight Media.

Conyne, R., Wilson, F. R., & Ward, D. E. (1997). *Comprehensive group work: What it means & how to teach it.* Alexandria, VA: American Counseling Association.

Cooley, C. (1965). Primary groups. In A.P. Hare, E. Borgatta, & R.F. Bales (Eds.), *Small groups: Studies in social interaction* (pp. 15–19). New York: Knopf.

Corey, G. (2000). *Theory and practice of group counseling* (5th ed.). Pacific Grove, CA: Brooks/Cole.

Devall, B., & Sessions, G. (1985). *Deep ecology.* Salt Lake City, UT: G.M. Smith.

Draguns, J. (1988). Personality and culture: Are they relevant for the enhancement of quality of mental life? In P. R. Dasen, J. W. Berry, & N. Sartorius (Eds.), *Health and cross-cultural psychology: Toward applications* (pp. 141–161). Newbury Park, CA: Sage.

Fenster, A. (1996). Group therapy as an effective treatment modality for people of color. *International Journal of Group Psychotherapy, 46*(3), 399–416.

Fujishin, R. (2001). *Creating effective groups: The art of small group communication.* San Francisco: Acada Books.

Gazda, G., Ginter, E., & Horne, A. (2001). *Group counseling and group psychotherapy: Theory and application.* Boston: Allyn & Bacon.

Gladding, S. (1999). *Group work: A counseling specialty* (3rd ed.). Upper Saddle River, NJ: Merrill.

Gregory, R. (1994). Deep ecology: An opportunity for rehabilitation counselors. *Journal of Applied Rehabilitation Counseling, 25,* 45-47.

Hofstede, G. (1983). Dimensions of national culture in 50 cultures and 3 regions. In J. B. Deregowski, S. Dziurawiec, & R. C. Annis (Eds.), *Expectations in cross-cultural psychology* (pp. 335-355). Lisse, the Netherlands: Swets & Zeitlinger.

Horne, A., & Rosenthal, R. (1997). Research in group work: How did we get where we are? *Journal for Specialists in Group Work, 22,* 228-240.

Kunkel, J. H. (1970). *Society and economic growth: A behavioral perspective of social change.* New York: Oxford University Press

Lee, C. L. (1997). The promise and pitfalls of multicultural counseling. In C. L. Lee (Ed.), *Multicultural issues in counseling: New approaches to diversity* (pp. 3-13). Alexandria, VA: American Counseling Association.

Lieberman, M., Yalom, I., & Miles, M. (1973). *Encounter groups: First facts.* New York: Basic Books.

Marsella, A. J. (1998). Toward a global-community psychology: Meeting the needs of a changing world. *American Psychologist, 53,* 1282-1291.

McLuhan, M. (1968). *War and peace in the global village.* New York: McGraw Hill.

McLuhan, M. (1989). *The global village: Transformation in world life and media in the 21st century.* New York: Oxford Press.

Rapin, L., & Conyne, R. (1999). Best practices in group counseling. In J. Trotzer (Ed.), *The counselor and the group: Integrating theory, training, and practice* (3rd ed., pp. 253-273). Philadelphia: Accelerated Development.

Segall, M. H., Lonner, W. J., & Berry, J. W. (1998). Cross-cultural psychology as a scholarly discipline: On the flowering of culture in behavioral research. *American Psychologist, 53,* 1101-1110.

Sutton, A. (1996). African American men in group therapy. In M. P. Andronico (Ed.), *Men in groups: Insights, interventions, and psychoeducational work* (pp. 131-149). Washington DC: American Psychological Association.

Triandis, H. C. (1980). Introduction. In H. C. Triandis & W. W. Lambert (Eds.), *Handbook of cross-cultural psychology* (Vol. 1). Boston: Allyn & Bacon.

Triandis, H. C. (1990). Cross-cultural studies of individualism and collectivism. In J. Berman (Ed.), *Cross-cultural perspectives* (pp. 41-134). Lincoln: University of Nebraska Press.

Trotzer, J. (1999). *The counselor and the group: Integrating theory, research, and practice* (3rd ed.). Philadelphia: Accelerated Development.

U. S. Bureau of Census. (1996). *Current population reports. Population projections of the United States by age, sex, race, and Hispanic origin: 1992-2050* (pp. 25-1130). Washington, DC: U.S. Government Printing Office.

U. S. Bureau of Census. (1997). *Current population reports: Special studies* (pp. 23-193). Washington, DC: U.S. Government Printing Office.

Walton, R., & Hackman, J. (1986). Groups under contrasting management strategies. In P. Goodman (Ed.), *Designing effective work groups* (pp. 168–201). San Francisco: Jossey-Bass.

Wilson, G. (1996). *Groups in context: Leadership and participation in small groups* (4th ed.). New York: McGraw-Hill.

Yalom, I. (1995). *The theory and practice of group psychotherapy* (4th ed.). New York: Basic Books.

Chapter 9

# Career Counseling From an Ecological Perspective

*Ellen P. Cook, Karen M. O'Brien, and Mary J. Heppner*

---

*Chapter Highlights*

- *Diversity is at the heart of ecological career counseling: diversity of client issues and environmental interactions considered relevant in career counseling, of ways that counselors can facilitate career development, and of settings in which counselors can perform career development services.*

- *Ecological career counseling expands common conceptual boundaries of where, and in what manner, career counselors work, by recasting familiar ideas and strategies into a broader multilevel, interactional framework.*

- *The ecological perspective places renewed emphasis on the centrality of meaning making in career development, and on the complexity of the person-environment interactions forming lifelong career paths.*

- *Ecological career counselors try to empower clients to establish intrapsychic, interpersonal, and environmental congruence in order to experience meaning and personally defined success in their careers.*

- *Counselors use diverse methodologies to modify and enhance person-environment interactions, and to combat influences that oppress individuals and serve as barriers to their career development.*

---

Person-environment psychology has had a long and venerable history within the field of career development. For career counselors, the question of interest has not been *whether* to include both personal and environmental variables in understanding career development, but *how* variables and processes interact to influence vocational paths. The success of career counseling is commonly framed in terms of a successful person-environment interaction: How successful and/or happy is a client in a particular job? At a broader level, the importance of civil law, opportunity structures, the nation's economic health, and other environmental factors in shaping individual behavior have been discussed more explicitly in career psychology than in other counseling specializations.

Despite the popularity of person–environment approaches in career counseling, variables and processes crucial to explaining the career development of many individuals, particularly women and people of color, have until recently been virtually ignored. The ecological perspective offers fertile ground for expanding our understanding of career development and the range of interventions typifying career counseling. Specifically, by acknowledging the contributions of the micro-, meso-, exo-, and macrosystems on vocational choice and success, counselors can assist career clients in understanding the complexity of forces that interact to influence their vocational lives. Career behaviors are affected by factors at multiple levels: individual (e.g., motivations, skills, self-efficacy beliefs); microsystem—family and other significant people (e.g., family work values or dreams, peer group influences); mesosystem— relationships between microsystems (e.g., parental vs. school-based aspirations for achievement); exosystem—broader systemic influences, including the community or media (e.g., regional labor market); and macrosystem—broader social/cultural blueprints organizing life (e.g., patterns of racial or gender discrimination, societal stereotypes of class status). (See Bronfenbrenner, 1977, for a complete description of these systemic levels.)

By addressing these systemic influences on client behaviors, career counselors can work toward additional salient counseling goals. For example, to what degree can the client articulate the myriad influences on his or her career development? In what ways might the client be able to positively use the environmental influences that shape his or her vocational life? In what ways can environmental factors be changed to better the client's educational and occupational opportunities? How can the client develop tools to assist him or her in making complex career choices in his or her future? What environmental constructs can assist the client in achieving his or her vocational dreams?

In this chapter, we first explore in some detail how career development is influenced (both positively and negatively) by complex person-environment interactions, particularly within the career development of women. The occupational structure in the United States clearly illustrates the power of race, class, and gender to shape life patterns. The diversity of career patterns among women as a group also makes it clear that race, class, and gender dynamics effectively derail some individuals' career aspirations and seem to have little impact on others. For some, environmental factors (e.g., presence of supportive mentors in higher education) might provide the necessary supports for educational and occupational success.

We believe that an ecological perspective assists in articulating the myriad factors influencing the career paths of diverse individuals. Thus, we devote the remainder of the chapter to outlining features of an ecological perspective on career development, and illustrating its applicability through an extensive case study.

## Traditional Career Counseling Theory and Practice

From the earliest years of the career guidance movement, the interaction between personal and environmental factors has been crucial to career satisfaction and success (Dawis, 2000). As described in Swanson and Fouad (1999), many career theories explicitly acknowledge the role of the environment in individuals' career choices and their functioning. These include Holland's (1997) theory of work adjustment, Super's (1990) and Gottfredson's (1981) developmental theories, and Krumboltz's (1998) and Lent, Brown and Hackett's (1994) social learning theories.

Historically—and consistent with an individualistic psychology paradigm—vocational interventions were often based on the belief that career behaviors predominantly were a function of person characteristics, or $B = f(P)$. Career success was the consequence of good choices and hard work. To facilitate the decision process, career counseling often followed a brief, three-step model incorporating interviewing, standardized assessment measures, and summative test interpretation with recommendations for action steps. The focus was on enhancing and organizing a client's self-knowledge into constructs considered central to career decision making (e.g., interests, abilities, values, personality style). Clients were expected to gather a sufficient quality and quantity of personal and career (environmental) information that they could then evaluate to make the best match. The counselor's role was to provide the client access to sufficient information about self and work, structure it in a way conducive to matching personal and environmental characteristics, and, if necessary, improve the client's rational decision-making skills. Successful career counseling resulted in an optimal matching of personal givens with environmental opportunities, thus promoting career longevity and satisfaction.

There is little question that career development represents the end product of individual behavior within environmental contexts. Individuals typically make choices of where to work and how to perform the job tasks; employers select certain persons for the job and reward their performance or terminate them. However, we believe that the traditional model of career development as just sketched is at best incomplete; at worst, it fails to acknowledge the role of meso-, exo-, and macrosystemic influences on career development. For example, critical contextual variables such as gender, class, and race (and the way society responds to these variables) exert powerful forces on the vocational choices and accomplishments of most individuals.

Moreover, this model is incomplete or inaccurate because it paints an unduly static and objective model of the person–environment interaction inherent in career development. Prospective workers try to weight heavily the most salient person/job characteristics, but what is most salient varies within and across groups of people. Research has suggested that matching along traditional criteria (e.g., interests) may be associated with career satisfaction and success for some individuals, but other factors are also likely to determine outcome (e.g., see Betz, 1994, for an overview of constructs affecting women's career development). Individuals with a certain pattern of interests, abilities, and values may prove to be an ideal or uncomfortable match for a job's requirements, and a successful marriage of personal and job requirements may later sour into discordance. Career counseling clients sometimes make choices inconsistent with the most carefully derived psychometric information and are still delighted with the outcome. Individuals can be satisfied with choices motivated by reasons other than self-enhancement, such as to carry on the family business, to derive spiritual meaning from their daily labor, or to use on-site day care facilities. Even the best-laid plans can go awry because of environmental factors impossible to ascertain ahead of time, such as an emotionally unpredictable boss or a plummeting national economy.

The traditional model of career decision making can be unfair to many clients as well. We have argued elsewhere (Cook, Heppner, & O'Brien, 2002) that this paradigm for career counseling reflects certain assumptions about the nature of career development within a free enterprise system. In the United States, it is commonly believed that occupational success depends primarily on individual initiative within a system that offers everyone equal access to opportunities. The harsh reality is that race, gender, social class, physical attractiveness, ability, and many other variables render success comparatively easy for some and illusory for others. To use the metaphor of the ladder of success: being White, Anglo, well-educated, able-bodied, male, and heterosexual has commonly meant that the bottom ladder rungs are carpeted and relatively easy to climb. For others, discrimination removes the bottom rungs entirely, forcing the person to jump unaided over the gap or remain grounded in subsistence level jobs or unemployment. Movement upward may be possible, but the ladder for these individuals is not constructed the same.

For women and racial and ethnic minorities, the macrosystemic influences can be dramatic. For example, even though the number of women in the labor market has continued to rise, their earning ratios compared with men peaked in 1993 at 77% of men's earnings. More recently, these earning ratios have reversed direction, plateauing at 75% in 1997 (Lewin, 1997). Once in the labor force, women continue to feel the influence of macro-level racism, sexism, and homophobia. For example, Croteau, Anderson, Distefano, and Kampa-Kokesch (2000) found that 25% to 66% of respondents in studies had experienced discrimination at work based on sexual orientation. In one of the largest studies of sexual harassment ever conducted, the Pentagon found that of the 20,000 respondents in their survey, 64% reported having been sexually harassed (Webb, 2001). Thus, although there have been positive changes in our civil rights legislation and in rights aimed at protecting workers, macrosystemic influences are still pervasive and continue to negatively influence the career development patterns of many individuals.

An ecological model of career development places individual choice within the context of a dynamic person–environment interaction, an interaction whose very nature is continually revised by contextual changes and shaped by meaning making. Diversity occupies center stage in an ecological model: Why do some individuals attain career success easily, while their peers seem to stumble on their career path in terms of interests, talents, and background? What factors help to explain why certain groups of people display unique career patterns collectively (e.g., women's home/career blending compared to men) and yet seem so diverse when examined as individuals? Why do various forms of discrimination seem to paralyze the efforts of some and catalyze the efforts of others? What makes a job a reason for living for some yet a declaration of defiance, a pleasant diversion, or a necessary evil for others?

We believe that the ecological perspective offers an integrative view of these puzzling anomalies. What the ecological perspective contributes to person–environment psychology is a renewed emphasis on the centrality of understanding the myriad environmental influences and the dazzling complexity of the person–environment interactions that shape a career path over an individual's lifetime. The ecological model reminds counselors that what is best for a client can be determined only within the unique contexts of his or her life at the present time, and that we must equip clients with the tools to handle the only constant: change.

The philosophy that career choice is the ultimate and appropriate outcome is being called into question (Krieshok, 2002). In a fast-moving labor market, vocational openness and adaptability should be the sought-after outcome rather than choice. Change is the only constant, and yet we engage with our clients as though choice is the ultimate goal. What may have worked quite well at a period in history where individuals made career choices and stayed with those choices for their working lives may not be serving us well in a world of rapid employment change. This contextual factor is critical when counseling the individual and determining whether choice should really be our goal or rather, as Krieshok (2002) argued, promoting an adaptive vocational personality style may help our career clients most.

## An Ecological Perspective on Career Development and Counseling

We have explored facets of ecological career counseling over the past several years, focusing primarily on applications to women, particularly women of color (Cook, Heppner, & O'Brien, 2002, 2003, in press). In this chapter, we organize our discussion around selected features of ecological counseling.

### Ecological Career Counseling Is Metatheoretical and Interdisciplinary

It has long been argued in vocational psychology (e.g., Savickas & Lent, 1994) that no single career theory encompasses all aspects of career development. Using Subich and Taylor's (1994) analogy of a metamap, "different routes may be necessary to apprehend different people's vocational behavior and the obstacles they may encounter" (p. 171). In ecological career counseling, different theories may be needed to explain the micro-, meso-, exo-, and macrosystemic influences on career development. For example, Holland's (1997) theory may help counselors understand the ways in which the client's family influences the development of interests. Social cognitive theory can shed light on societal conditions and values (i.e., macrosystem) that may affect the development of efficacy and outcome expectations. It is also clear that a comprehensive understanding of the labor market demands input from numerous disciplines, including economics, political science, and sociology. Although it is unreasonable to expect career counselors to become experts in all these diverse disciplines, counselors may turn to other experts for insights to broaden their understanding. For example, what long-term impact on the labor market may we expect because of the September 11 terrorist attacks?

## Ecological Career Counseling Is Interactional in Focus

Part of the interactional nature of career development is that career behavior is inseparable from other aspects of a person's life. Super (1980) has been widely credited with introducing this everyday observation into career development theory. For some individuals, work can be a source of personal meaning and close relationships. For others, work provides a paycheck that supports their family. Work influences, and is influenced by, other life roles such as parent, partner, student, and community citizen. How a person perceives self as a gendered/ethnic/ religious/class identified/able or disabled/sexual being is often expressed in career behavior. This recognition of how work and other life domains interact with one another has especially enriched our understanding of the career development of women, who as a group are more likely than men to make career decisions in the context of home and family commitments (Betz, 1994). This understanding of the interconnectedness of myriad influences is also demonstrated in the work of vocational psychologists who proposed career counseling models that account for the interaction of personal, environmental, and cultural factors in vocational interventions (i.e., Fouad & Bingham, 1995; Gysbers, Heppner, & Johnston, 2003; Hansen, 1997; Leong & Hartung, 1997; Leung, 1995).

## Ecological Career Counseling Considers Multiple Contextual Levels

Career behavior is fascinating to analyze because it is an easily observable, classifiable representation of extremely complex person–environment dynamics. By looking at a factual listing of a person's labor market involvement in terms of positions and duties, an astute counselor can often make reasonably accurate guesses about gender, ethnicity, socioeconomic status, education, abilities, values, and personality styles. Yet every counselor knows of times when such hypotheses about a particular person can be off target.

Career behavior at any time is a one-dimensional snapshot of a multidimensional story played out over time. At any point in time, career behavior is shaped by factors at multiple levels: individual, microsystem, mesosystem, exosystem, and macrosystem. At any time, these levels of contextual factors are likely to influence an individual's career path, although some may be much more powerful than others.

Career counselors are likely to find it most helpful to emphasize the person's ecological niche and personally constructed life context (see chapter 1). What contextual factors describe the client's life as he or she currently experiences it? What influences, roles, significant others, or barriers does he or she view as most salient? What important influences appear to be present, but are not recognized by the client?

This explicit focus on multiple contextual levels distinguishes ecological career counseling from traditional person–environment models. For example, one's status of racial identity may drastically affect one's view of life choices. One's sexual orientation may make otherwise interesting career choices seem out of bounds. One's lower class background may make one feel like an imposter, always trying to pass in a career field dominated by the privileged. Instead of examining the client's career behavior as an individual action, an ecological counseling model examines client behaviors as acts-in-context, where the multiple nested layers that comprise the individual's unique ecosystem are studied to determine the role they play in influencing current behavior.

## Ecological Career Counseling Is Concerned With Meaning

Collin and Young (1992) asserted that for many people meaning is "at the heart of career" (p. 12). The familiar paradigm of career counseling that we outlined at the beginning of the chapter reflects an implicit consensus or meaning making among experts about the nature of career and how it can be intentionally shaped. Ideally, career counselors strive to create opportunities for people to find meaning in their work. Career counselors can become dream restorers, helping those who have felt the need to compromise choice for all kinds of contextual reasons. This goal is often addressed through administration of work or life values inventories, fantasy exercises oriented around clarifying central values, focused interviewing, and so on.

In career counseling, changes in clients' meaning-making processes are often crucial to resolution of the career dilemma. Structured inventories (e.g., interest, values) organize bits of clients' self-knowledge into constructs (e.g., creative interests, an artistic personality type) that can be more readily compared with each other. Clients evaluate or attach relative significance to various pieces of information about themselves and job opportunities. Finally, clients decide what is worth doing for fun, financial reward, or perhaps a more transcendent purpose in the context of their lives over time.

In ecological career counseling, the importance of meaning making within career behavior is explicitly recognized. Individual behaviors may reflect meaning making at multiple levels of abstraction, ranging from construals of specific events to life stories reflected in patterns of choices over time (e.g., Savickas, 1997). Throughout life, individuals try to understand the nature and value of their personal qualities; their place in the world at large; rules governing interpersonal interactions, both formal and informal; distinctions among attractive vs. unattractive jobs; work possibilities both available and feasible for "people like me" (however they define that); strategies for handling multiple role responsibilities; and the importance of honoring family, gender-based, religious or ethnic, or other broadly defined criteria for appropriate occupations. In certain work settings or demographic groups, people may develop some general consensus about shared events; however, individuals' personal life goals, prior experiences, and unique interpretations maintain meaning making as an idiosyncratic process (Wicker & August, 2000). Moreover, systemic influences make it difficult for many individuals to have access to jobs that feel meaningful. For much of the population, the meaning attached to work may be survival.

In counseling, we apprehend clients' career dilemmas primarily through how they describe, understand, react to, and perceive opportunities (or not); compare themselves positively or negatively to desired models; conceive of the future as rosy or a dead end; and internalize other individuals' job, gender, class, or racial/ethnic stereotypes as personally salient or dismiss them as irrelevant. Laypersons may mistakenly believe that career counseling somehow transcends irrational thinking by exclusive reliance on psychometric results and employment facts. Instead, how a client perceives and integrates such information with other aspects of his or her life determines its usefulness in the career planning process.

## Ecological Career Counseling Seeks Improved Concordance

Clients typically initiate career counseling when they face a choice that either will transform their current person–environment interactions or will introduce essential new contexts into their lives. Career counselors try to empower clients to maximize their individual and environmental potentials and experience congruence, meaning, and success in their vocational endeavors. This process involves matching and establishing intrapsychic, interpersonal, and environmental congruence (thus extending beyond traditional definitions of congruence; cf. Spokane, 1994).

As noted in earlier chapters, ecological counseling uses the construct of ecological concordance to describe counseling goals. Career counselors implementing this perspective need to be reminded that rarely is the process as simple as matching measured interests, abilities, and values with a corresponding list of occupational requirements. Clients may interpret their test scores in a markedly idiosyncratic manner; act out a life narrative constructed within their family of origin; choose a career consistent with a collectivist worldview characteristic of their culture; need to confront multiple barriers erected by institutionalized discrimination; or fail to find desired job openings because of an economic recession.

In other words, what will accomplish concordance for a person in the world of work may need to be defined uniquely for the individual. Consistent with an ecological metaphor, counselors strive to root the organism in fertile soil with the nutrients it needs to develop over time. Ideally, the developing organism contributes to its surroundings while it thrives. Only human organisms can transplant themselves, however, and participate in determining the manner of their growth patterns. Career counselors can help them envision the range of possibilities open to them, identify and draw on the particular nutrients they need, and affirm the special value of growing within their ecosystem as they experience it. This process is the essence of empowerment within ecological career counseling.

## Ecological Career Counseling Uses a Full Range of Intervention Targets

When intervening with career clients, the ecological perspective seeks to expand the conceptual boundaries of where, and in what manner, career counselors do their work (Blustein & McWhirter, 2000). Thus, career issues are addressed on the individual, institutional, and societal levels. Interventions are aimed at helping the client recognize how various environmental factor levels can create barriers or promote career development. Counselors use diverse methodologies to modify and enhance person–environment interactions and to combat influences that oppress individuals and serve as barriers to their career development. As Cook et al. (2002) discussed, "An ecological perspective reminds counselors that person–environment interactions can be changed in numerous ways for any given client, for example by changing the environment through the counselor's or client's initiative, thereby making systems more helpful or affirming; helping clients identify and practice skills to cope with the environment more effectively; or

228

addressing clients' cognitive processes that shape their transactions with the environment" (p. 297). Thus, the ecological model expands the job description of career counselors and challenges us to be flexible and holistic in our thinking and actions related to empowering clients to achieve concordance and success.

## Case Study

Kathleen is a 29-year-old biracial heterosexual woman who entered counseling because of difficulty finishing her undergraduate degree and selecting a career. Although very intelligent, Kathleen has recently demonstrated a pattern of underachievement in her courses. She indicated that dealing with emotional concerns and family problems prevented her from making timely progress in the completion of her undergraduate degree, which she began about 10 years ago. Kathleen is considering changing her major from communication to education, but she is worried that the requirement for student teaching will delay her graduation even longer. She currently owes the university several thousand dollars, and she is concerned she will not be allowed to enroll in subsequent semesters until she pays her outstanding bills.

Kathleen is the second daughter of three children. She has an older brother who works in a sports equipment retail store and a younger brother who has difficulty keeping jobs and is currently unemployed. Kathleen's mother is Caucasian and in her early 60s. She is employed as an aid in a nursing home and rarely keeps a job for more than 2 years. Kathleen has lived most of her life in poverty, and her mother often moved the family from one location to another.

Kathleen's father (who is African American) divorced her mother shortly after Kathleen's younger brother was born. He has since remarried, graduated from law school, and had two additional children. Kathleen's father has had minimal contact with her and her siblings; she was 8 years old the last time she saw him, when he left their home.

For many years, Kathleen excelled at school. She was bright, learned quickly, and received much attention and praise from teachers. She dreamed of being a doctor and was encouraged by her teachers to pursue a college degree. Kathleen's school counselor arranged for her to receive a scholarship for her first 2 years in college.

Kathleen progressed well during those first 2 years of college and maintained a B+ average in introductory courses. She majored in biology and lived on campus. She made friends easily, but did not become emotionally close to any one person. Kathleen had a series of casual romantic relationships, and never dated anyone for more than 6 months.

After her scholarship ended, Kathleen moved to an inexpensive apartment and began to work full time as a waitress while attending school. Her grades began to fall, and she had difficulty managing work and school demands simultaneously. She changed majors to communications and began to take one or two classes a semester. Recently, Kathleen has begun to have nightmares in which she is following her mother's path of wandering from one job to another. She feels frustrated, since she knows she can succeed in school, but has become overwhelmed by work and by family problems. Kathleen is often drawn in to helping her mother find affordable housing, and her brothers do not assist with this process. Kathleen's mother reminds her that she needs to care for her as she ages, since she alone provided for Kathleen during her childhood. Kathleen harbors much anger toward her father for leaving the family, and yet she has often dreamed that he would return to the family and rescue them from poverty and despair. She feels estranged from the African American community, but at times is drawn to learn more and belong to a group where she could interact more with African Americans. Most African Americans (and others) do not recognize her as the daughter of an African American parent. She often is asked, "What are you?" and is commonly considered to be of Hispanic origin. Her secret dream is to teach kindergarten in a predominantly African American school district. Kathleen acknowledges that she is conflicted about embracing a biracial identity, since her mother consistently makes disparaging remarks about Kathleen's father and the children's African American heritage.

Kathleen entered counseling because she is increasingly worried that she will not complete college, and she is very confused about which career path to pursue. She also indicated that she has difficulty being motivated enough to go to work, get out of bed, or complete minor tasks. Kathleen is afraid of becoming like her mother and wants to make a difference in the lives of neglected children through her work. She indicated that she is scared, lonely, confused, and angry.

## Assessment Questions and Strategies

The Ecological Model of Career Development (Cook et al., 2002) provides a series of nested lenses with which to assess Kathleen's situation. The Ecological Model encourages a creative approach to assessment and interventions informed by the life situation of each client. Each subsystem in the model can be thought of as a different layer which, when uncovered, can help the client and her counselor understand more deeply and fully the various life circumstances that have influenced her career development and choices. The focus on meaning making continually reminds the counselor that how Kathleen perceives and understands these diverse life circumstances is crucial to shaping her responses to them.

It is clear that Kathleen does not experience her present life circumstance as one in which she can develop her career, and she needs help in making and perhaps implementing some career decisions. Consistent with the ecological model presented in chapter 5, the counselor in the assessment phase attends to the following tasks: (a) situate the career problem within Kathleen's life space; (b) elaborate the person–environment interactions implicit in the career problem; and (c) identify resources and challenges relevant in initiating ecosystem change. This analysis should occur at multiple levels of contexts to obtain a complete picture of the issues Kathleen faces. The counselor needs to use ecological empathy to appreciate fully the multiple contexts involved in Kathleen's concerns, and the meaningfulness of these issues to Kathleen. The goal of career counseling is to improve the ecological concordance of Kathleen's life space so it facilitates her continued growth and development as a person. The relevant person–environment interactions should provide her with both support and challenge as she negotiates the career tasks confronting her in the near future.

It seems clear that both assessment and intervention will occur primarily at the individual level, because Kathleen needs assistance in making some decisions for which she has personal responsibility. The counselor recognizes, however, that relevant factors at the group, organizational, and perhaps the community level need to be considered for a complete picture of Kathleen's problem.

The counselor keeps several guiding questions in mind as Kathleen explores her career concerns. What contextual features describe Kathleen's life space as she experiences it? In other words, what does her ecological niche look like to her? The W questions are usually helpful in this regard: Who? What? When? Where? Why (i.e., what do these features mean to her)? What influences does she view as particularly salient? What patterns of meaning might be present? Are there life themes, recurrent attitudes, attributional patterns, and self-concepts, that seem to be reflected in her life as a whole? What influences or patterns are present but implicitly rather than explicitly recognized by Kathleen? Finally, how can all of this ecologically relevant information be integrated into a conceptualization of Kathleen's career dilemma that empowers her to take positive action? What resources can be mobilized and challenges confronted on her behalf?

It appears that Kathleen may be depressed, and the counselor must determine the extent of her depression (e.g., its duration, associated symptoms, and suicidal ideation). The counselor may want to use a formal assessment measure to assess level of depression such as the Brief Symptom Inventory (BSI) (Derogatis, 1993) or the Beck Depression Scale (BDI) (Beck, Rush, Shaw, & Emery, 1979). Kathleen may benefit from medication, or from improving personal health habits that may help her feel better (e.g., sleeping habits, exercise, diet). Depending on the setting in which the counselor works, these issues may be explored more extensively in the counseling relationship, or the counselor may wish to refer Kathleen to a mental health counselor specifically for the depression. However, the counselor is well aware that her depression may abate when the career issues are resolved. The counselor might consider reframing her depression not as a sign of personal weakness but as consistent with how her life as a whole is at this point. Assuming that Kathleen is not in immediate danger from her depression, an ecologically oriented career counselor will present the options and help her decide how she wishes to address this part of her life.

It is important at the outset to ask Kathleen directly about her own understanding of her career issues thus far (meaning making). Why has she made the choices and changes that she did? What combination of personal and environmental issues help explain her career path? Why does she believe she needs expert assistance now? What does she view as her resources and challenges? Ecological career counselors assume that a client's description of her life space is valid, although there are likely to be some processes operating outside the client's awareness or meaning-making capacities. The client's perceptions may be changed as a consequence of counseling, but the perceptions are honored as representing the reality in which the client currently lives (life space).

A career counselor will note that career indecision and floundering are quite common for individuals of Kathleen's age, although by the age of 30, young adults are typically in the process of implementing some (often provisional) choice. Kathleen obviously has some anxiety about timing, although it is not clear why. Does she feel she is off the social clock of her peers? Does she feel some pressure from others or from within to make these commitments? Is she simply tired of being in a transitive phase? The counselor will wonder why she is a bit off schedule. Does she have the necessary knowledge of self and the world of work, and the career decision-making skills important for making sound decisions?

As is true in any career counseling, it is important to address Kathleen's work experiences and relationships. What aspects of Kathleen's current job are satisfying? How would she change her job to improve her satisfaction with work and her productivity? The counselor will want to assess her understanding of her interests, abilities, values, and decision-making skills using some combination of structured inventories and interview techniques. For example, Kathleen might benefit from an interest inventory, a fantasy exercise to clarify job relevance or broader life values, or various interview questions (cf. Brown & Brooks, 1991; Gysbers et al., 2003, and others for career exploration strategies). The counselor is aware that such exploration can help alleviate Kathleen's depression and anxiety, and serves as a career intervention as well as assessment.

Such career exploration is likely to be necessary but not sufficient for Kathleen. Ecological counselors remember that individuals function as integrated beings, and distinctions between career and non-career issues are frequently illusory and misleading. Kathleen provides many clues that her career issues are—as they are for many clients— inseparable from pervasive life issues, and that these issues must also be addressed in resolving Kathleen's presenting career concerns.

Kathleen seems to be struggling with key identity issues concerning race, gender, and perhaps also class. These core identity issues are intensely personal meaning-making matters for Kathleen, but they are strongly influenced by family and other relationships (microsystem) and broader societal (macrosystem) patterns of domination, power, and discrimination.

Kathleen directly acknowledges her struggles with racial identity. In terms of race, Kathleen does not know who she is, where she belongs, and what it means to her life. These struggles are linked to Kathleen's relationships in multiple contexts. Her mother, who raised her as a single parent, is contemptuous of half of Kathleen's genetic heritage. Kathleen has probably internalized some of her mother's attitudes in the form of self-hatred, yet she also longs to reconcile this part of herself. It appears that Kathleen has had little contact with African Americans who might have helped her embrace this half of her heritage; the counselor may want to confirm this. As a role model, her father is both negative (because of his abandonment of his children) and positive (because of his educational and career success). Conversely, Kathleen seems to love her mother, but wants to avoid her mother's erratic and marginal job history. These mixed messages about parents are extremely difficult to reconcile, especially since Kathleen's father is not physically present for her to conduct any reality testing of her idealized perceptions about him.

The counselor will also wonder about other contributors to Kathleen's racial identity issues. What were the race, attitudes, and behaviors of significant others in her past? Was she a minority in her schools and neighborhoods? Did others affirm, disparage, or ignore her as a biracial person? It seems as though Kathleen's true identity has been invisible to others who misidentified her as Hispanic. The counselor will wonder if the theme of invisibility might also apply to other areas of Kathleen's life (life pattern).

Ecological career counselors understand that racial identity development may play a role in finding, selecting, and succeeding in a satisfying career (Robinson & Howard-Hamilton, 2000). Clarifying the impact of this issue may be important to Kathleen's career development. Multicultural texts (e.g., Helms & Cook, 1999) provide counselors much useful information about racial identity development. Formal assessment using such instruments as the Colorblind Racial Attitudes Scale (CoBRAS) (Neville, Lilly, Duran, Lee, & Browne, 2000) or Swartz and Martin's (1999) Cultural and Contextual Guide Process may be useful in helping Kathleen assess her own recognition of racism. Kathleen may also find it enlightening to read about biracial individuals and their struggles to find their own place in a world that typically assigns individuals a particular status based on race.

There are hints that macro-based issues related to gender and class may also be important for Kathleen. She may have internalized broad social expectations for women to serve as caretakers, an expectation that complicates her efforts to reconcile her career aspirations with her mother's expectation that Kathleen as her daughter will take care of her. She has also abandoned a challenging, traditionally male-dominated career choice of physician in favor of more traditional options for women. It will be important to assess whether her perceptions and experiences of herself as a woman have influenced her career path thus far. In addition, Kathleen has been living in poverty and may very well have internalized classist macrobased attitudes about appropriate roles and aspirations for people in her social class. Promising new assessment measures (e.g., The Social Class Attitude Scale—Patterson, 2001) may provide formal assessment of these attitudes.

Informal assessments, such as simply asking about the role macro-level racism, sexism, and classism have played in Kathleen's life, may also be fruitful. A racial/cultural career genogram (Gysbers et al., 2003) can encourage Kathleen to clarify how race/gender may have shaped the career development of generations on both sides of her family. These and other assessment strategies affirm potentially empowering insights for Kathleen concerning, for example, macrofactors that have been an important part of her ecosystem and that may have had a profound effect on both the real structure of opportunity open to her as well as her internal view of that structure. Finally, through awareness, she can make decisions about how she will deal with these influences in the future.

Throughout the interview, the counselor will pay attention to Kathleen's interactions with important individuals. Kathleen's father clearly has been an extremely powerful part of her life space, even though he has not been physically present for years. Her relationship with her mother is also likely to influence her career development in upcoming years. Can Kathleen look to her for support, or must Kathleen be prepared to deal with emotional roadblocks from her mother? Will her brothers likewise serve as resources or challenges? How does she compare herself to them? It appears that her precollege education was characterized by particularly positive ecological concordance. Has she enjoyed such support and validation from any school personnel since then? What blatant or subtle messages has she received from teachers, peers, or staff about her ability to succeed?

We know from a host of research that the most consistent predictor of staying in college and doing well is connection with an adult, usually a faculty or staff member. To what degree has Kathleen encountered a null environment (Freeman, 1975), where her progress is neither encouraged nor discouraged? Particularly for individuals who are courageously trying a path new to their family, race, or gender, a null environment essentially functions as discouragement.

The counselor will also want to explore other diverse features of her environment. Financial problems have posed a real challenge to her education. What other options has she explored (grants, loans)? She also does not report many supportive, enduring relationships in her life thus far, whether friendships or romantic relationships. How might the presence or absence of these relationships shed light on the person she has become? Such relationships can also provide an important base of support for career and general life exploration in the adult years, and certainly are relevant as factors involved in her depression. Does she belong to a church, neighborhood group, or hobby club? All can serve as resources in future life changes.

Also of importance seems to be an internal examination of the challenges Kathleen faces in managing the multiple roles of worker and student. Kathleen's progress in college apparently was seriously undermined by her need to work full time to support herself. The challenges (and rewards) of balancing multiple roles will be useful to understand. Moreover, advocacy to assist Kathleen in obtaining sound financial advice and help in managing her loans and expenses may also be necessary.

Although the ecologically based counselor works to empower the client to accomplish as much of this work on his or her own as possible, the counselor also must recognize the important advocacy role that often is necessary in helping to obtain appropriate resources for clients who might not be used to assertively seeking these services on their own.

Kathleen's counselor will wonder about pervasive life themes or patterns of meaning that may be expressed in how she understands her life and makes choices within her life space. Such patterns are likely to recur in the future. With help, Kathleen can learn how to express these in productive and satisfying rather than self-defeating ways. She can also learn to replace these patterns with other methods of experiencing her life (Savickas, 1997). The counselor will wonder whether Kathleen experiences her real self as invisible and possibly unlovable—her race, her skills, her dreams. She may need to learn ways of revealing herself to the outside world, safely testing how others will accept her. It will be important to determine whether her earlier dream of becoming a physician reflected her own interests or a goal set by others in school whose approval was so life-giving to her. Which of her career choices—physician, communication, or teaching—represents her unique self? How can that self be affirmed and nurtured?

In addition, Kathleen may feel herself a misfit, caught between two worlds and two unresolvable choices. She may feel that she must choose to be her mother or her father, Black or White, responsible for family or successful at work. Resolution of her impasse may require her to affirm that she can become the best of both worlds, her own unique blending of possibilities.

## Interventions

Ecological career counseling can use the full range of career interventions already familiar to career counseling, including interpretation of inventories, teaching and practice of career-relevant skills, gathering occupational information from a variety of sources (e.g., literature, interviews, the Internet). It should be clear, however, that career counseling may also involve exploration and resolution of many issues generally addressed in counseling, including emotional, interpersonal, and self-identity issues. For example, it seems crucial for Kathleen to explore and resolve the myriad feelings she has toward her father. Helping her decide whether and how to reconnect with him may free her to make career decisions uncomplicated by her father-daughter relationship.

The ecological counselor also recognizes that clients may need assistance in exiting present environments, or in locating or enhancing more

236

desirable environments. Kathleen, for example, may decide to find a job more directly relevant to longer term career interests, or one that provides direct support for continuation of her education through flexible scheduling or tuition remission. Joining a biracial discussion group or a counseling group may provide Kathleen with the opportunity to talk with others about her feelings and assuage her loneliness. She may become involved in activities sponsored by the African American student association on campus. The counselor may even help Kathleen obtain assistance in finding housing for her mother, by connecting her with appropriate human service agencies.

Vocational researchers (Gysbers et al., 2003; Savickas, 1997) are increasingly encouraging career counselors to assist clients in identifying how they find meaning in their lives. Assisting Kathleen in determining what is meaningful about her life, and helping her to develop the tools and resources to pursue meaningful life and work roles, is central to the success of vocational interventions with Kathleen. The counselor and Kathleen could work together to identify some changes in her life that ultimately will support the career and life space where she not only could be happy but also productive in satisfying ways and hopeful about her future.

## Training Implications of the Ecological Model

Recently, Swanson and O'Brien (2003) provided suggestions for how training programs in counseling psychology could improve their training so career counselors can better meet the challenges of diverse clients in the 21st century. Many of their suggestions are consistent with the methods needed to apply an ecological model of vocational interventions in work with clients like Kathleen, who need more than a trait-factor-matching approach to career counseling. Specifically, Swanson and O'Brien advocated for a multicultural, contextual, holistic, and ecological approach to training career counselors. To facilitate this type of training, these authors proposed that graduate programs use an integrative approach in training such that career-related training opportunities are infused throughout the curriculum. Career counselors must be skilled in basic and advanced helping skills so they can address the complexity of issues facing career clients today. For example, Kathleen needs a counselor who can listen well, administer and interpret a range of assessment tools, address the intrapsychic and interpersonal core issues confronting her, be multiculturally skilled and gender and class aware, and be able to make appropriate recommendations for community resources.

Historically, career counselors have been trained to intervene at the individual level with consideration of the micro- and macrosystems influencing the client. It is imperative the counselors understand the role of race/ethnicity, gender, and class in career development. In addition, career counselors should be trained to extend beyond the traditional method of career counseling to directly intervene in the micro- and macrosystems. For example, counseling students might be trained to work with clients like Kathleen and her mother in several sessions to begin to process unresolved issues. This counselor should have confidence in intervening in Kathleen's microsystem by connecting her with community resources and helping her to build supportive networks. Group counselors working with Kathleen (or similar clients) could receive instruction in how they might encourage the group microsystem to exert positive feedback and motivational support related to difficulty completing college, deciding on a career, and taking responsibility for future life choices.

The training of career counselors might also address macrosystemic influences in which career counselors work for social change (Fassinger & O'Brien, 2000), confront unhealthy messages promulgated from society and the media, and encourage clients to address inequities in larger academic, work, and social environments. Career counselors can serve as role models in working to change oppressive systems by serving on boards and committees that foster social justice.

## Conclusion

The ecological approach to career counseling asks a great deal of the counselor. No longer is it simply enough to be knowledgeable about interest inventories, career information, and the world of work (and we would argue that this was rarely so). The ecological model requires a large repertoire of skills that can be used creatively and flexibly. The ecological counselor is likely to continue to be in training, learning how to intervene effectively at all levels of the ecosystem. Only then can counselors be certain to maximize their ability to apply the ecological model of career counseling to assist clients in living full and meaningful lives.

## Learning Activities

1. Write your own career autobiography from an ecological perspective. What ecological factors and processes have influenced your own career development thus far? What role has personal

meaning making played? What might influence how your career develops in the future?

2. As noted in the chapter, career counseling often follows a brief, three-step process using interviewing, standardized assessment measures, and summative test interpretation with recommendations for action. What if Kathleen's counselor had used this brief model rather than the ecological perspective described here? Compare the possible process and outcome of career counseling for Kathleen using both approaches. How might Kathleen have reacted to each approach?

3. Choosing one service delivery system (e.g., in schools or employee assistance programs), discuss how an ecological perspective might change the way career counseling is conducted there. What must happen for such changes to take place? Do you think such changes are desirable and feasible? Why or why not?

## References

Beck, A. T., Rush, A. J., Shaw, B. F., & Emery, G. (1979). *Cognitive therapy of depression*. New York: Guilford Press.

Betz, N. E. (1994). Basic issues and concepts in career counseling for women. In W. B. Walsh & S. H. Osipow (Eds.), *Career counseling for women* (pp. 1–42). Hillsdale, NJ: Erlbaum.

Blustein, D. L., & McWhirter, E. H. (2000, August). Toward an emancipatory communitarian approach to career development theory. In N. A. Fouad (Chair), *Building the next stage of career development: New theoretical innovations*. Symposium conducted at the annual convention of the American Psychological Association, Washington, DC.

Bronfenbrenner, U. (1977). Toward an experimental ecological of human development. *American Psychologist, 32*, 513–531.

Brown, D., & Brooks, L. (1991). *Career counseling techniques*. Boston: Allyn & Bacon.

Cook, E. P., Heppner, M. J., & O'Brien, K. M. (2002). Career development of women of color and White women: Assumptions, conceptualizations, and interventions from an ecological perspective. *The Career Development Quarterly, 50*, 291–305.

Cook, E. P., Heppner, M. J., & O'Brien, K. M. (2003). Multicultural and gender influences in women's career development: An ecological perspective. In S. Niles (Ed.), *Adult career development: Concepts, issues, and practices* (pp. 169–189). Tulsa, OK: National Career Development Association.

Cook, E. P., Heppner, M. J., & O'Brien, K M. (in press). Feminism and women's career development: An ecological perspective. *Journal of Multicultural Counseling and Development*.

Croteau, J. M., Anderson, M. Z., Distefano, T. M., & Kampa-Kokesch, S. (2000). Lesbian, gay, and bisexual vocational psychology: Reviewing foundations and planning construction. In R. M. Perez, & K. A. DeBord (Eds.), *Handbook of counseling and psychotherapy with lesbian, gay, and bisexual clients* (pp. 383–408). Washington, DC: American Psychological Association.

Dawis, R. (2000). The person-environment tradition in counseling psychology. In W. Martin, Jr., & J. Swartz-Kulstad (Eds.), *Person-environment psychology and mental health: Assessment and intervention* (pp. 91–111). Mahwah, NJ: Erlbaum.

Derogatis, L. R. (1993). *The Brief Symptom Inventory (BSI): Administration, scoring, and procedures manual-III.* Minneapolis: National Computer Systems.

Fassinger, R. E., & O'Brien, K. M. (2000). Career counseling with college women: A scientist-practitioner-advocate model of intervention. In D. A. Luzzo (Ed.), *Career development of college students: Translating theory and research into practice* (pp. 253–265). Washington, DC: American Psychological Association.

Fouad, N. A., & Bingham, R. (1995). Career counseling with racial/ethnic minorities. In W. B. Walsh & S. H. Osipow (Eds.), *Handbook of vocational psychology* (2nd ed., pp. 331–366). Hillsdale, NJ: Erlbaum.

Freeman, J. (1975). How to discriminate against women without really trying. In J. Freeman (Ed.), *Women: A feminist perspective* (pp. 194–208). Palo Alto, CA: Mayfield.

Gottfredson, L. S. (1981). Circumscription and compromise: A developmental theory of occupational aspirations. *Journal of Counseling Psychology, 28,* 545–579.

Gysbers, N. C., Heppner, M. J., & Johnston, J. A. (2003). *Career counseling: Process, issues, and techniques.* Boston: Allyn & Bacon.

Hansen, L. S. (1997). *Integrative life planning: Critical tasks for career development and changing life patterns.* San Francisco: Jossey-Bass.

Helms, J. E., & Cook, D. A. (1999). *Using race and culture in counseling and psychotherapy: Theory and process.* Boston: Allyn & Bacon.

Holland, J. L. (1997). *Making vocational choices.* Odessa, FL: Psychological Assessment Resources.

Krieshok, T. S. (2002). *The postmodern virtues of being an undecided major.* Unpublished manuscript, University of Kansas.

Krumboltz, J. D. (1998). Serendipity is not serendipitous. *Journal of Counseling Psychology, 45,* 390–392.

Lent, R. W., Brown, S. D., & Hackett, G. (1994). Toward a unifying social cognitive theory of career and academic interest, choice, and performance. *Journal of Vocational Behavior, 45,* 79–122.

Leong, F. T. L., & Hartung, P. J. (1997). Career assessment with culturally different clients: Proposing an integrative-sequential conceptual framework for cross-cultural career counseling research and practice. *Journal of Career Assessment, 5,* 183–201.

Leung, S. A. (1995). Career development and counseling: A multicultural perspective. In J. G. Ponterotto, J. M. Casas, L. A. Suzuki, & C. M. Alexander (Eds.),

*Handbook of multicultural counseling* (pp. 549–566). Thousand Oaks, CA: Sage.

Lewin, T. (1997, September 15). Women losing ground to men in widening income difference [Electronic version]. *New York Times*, pp. A1, A12.

Neville, H. A. Lilly, R. I., Duran G., Lee, R. M., & Browne, L. (2000). Construction and initial validation of the Color-Blind Racial Attitudes Scale (CoBRAS). *Journal of Counseling Psychology, 47*, 59–70.

Patterson, E. (2001). *The development of the Social Class Attitudes Scale (SCAS): Instrument construction and estimates of reliability and validity.* Unpublished doctoral dissertation, University of Missouri, Columbia.

Robinson, T. L., & Howard-Hamilton, M. F. (2000). *The convergence of race, identity, and gender: Multiple identities in counseling.* Columbus, OH: Merrill.

Savickas, M. L. (1997). The spirit in career counseling: Fostering self-completion through work. In D. P. Bloch & L. Richmond (Eds.), *Connections between spirit and work in career development* (pp. 3–25). Palo-Alto, CA: Davies-Black.

Savickas, M. L., & Lent, R. W. (Eds.). (1994). *Convergence in career development theories.* Palo Alto, CA: CPP Books.

Spokane, A. R. (1994). The resolution of incongruence and the dynamics of person–environment fit. In M. L. Savickas & R. W. Lent (Eds.), *Convergence in career development theories* (pp. 119–135). Palo Alto, CA: CPP Books.

Subich, L. M., & Taylor, K. M. (1994). Emerging directions of social learning theory. In M. L. Savickas & R. W. Lent (Eds.), *Convergence in career development theories* (pp. 167–175). Palo Alto, CA: CPP Books.

Super, D. E. (1980). A life-span, life-space approach to career development. *Journal of Vocational Behavior, 16*, 292–298.

Super, D. E. (1990). A life-span, life-space approach to career development. In D. Brown, L. Brooks, & Associates (Eds.), *Career choice and development* (2nd ed.). San Francisco: Jossey-Bass.

Swanson, J. L., & Fouad, N. A. (1999). *Career theory and practice: Learning through case studies.* Thousand Oaks, CA: Sage.

Swanson, J. L., & O'Brien, K. M. (2003). Training career counselors: Meeting the challenges of clients in the 21st century. In S. Niles (Ed.), *Adult career development: Concepts, issues, and practices* (pp. 351–366). Tulsa, OK: National Career Development Association.

Swartz-Kulstad, J. L., & Martin, W. E., Jr. (1999). Impact of culture and context on psychosocial adaptation: The cultural and contextual guide process. *Journal of Counseling & Development, 77*, 281–293.

Webb, S. L. (2001). History of sexual harassment on the job. In L. Lemoncheck & J. P. Sterba (Eds.), *Sexual harassment: Issues and answers.* Oxford, United Kingdom: Oxford University Press.

Wicker, A. W., & August, R. A. (2000). Working lives in context: Engaging the views of participants and analysts. In W. B. Walsh, K. H. Craik, & R. H. Price (Eds.), *Person-environment psychology: New directions and perspectives* (pp. 197–232). Mahwah, NJ: Erlbaum.

Chapter 10

# The Ecology of Community and Agency Counseling: An Administrator's Perspective

*William O'Connell and Alan Mabry*

---

*Chapter Highlights*

- *Historical events have helped shape the landscape of community counseling.*
- *Managed care has had the greatest impact on counselor functioning.*
- *An ecological counselor understands the interaction of multiple systems of influence on the counseling relationship.*
- *Counselor training must foster proficiency in understanding agency management and skills to function and thrive in a complex behavioral health system.*

---

As we consider ecological interventions in counseling, we are aware that the client and the counselor each bring an ecological history to the counseling process (Blocher, 1981; Volker, 1994). Conversely, the service delivery system surrounding the counseling relationship also brings an ecological history and context to the process (Gladding, 1997; Liddle, 1995; Myer, 2001; Yank, Barber, & Spradlin, 1994). The counseling process is born from the reciprocal communication between the ecological domains of the client and the counselor, the coproviders of service, and the service delivery environment (Blocher, 1981; Bronfenbrenner, 1979; Conyne, 1985; Gopaul-McNicol, 1997; Henggeler & Borduin, 1990; Munger, 1997).

In our view, counselors and human service providers have historically become experts in the nature of counseling, yet often lack awareness of the environment surrounding the counseling relationship (Blocher, 1981; Mowbray & Holter, 2002; Warnath, 1977). The counselor and client are embedded in a complex service delivery matrix that influences every detail of the counseling process. Counseling cannot be understood apart from these relationships and the multiple domains that influence counseling (Boyd-Franklin, 2001; Conyne, 1985; Gopaul-McNicol, 1997; Henggeler & Borduin, 1990; Van Voorhis, Braswell, & Morrow, 1997). It is our experience that community counselors have not been trained to think in an ecological, multisystemic context. In this chapter, we first examine the historical backdrop linking the service delivery environment with counselor behavior and then an ecological model for increasing counselor efficiency and reducing counselor burnout. We also summarize counselor competencies to practice as an ecological community counselor and evaluate a case study.

## History of Community Counseling

Since passage of the Community Mental Health Act in 1963, professional counselors have provided services in myriad treatment settings to prevent and intervene in major social problems (Gladding, 1997). While the number of community counselors burgeoned in the late 1960s and early 1970s, several movements transformed the service delivery landscape: (a) government funding of community mental health centers; (b) the growth of grassroots advocacy groups on behalf of people with mental illness; (c) the evolution of managed care in behavioral health services; (d) political division in obtaining parity for mental health; and (e) the use of technology in mental health care administration.

### Government Funding of Community Mental Health Centers

In the 1950s, the psychiatric, psychological, social work, and counseling professions began advocating for the deinstitutionalization of people with mental illness who might thrive in society with outpatient assistance (Mowbray & Holter, 2002). Many mental health professionals believed that institutionalization deterred recovery for many clients diagnosed with mental illness (Gladding, 1997; Mowbray & Holter, 2002). In addition, because of the introduction of new psychotropic medications, some medical professionals and quite a few public health administrators were confident that people diagnosed with mental illness could function independently (Visotsky, 1993). The Community Mental Health Act of 1963 dispersed federal funds to establish programs to serve people who are mentally disturbed and mentally disabled. Funding was also set aside to train practitioners serving this at-risk population.

Government funding of community mental health centers ignited the community counseling profession. Federal and state assistance fueled enthusiasm to train and hire counselors to work with people who are mentally ill and mentally disabled in outpatient settings. Some historians, however, believe that many counselor education programs in the 1960s and early 1970s were ill prepared to effectively train counselors to work with a transient, ethnically diverse, and high-risk population (Blocher, 1981; Warnath, 1977). Most counselor education programs based training on psychodynamic and human growth theories. These theoretical approaches may have been helpful for mental health clients living in long-term care facilities, but they were inadequate for the typical outpatient client. Because of the mismatch between this new population and traditional approaches, counselors began to discuss ecological theory and multisystemic approaches that considered clients in the context of their environment as opposed to the client's intrapsychic needs and feelings (Blocher, 1981; Bronfenbrenner, 1979; Conyne, 1985). For example, Salvador Minuchin pioneered strategies for improving counseling services to poor, urban families. He opposed traditional child psychiatry and believed that home-based therapy was more likely to effect change than treatment in a clinic. Minuchin reasoned that a child is best understood according to the complex network of relationships in his or her family (Minuchin, 1967; Nichols & Schwartz, 2001).

Despite these early critiques of counselor training and the use of psychodynamic- and growth-oriented approaches, counselors typically continued to work in an environment in which the type of treatment clients received depended on the counselor's personal preferences (Mowbray & Holter, 2002). In other words, counselor practice was not guided by research into best practice approaches. Clients, therefore, may have suffered from ineffective intervention, while counselors may have suffered from the frustration of being ineffective (Blocher, 1981; Lawless, Ginter, & Kelly, 1999; Warnath, 1977).

The launch of government funding of community mental health centers and the subsequent effect on counselor and client relationships is critical in understanding the current emphasis on best practice approaches to the treatment of people who are mentally ill. As Kaplan (2002) stated, "mono-theoretical approaches gave way to eclecticism, then to technical eclecticism, whereby counselors utilize a theoretical approach aimed to best serve an individual client." Counseling and human services research is now aimed at discovering which theoretical approaches have the highest efficacy when considering multiple factors, such as type of disorder, gender, cultural background, and available resources (Lloyd, 2000; Mee-Lee, 2000; Messina, 1999). Professional community counseling has evolved into a complex but necessary service to prevent and treat mental illness.

## Grassroots Advocacy for People Who Are Mentally Ill

In the 1970s, community-based mental health practitioners found themselves responding to deinstitutionalization with innovative but clinically unproven programming (Mowbray & Holter, 2002). Poor programming may have proved frustrating for clients and counselors, yet those experiencing the impact of deinstitutionalization firsthand were client families. The most prominent grassroots organization to emerge in response to concern for the care of people who are mentally ill and mentally disabled was the National Alliance for the Mentally Ill (NAMI). In 1979, 234 family members started NAMI; currently, approximately 70,000 families in the United States claim affiliation. NAMI provides emotional support and education to family members of people who are mentally ill while advocating in the political arena and sponsoring research aimed at eradicating mental illness. The members of NAMI are passionate about improving the quality of care for people who are mentally ill. In fact, the organization awards more than $1 million annually in research grants (Flynn, 1989).

The energy unleashed by members of NAMI and similar advocacy groups (e.g., the National Mental Health Association) is critical to the historical backdrop of current community mental health practices. NAMI and its political allies began to unite to encourage government support for maintaining quality care for people who are mentally ill while preserving the autonomy of the mental health client. Historically, some community counseling centers relied completely on government funding, such as Medicaid and Medicare, to operate. When government funds were transformed to block grants to states in the 1980s, some community counseling centers closed their doors due to a complete loss in funding for operations.

This vulnerability still occurs today. Many counseling agencies face uncertain futures given the ebb and flow of monetary resources. Grassroots organizations advocating for people who are mentally ill have taught counselors that it is impossible to commit to working with this population without stomping the streets to gain support for services. The expectation that someone else will do it leaves the client at risk of losing services and the counselor at risk of losing his or her job. Successful community mental health centers work at creating a team environment based on the social advocacy model witnessed in organizations such as NAMI (Messina, 1999; Welfel, 2002; Yelton, 1989).

## Managed Care and Service Delivery

The competing forces between an increase in the demand for counseling-related services and rising health care costs helped launch managed care (Lloyd, 2000; Mee-Lee, 2000). The implementation of managed care in both the private and public sector has had the most significant impact on behavioral health care of any development in the past 20 years. Among myriad important changes are (a) less inpatient and more outpatient care; (b) shortened intensive treatment episodes; (c) an increase in performance utilization reviews; (d) a decrease in reimbursement for services; and (e) an increase in accountability, responsibility, and risk for the provision of behavioral health care (Mee-Lee, 2000).

In many ways, managed care has been helpful (Lawless et al., 1999; Smitson, 2001). Mental health care is available in communities where clients live rather than distant institutions. Managed care has forced providers to measure and achieve positive outcomes, reduce waste, and adopt best practice care models (Smith, 1999). Clients are more likely to receive treatment targeted at resolving presenting problems than in the past, when outpatient treatment was provided based on a counselor's personal theoretical model. From one perspective, the lives of clients and families are less disrupted now.

Managed care models may not work as well for people who are chronically mentally ill, however, since behavioral health care benefits have been reduced in order to protect physical health care benefits and to offset increasing costs for high tech treatment (Danzinger & Welfel, 2001; Lawless et al., 1999). Residential care and case management are costly services often left out of managed care plan designs. Funding for community counseling centers has noticeably declined (Lloyd, 2000; Smitson, 2001).

Many mental health professionals and mental health consumers have blamed the managed care system for creating a landscape that emphasizes profitability over quality of care. From the perception of direct service staff, problems include numerous forms to complete, lack of adequate compensation for services, inconsistent rules for continuing client care, and the belief that persons in management and administration are impersonal and uncaring individuals. The bifurcation between care providers and administration presents an ongoing challenge to community mental health agencies (Smitson, 2001). The negative perceptions of managed care that counselors hold risk being transferred to clients. In turn, clients may be burdened with problems of the counselor and the agency in addition to their presenting issues.

## Politics of Mental Health Parity and Health Care Integration

A major stumbling block to the care continuum for mental health clients in the United States today is the lack of parity between reimbursement for general health care, mental health care (behavioral health care), and chemical dependency treatment. Continuum of care refers to the natural progression from intensive dependent levels of care (e.g., residential treatment, day treatment) to independent levels of care (e.g., outpatient and aftercare). Behavioral health care has become a low priority in terms of funding policies compared to general health care, while the demand for behavioral health care has increased at a rate exceeding general health care (Smith, 1999).

Parity is important to the prevention of medical illnesses and to controlling primary health care costs. Research has demonstrated the benefits of behavioral health care in reducing stress, anxiety, and poor health practices that contribute to the onset of major medical illnesses (Dorfman & Smith, 2002). The federal government is examining the efficacy of integrating physical health, behavioral health, and substance abuse treatment through Medicaid and Medicare funding. This means agencies would support general medical and behavioral health under one roof. Such an experiment may increase parity; however, the organizational processes to achieve integration are complex.

From another perspective, parity offsets the burden of primary health care for employers and consumers. The Mental Health Parity Act of 1996 requires parity, but the law is limited to large employers and does not stipulate the type and quality of accessible care for the insured. For many mental health consumers who do not qualify for public assistance, mental health care treatment must be paid for out-of-pocket.

Counselors need to be aware of the stigma attached to mental illness in society today. If society fails to acknowledge the need to care for people who are mentally ill, then it is unlikely that voters will approve increases in monies aimed at improving services. Counselors can help advance the ongoing battle for parity by demonstrating to the community that behavioral health counseling works.

## Impact of Technology on the Field of Community Counseling

Advances in technology have fueled rapid changes in American and global society. Counseling agencies are quickly adopting technology to manage and reduce operational costs. Agencies have developed computerized databases and are implementing computerized clinical files. The increases in the availability of data drive the demand for information by those in the larger treatment environment. Funding sources, both public and private, now want and demand information from providers. This information is used to justify reimbursement for services as well as help politicians secure funding for public mental health services. For some funding sources, the more information available, the better.

The demand for information means counselors are now expected to have a basic set of computer skills (CACREP, 2001). Today, technology is essential to effective record keeping, accurate billing reports, compilation of outcome data, and maintenance of corporate compliance records. If counselors do not possess these basic skills, they are often overwhelmed in the work setting. Counselors must be experts at obtaining as much information and history from clients as possible. It is common for counselors to be trained in the use of one assessment and learn that the assessment is outdated within weeks. Many new counselors become angry and disillusioned at this point. Administrators, of course, need to decrease repetitive documentation and unnecessary workloads. Counselors, however, need to become competent in using basic technology to meet the demands of the modern workplace.

## Summary

This overview of historical trends helps the reader envision the inextricable link between counselor behavior and the service delivery environment. Events have led to the evolution of best practices, political advocacy for mental health, corporate compliance standards, outcome-oriented treatment services, and competition to maintain funding for services. As stated, the counselor, client, and service delivery environment each bring an ecological history to the counselor–client relationship. It is impossible to shield the counselor and client from the impact of decisions and processes made by agency administrators and the larger service delivery environment. Examining the network of relationships in the behavioral health service field helps the counselor understand his or her professional role.

## The Ecology of the Community Mental Health Agency

Funding sources, administrators, and counselors need to understand the responsibilities and challenges of one another's roles in order to appreciate fully the counseling business. Community counseling is an industry whose customer base is the funding source providing the monetary resources to fulfill a specific mission in the community. The agency and counselor play a role in continuing that mission by meeting the demands of the corporate environment and finding ways to increase quality, decrease redundancy, and increase efficiency in the delivery of services.

At the macrolevel, funding sources and philanthropic groups assess and identify needs in local communities. These funding sources then develop strategic plans to initiate or sustain services that help meet community expectations. Depending on the funding source, a public or private regulatory body is appointed to monitor efforts to achieve the mission defined by the funding source. It does this by establishing compliance standards for delivering services in a community. State or local agencies contract with the government or private foundation with the promise to use funds to meet the funding source's mission. Agencies build the physical operation and infrastructure to set this mission in stone. Finally, at the microlevel, direct service providers contract to provide counseling services to clients in the community and help fulfill the mission. Decisions made at the macrolevel impact behavior at the microlevel. Behavior at the microlevel eventually filters back to decisions made at the macrolevel. This concept is key to an ecological approach (Bronfenbrenner, 1979, 1995).

To illustrate the complex nature of the modern counseling context, we have adapted Carter and McGoldrick's (1989) family life stressor model (see Figure 10.1), which we have renamed "The Ecology of the Counselor–Client Relationship." In the center of the diagram, the first system consists of the counselor–client relationship, the coproviders of service, and the different philosophies regarding treatment. The system immediately surrounding this relationship is the community agency, its mission, administrative organization, and monetary resources. The third system involves those organizations that regulate the practice of counseling at the state level—organizations that audit direct care providers and grant sources. This third system of regulatory bodies and funding sources is driven by cultural and political attitudes in society.

In the model, vertical and horizontal stressors influence multiple domains. Vertical stressors are the patterns of relating and functioning that bring past and present issues to bear reciprocally, including attitudes, expectations, legacies, and unresolved conflicts. These stressors are historical and inherited from previous generations (Gladding, 2002). They are the knapsack a counselor carries into the counselor–client relationship. Horizontal stressors are the demands placed on a system as it moves through time, including normative and nonnormative events (Gladding, 2002). Horizontal stressors are the obstacles a counselor may encounter, or run into, while working for a community agency.

Counselor education programs can prepare counselors to cope with vertical stressors in a number of ways. For instance, counselor educators may teach agency management and finance, clinical best practice

# Figure 10.1

# The Ecology of the Counselor–Client Relationship

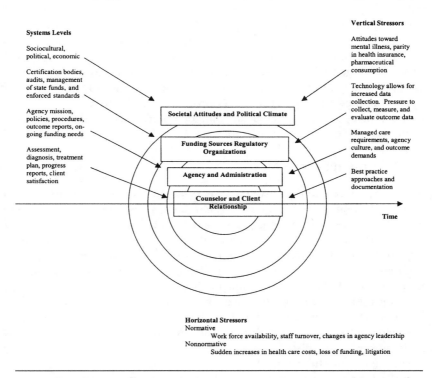

*Note.* From *The Expanded Family Life Cycle: Individual, Family, and Social Perspectives* (3rd ed.), by B. Carter and M. McGoldrick, 1999. Copyright © 1999 by Pearson Education. Adapted with permission.

approaches, electronic data entry, needs assessment, and grant writing strategies. In other words, counselors in training have the opportunity to learn what is in the knapsack prior to beginning work at a community agency. It is much more challenging to prepare counselors for the horizontal stressors, especially the nonnormative stressors they may face in their career (e.g., termination of funding contracts and potential job loss). By discussing some of the more contentious issues in community counseling today, the reader will learn how funding sources, agency administration, counselors, and clients interact reciprocally to meet the challenges of vertical and horizontal stressors.

The most exigent issues facing the community counselor today are issues regarding documentation, reporting outcome data, and meeting utilization rates. These issues are vertical stressors resulting from historical developments over time. When these issues are ignored or mishandled by funding and regulatory sources, agency administrators, or direct service providers, the consequences may include nonnormative horizontal stressors such as sudden loss of funding or damaging litigation against an agency. We address each of these vertical stressors, while simultaneously discussing the tasks and responsibilities of the funding source, agency administrator, and counselor. In addition, we introduce competencies that the ecologically minded community counselor needs to increase efficiency and avoid burnout.

## Documentation Issues

A funding source is responsible for securing an accurate assessment of need in the community and raising the monetary resources necessary to address this need (Roth, Siegel, & Black, 1994; Swift, Fine, & Beck, 1985). The continuation of services depends on the degree to which the expectations of the community are met. For example, Medicaid is a government funding source for behavioral health care. Since this program is ultimately funded by taxpayer dollars, the political environment shapes the allocation of money each year during the federal and state budgetary processes. In the late 1980s and early 1990s, stories of welfare fraud in the media pushed the U.S. Congress to form subcommittees that drafted new legislation for distributing and monitoring Medicaid dollars. State governments and their regulatory boards held agencies accountable for spending the allotted money under federal parameters. Agencies found guilty of violating federal regulations were penalized through fines or dollars withheld in the next annual budget (Sands, Cullen, & Higuchi, 1996).

Depending on the state or locale, a regulatory organization is either appointed or formed to monitor effectiveness, efficiency, and accountability for behavioral health care dollars. The primary function of a regulatory organization is to conduct audits to determine whether agencies using funding source dollars are in compliance with established standards, including medical necessity. Medical necessity implies a treatment provider has accurately diagnosed a problem condition and determined the appropriate course of treatment. When the regulatory organization can report to the funding source that agencies using Medicaid funds did so in good faith and according to guidelines, politicians can then report to their constituencies that taxpayer money has been put to good use. Positive audits often result in ongoing political and public support. If fraud is unveiled in an audit, the fraudulent act can threaten the agency's existence. For example, if an agency provides services that do not meet medical necessity criteria, the sessions billed might be considered fraudulent (Lloyd, 2000; Sands et al., 1996). Counselors in training need to understand the differences between Medicaid and Medicare and the rigid requirements regarding reimbursement.

When a counselor is asked to complete his or her documentation and billing tickets by the end of the day, it is imperative to understand how this activity is connected with reimbursement and compliance. Reimbursement refers to the dollar amount agreed to in contract per period of billable service. Compliance means that an agency and the employees of that agency follow the rules of providing service and billing for that service. Noncompliance by today's rules may mean severe penalties for agencies, including monetary restitution and prison (Lloyd, 2000). Agencies cannot afford to withstand the consequences of such major mistakes. Administration and direct service providers benefit from clear negotiation of expectations on the job. Such efforts prevent potential cutbacks in services to consumers and legal action against counselors and agency administrative staff.

Clients often struggle with paper work at the intake process and periodically throughout treatment. Agencies are mandated to follow state and federal regulations to collect certain data. Some of this will make sense to the client, though most may not. The counselor can help clients understand the clinical and operational importance of this process and even assist them if necessary. When clinical documentation is a problem, the agency may be vulnerable to litigation or denial of payment for services rendered when documentation is not submitted or submitted incorrectly (Lloyd, 2000). Agencies hold certifications from state or national organizations that routinely, and sometimes randomly, audit for compliance. To fail such audits puts the agency's existence at risk. Medicaid, for example, may suspend an organization's Medicaid contract for 1 year with proof of inadequate clinical documentation (Lloyd, 2000). Such a penalty is tantamount to a death sentence for most organizations. Documentation is an area where the ecology of the client, counselor, and agency is more apparent, and it has the potential to negatively impact the treatment outcome.

## Utilization Rates

Funding sources are pressuring agencies to be more efficient (Lawless et al., 1999; Visotsky, 1993). That means providing good clinical care while meeting revenue targets. Counselors need to understand the demands of their job not only include providing good clinical care but also meeting expectations for utilization rate (UR). Agency revenues are based on assumptions about the number of services to be delivered in the next fiscal or calendar year. Revenues are calculated by multiplying the number of counselors by the UR and, finally, by the contract rate for the specific services. UR for counselors can range from 50% to 80% of available time, depending on the nature and culture of the agency, contract demands, and the type of services delivered.

The counselor is responsible for fulfilling an obligation to provide quality care and to generate income for services rendered to clients. These revenues must be sufficient to pay for counselor salary and benefits as well as the organization's operational and overhead expenses. Ideally, counselors in an agency can generate enough revenues to create a surplus by year's end. These surpluses can then be reinvested to expand care the following year, increase staff salaries, and purchase equipment and technology. Conversely, failure to generate revenue means a cut in programs and staff, and a delay in purchasing equipment.

Counselors who are ill prepared to meet utilization rate expectations will find their employment environment to be stressful. The reciprocal impact on clients is clear. Counselors may appear distracted and unsympathetic, especially toward clients who do not show for appointments. The client may feel as if he or she is just a number. It is paramount that the counselor communicates any pertinent policies to the client to prevent instances that might impede treatment.

## Outcome-Oriented Treatment Planning

The ability to measure outcomes is critical for the ecological counselor. In the early 1990s, Simon Budman led a series of workshops on brief solution-focused therapy. One of the most important messages from those sessions was that intermittent therapy or treatment over a long period may be more efficacious than long-term therapy with no interruption or break (Budman, Hoyt, & Friedman, 1992). Counselors need to learn to set realistic treatment goals that a consumer of services can achieve during a brief period. When clients achieve goals, this increases the validity of the treatment process and reflects positively on counseling as a means of working on personal and social problems.

Agencies are now measuring treatment outcomes and progress in a number of ways. Many times this evaluation process results from awareness of the client, such as measuring the length of stay in treatment or the number of hospitalizations in a specific population. Other times, the client may be aware that outcomes are being tracked. These examples are usually a part of the treatment plan and may require the client to complete an assessment instrument that measures levels of depression or areas of life functioning (e.g., client satisfaction survey). Clients generally see this as helpful in demonstrating the counselor's interest and concern (Lloyd, 2000; Mee-Lee, 2000). Some counselors, however, may see outcome measures as unnecessary and as an invasion of their professional management of client care. Since they assess the client's progress at each contact, they may consider this redundant. Counselors may see this as one more imposition from management when they are struggling to achieve utilization rate and complete paperwork. The counselor must be careful not to let these factors deter his or her enthusiasm for the work. Appropriate training should help the counselor realize that outcomes have value for the treatment process and demonstrate organizational effectiveness to funding sources. The formal measurement of treatment outcomes becomes another clinical tool for the therapeutic relationship.

## Summary of Counselor Competencies

Developing competence as an ecological community counselor means working to create hospitable environments for clients while understanding the responsibilities of administrators, regulatory organizations, and funding sources. The ideas we propose here are meant to be a guide for enhancing counselor competence. We concur with the recommendations of Favier, Eisengart, and Colonna (2000) and other authors (Anderson, 2000; Chandras, 2000; Myer, 2001; Smith, 1999; Warnath, 1977) who suggested that counselors should be competent in the following: (a) understanding health care delivery systems, and their organization and financing systems; (b) knowledge and skills in management and administration; (c) ability to complete outcome-oriented treatment planning; (d) basic skills in the use of technology; (e) knowledge of best practices in treatment; (f) time management; and (g) advocacy skills. These competencies help decrease burnout.

We referenced the first five competencies earlier in the chapter. Time management and advocacy skills are illustrated further for clarity.

### Time Management

Time management skills follow from understanding priorities and negotiating learning goals with one's administrative or clinical supervisor. Many counselors with good intentions focus on issues irrelevant to an agency's mission. Nonbillable time with clients (e.g., time on the phone) and counseling sessions that do not address treatment goals are examples of counselor misuse of time. Often, counselors enter agencies with little or no mentoring experience due to time constraints placed on managers and supervisors. Regular and consistent supervision is essential to counselors in developing time management skills (Sexton, 2000). Agency administrators cannot ignore this responsibility to the counselor and client.

Supervisors are responsible for helping shape the behavior of counselors in an agency setting. Ecologically based supervision assists the counselor in gradually understanding all aspects of agency functioning in addition to developing clinical skills with clients. Explaining utilization expectations, documentation, charting procedures, peer review, and other continuous quality improvement processes helps incorporate the counselor into the agency culture.

In supervision, counselors can develop appropriate linkage skills to help a client access needed services and decrease the burden on the counselor to manage all aspects of client care. Counselors who fail to connect with resources available in the client's support network often contribute to a client's poor adjustment skills in the community. Linkage is a necessary function of the counseling process. It is not enough to provide therapy in isolation from other resources (Van Hook & Ford, 1998).

## Advocacy

As already mentioned, counselors who become involved in the political process regarding client care and agency funding develop a greater stake in the organizational mission. Universities play an important role in developing advocacy skills. Programs that encourage writing politicians to advocate for a special population, service learning projects, or scholarly research to understand the needs of the local community contribute to advocacy training (Garcia, 2000; Kiselica & Robinson, 2001).

Advocacy in the counseling profession is rooted in understanding the political processes involved in sustaining the agency mission. A reality for counselors and communities is that human services agency funding is a political process. Aside from a few agencies funded by private donations, most agencies rely on government funding. Counselors ought to become familiar with the lobbying efforts of agencies in state, county, and city governments that impact funding decisions. Counselors can influence the political process by staying in touch with legislative procedures and writing representatives on behalf of clients in the community who benefit from services, as demonstrated in outcome research.

It is important to recognize that the administrative staff of an agency or funding authority will be involved in political lobbying and advocacy to a greater extent than direct service staff. Members of the boards of directors of those organizations will also be in a better position to advocate at the state and national levels. Trade associations such as the National Council for Community Behavioral Health take an active and visible role in lobbying and advocating for policy at the national level. Counselors will not be in position to influence policy at that level. Rather, counselors can communicate with their legislative representatives or work with their professional organization (e.g., the American Counseling Association). We recommend that counselors educate themselves to the issues in support of these larger efforts.

## Case Study

### The Case

Jim has been employed for 2 years as a full-time counselor at the local mental health clinic. He schedules approximately 20 individual clients per week for 1-hour sessions, and facilitates three 1.5-hour psychoeducational sessions for men convicted of domestic violence and one 1.5-hour group for individuals with chronic depression. In addition, Jim receives 2 hours of supervision a week: 1 hour from a clinical psychologist and 1 hour from a professional counselor specializing in forensic services. Jim receives a salary of approximately $26 thousand a year plus health benefits. He works approximately 45 to 50 hours a week in order to stay up to date with documentation.

The local mental health authority for his county is sponsoring a tax levy. The levy failed the year before. The message Jim understands from his administrative supervisor is that if the levy does not pass this year, the mental health agency might need to cut services and lay off counselors for an indefinite period. Several counselors are upset by this news. There is a general fear that jobs will be cut.

A few of Jim's clients have been especially difficult in recent weeks. One client is diagnosed with borderline personality disorder. She frequently calls the agency and leaves vague messages that she might harm herself. She leaves no phone numbers and cancels her next appointment. In one of the psychoeducational groups referred for domestic violence, Jim is having particular trouble with a man demonstrating narcissistic characteristics. He continually challenges Jim in the session, claiming the only reason he is in the group is because he is dating the municipal court judge's ex-wife. Jim is overwhelmed with some of the issues generated in his client caseload.

The agency administrator calls a staff meeting and asks all counselors and therapists to reschedule their appointments the day before voting day. She instructs the counselors to hand out pamphlets promoting the levy at select voting stations. In addition, she informs the counselors that each employee will need to make up the hours rescheduled in order to meet utilization for that month. The counselors comply with the administrator's demands, but are very angry. Among the statements they make are, "We hardly make enough money to live, and now we have this added to our plate" and "Who does she think she is demanding that we spend all day outside a voting booth . . . I should have a choice" or "Why isn't someone else doing this . . . why are the counselors promoting the levy . . . shouldn't the clients and their families be doing this?"

The levy passed by a narrow margin, but in the coming weeks Jim considers leaving the agency. He feels pressured to do more than he can handle in a given week and the stress of the job is taking a toll on his personal health and well-being.

## Discussion of the Case

A discussion of local fund raising best illustrates how the staff counselor can be involved in reciprocal activities with the larger delivery system, although many times counselors will say, "That's not my job." In the case of Jim and the local mental health clinic, neither counselor nor administrative supervisor realized that counselor involvement is critical to the quality of employment, the viability of the organization, and the success of the mission to help clients. If the administrative supervisor and Jim had talked about the importance of activities outside the counseling relationship when Jim was first employed, Jim might have been more receptive to scheduling clients so he did not feel overwhelmed or dumped on at the last minute.

In some locales, tax levies generate significant amounts of money that support services to the working poor and sometimes can be used to leverage grants and Medicaid matches. Levy campaigns are generally organized by the local system at large, require money to finance, and include activities to publicize the importance of the mission. The counselor can be involved in a number of ways as the campaign unfolds. Generally, the campaign committee has a schedule of planned activities. Counselors can solicit and donate contributions to support the campaign. Even small donations add up and demonstrate wide support for the levy. Counselors can help clients and their families understand the importance of voting to support the levy. They may also be involved in voter registration for clients.

As the campaign begins, counselors may be asked to speak to service organizations, social groups, or churches to explain the agency services and their importance. These groups may have technical questions about the use of tax dollars, and the counselor must be knowledgeable enough to answer such questions. Counselors may also be asked to appear on television and radio talk shows to answer similar questions. Many times, local forums are scheduled where representatives of various levies appear together to answer voter questions. These appearances are usually outside the normal workday and schedule, requiring the counselor to donate his or her time. Counselors can educate their families and friends about the levy and encourage their support by voting and campaigning for it.

As the election draws near, yard signs and posters must be erected. Counselors may be asked to attend rallies, wear campaign buttons, conduct honk-ins, and serve as poll workers. Rallies generally are held to show support and capture news media attention. Honk-ins are mini rallies held just before election day where staff members stand on busy intersections with posters. The goal is to attract attention and encourage drivers to honk in support of the levy, activities that generate a great deal of enthusiasm, attention, and support. In addition, counselors may be assigned to local voting polls to hold posters and encourage support for the levy.

At first glance, these activities do not seem to fit the role of the counselor, but from an ecological perspective, we propose they should be incorporated into the counselor's mission. This kind of participation in the larger system ensures input and dialogue among all parties and strengthens the reciprocal relationships when clinical policy issues surface. Counselors thereby take responsibility for the care and development of the larger delivery system.

## Conclusion

The counseling relationship cannot be understood apart from the multiple domains of influence surrounding it. The counselor is one of many important people in a service delivery system that extends beyond the immediate helping relationship with clients. For community counseling to be truly effective, there must be shared dialogue and understanding between the multiple systems in which the counseling relationship is embedded. These systems include the counselor-client relationship, the agency setting, the coproviders of service in the community, the local funding authority, the state and federal regulatory systems, and the larger political arena. Counselors must possess certain competencies to function in a complex service delivery environment. Knowledge of the health care delivery system, knowledge of management and administration, skills in outcome-oriented treatment planning, technological preparedness, advocacy skills, and time management are essential for the ecological counselor. We believe that the knowledge and skills recommended here must be taught in graduate level counseling programs nationwide.

We acknowledge the complexity of these concepts and the challenges posed to counselors in training, counselor educators, and agency supervisors and administrators. Still, we believe counselors who understand the reciprocal nature of these aforementioned domains of influence will provide more effective counseling services and find greater satisfaction in the work environment. Participation in these multiple systems at some level enhances the counselor's insight into issues in the larger service delivery environment. It also helps advance the community counseling agency's mission of providing high-quality services to clientele.

## Learning Activities

1. You read in this chapter how working on a local campaign levy to raise funds for mental health services is one way for counselors to interact with the larger delivery system. Identify two or three other activities that would include interaction between the counselor and larger delivery system. How would these activities promote the mission of service to others in need?

2. Search the Internet for homepages of two or three local counseling agencies in your community. Find the mission statements for these organizations. Using Figure 10.1 (The Ecology of the Counselor–Client Relationship), consider what vertical or horizontal stressors might inhibit a community counseling agency from sustaining its mission in the community.

3. Visit a local funding authority public meeting. Take notes of issues discussed, including the disbursement of public funds, standards for decision making, and plans for future funding.

4. Schedule a meeting with an experienced community counselor and discuss how that individual manages time, advocates for his or her respective population, manages documentation, plans to meet the agency's utilization rate, and avoids burnout.

5. Search local, state, and national Web sites for information on the debate regarding Medicaid, Medicare, and parity in funding for behavioral health care and drug and alcohol counseling services.

# References

Anderson, C. E. (2000). Dealing constructively with managed care: Suggestions from an insider. *Journal of Mental Health Counseling, 22*(4), 343-353.

Blocher, D. H. (1981). Human ecology and the future of counseling psychology. *The Counseling Psychologist, 9*, 69-77.

Boyd-Franklin, N. (2001). Using the multisystemic model with an African American family: Cross-racial therapy and supervision. In S. H. McDaniel, D. Lusterman, & C. Philpot (Eds.), *Casebook for integrating family therapy* (pp. 395-400). Washington, DC: American Psychological Association.

Bronfenbrenner, U. (1979). *The ecology of human development*. Cambridge, MA: Harvard University Press.

Bronfenbrenner, U. (1995). Developmental ecology throughout space and time: A future perspective. In P. Moen, G. H. Elder, & K. Luscher (Eds.), *Examining lives in context: Perspectives on the ecology of human development* (pp. 619-648). Washington, DC: American Psychological Association.

Budman, S. H., Hoyt, M. F., & Friedman, R. M. (1992). First words on fit sessions. In S. H. Budman, M. F. Hoyt, & R. M. Friedman (Eds.), *The first session in brief therapy* (pp. 3-8). New York: Guilford Press.

Chandras, K. V. (2000). Technology-enhanced counselor training: Essential technical competencies. *Journal of Instructional Psychology, 27*(4), 224-227.

Conyne, R. (1985). The counseling ecologist: Helping people and environments. *Counseling and Human Development, 18*(2), 2-10.

Council for Accreditation of Counseling and Education Related Programs (CACREP). (2001). *The 2001 CACREP standards*. Alexandria, VA: Author. Retrieved December 8, 2002, from http://www.counseling.org/cacrep/

Danzinger, P. R., & Welfel, E. R. (2001). The impact of managed care on mental health counselors: A survey of perceptions, practices, and compliance with ethical standards. *Journal of Mental Health Counseling, 23*(2), 137-150.

Dorfman, S. L., & Smith, S. A. (2002). Preventive mental health and substance abuse programs and services in managed care. *Journal of Behavioral Health Services and Research, 29*(3), 233-258.

Flynn, L. M. (1989). The family phenomenon: The story of the National Alliance of the Mentally Ill. In R. M. Friedman, A. J. Duchnowski, et al. (Eds.), *Advocacy on behalf of children with serious emotional problems* (pp. 134-139). Springfield, IL: Charles C Thomas.

Garcia, R. M. (2000). Service learning and community collaboration. *Community College Journal, 70*(3), 33-35.

Gladding, S. (1997). *Community and agency counseling*. Upper Saddle, NJ: Prentice-Hall.

Gladding, S. (2002). *Family therapy: History, theory, and practice* (3rd ed.). Columbus, OH: Merrill Prentice Hall.

Gopaul-McNicol, S. (1997). *A multicultural/ multimodal/multisystems approach to working with culturally different families*. Westport, CT: Praeger.

Henggeler, S. W., & Borduin, C. M. (1990). *Family therapy and beyond*. Pacific Grove, CA: Brooks/Cole.

Kaplan, D. (2002). Excellence in practice. *Counseling Today, 45*(2), 5.

Kiselica, M. S., & Robinson, M. (2001). Bringing advocacy counseling to life: The history, issues, and human dramas of social justice work in counseling. *Journal of Counseling & Development, 79*(4), 397.

Lawless, L. L., Ginter, E. J., & Kelly, K. R. (1999). Managed care: What mental health counselors need to know. *Journal of Mental Health Counseling, 21*(1), 50-65.

Liddle, H. A. (1995). Conceptual and clinical dimensions of a multidimensional, multisystems engagement strategy in a family-based adolescent treatment. *Psychotherapy, 32*(1), 39-58.

Lloyd, D. (2000). *Our future is excellence—let's build it!—eliminating barriers to quality services*. Paper presented at the second biennial conference of the Ohio Council of Behavioral Healthcare Providers, Columbus, OH.

Mee-Lee, D. (2000). *Keeping the behavioral health team healthy: Communication, conflicts, coping*. Paper presented at the second biennial conference of the Ohio Council of Behavioral Healthcare Providers, Columbus, OH.

Mental Health Parity Act. (1996). Centers for Medicaid and Medicare. Retrieved August 14, 2002, from http://cms.hhs.gov/hipaa/hipaa1/content/mhpa.asp

Messina, J. (1999). What's next for the profession of mental health counseling? *Journal of Mental Health Counseling, 21*(3), 285-294.

Minuchin. (1967). *Families of the slums: An exploration of their structure and treatment*. New York: Basic Books.

Mowbray, C.T., & Holter, M. C. (2002). Mental health and mental illness: Out of the closet? *Social Service Review, 76*(1), 135-179.

Munger, R. L. (1997). Ecological trajectories in child mental health. In S. W. Henggeler & A. B. Santos (Eds.), *Innovative approaches for difficult-to-treat populations* (pp. 3-26). Washington, DC: American Psychiatric Press.

Myer, R. (2001). Community agency counseling: Teaching about management and administration. In K. Eriksen & G. McAuliffe (Eds.), *Teaching counselors and therapists: Constructivist and developmental course design* (pp. 275-291). Westport, CT: Bergin and Garvey.

Nichols, M. P., & Schwartz, R. C. (2001). *Family therapy: Concepts and methods* (5th ed.). Needham Heights, MA: Allyn & Bacon.

Roth, J., Siegel, R., & Black, S. (1994). Identifying the mental health needs of children living in families with AIDS or HIV infection. *Community Mental Health Journal, 30*(6), 581-593.

Sands, H., Cullen, E., & Higuchi, S. (1996). Practitioner's alert: Health care fraud and abuse. *Psychoanalysis and Psychotherapy, 13*(1), 86-88.

Sexton, T. L. (2000). Reconstructing clinical training: In pursuit of evidence-based clinical training. *Counselor Education and Supervision, 39*(4), 218-227.

Smith, H. B. (1999). Managed care: A survey of counselor educators and counselor practitioners. *Journal of Mental Health Counseling*.

Smitson, W. S. (2001). Managed mental health care: A home grown product. *Administration and Policy in Mental Health, 28*(3), 229-234.

Swift, C. F., Fine, M.A., & Beck, S. (1985). Early intervention services of young children: National implications from a key informant look at Ohio. *Mental Retardation, 23*(6), 308-311.

Van Hook, M. P., & Ford, M. E. (1998). The linkage model for delivering mental health services in rural communities: Benefits and challenges. *Health and Social Work, 23*(1), 53-60.

Van Voorhis, P., Braswell, M., & Morrow, B. (1997). Family therapy. In P. Van Voorhis, M. Braswell, & D. Lester (Eds.), *Correctional counseling and rehabilitation* (3rd ed., pp. 155-174). Cincinnati, OH: Anderson.

Visotsky, H. M. (1993). Twenty years of progress. *Administration and Policy in Mental Health, 21*(2), 133-137.

Volker, T. (1994). Value analysis: A model of personal and professional ethics in marriage and family counseling. *Counseling and Values, 38,* 193-204.

Warnath, C. F. (1977). Relationship and growth theories and agency counseling. *Counselor Education and Supervision, 17*(2), 84-91.

Welfel, E. R. (2002). *Ethics in counseling and psychotherapy: Standards, research, and emerging issues.* Pacific Grove, CA: Brooks/Cole.

Yank, G. R., Barber, J. W., & Spradlin, W. W. (1994). Mental health treatment teams and leadership: A systems model. *Behavioral Science, 39,* 293-310.

Yelton, S. W. (1989). Advocacy efforts from a state mental health administrator's perspective. In R. M. Friedman, A. J. Duchnowski, & E. L. Henderson (Eds.), *Advocacy on behalf of children with serious emotional problems* (pp. 114-124). Springfield, IL: Charles C Thomas.

Chapter 11

# Ecological Applications to Organizational Consultation

*Lynn S. Rapin*

---

*Chapter Highlights*

- *A core ingredient of a successful organizational intervention is an ecological understanding of potential person–environment fits.*
- *An ecological perspective helps protect the consultant from having a myopic view of the factors prompting counseling interventions.*
- *The Work Environment Scale is a social climate measurement tool that identifies organizational consultation goals and gauges changes in personal and group perceptions of organizational characteristics that have been targeted for intervention.*
- *Work groups and organizations can be developed by focusing on the social climate characteristics of work relationships, personal growth supports, and system maintenance and system change attributes.*

---

Organizations comprise a number of groups in complex interaction. In applying Lewin's famous ecological equation, an organization consists of many layers of P × E interactions (Lewin, 1936). The layers of group interactions are influenced by the larger social cultures around them, and they, in turn, influence organizational members, organizational subgroups, and the larger environment.

In this chapter, ecological approaches to organizational consultation that target the organization and its characteristics are described using the common organizing elements of (a) conceptual linkages to ecology, (b) ecological principles guiding organizational consultation interventions, and (c) essential counselor competencies. In addition, two case studies are provided.

# Conceptual Linkages to Ecology

## Person–Environment Fit

Central to any assessment or intervention in complex organizations is a need to understand how organizational members fit with each other, with their work tasks and products, with relationships to other levels of the organization, and with their customers in order to perform as an effective and efficient institution. The missions and values of organizations are intrinsically tied to work products, which often means subrogating the needs of individual organizational members and subgroups. Organizational goals and their fit with individual departments and employees depend on many factors, including status, gender, the dominant work culture, the organization's life cycle, business cycles, larger community elements, and economies at the local, regional, national, and global levels. An ecological understanding of the potential person–environment fits within an organization is a core ingredient of successful organizational interventions.

Three considerations on the positive and negative consequences of good person-environment fit for organization—good fit for whom, good fit of what, and good fit when—have been discussed by Schneider, Smith, and Goldstein (2000), who suggested that fit is contextual. Homogeneity in general subordinates may be desirable, for instance, but heterogeneity for individuals in key problem solving and strategic decision making may be detrimental to the organization's long-term health. Good fit between a particular employee and the other organizational members who make up the interpersonal environment is known as *supplementary congruence*, whereas *complimentary congruence* occurs when an individual's skills and talents are consistent with the needs of the organization (Muchinsky & Monahan, 1987). Schneider et al. (2000) proposed that less-than-perfect fit (i.e., heterogeneity) may be most desirable.

Turner, Barling, and Zacharatos (2001) argued that healthy work includes the promotion of both the psychological and physical well-being (p. 715). Job-related well-being, posited by Warr and cited in Turner et al. (2001), involves many potential measures, such as job satisfaction, job involvement, and organizational commitment. These three factors contribute to individual and organizational perceptions of the work climate. As the structure of work organizations has changed to include leaner staffing, increased demands for employee flexibility, and a greater attention to productivity, efforts to define and promote healthy and positive work environments must come from individual employees and their organizations (Turner et al., 2001).

266

## Ecological Models

A number of stimulating models have been developed to conceptualize the interactions and effects that individuals, groups, organizations, communities, countries, and the world have on each other.

Bronfenbrenner's theory of human ecology enumerated four ecological levels with which the individual interacts (Bronfenbrenner, 1988). These levels, previously described in this book, include the microsytem (in which the individual has face-to-face contact with key others), the mesosystem (in which two or more microsystems relate), the exosystem (larger cultural systems that influence the individual by the impacts of their decisions), and the macrosystem (overarching values, structures, and norms that define society).

In considering the increasing interrelatedness of the global world, Kasambira and Edwards (2000) added an additional level to the Bronfenbrenner model: the globalsystem (defining those elements at the international and global levels that affect individuals). They also visually reconfigured the model from a series of concentric circles surrounding the individual to a double helix, demonstrating the spiraling and interconnected nature of each of the levels and their impacts.

Ogbu (as cited in Rudkin, 2003) reversed the Bronfenbrenner diagram, which has at its center the individual, by beginning analysis at the macrosystem level. In addition, Ogbu postulated that ecological understanding is culture bound and proposed a cultural-ecological perspective that emphasizes the effects of long-standing cultural patterns of coping and requires interventions at the larger system levels.

Maton (2000) also designed an interrelated ecological model to demonstrate the embeddedness and interconnectivity of ecological environments that impact the individual, radiating from the person, to setting, to community, to society, and to the world. One of the overlapping ovals related to work settings includes the person, workplace, and the local, national, and international economic systems, which in turn interact with other life space systems.

Each of these models shares central ecological assumptions—that levels of ecological influence can be identified, and that they influence and are influenced by each other. These ecological models can assist in conceptualizing the consultee organization in a dynamic relationship and as part of a larger ecological system. This perspective allows and demands that the consultant be informed of the larger ecological realities facing a potential consultee organization. Further, it helps protect the consultant from having a myopic view of the factors prompting the consultation. For example, in planning a consultation with a service unit, it is important not just to understand the characteristics of the unit, but also to understand the larger organization's impact on that unit.

## Environmental Units and Behavior Settings

Barker (1974) conceptualized the defining elements of an environmental unit to include a natural phenomenon with a time and space orientation (i.e., within a defined, self-generated boundary, and with balance in its components). Barker described the relationship between the pattern of behavior in the environmental unit and the pattern of its nonbehavioral components as *synomorphic*, meaning similar in structure. To explain this, Barker used a description of a school class session and its components of behavior (e.g., sitting, raising hands, listening) and of the objects with which the behavior is transacted, such as chairs, the room, and the blackboard (p. 265). In this example, there is synomorphy between the behaviors of the children and teacher within the classroom setting.

Barker and his colleagues (Barker, 1965; Gump, 1974; Wicker, 1974) further described and studied one type of ecological unit called the behavior setting, in which predictable behaviors occur among people and physical objects in naturally occurring events (e.g., behavior on a baseball field or in a restaurant). Using rigorous observation, Barker documented and categorized behavior settings. His applications included the study of how different setting characteristics influence the behavior of its inhabitants. For example, students in an undermanned school (say, a high school class of about 22 individuals) have many more opportunities to participate in academic and organizational activities at the school and in the community. Students in an overmanned setting (e.g., a high school class of about 800) by contrast have fewer opportunities to participate in these activities because of the sheer number of candidates for any slot.

In considering the application of behavior settings to consultation within an organization, Barker and colleagues highlighted the importance of examining both the behaviors in an organizational setting (i.e., what happens) and the effects on its members. In the decades following Barker's initial research, changes in behavior settings have been noted (Rudkin, 2003), including changes in levels of participation and influences of technology. For example, Putnam (2000) has detailed the severe decline in organizational (e.g., social, religious, work) participation in the United States since the 1960s.

## Ecological Principles Guiding
## Organizational Consultation Interventions

Scientific fields, including physics and field biology, have served as models for community and counseling ecological theories and interventions (cf. Moos, 1974; Moos & Insel, 1974). The following ecological principles have direct application to organizational consultation efforts.

### Social Climate

Development of social climate measurements has been influential in the application of ecological principles to organizations. Moos and colleagues (Moos, 1986, 1994; Moos & Insel, 1974) developed nine social climate scales that have been used widely in organizational settings to describe individual and group perceptions of environments, to measure distinctions between Real and Ideal environmental characteristics, to compare groups and settings, and to measure changes in perception over time. The social climate scales have been translated into 25 languages and have been used widely in research on organizational characteristics (Holahan, 2002). These instruments can be administered to assist organizations in determining the current ecological characteristics on several indices in order to identify organizational consultation goals. Further, they can be used to measure change on organizational characteristics that have been targeted for intervention. Examples of the scales include the Work Environment Scale (WES) (Moos, 1986, 1994), which is described by example later in this chapter; the Group Environment Scale; the School Environment Scale; and the Family Environment Scale.

All of the social climate scales have three dimensions that reflect areas of potential growth and development within settings through (a) relationship characteristics, (b) personal growth supports, and (c) system maintenance and system change attributes. These com ponents are described in greater detail later in the chapter. The social climate scales reflect personal and group perceptions of environments, and when used with other tools, can promote ecological congruence.

### Four Ecological Principles in Mental Health Consultation

Trickett, Barone, and Watts (2000) described four ecological principles as fundamental considerations in mental health consultation. Each of the

269

principles reflects the need to understand the environmental context within which consultation takes place. Further, the principles can be used to assess macro (community or organization) or micro (individual or work unit) aspects of the person–environment fit in order to design appropriate interventions. Each can be employed in determining the goals of consultation, the outcomes of consultation interventions and their positive and negative side effects (Craig, 1978), or intended and unintended consequences (Trickett et al., 2000).

### Adaptation

Any organization setting, from community to work unit, has a unique set of characteristics, each influenced by the values, norms, goals, and particular set of inhabitants in the setting. As Trickett et al. (2000) stated, "The general task for the ecologically oriented consultant is to 'tune in' to how the particular setting functions and what combination of influences *in that particular setting* [italics in original] provide the most useful framework for designing and carrying out the intervention" (p. 308). For example, two organizations may experience the same outcome or problem, but from different combinations of environmental influences. One organizational unit experiencing lowered work productivity may be influenced by physical factors, such as poor lighting or a safety issue. In another unit with similar productivity results, the influences may generate from inattention to work tasks or from conflict between supervisor and supervisees.

Understanding the ecology of the organizational setting is enhanced by understanding the perceptions of the individuals in the environment and those of key agents with whom the organization unit interacts. Assessment of these influences prior to intervention provides a base from which an evaluation plan can be formulated. Individual perceptions of the environment can be gathered to form the perception of the whole, and measurements of intervention effects can be provided at the organization, group, or individual levels.

### Cycling of Resources

Organizational consultations may have a number of phases, beginning with the assessment process and continuing with intervention(s), formative and summative evaluations, and potential redesign. At each of these intervention points, it is important to identify the necessary and sufficient resources to promote the desired changes. For example, if a consultant is contracted by the head of an organization to engage with a particular work unit, it is imperative to assess the perceptions and strengths of those in the work unit who are subjects of potential interventions.

### *Interdependence*

This principle pertains to the interrelated nature of organizational or system parts. According to Kelly, Ryan, Altman, & Stelzner (2000), "the concept of interdependence is the basic axiom of the ecological perspective" (p. 133). Trickett et al. (2000) pointed out that interdependent relationships may be tight, in which change in one system part may have far-reaching effects in other parts of the system, or they may be loose, where an intervention in one part of the system may minimally affect other parts. It behooves the consultant, therefore, to understand the potential interactions and to anticipate a wide range of potential outcomes of any consultation intervention.

Not only are the elements of an organizational system interdependent, but the consultant must also attend to these elements in considering entry into a client system. Ecological approaches to consultation are predicated on the collaboration, interaction, and interdependence of the consultant and the consultation organization. In contrast to other intervention modes, this type of consultation assumes a collaborative process in assessment, implementation, and evaluation.

### *Succession*

Organizations are not static. They develop histories, patterns of success and failure, and internal and external perceptions. Enron Corporation, for example, moved from internal and external perceptions as one of the most successful and profitable corporations in the United States to the embodiment of a failed organization in which alleged greed and profit motives at the highest levels destroyed the corporation's reputation and brought it to bankruptcy. In considering consultation options, it helps to consider the life cycle position of the organization as well as its current culture. As Schneider, Smith, and Goldstein (2000) have described in their Attraction–Selection–Attrition model, organizational goals reflect the personality of the founder. Structure, rules, and policies flow from those goals. Early employees find good fit with the organization as they match the values of its founder and create a homogeneous workforce. This outcome may produce positive consequences in the short run (through shared vision and focused efforts), but may lead to negative long-term outcomes (e.g., group think, stagnant problem-solving models, inability to respond to changes affecting the organization, industry, or larger environment).

## Diversity

Ecological approaches value diversity (Bond, 1999). Multiple experiences of diversity within organizations can both contribute to existing problems and aid in their solutions. In her article presenting organizational contexts that support the productive participation of diverse groups, Bond identified two critical values: (a) a culture of connection; and (b) recognition of multiple realities. Bond used common sources of diversity, including race, gender, and class, to articulate potential supports for and inhibitions to participation among nondominant groups in organizations. For example, the commonly held value of autonomy and independence within U.S. culture may, on one hand, promote individual excellence and independent solutions to organizational problems. The culture of connection, on the other hand, may support the presentation of numerous points of view and collaboration in generating potential solutions. As a personal example, while working with various nursing units, I have heard staff discuss what is actually done on a unit in a particular situation, as opposed to what may be written as a policy or procedure. Newcomers, following printed guidelines and working in a climate of individual assimilation of meaning, learned informally that the written procedure was either outdated or not used for some other reason. In this type of situation, the newcomers were challenged to learn through trial and error, rather than being provided accurate guidance. Only with more rigorous implementation of external controls (e.g., through accreditation audits), or through intentional organizational planning or consultation, have such informal traditions been modified.

A similar situation is frequently heard in counseling training situations in which counselors in training are placed in community agencies for practica or internships. There are often no clear ground rules for the counselors, prompting the suggestion from trainees that the agency needs a manual for trainee orientation. This often results in the presumption that the organizational members (other than trainees) would value such a manual, and that it would actually reflect agency policy. Unless there is an ongoing commitment to keep such a tool updated, these manuals can become obsolete quickly.

Diversity can be a positive experience when multiple perceptions of the organization are valued. Some consultation tools, such as the social climate scales (Moos, 1986, 1994), can enumerate similarities and disparities in perception among members of different units of an organization, and among individuals in different positions within the same work unit. The following case studies demonstrate similarities and differences in the perception of organizational supports among staff at administrative, supervisory, and line staff levels. Establishing and nourishing a culture of connection includes interdependence, accountability to the team, and attention to the work products of the entire unit (Bond, 1999).

Some diversity issues are tied to the preceding discussion of succession. When an organization replicates its goals and values in its staffing practices, homogeneity in performance and approach are valued and reinforced. In these situations, continuity and low turnover is to be expected. By contrast, Bond (1999) noted that heterogeneous work groups often produce more creative solutions to problems, thereby contributing to long-term organization health.

## Consultation Case Studies

These consultation case studies are taken from my consultation experience, and are provided to demonstrate ecological assessments and interventions.

### Case Study 1: The Laundry and Linen Department— Targeting the Organization

***Consultation Background***
This example is taken from an organizational development and training consultation that established process/quality improvement groups within a 17-department facilities management division of a large urban university hospital (Rapin, 1985). Although the intent of this example is not to give a thorough review of specific iterations of quality performance groups that have been implemented in the past three decades, I provide a brief overview of key group process elements to orient the case illustration. (For a more complete review of quality circles and a more detailed description of the consultation, see Rapin, 1985.)

The process/quality improvement groups implemented in the hospital are an example of a structured, group-based, organizational development intervention that targets the entire organization. Designed to increase employee participation in resolving work-related problems, task groups are introduced into the formal structure of the organization. Rather than creating a new structure for implementation of any identified problem and recommendations, the groups use the formal management channels already existing in the organization to implement any changes.

Structured, group-based consultation methodologies must be endorsed at the highest level of any organization considering their implementation and be tailored to its specific needs. Organizational leaders, managers, employees, and counselors working as consultants must have a shared understanding of the goals for such a group intervention as well as the particular benefits to the specific organization and its members. With careful implementation and ongoing monitoring of effectiveness, these group structures can be modified to reflect the impact of changes in the organization, its business focus, and larger environmental effects.

Since the 1960s—when quality circles seemed to contribute significantly to the success of Japanese industry and were widely adopted in the United States—to present efforts that incorporate participatory management in decision making and work product/process improvements, core sources of success and failure have been consistent. Many of the models have been adopted as the latest business craze, and then discarded and replaced almost as quickly.

One of the dangers in implementing any new organizational structure is that the organization's administration and employees alike might perceive it as an immediate resolution to long-standing problems. Such implementations take time to prepare and produce results. Many organizations have enthusiastically embraced management and employee improvement practices and then have not provided the necessary resources to support them as a long-term intervention. To be successful, structured organizational development groups must reflect how an organization values the contributions and experiences of employees in their areas of responsibility.

### Small Group Structure

Small groups of 6 to 10 employees meet together because they are part of the same work unit (in this case study, the 44 employees of an industrial laundry) or because of common responsibilities (e.g., the managers in the 17 departments). The goals focus on the $P \times E$ interactions among participants working toward task improvement, and on the direct benefits to the work organization, including more proactive problem solving and a reduction in work errors. Indirect benefits to members (P) may include increased individual problem-solving skills and enhanced speaking, presentation, and writing skills as well as increased positive interactions among divergent staff. Membership is voluntary, and the groups typically meet weekly with a trained facilitator for 1 to $1\frac{1}{2}$ hours on company time.

### Environmental Context

The Laundry and Linen Department was selected as an initial implementation site for several reasons. First, it was a production department with specific volume and timeline requirements, similar to industrial settings that had successfully implemented group process improvement models. Second, of the 17 departments in the division, this was the one with most chronic workforce problems and visible signs of organizational stress and discord. There was conflict among the line staff employees and poor supervisory relationships between the employees and their supervisors, and between the supervisors and their manager. The department was infamous for filing employee grievances (Quick, Quick, Nelson, & Hurrell, 1997). In addition, the staff ranked among the lowest in state pay grade and generally suffered from low morale. Equipment failed routinely; needles and other dangerous products arrived entangled with the soiled laundry; and complaints from the laundry and about the laundry proliferated. In some respects, the organization selected this department because it had nothing to lose. The prospects for success were modest, and any improvements were anticipated as welcome outcomes.

Although these conditions were not ideal, to say the least, they provided a venue for positive intervention. Administration was willing to support any relevant identified problem and appropriate solution, thus demonstrating trust that the employees could act on their knowledge. The employees union, likewise, supported the efforts, though employees and supervisors remained both interested in and skeptical of the opportunity to participate. Twenty eight of the 44 department employees volunteered for participation. From that volunteer pool, 10 were selected, based on diversity in level of experience and workstation. The remaining volunteers participated initially as supports and data gatherers, and then later in additional groups.

### Process and Products

The group, named the Quality Century Team for its more than 100 years of accumulated experience in the department, became a new department subteam. Selecting the team name demonstrated the pride participants had in their department. Thus, the intervention with them became mesosystem focused (each individual as part of the department unit and also part of the intervention group), while the division and larger organization (macrolevels) influenced their work and outcomes by providing organization supports, including time and space to meet during work hours, specific training in group process and problem-solving models, a trained facilitator, direct access to the organization consultant through the entire first round of the problem-solving process, access to institutional decision makers, and the opportunity to be recognized for their organization contributions.

Following two 4-hour training sessions in team building and group member skills training, a series of problem identification and problem-solving steps were introduced, employed, and reinforced. The team generated a list of 48 potential problems, narrowed the list to a target problem, converted their problem statement to an objective, presented the problem to the department director for approval, presented the problem and data-gathering process to all department employees and gained their cooperation, researched the problem and potential solutions, used three technical consultants, devised a budgeted plan for implementation, presented the plan to hospital administration, gained approval, and implemented the plan.

### The Identified Problems

Two chronic problems in the laundry's physical environment (E) were identified for intervention: the large laundry processing machines emitted excess shocks to employees, and an unacceptable amount of static remained on linens throughout the laundry process. It was discovered through technical consultation that certain staff members were being shocked by the machines because of their body chemistry, not because of lax attention to safety regulations.

### The Solutions

After data gathering on each machine and assessments of eight potential solutions, two were chosen for implementation. Group members elected the simplest and least expensive strategies to see whether they would eliminate the problems. These were to install Formica® (a nonconducting product) as insulation on the worktable portions of four selected machines and to install discharge bars on all machines (so that during a work shift, an employee could occasionally touch the bar to reduce electrical flow between body and machine). In trying to solve the problems these workers faced, a specific ecological intervention (B) was made in the physical environment (E) because of its negative and discordant (Conoley & Haynes, 1992) interaction ($\times$) with certain individuals' personal characteristics (P), following the formula B = f(P $\times$ E)]

The strategies adopted were successful in reducing the identified problem. When considering the relationships among individual members of the Laundry and Linen Department and the larger organization of the hospital, interventions were multimodal. Ecological interventions were implemented at the whole hospital organizational level (exosystem), in introducing a new management process. They were also implemented at the division level (macrosystem), as the initial implementation site for organizational implementation of a process, and at the department level (micro- and mesosystems), as participants worked with their small group and their department peers. For the year following implementation, no employee grievances were filed, a testament to the positive impacts of attention to physical and social climates. What had been a discordant department was transformed into one of vastly improved concordance among the members of the Laundry and Linen Department, their physical environment, and the members of the hospital with whom their department interacted (Conoley & Haynes, 1992).

### Side Effects and Intended and Unintended Consequences

There were a number of side effects (Craig, 1978), some anticipated and some not (Bond, 1999; Trickett et al., 2000). Early in the implementation process, there were concerns that there might be too few volunteers to staff a workable group. Contrary to that fear, and with specific education of the employees to the process, more than half of the department volunteered to participate. Once the training began, more employees expressed interest in participating (perhaps from the perception they would get relief from duty at hot machines for a set time each week, or perhaps because they truly expected positive social or work consequences from participation). Some of this interest was expressed positively, and some was expressed in the form of jealous and bullying comments toward participants. Based on past staff relationships, however, that particular response was anticipated. Department members who were not selected for direct involvement in the group were given opportunities to participate indirectly via machine monitoring.

Because of the success of the first group, a second group was added. A further unanticipated and positive outcome was that supervisors, who had been reluctantly positive about the potential success of the intervention, formed their own peer-level group. When the Laundry and Linen Department was identified for implementation, the department supervisors and their department manager were concerned that the employees would be unable to learn and implement the required skills and problem-solving processes. It was learned after the fact that these managers did not know whether their employees could read or write and were afraid to ask whether they could. The managers learned during training and implementation that the group members had the requisite communication and writing skills and were cooperative and supportive of each other's learning.

### Counselor Skills Required

Counselors providing any organizational consultation intervention must be skilled in the theory and practice of group work. Because organizations present innumerable complexities, it is important to be competent in basic group facilitation, in task group facilitation, in issues of diversity, and in best practice considerations for organizational group work (ASGW, 1998, 1999, 2000; Conyne, Rapin, & Rand, 1999). Further, in providing training in group skills as part of the consultation process, counselors need to be familiar and experienced in teaching methodologies appropriate to the tools they choose to use (Casella, 1979; Conyne, Wilson, & Ward, 1997). Those counselors who do specific group problem-solving consultation also need to be skilled in program development and evaluation processes and techniques (Craig, 1978; Joint Committee on Standards for Educational Evaluation, 1994; Kettner, 1999; Patton, 1997). It is insufficient for counselors merely to know the steps in a problem-solving model.

Many organizations have experienced failure with group process improvement strategies because they implement the mechanics of an intervention without adequate attention to group skills and group process (Conyne, 1989, 1999; Hulse-Killacky, Killacky, & Donigian, 2001). The working relationships among the participants (i.e., the interactions in the $P \times E$ relationship) mediate the content work. As individual participants are recognized for their contributions—whether diverse opinion, novel suggestion, gripe, facilitative comment, excellent summary, or the like—they will internalize critical process skills. These must be modeled by a competent facilitator or consultant.

Any consultation intervention requires knowledge of organizations, organizational processes, consultation models, and consultation processes (Dougherty, 1995; Herr & Fabian, 1993; Wallace & Hall, 1996). Because recipients of organizational consultation are often under stress, it behooves the ecologically grounded consultant to be cognizant of organizational aspects of stress and environmental contexts within which any consultation occurs (Allcorn & Diamond, 1997; Goldberger & Breznitz, 1993; Lewis, Lewis, Daniels, & D'Andrea, 1998; Lewis, Lewis, Packard, & Souflee, 2001; Lowman, 1998; Quick et al., 1997).

## Case Study 2: Assessing an Organization's Ecological Climate

### Consultation Background

This example is taken from a 17-month consultation with an in-house laboratory serving the needs of a large research medical center. Aspects of the consultation pertaining to social climate assessments are highlighted.

### Environmental Context

The laboratory interacted with several research departments in three institutions, thus producing a plethora of $P \times E$ interactions across many ecological levels. The host institution (the macrosystem), affected by larger economic pressures in the exosystem, had made a significant conversion in its accounting of ancillary services, which included the identified laboratory. Services that had been funded by research grant monies from user departments and augmented by general revenues were converted to self-sustaining accounting units. This trend was consistent with changes in research medical centers throughout the country (exosystem). The accounting change had a dramatic impact on the department in that it had to become more economically viable and institute measures to pass on additional costs to user departments. The laboratory was highly critical to the research mission of the institution because it was responsible for central aspects of the research agenda and accountable to a number of accreditation and funding units, including the federal government. Any serious accreditation problems could have resulted in suspension of federally funded research grants.

The laboratory, however, was already experiencing negative relationships with various user departments, and had fairly public interstaff and laboratory-user department conflicts. When initially contacted by senior medical center administrators about a consultation with the unit, I learned that the administrators were unsure which aspects of the department's management, practices, and relationships would be most appropriate to target for improvements. The administrators and users perceived the laboratory director as knowledgeable, but they also felt his interpersonal style often defeated efforts at good laboratory-user relationships. I learned that the director's work environment background had been in the military. Many considered his heavy-handed, top-down, authoritarian style discordant with the larger research community, though it was effective in improving quality standards. A conflict of contexts was in place, meaning several person–environment interaction ($P \times E$) misfits could be potential targets for consultation.

### Assessment

The consultation was initiated with an assessment phase designed to highlight issues most in need of intervention (i.e., those most discordant) and issues immediately amenable to intervention (with potential for parsimony). Specific interventions were contracted upon analysis and presentation of the assessment data. Consistent with ecological consultation approaches (Conoley & Haynes, 1992; Moos, 1996; Trickett et al., 2000), this process was intended to measure several ecological realities of the laboratory.

Information was gathered from multiple sources and through varied techniques in order to determine an accurate measurement of the ecological conditions and interactions in the laboratory and to prepare for appropriate interventions. The following elements were included in the assessment: (a) preliminary group meetings with key medical center and laboratory administrators to determine scope of assessments; (b) document review; (c) individual assessment interviews with key medical center administrators (n = 2), laboratory management (n = 5), a subset of laboratory staff (n = 7), and representatives from key user departments (n = 4); (d) group administration of the Real and Ideal forms of the Work Environment Scale (Moos, 1986, 1994) to all laboratory staff (n = 25); and (e) administration of a personal work style inventory—the Personal Profile System (PPS)—to top laboratory management (n = 4). Space considerations preclude a full discussion of each assessment component.

By contract, all raw data except for individual WES and PPS profiles remained the property of the consultant. All data reported were in aggregate form and provided to all participants in the assessment. Individual instrument data were provided to each participant for their own assessment and comparison with group data, thereby giving them opportunities to engage in individual processing of P $\times$ E fits.

### Social Climate Measurement via the Work Environment Scale

The WES, administered to all laboratory staff, provided valuable information on staff perceptions of the social climate. Data from the Real–Ideal comparisons are provided here to highlight specific ecological features of the instrument and to demonstrate how it was used in this consultation assessment. The Real and Ideal forms of the WES are parallel questionnaires composed of 90 true/false items. The scales were used in this consultation assessment to compare laboratory employees' perceptions of their current work environment (Real) with their desired work environment (Ideal). Magnitude of perceptions, using the standard score mean of 50 and the standard deviation of 10, were compared with normative data from health care settings and with subsets of employees in the laboratory. Scale descriptions reflect WES manual information (Moos, 1986, 1994).

*Relationship dimension.* Three subscales measure aspects of the work environment that emphasize the quality of interpersonal relationships. Involvement (INV) measures the extent to which employees are concerned about and committed to their jobs. Peer cohesion (PC) assesses the extent to which employees are friendly and supportive of one another. Supervisor support (SS) indicates the extent to which management is supportive of employees and encourages them to support one another.

280

*Personal growth dimension.* Three scales comprise the focus on personal growth and task orientation. Autonomy (AUT) measures the extent to which employees are encouraged to be self-sufficient and make their own decisions. Task orientation (TO) is indicated by the degree of emphasis on good planning, efficiency, and getting the job done. Work pressure (WP) monitors the degree to which the presses of work and time urgency dominate the job milieu.

*System maintenance and system change dimension.* Four subscales contribute to the measured focus on the organizational structure of the work environment. Clarity (CLA) reflects the degree to which employees know what to expect in their daily routine and how explicitly rules and policies are communicated. Control (CTL) is the extent to which management uses rules and pressures to keep employees under control. Innovation and change (INN) measures the degree of emphasis on variety, change, and new approaches in the work setting. Physical comfort (COM) reflects the extent to which the physical surroundings contribute to a pleasant work environment.

### Health Care Norms
Health care norms were employed as the appropriate reference group for the consultation. General normative data about the WES (Moos, 1986, 1994) indicate that scores for employees in general work settings are higher than for health care employees on three subscales: supervisor support (from the relationship dimension), clarity (of expectations), and physical comfort (from the system maintenance and system change dimension). General work groups are seen as more involving, more cohesive, and allowing for more autonomy than typical health care groups. Health care work groups are generally found to have more work pressure and management-induced controls than general work groups.

### Whole Staff Real vs. Ideal Comparison
As shown in Figure 11.1, whole staff perceptions of the current work environment clustered around the health care mean. The staff's perception of a very positive level of physical comfort (COM), scored at 11/2 standard deviations above the mean for health care settings, reflected the attention and regular upgrading of the physical facility. The laboratory was also characterized with a higher than average degree in autonomy (AUT), reflecting more independence in individual accomplishment of work responsibilities.

Ideal ratings were generally in the predicted direction, with whole staff preferences for greater amounts of supportive aspects in the relationship dimension. This desire for increases in relationship supports was consistent with interview data. Although they reflected a different

## Figure 11.1

### Laboratory Management and Technicians Real vs. Ideal Work Environment Standard Score Comparison

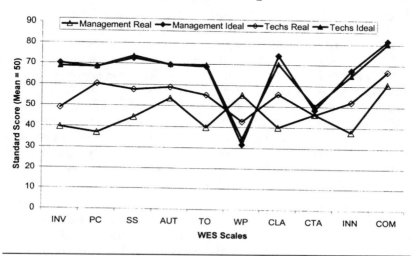

*Note*. Relationship dimension: Involvement (Inv), Peer Cohesion (PC), Supervisor Support (SS); Personal growth dimension: Autonomy (AUT), Task Orientation (TO), Work Pressure (WP); System maintenance and system change dimension: Clarity (CLA), Control (CTL), Innovation and Change (INN), Physical Comfort (COM).

lens for observation of the environment of the laboratory, interviewees identified the need to improve relationships within the department and between the laboratory and its users. In the personal growth dimension, staff preference in the Ideal called for increased autonomy, despite the AUT baseline being higher than health care norms. Similar findings are revealed with task orientation. Work pressure would be lowered for the staff in the ideal work environment, but the real work pressure score was at the health care mean.

### *Management and Technicians Comparison of Real vs. Ideal*
When the Real and Ideal comparisons were broken down further to reflect staff levels, as shown in Figure 11.2, additional valuable information was gained which helped in planning interventions. In looking only at the whole staff data, it was revealed that the staff paralleled health care norms on their shared perception of the work environment.

## Figure 11.2

### Laboratory Whole Staff Real vs. Ideal Work Environment Standard Score Comparison

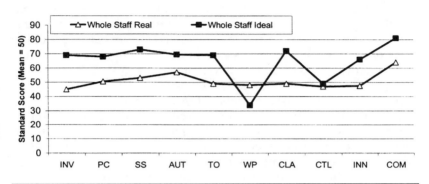

*Note.* Relationship dimension: Involvement (Inv), Peer Cohesion (PC), Supervisor Support (SS); Personal growth dimension: Autonomy (AUT), Task Orientation (TO), Work Pressure (WP); System maintenance and system change dimension: Clarity (CLA), Control (CTL), Innovation and Change (INN), Physical Comfort (COM).

When observing the management/staff composite results, however, it is apparent that there is a discrepancy (an environmental discordance) between the perceived levels of relationship supports in the current work environment. Managers had low scores on each of the relationship subscales. It is noted that managers in health care settings sometimes perceive their work environments more negatively than do health care workers in general (Moos, 1986). By contrast, managers in general work settings typically perceive the work environment more positively than do line staff.

On the three scales indicating environmental sources of personal growth, managers and line staff agreed closely in how they perceived the degree of autonomy of responsibility present in current work expectations. Managers saw lower than average focus on task orientation, scoring about 1 standard deviation below the health care mean, while staff perceived slightly higher than average attention to work tasks. Work pressure scores were in the expected directions, with managers feeling more work pressure than line staff.

In observing the results in the system and physical support areas, managers perceived lower levels of clarity of daily routines, and less innovation and change, than did staff. All staff considered the use of controls in the laboratory equivalent to health care norms. The subscale on use of controls and the subscale of physical comfort provided close matches on environmental perceptions, which ruled these areas out for further intervention.

When reviewing the information on the desired work environment via Ideal scores, there was virtual consistency among all staff. This was good news because it reflected a common set of values about the levels of social climate supports all staff desired, and it served to unify the laboratory's goals for further development.

### Applications of the Social Climate Information

The social climate results were integrated with the other assessment components to formulate a consultation intervention plan. Because the consultation was established to be longer term, several elements of the organization were identified for intervention. Among them was team building within the management staff and between the management team and line staff. Communication with users was identified as a key deficiency. Several specific procedures were introduced to provide better information to users and to provide a more consistent flow of information from the laboratory. One dramatic consequence was that the communication patterns became more open. For example, the laboratory instituted a monthly newsletter for users and, in its first edition, reported on the organizational consultation and its progress to date. Management elected to share information on its work style to improve communication and decision making and to reduce overpersonalized interpretations of work events.

### Counselor Skills Required

In addition to the broad set of skills enumerated in Case Study 1, counselors who work with organizations need to be qualified to use any instruments they determine appropriate for administration. Publishers of instruments often require specific documentation of requisite skills and training in order to make purchases. This is the case for both commercial instruments used in Case Study 2. Interviewing skills honed in counselor education training must be used in context with organizational needs and consultation purposes. Further, it is essential to be aware of political and ethical considerations when working with organizations. Any reports provided to organizations must be protected from potential misuse. After all, exposing the social climate characteristics of any work organization can be used for political or personal fodder.

# Conclusion

In summary, many opportunities exist for ecological counselors to use their skills in complex organizations. The ecological models presented prepare the consultant to conceptualize the organization in dynamic relationship with its larger ecological system. The ecological principles identified have direct and positive bearing on organizational consultation efforts. Of the two such consultations described in the case studies, the first highlights group skills training for organizational development and improvement of the physical work environment. The second focuses on the elements of social climate in relation to improving management practices. Both of the cases present examples and opportunities to understand and improve work environments through careful attention to specific attributes of the organization and its members. Counselors who practice ecological approaches have rich potential to consult successfully with groups and organizations. Preparation, understanding of contexts, and an ecological perspective can only contribute to a healthy organization.

# Learning Activities

1. This chapter provides descriptions of several models that share central ecological assumptions: that levels of ecological influence can be identified, and that they influence and are influenced by each other. With a partner, identify key elements of these models and how they might be applied in an organization.
2. Several ecological principles central to consultation interventions are presented in this chapter. Identify three of these principles and discuss with a partner how they could apply to your academic department.
3. In the case studies of organizational consultation, two aspects of the work environment are targeted for intervention. How might you decide to conceptualize a potential consultation with your immediate work group (class or work environment)? Discuss this with a partner or small group.

# References

Association for Specialists in Group Work (1998). Best practice guidelines. *Journal for Specialists in Group Work, 23*(3), 237-244.

Association for Specialists in Group Work (1999). Principles for diversity-competent group workers. *Journal for Specialists in Group Work, 24*(1), 7-14.

Association for Specialists in Group Work (2000). Professional standards for the training of group workers-2000 revision. *Journal for Specialists in Group Work, 25*(4), 327–342.

Allcorn, S., & Diamond, M. A. (1997). *Managing people during stressful times: The psychologically defensive workplace.* Westport, CT: Quorum.

Barker, R. G. (1965). Explorations in ecological psychology. *American Psychologist, 20,* 1–14.

Barker, R. G. (1974). The ecological environment. In R. H. Moos & P. M. Insel (Eds.), *Issues in social ecology: Human milieus.* Palo Alto, CA: National Press Books.

Bond, M. A. (1999). Gender, race, and class in organizational contexts. *American Journal of Community Psychology, 27,* 327–355.

Bronfenbrenner, U. (1988). Interacting systems in human development. In N. Bolger, A. Caspi, G. Downey, & M. Moorehouse (Eds.), *Persons in context: Developmental processes* (pp. 25–49). New York: Cambridge University Press.

Casella, C. (1979). *Training exercised to improve interpersonal relations in health care organizations.* Greenvale, NY: Panel.

Conoley, J. C., & Haynes, G. (1992). An ecological approach to intervention. In R. C. D'Amato & B. A. Rothlisberg (Eds.), *Psychological perspectives on intervention* (pp. 177–189). White Plains, NY: Longman.

Conyne, R. K. (1989). *How personal growth and task groups work.* Newbury Park, CA: Sage.

Conyne, R. (1999). *Failures in group work: How we can learn from our mistakes.* Thousand Oaks, CA: Sage.

Conyne, R. K., Rapin, L. S., & Rand, J. M. (1999). A model for leading task groups. In H. Forester-Miller & J. Kottler (Eds.), *Issues and challenges for group practitioners* (pp. 117–131). Denver, CO: Love.

Conyne, R. K., Wilson, F. R., & Ward, D. E. (1997). *Comprehensive group work: What it means and how to teach it.* Alexandria, VA: American Counseling Association.

Craig, D. P. (1978). *HIP pocket guide to planning and evaluation.* Austin, TX: Learning Concepts.

Dougherty, A. M. (1995). *Consultation: Practice and perspectives in school and community settings* (2nd ed.). Pacific Grove, CA: Brooks/Cole.

Goldberger, L., & Breznitz, S. (Eds.). (1993). *Handbook of stress: Theoretical and clinical aspects* (2nd ed.). New York: Free Press.

Gump, P. V. (1974). The behavior setting: A promising unit for environmental designers. In R. H. Moos & P. M. Insel (Eds.), *Issues in social ecology: Human milieus* (pp. 267–275). Palo Alto, CA: National Press Books.

Herr, E. L., & Fabian, E. S. E. (1993). Consultation: A paradigm for helping. Consultation II: Prevention, preparation, and key issues [Special issue]. *Journal of Counseling & Development, 72*(2).

Holahan, C. J. (2002). The contributions of Rudolf Moos. *American Journal of Community Psychology, 30,* 65–66.

Hulse-Killacky, D., Killacky, J., & Donigian, J. (2001). *Making task groups work in your world.* Upper Saddle River, NJ: Prentice-Hall.

Joint Committee on Standards for Educational Evaluation, J. R. Saunders, Chair. (1994). *The program evaluation standards: How to evaluate educational programs.* Thousand Oaks, CA: Sage.

Kasambira, K. P. & Edwards, L. (2000). Counseling and human ecology: A conceptual framework for counselor educators. In *Proceedings of the Eighth International Counseling Conference: Counseling and Human Ecology* (pp. 43–52). San Jose, Costa Rica.

Kelly, J. G., Ryan, A. M., Altman, B. E., & Stelzner, S. P. (2000). Understanding and changing social systems: An ecological view. In J. Rappaport & E. Seidman (Eds.), *Handbook of community psychology* (pp. 133–159). New York: Kluwer Academic/Plenum.

Lewin, K. (1936). *Principles of topological psychology.* New York: McGraw-Hill.

Lewis, J. A., Lewis, M. D., Daniels, J. A., & D'Andrea, M. J. (1998). *Community counseling: Empowerment strategies for a diverse society* (2nd ed.). Pacific Grove, CA: Brooks/Cole.

Lewis, J. A., Lewis, M. D., Packard, T., & Souflee, J. F. (2001). *Management of human service programs* (3rd ed.). Pacific Grove, CA: Brooks/Cole.

Lowman, R. L. (Ed.). (1998). *The ethical practice of psychology in organizations.* Washington, DC: American Psychological Association and Society for Industrial and Organizational Psychology.

Maton, K. I. (2000). Making a difference: The social ecology of social transformation. *American Journal of Community Psychology, 28,* 25–57.

Moos, R. H. (1974). Systems for the assessment and classification of human environments: An overview. In R. H. Moos & P. M. Insel (Eds.), *Issues in social ecology: Human milieus* (pp. 1–28). Palo Alto, CA: National Press Books.

Moos, R. H. (1986). *Work Environment Scale manual* (2nd ed.). Palo Alto, CA: Consulting Psychologists Press.

Moos, R. H. (1994). *The social climate scales: A user's guide* (2nd ed.). Palo Alto, CA: Consulting Psychologists Press.

Moos, R. H. (1996). Understanding environments: The key to improving social processes and program outcomes. *American Journal of Community Psychology, 24,* 193–201.

Moos, R. H., & Insel, P. M. (Eds.). (1974). *Issues in social ecology: Human milieus.* Palo Alto, CA: National Press Books.

Muchinsky, P. M., & Monahan, C. J. (1987). What is person-environment congruence? Supplementary vs. complementary models of fit. *Journal of Vocational Behavior, 31,* 268–277.

Putnam, R. D. (2000). *Bowling alone: The collapse and revival of American community.* New York: Simon & Schuster.

Quick, J. C., Quick, J. D., Nelson, D. L., & Hurrell, J. J. (1997). *Preventive stress management in organizations.* Washington, DC: American Psychological Association.

Rapin, L. S. (1985). Organization development: Quality Circle groups. In R. K. Conyne (Ed.), *The group workers' handbook: Varieties of group experience* (pp. 214–232). Springfield, IL: Charles C Thomas.

Rudkin, J. K. (2003). *Community psychology: Guiding principles and orienting concepts*. Upper Saddle River, NJ: Pearson Education.

Trickett, E. J., Barone, C., & Watts, R. (2000). Contextual influences in mental health consultation: Toward an ecological perspective on radiating change. In J. Rappaport & E. Seidman (Eds.), *Handbook of community psychology* (pp. 303-330). New York: Kluwer Academic/Plenum.

Turner, N., Barling, J., & Zacharatos, A. (2001). Positive psychology at work. In C. R. Snyder & S. L. Lopez (Eds.), *Handbook of positive psychology* (pp. 715-727). New York: Oxford Press.

Wallace, W. A., & Hall, D. L. (1996). *Psychological consultation: Perspectives and applications*. Pacific Grove, CA: Brooks/Cole.

Wicker, A. W. (1974). Processes which mediate behavior-environment congruence. In R. H. Moos & P. M. Insel (Eds.), *Issues in social ecology: Human milieus* (pp. 598-615). Palo Alto, CA: National Books Press.

Chapter 12

# Advocacy and Social Action in the Context of Ecological Counseling

*Albert L. Watson, Roger L. Collins, and*
*Felicia Collins Correia*

---

*Chapter Highlights*

- *Advocacy implies arguing for a particular idea, cause, or policy; however, in social services, advocacy and social action typically involve assisting the oppressed and disenfranchised, and assuming that those with resources will advocate for themselves or hire advocates.*
- *Social action, sometimes referred to as citizens advocacy or political advocacy, is implemented to modify a harmful environment, institution, or community on behalf of the entire category of clients.*
- *The long-running debate among practitioners regarding whether clients are empowered, and whether it is within the ability of practitioners to redistribute power within institutions, continues today.*
- *The goal of counselor education programs is not to develop advocates, although that does not mean a counselor will not develop the skills to function as an advocate. There are ethical issues regarding counselor training and advocacy as well as counselor practice and advocacy that require clarification beyond this chapter.*
- *Advocacy and social action are interventions that focus on the environment rather than the individual.*

---

Advocacy and social action are two approaches to counseling services that emphasize the significance of the client's interaction with his or her environment. Basic definitions of advocacy refer specifically to the client's environment as focus for intervention. For example, Lewis and Bradley (2000) defined advocacy as "the act of speaking up or taking action to make environmental changes on behalf of the client" (p. 3). Given the emphasis on environment, advocacy and social action have a great deal to offer counselors in conceptualizing person–environment interactions.

As with any approach to counseling, advocacy and social action have their share of both critics and proponents, although even their supporters respond with mixed emotions. In this chapter, we first describe that diversity and the rebuttals these supporters offer their critics, emphasizing the implications of these debates for ecological perspectives on counseling. We then discuss the implications of advocacy and social action approaches for counselor training. We also describe how advocacy can be used as an intervention on behalf of victims of domestic violence. The case study introduced is based on a seven-step ecological assessment intervention approach (Pardeck, 1988; Pardeck & Chung, 1997). Finally, we discuss issues related to implementation of advocacy.

## Definitions: Advocacy and Social Action in the Context of Ecological Counseling

Literally, advocacy implies the act of arguing in favor of a particular idea, cause, or policy on one's behalf. Within the context of daily civic activity, advocacy can include professional lobbying, adopting legal representation, conducting an advertising or letter writing campaign, even engaging in public protests. Within the context of counseling, however, advocacy has acquired a unique meaning regarding very specific groups of clients.

Most proponents of advocacy and social action recognize that advocacy in the social services typically involves assisting the oppressed and disenfranchised, making the assumption that the wealthy can either advocate for themselves or pay others to support or defend their interests. Others have identified the oppressed and disenfranchised as prime candidates for advocacy because the needs of these groups are often treated as irrelevant or ignored by those in power (D'Andrea & Daniels, 2000). It is not surprising, therefore, that recent publications on advocacy have identified women, ethnic minorities, people with mental illness, and older persons among the groups who might benefit most from this approach to counseling (Lewis & Bradley, 2000; Toporek & Liu, 2001).

Counselors working with clients from these groups encounter two principal challenges to traditional service delivery approaches. First, they discover that clients often suffer from institutional sources of oppression that contribute to their problems (Atkinson, Morten,

& Sue, 1993). Second, it becomes clear that the traditional focus on helping the client adapt to his or her environment is untenable when that environment is unjust or otherwise flawed in its treatment of these clients. Not only does the environment become salient in the counselor's conceptions of the problem, but it also becomes a primary target for change as a means of improving the mental health of clients.

Although the counseling profession has historically viewed the environment as a contributing factor to emotional problems, it only recently began to recognize a relationship to environment and intervention. Consequently, as Morrill, Oetting, and Hurst (1974) noted, the profession thus far has relied almost exclusively on intrapsychic approaches. These authors suggested that counseling interventions aimed at institutions and communities that influence clients may be goals in and of themselves. When mandates are established for large institutions or communities to recognize the individual and respond in a different manner, this may be a signal for that individual to begin expecting the same consideration from other institutions. Expectation often leads to request. Requests are sometimes granted. This may be a new experience, especially for individuals who have been ignored, unrepresented, and mistreated. As the environment, including inhabitants, begins responding differently, those who have been excluded often have greater access. They may also learn to influence institutions and communities to gain access whenever it is needed.

Reflective of the intervention approaches outlined by Cook, Conyne, Savageau, and Tang in chapter 5, we propose the following extrapsychic targets for counselor intervention: (a) the primary group, such as the family, couples, and close friends; (b) associational groups, such as classes, clubs, or a dormitory; (c) institutions, such as community mental health programs, alcohol and drug treatment programs, and a department of corrections; and (d) the community-at-large category of clients (e.g., battered partners, people with disabilities, seniors). Advocacy for women within the context of family therapy is an example of an intervention targeted at the primary group level (cf. Goodrich, 1991). The underlying assumption of this application is that the emotional distress experienced by women in many families is caused by gender inequality with regard to marital intimacy, household decision making, physical and/or emotional coercion. Repeatedly, a counselor's attempts to empower female clients experiencing distress within such family environments are one form of advocacy enacted at this primary level (Avis, 1991; Kaslow & Carter, 1991).

Many who espouse this application of advocacy at the family level are hopeful, yet guarded. For example, Hare-Mustin (1991) wrote that

> the possibility of reorganizing families through therapy is limited by the gender relations sanctioned by the larger society. If the therapist is to do more than encourage [women] to conform to existing norms, he or she needs to recognize how the dominant discourses influence behavior and support the power difference in the relations of women and men. (pp. 81, 82)

This warning by Hare-Mustin suggests that the different targets of intervention can overlap and that boundaries among the categories are more convenient than genuine. This caveat is important when considering the subsequent targets of intervention. Associational groups are usually nested within institutions, and institutions are nested within communities; interactions across these categories, therefore, can be expected. Extending advocacy to these intervention targets, however, introduces another complexity: the possibility that any one client is not the sole victim of a harmful institution or community. This possibility creates another form of advocacy: class advocacy (Lewis, Lewis, Daniels, & D'Andrea, 1998, pp. 191-192).

Class advocacy is conducted to change harmful environments, either institutional or communal, on behalf of an entire category of clients (e.g., battered partners, people with disabilities, seniors). Increasing the number of clients from a single case to an entire class permits a specific intervention strategy associated with this form of advocacy: social action. The social action form of advocacy involves the empowerment of a class of clients, including the development of leadership and other resources among members of this class (Lewis, Cheek, & Hendricks, 2000; Toporek & Liu, 2001). This form of advocacy is sometimes referred to as political advocacy (Lewis & Bradley, 2000) or citizen advocacy (Kiselica & Robinson, 1979); however, it always involves consultative efforts to empower a socially disfranchised group of clients.

Although the schema proposed by Morrill et al. (1974) concluded with community as the broadest macro social level affecting clients' mental health, it may be useful to add a more intangible yet ubiquitous sphere of influence we can call cultural or societal. Hare-Mustin (1991) attested to the significance of this domain in her warning that male prerogatives enacted in the family reflect male privilege in a patriarchal culture. Inequities in the family represent inequities in the society. Challenging inequities on the macro social level may require ongoing interventions that suggest yet another from of advocacy: preventive advocacy (Lewis & Lewis, 1983). Theoretically, this form of advocacy could take place with or without a designated client or class of clients. In either case, the counseling professional needs to change troubled institutions, communities, and other propagators of culture that harm different classes of clients.

## Advocacy Approaches to Counseling: Opposition and Rebuttal

Attention to the causes of client distress rooted within the client's associations, institutions, communities, and/or culture is often at odds with the more accepted practice of providing counseling to individuals. Some have argued that a counselor's commitment to intervene in the client's social environment politicizes an otherwise politically neutral process (Weinrach & Thomas, 1998). Still others maintain the primacy of enlightened self-interest as a motivational factor among clients, driving them away from sociocentric values (Ramm, 1998). In other words, as clients become clear about the issues and gain a voice for themselves, they are better able to understand why they feel the stress and recognize there is no need to internalize stress. Advocacy can reduce some stress and helps to empower the individuals.

Even those who espouse advocacy approaches to counseling have noted the intermittent ascendancy in the United States of "a larger cultural ethos of self-contained or romantic individualism that promotes personal gain rather than mutual benefit" (Enns, 1993, p. 51). Some argue that individualistic problem-solving prevails over systemic approaches as a profession matures. As Enns (1993) observed, citing Withorn (1984), "historically, members of sanctioned professions have tended to privatize problems, narrowly define clients as recipients of direct services, become overly concerned with legitimizing their own expertise and competence, and show limited willingness to form alliances with grass-roots organizations" (p. 53). Professional counselors tend only to view others similarly trained as legitimate providers of human services, and many even challenge legitimacy of their own counterparts to provide advocacy.

In addition to opposition based on values, others have objected to advocacy as a practical alternative to individualistic approaches, noting the pervasive nature of social problems and/or the lack of training of advocacy counselors (Weinrach & Thomas, 1998). Several proponents of advocacy counseling have raised concerns that some paternalistic practitioners run the risk of fostering dependency and helplessness among their clients (Lee, 1998; McWhirter, 1994; Pinderhughes, 1983). In sum, opposition to advocacy approaches to counseling has been based on conflicts over values and on questions about the efficacy of this approach. Major issues seem to be (a) whether advocacy or the functions of advocacy fall within the scope of professional counseling, (b) whether the present counselor training prepares counselors to serve as advocates, and (c) whether trained counselors will be equipped to address undesirable client characteristics (e.g., client dependency).

The argument that advocacy approaches to counseling add a political quality to an otherwise politically neutral practice fails to take into account the hidden political dimensions of traditional practice. For example, removing the client from his or her sociopolitical environment can be viewed as particularizing the problem within the client, or at least making the client more prominent in construing the problem. Similarly, isolating the client from others who may share his or her problem can be viewed as the opposite of collectivizing clients—and no less political even if less questioned. Several proponents of advocacy have noted the implicit politics underlying traditional counseling practices and have distinguished advocacy as merely explicitly political (e.g., Katz, 1985; Sue & Sue, 1999).

The efficacy arguments are more difficult to rebut because the momentum of the status quo is, in part, a major obstacle advocacy approaches must overcome. The fact is that many counselors are not sufficiently trained in advocacy approaches to be effective. It is no surprise, therefore, that the context in which personal problems are rooted can seem overwhelming: problem finding becomes as formidable as problem solving. Left to their own devices and in the absence of specific ethical guidelines, it is not surprising that many counselor advocates can lapse into benevolent paternalism. Nevertheless, there is a sufficient knowledge base about advocacy counseling to offer guidance in addressing problems of implementation, to which we now turn.

## Knowledge About Advocacy in Counseling Empowerment

As mentioned earlier, advocacy approaches to counseling are most often used with people or groups that lack the means to advocate for themselves. Often, their most conspicuous shortcoming is power to effect changes in their own lives. McWhirter (1994) defined empowerment as

> The process by which people, organizations, or groups who are powerless
> or marginalized (a) become aware of the power dynamic at work in their life

context, (b) develop skills and capacity for gaining reasonable control over their lives, (c) which they exercise (d) without infringing on the right of others, and (e) which coincides with actively supporting the empowerment of others in their community. (p. 12)

McWhirter's (1994) ecological notion of empowerment contrasts with more traditional intrapsychic definitions of empowerment, where the focus of counseling is to facilitate the client's sense of self-efficacy during counseling. Toporek and Liu (2001) wrote that traditional definitions of empowerment typically "have avoided references to sociopolitical variables affecting barriers to client action" (p. 387). Others have been more critical of intrapsychic perspectives that are forced on clients experiencing oppressive environments: "Focusing on childhood experiences, developing self concept, or attempting to modify behavior from a traditional counseling perspective does little to address environmental factors such as racism or sexism" (Katz, 1985, p. 618).

In fact, traditional counselors can effectively disempower clients. One of the most unfortunate situations that can occur is when the helping process contributes to a client's feeling of powerlessness. If we consider some of the major ways in which clients experience disempowerment, we are better able to understand how advocacy can be used to empower clients. First, clients experiencing mental health problems are isolated because, among other factors, those professionals who understand and are able to discuss client issues (e.g., psychological counselors) appear to be very different from the clients themselves. The professionals differ in that they often possess a graduate education, specialized training, and other experiences. Many clients find therapy and therapists very alienating and seek other forms of support more consistent with their lifestyles.

Some have argued that the idea of empowering clients represents a paradox in which the powerful impart power to the powerless, but the power hierarchy remains intact. Documented failures to redistribute power within institutions seem to support this proposition (e.g., Gruber & Trickett, 1987). A related fear is that resourceful counselors can apply personal and political power to affect social change on behalf of their clients, but their clients never develop a sense of empowerment, and again, the power differential remains unchanged.

Toporek (2000) offered a theoretical framework in which empowerment is situated on one end of a continuum and social action on the other end. According to this model, counselor actions that tend to focus within the individual or group counseling environment and assist clients in recognizing and addressing sociopolitical barriers to well-being lie toward the empowerment end of the continuum. Counselor actions that advocate for change in the context of a large, public arena lie toward the social action end of the continuum. Although the scope of social change ranges from local to regional to national, this model views personal problems of powerlessness and marginality as rooted in flawed social systems.

The difference between failure and success with regard to client empowerment may be found in the details of implementation. The process of empowerment is complex, and guidelines need to be specified and theoretically coherent.

Several practitioners and theorists have suggested principled and logical approaches to client empowerment within the context of advocacy. Toporek and Liu (2001) recommended the client and counselor-advocate collaborate in problem finding and problem solving, where the collaborative alliance is driven by the client, and the goals of the collaboration are mutually determined. These authors cited the descriptors of collaboration encouraged by Keiffer (1984) when he used the terms *external enabler* and *mentor* to describe how the counselor advocate can act in the best interest of the client.

External enabler and mentor can be used interchangeably to refer to the counselor acting as a third-party consultant to the client (Keiffer, 1984). In this capacity, the external enabler has two major functions. First, it is to share information with the client so that he or she is better prepared to understand the rules of the game. Of course, these rules may be relevant in the client's work setting, community setting, or a number of other settings where advocacy may be useful. Second, the external enabler can intervene on behalf of the individual, which may be done in the presence of clients. Intervening in the presence of clients gives them an opportunity to observe the process. They can also learn how to serve as their own advocates in future situations.

Galper (1975, 1978, 1980) offered a more radical approach to collaboration. In this view, the client and counselor advocate are both victims of flawed social systems, although each may confront systemic injustices with different resources and liabilities. In traditional counseling approaches, the counselor is considered to be all right, at least for the purposes of the helping interaction, whereas the client is seen as having the problem. From a social systems perspective, however, it is quite possible that the counselor and client have the same problem, perhaps rooted in the social structure, such as racism or sexism. In this circumstance, helping the client solve his or her problem will also help the counselor (Galper, 1978).

This perspective does not imply that the client and counselor are equally powerful or equally able to effect social change: a power hierarchy still exists. Yet by rooting the counselor's life space in the same ecological context as the client's, Galper negated the notion of detachment between the two and traced the mutual interest of their alliance. The helping relationship is thus symbiotic, removing the temptation of benevolent paternalism.

Empowerment refers not only to systems change, but also to enabling clients to understand how social systems may oppress them. Edelman (1974) criticized social service providers for underestimating clients' abilities to understand the intersection between their lives and the social systems that affect them. Further, he challenged the profession to demystify the helping process and the interventions counselors make on behalf of their clients.

Proponents of advocacy and client empowerment do not shrink from the political elements inherent in the educative process. According to Galper (1978), every helping interaction contains components of education implicitly or explicitly. In addition, each of these components has a political dimension. Furthermore, when radical politics are introduced into a context, it is not introducing politics into an otherwise politics-free environment. Rather, radical politics are substituted for what is often implicitly conservative politics.

Models of empowerment also inevitably question the prevalence of individualized treatment of separate clients, which is logical when the problem is seen as an individual failure in otherwise viable social systems. When the problem is located within the system, however, collective action may be more appropriate than isolating individuals from one another. Together, clients may be better able to identify the ecological components of their personal problems and better able to organize and initiate activities that can contribute to their resolution (Galper, 1978).

Empowerment also can be achieved by increasing knowledge—knowledge unavailable to counselor advocate and client alike. Research, therefore, can play an important role in advocacy, though traditional research paradigms have placed clients outside the decision-making process. However, the emergence of participatory action research (PAR) offers new possibilities for empowering counselor advocates and their clients with the information they need to effect systems change (Walz, 1997). Researchers using this approach typically commit to working with members of communities who have traditionally been exploited and oppressed, in a united effort to bring about fundamental social change (Brydon-Miller, 2001).The PAR model involves participants in the design of research questions, data collection, and utilization of results; the method itself is an act of empowerment.The literature includes many examples of successful implementation of this research model of advocacy and social action (Dobash, & Dobash, 1992; Naples, 1998; Pederson et al., 1993).

Evidence clearly shows that issues of empowerment are important to the client as well as the counselor. It also is very clear that empowerment can be obtained most easily through the joint efforts of both parties. Counselors, however, often work with clients who experience problems on multiple levels: individual, family, neighborhood, community. Consequently, many of the problems clients bring to counselors are beyond the scope of intrapsychic counseling alone.

Considering this situation, what seems to be needed is an intervention with the ability to be used efficiently by various individuals, such as the counselor and client.A second need is an intervention strategy that can be reproduced or modified and used for various situations. Advocacy, as opposed to traditional intrapsychic approaches, tends to address these needs more efficiently.

## Training Individuals to Function as Advocates

Several aspects of advocacy in order to train individuals to function as advocates can be considered. One aspect of interest is the development of self-advocates, wherein individuals learn to advocate on their own behalf.A second aspect that perhaps touches on various areas of advocacy training is the issue of ethical concerns (e.g.,What is appropriate acceptable behavior for the advocate?). Of particular interest is the third aspect: the training of advocates in counselor education programs. Each of these topics is discussed here.

### Development of Self-Advocates

Gould (1986) described an innovative self-advocacy program designed for high school students with disabilities—high school seniors anticipating graduation before making the transition from school to work.The self-advocacy program was designed to address several major issues.These students were required to become familiar with how their needs were associated with a new setting and new situation. Central to this change in setting and situation was a need to learn about (a) their legal or statutory rights, which are protected by law, and (b) their personal or human rights, which are guaranteed to everyone by societal agreement. The self-advocacy curriculum included the following: (a) definition of rights; (b) exploration of significant human rights; (c) civil rights for the disabled; (d) how laws are made; and (e) what consumers can do when their rights are violated. This curriculum represented an important development which coincided with other changes in society, namely the expansion of educational and employment opportunities for young adults with disabilities.

Options useful in maintaining this program may be directed at the consumer level (microsystem), direct service level, or the policy level (exosystem). At the microsystem level, parents may incorporate the transition as part of an individualized education plan (IEP) or arrange it informally; students also may request this service. At the direct service level, teachers may incorporate self-advocacy into existing course content. At the exosystem level, state or federal agencies may view self-advocacy as valuable and establish policy requiring it for all seniors with disabilities.

Just as this self-advocacy program may fit for one disenfranchised group, we believe it will also benefit survivors of domestic violence and other forms of disenfranchisement. What can be more empowering than learning to advocate for oneself?

## Ethical Concerns in Advocacy

Most groups of counselors (e.g., school, mental heath, rehabilitation) have adopted a code of ethics, which is considered an indication of professionalism in the field (Collinson et al., 1998). Ethics provide broad guidelines that counselors can use in deciding what behaviors are acceptable. The American Counseling Association (1995) Standards of Practice, for instance, represent minimal behavior standards that are consistent with its Code of Ethics, and counselors are required to adhere to both. Professional counselors adopt codes of ethics to protect the public from unscrupulous and incompetent practitioners.

Lewis, Cheek, and Hendricks (2000) highlighted a dichotomy in attitudes among many professional counselors. In adhering to their Code of Ethics, counselors have a responsibility to promote the welfare of clients. Lewis et al. pointed out that there are counselors who still believe they can promote the welfare of their clients solely through direct services, while they have the "luxury of ignoring everything that is going on outside the counseling room" (p. 330). Lewis et al. also pointed out that increasing numbers of counselors realize that their responsibility to clients exceeds what they can accomplish from their office. In fact, according to these authors, "advocacy is an integral part of every counselor's role" (p. 330).

This viewpoint suggests a number of interesting situations. First, who trains counselors to be advocates? Also, if counselor educators concur with Lewis et al. about counselors needing to function as advocates, what progress has been made within counselor education programs? Do employers have concerns that advocacy is not part of the traditional counselor education preparation? Has any research been conducted on the skills advocates possess and where they acquire these skills? Are counselors who graduate from traditional counselor education programs who accept jobs involving advocacy providing services beyond their expertise?

## Advocacy Training in Counselor Education

It should be acknowledged that signs exist within the profession that support advocacy. For instance, Chi Sigma Iota, the honorary fraternity of counselors and counseling students, sponsored a leadership conference in 1998, and ACA has supported an Emerging Leaders Workshop at its annual convention for the past several years. Counselor education programs have been encouraged to incorporate advocacy training into their curricula. Accrediting bodies such as the Council for the Accreditation of Counseling and Related Educated Programs (CACREP) also underscore the importance of counselor education by providing beginning students with knowledge of advocacy.

Professionals have identified the skills necessary to advocate for ethnic minorities (Arredondo & Vazquez, 2000; Herring, 2000; Sander, 2000), youth (D'Andrea & Daniels, 2000), older persons (Goodman & Waters, 2000; Myers, 1998), and a host of other disenfranchised groups. House and Martin (1988) provided a detailed list of functions that counselors need to perform in the role of advocate. The functions are categorized into three groups: (a) assisting students; (b) assisting the school system; and (c) assisting the community. Specific examples include (a) removing barriers to learning; (b) teaching students to help themselves; (c) teaching students and their families to access information and support systems; and (d) working collaboratively with school personnel.

Lee (1998) indicated that advocates must perform three important functions. First, in addition to traditional counseling skills, advocates must be able to view helping from a systemic change perspective. Second, advocates must attempt changes throughout various systems and partner with clients who lack the knowledge and skill to make changes. Third, advocates must possess knowledge of system change principles and the skills to implement principles into purposeful action.

Six generic advocacy competencies are generally useful with various group situations (Kiselica & Robinson, 2001). First, advocates must develop the capacity for commitment and an appreciation for the suffering experienced. Second, advocates need to be able to accurately convey and interpret verbal and nonverbal interactions. Third, advocates must possess a multisystemic perspective and be able to see issues from the individual, microsystemic, mesosystemic, exosystemic, and macrosystemic levels. Fourth, advocates must be able to intervene skillfully with individuals, groups, and organizations. Fifth, because advocates are often involved with social causes, they need to be adept at using media, technology, and the Internet. Sixth, advocates need research and research skills to inform their advocacy initiatives.

Lewis et al. (2000) offered valuable suggestions for supervising the training of advocates. Their model is designed to monitor and facilitate the changes that occur as counselors develop, including not only the skills but also the confidence to assume the role of advocate. This five-stage model is based on the work of Prochaska, DiClemente, & Norcross (1992) and Norcross & DiClemente (1994), on stages of change.

According to Collison et al. (1998), counselor education programs should contain social action as a core component of the curriculum. Suggestions for successfully developing social activism among counselor education students include the following. First, the counselor education program statement (e.g., mission statement, goals) should clearly display a commitment to activism. Second, course descriptions, syllabi, class assignments, and other materials should support social advocacy. Third, Internet sites that support socially responsible counselors should be used whenever possible. (The Internet is a wealth of timely and convenient information, often providing opportunity to connect with individuals who can provide feedback about the usefulness of information and resources.) Fourth, counseling professors should encourage students to participate in social advocacy projects. Fifth, in addition to learning about individual change, counseling students also should learn about societal change and organizational change. Sixth, evaluation following graduation should explore what graduates are doing to address social injustice. Seventh, counseling professors in a program that stresses social activism must be willing to model activist behaviors for their students; otherwise, their credibility is diminished.

Some advocacy-building efforts are finally being reported in the counseling literature. For example, Russo and Matchette (1998) described a service-learning project designed to introduce beginning school and community counseling students to social activism. The students were introduced to Bronfennbrener's social ecological theory (as cited in Russo & Matchette, 1998). This approach is a valuable orientation for counselors because it assumes that development is a reciprocal process of interaction and that accommodation occurs across the life cycle. Not only does this development occur across the life span, but it also occurs across different environments.

## Ecological Assessment–Intervention Approach

Ecological approaches have received considerable attention for the past 30 years. This particular assessment–intervention approach consists of seven phases (Pardeck, 1988; Pardeck & Chung, 1997). First, the "entering the ecosystem" phase is concerned with assessing relationships in the client's life and gathering information about clients and related subsystems. Second, "mapping the ecology" involves analyzing the client's various subsystems to identify the people and events pertinent to client problems. Third is "assessing the ecology." Strength, weakness, and influential factors are assessed and weighted for value or importance to the individual. Fourth is "creating the vision of change," in which practitioners identify areas to be changed while emphasizing existing strengths in the client's ecosystem. Fifth, in "coordinating-communicating," the role of the practitioner is to communicate with those in the client's ecosystem, and to coordinate appropriate actions. Sixth is the "reassessing," which involves practitioners, clients, and significant persons reviewing the progress made, and then moving toward termination. Finally, "evaluation" may take various forms depending on the client's problems and interventions designed (e.g., feedback of client or significant others).

The ecological assessment provides detailed information useful in implementing either advocacy or social action interventions. Pardeck & Chung's (1997) seven-phase procedure allows the counselor to clarify important issues such as, What supports exist in a client's life? What are the problems, and how are others affected? What are the goals of counseling or client expectations?

Once the assessment process is complete, the advocacy functions can begin. Advocacy functions might include providing the client specific information about his or her situation, and arranging for the client to obtain services from other professional helpers. In addition, social advocacy can be performed at the macro level to initiate social change and social justice. Social advocates promote social justice by influencing letter-writing campaigns, the allocation of resources, lobbying for legislative changes, and initiating legal action. Although not presented in Michelle's case study, which follows, the counselor could work with Michelle and others experiencing similar concerns to develop a social advocacy movement to address the clients' concerns.

## Case Study

In 1999, Michelle K. divorced her husband, William K., both residents of California. Because the divorce was the result of domestic violence, Michelle was granted sole custody of her children. Her husband requested supervised visitation, but the judge denied it, explaining that his past behavior had been unpredictable and violent, and that he was an unacceptable role model for young developing children. Michelle was pleased with the decision; however, she reported to the court that she felt as though her safety depended merely on one piece of paper. That night, Michelle and her two daughters left California.

Just as the sun rose the next day, she drove into Coweta, Oklahoma. It was perfect. She knew no one there. It was a relatively small town, but large enough for her to open a business as a seamstress. She got the girls settled and started taking classes. Soon enough, her business was doing well. She was making it without child support from the girls' father.

One beautiful Friday afternoon, a neighbor called Michelle at the seamstress shop to tell her that she had noticed a prowler. As the neighbor described the prowler, reality slapped Michelle as hard as William ever had. He had tracked her down! He had found her! He was in her backyard!

Michelle quickly contacted the police, presented the protective order from the California court, and then realized the police would not be able to do anything. One officer explained that if her ex-husband were caught in her backyard he could be arrested. Michelle listened politely, taking a deep breath, because she was certain that by the time police came to arrest him she would be dead. Desperate and frightened, she and her daughters did not return to their home for 3 days, instead staying in a motel. She thought about packing and running, but to where this time? The third evening away from her business, she received a call from Ted, the owner of the florist shop adjacent to her shop. They talked for hours. She had not had the opportunity to share her dilemma, and Ted seemed helpful and confident. He suggested that she contact the Domestic Violence Intervention Service (DVIS). The following morning, she telephoned DVIS and scheduled an afternoon appointment with Mary Ellen, a counselor.

## The Seven Phases of Ecological Assessment-Intervention

### 1. Entering the Ecosystem

Mary Ellen met with Michelle and scheduled a 2-hour home visit with her and her family. This home visit allowed her to observe Michelle and her daughters, Catherine and Jane, in their home environment. During the initial contact, Mary Ellen provided Michelle with demographic information about domestic violence, with the intent that Michelle learn more about the seriousness of domestic violence, including its frequency, danger, and the resources available to help address it. Mary Ellen expected this information might help Michelle and her daughters feel less isolated. Mary Ellen noted both discord and strengths as Michelle interacted with her children. She arranged the next intervention, mapping the ecology.

### 2. Mapping the Ecology

This intervention often can be implemented during the initial visit. Mapping the ecology is intended to analyze the various subsystems, people, and events pertinent to Michelle's life. It became apparent to Mary Ellen that family and work were extremely important to Michelle. Two next-door neighbors, Dominic and Karen, played significant roles in Michelle's life, and Ted was a good friend. Unfortunately, Michelle's ex-husband was still important to her as well, but she explained that her independence was also essential to her. In fact, she was pleased with the success of the seamstress shop because it allowed her to refuse any child support. Financial freedom was just one other way of distancing herself from abuse, a marriage that failed, and a man she no longer loved.

Although Michelle no longer loved William, there were a number of issues to be resolved. For example, would the children have any contact with their paternal grandparents? How would visits be arranged, assuming that she wanted to avoid him? Financial support was not an issue at the time, but that could change after the children become older. It was even possible that Michelle would want to communicate with William concerning information involving hereditary conditions.

### 3. Assessing the Ecology

In this step, the counselor focused on the quality of the client's relationships. The counselor emphasized strengths and weaknesses among the client's significant relationships, with the intention of identifying and augmenting strengths. At this point, for example, Mary Ellen might help Michelle expand her social support system. In addition, considering the importance of her seamstress business, it might be valuable to assist Michelle in becoming actively involved with the Coweta Chamber of Commerce and other business outlets.

### 4. Creating the Vision of Change

This is critical to any change process. Mary Ellen can help identify areas that need to be changed, but only the client can change them, of course.

In Michelle's situation, a fundamental decision to be made is whether she will continue to run from William. No one can make that decision except Michelle. During the vision of change stage, it might be time for Michelle to volunteer for Court Watch, a volunteer program that monitors sentencing patterns in domestic violence cases. Such volunteer work might encourage Michelle to evaluate her own life possibilities.

### 5. Coordinating-Communicating
The master plan is implemented. The major role of the counselor is to communicate with those in the client's ecosystem and coordinate appropriate actions. Much of the change effort will be in the hands of those providing support. This can be very valuable for the client who chooses not to participate in traditional helping services. At the same time, professional counselors can be of assistance via telephone.

### 6. Reassessing
The sixth phase, reassessing, is consistent with traditional counseling approaches. Reassessment permits the counselor to reflect on the changes envisioned and what has been achieved. Feedback from the client and significant others may be helpful in determining how well the goal has been attained. During this stage, the counselor plans the termination.

Michelle was not clear about an exact goal for her situation. She wanted something done about the husband, but she was still not sure what. What she did come to realize is that she is better able to take care of herself and her children than she had believed. She also had come to understand that she does not have to be overwhelmed with fear of her husband. Although life was not what she thought it would be, it is manageable.

### 7. Evaluation
This is the seventh and final phase in this approach. As with traditional approaches, evaluation needs to consider process and outcome. Attention to ecological matters, however, extends the evaluation process to consider a broader range of effects.

## Issues, Barriers, and Concerns

According to Lewis and Bradley (2000), numerous unresolved issues are associated with the implementation of advocacy for professional counselors. Many of these issues involve the training that counselors receive (Lewis et al., 2000), as well as that of other professionals who become change agents or advocates (Bennis, Benne, Chin, & Corey, 1976).

Counselors traditionally focus on the client's intrapsychic concerns, which they attempt to resolve through counseling and other psychological procedures. Many of these practitioners focus solely on the client and rely exclusively on talk therapies. In their counseling sessions, their goal is to fix the client.

Some counselors practice this type of counseling all their lives. Others practice a different type. One notable difference is that these practitioners focus more on both the client and the client's environment. Attention to the client's environment frees them to use strategies other than talk therapy. For example, a counselor may want stressed clients to learn how they react to the different environments they encounter throughout the day. Which are warm and nurturing? Which produce stress? Perhaps even visiting and observing the client interacting in various environments will be within the range of appropriate conduct for the ecological counselor.

This shift in focus has obvious implications for changes in training advocates. Although counselor training is not intended exclusively to prepare individuals to become advocates, it can develop many of the skills advocates use. Also, there are other advocacy skills that typically are not part of counselor education, but should be included. One such area involves being able to analyze social contexts, and to develop environmental interventions aimed at organizations, governments, and other external factors.

Another consequence of emphasizing advocacy and social action models in counselor training is the need to rethink the research methods curriculum. The collaboration between counselor and client inherent in advocacy models should be reflected in data collection and analysis in assessing systemic, institutional, and individual change. Collaboration between researcher and subject is central to participatory action research, a model of research not typically available to counselor trainees (Maxwell, 1996).

It should be noted that recent efforts to diversify research methodology in counselor training programs have been slow to develop. Appeals to include qualitative research methods in the counselor training curriculum, for example, have encountered some resistance (e.g., Polkinghorne, 1984, 1991). Faculty members who are unfamiliar or uncomfortable with alternative research methods and already have a full curriculum are currently the principal barriers to diversifying research training. However, counseling programs can hire faculty members with proficiency in these methods, and they can use the expertise of research faculty outside their departments. In addition, the creative redesign of research methods courses and practice can create efficiencies and synergy of content such that a wider variety of methods can be included without overburdening the curriculum (e.g., Larson & Besett-Alech, 2000).

Another barrier to moving toward advocacy and social action counseling models is the financial infrastructure of the profession. With the increased involvement in managed care by counseling agencies and organizations, professional counselors need to more concerned with providing billable services. Funding sources tend to be more comfortable and willing to pay traditional service providers (i.e., those providing direct intrapsychic services on a one-to-one basis), and many third-party payers challenge the appropriateness of services directed toward the environment, or to organizational clients, rather than the individual.

As with managed care organizations, many employers of professional counselors are also conservative in their practices, with many counseling agencies reluctant to provide advocacy services. Sometimes, for instance, the provision of advocate services may put the counselors in a conflictual or adversarial relationship with other social service agencies or businesses. Administrators of some social service agencies may be concerned that advocacy will alienate important decision makers and cause financial risk. Other counselors could perceive advocacy as an inappropriate activity because they believe it exceeds the role and function of a professional counselor.

Most American adults, even those who receive graduate educations, do not learn to think about behavior from a systemic perspective. Counselors and other professional helpers usually have not been sensitized to the relationship between individual problems and the social context in which they occur. Likewise, many professional helpers rely exclusively on providing intrapsychic interventions, even when the outcomes of such interventions can be less than desirable.

In addition, many professional helpers are alienated from their clients because of class, race, socioeconomic status, and other factors. These professionals usually do not see themselves sharing the same or a similar life space as their clients, an alienation that is expressed in different ways. One example is the unwillingness of helping professionals to truly collaborate with clients as equals. We perceive advocacy as a process that can enable helping professionals to collaborate with clients in various manners, resulting in improved service delivery and greater client satisfaction.

## Conclusion

For decades, social scientists have recognized that many of the life problems Americans experience are rooted in the manner in which they tend to influence their environments and how their environments tend to influence them reciprocally. In the past two decades, however, many Americans best able to influence their environment have chosen not to do so (e.g., the decline in civic activities). Furthermore, those least able to influence their environment at any level, such as victims of violence, older persons, and poor people, comprise a significant proportion of the U.S. population. Professionals charged with assisting victims of violence, older persons, poor people, and other disenfranchised groups could vastly extend their reach if they were to function as advocates and prepare their clients to advocate on their own behalf.

For more than two decades, researchers involved with person–environment transactions have demonstrated that the problems many disenfranchised individuals experience are often embedded within their environments. Researchers have also described the efficacy of counselors functioning as advocates, and they have demonstrated the training methods and skills useful in developing such professionals.

Advocacy can be a vital resource for counselors and others serving disenfranchised clients. Advocacy facilitates empowerment so that the individuals and their advocates are able to create environments that contribute to the clients' personal and collective development.

## Learning Activity

### Premise

This chapter introduces an ongoing learning activity rather than several separate ones, as in the other chapters. The premise of this activity is that it is often instructive for students to discover their personal inclinations toward problem defining and problem solving by responding to problems they encounter as students. Thus in this activity, you are asked to write down your complaints as students. Your instructor may initiate brainstorming by mentioning any commonly heard grievance, such as insufficient parking; classes (training) scheduled too early (too late); poorly lit campus at night (concern for personal safety); sexual or racial harassment by faculty; inadequate advising; and thefts on campus.

### Instructions and Notes

#### Instructions
In groups or individually, develop a list of grievances, using the following prompt: "Campus problems I've encountered as a student/trainee."

Consider the nature of the problem, generate solutions, and rank-order the perceived effectiveness of those solutions, noting areas of agreement and disagreement if you are working in small groups.

## Purpose
The purpose of this activity is to activate the frameworks by which you define problems and envision solutions.

## Analysis
Each of these problems can be construed in terms of the individual's responsibility and/or institutional responsibility. For example, if the problem is insufficient student parking, one potential solution is for student drivers to arrive earlier, when more parking is available. From this perspective, the problem and the solution are viewed in individualistic terms. It is the student's responsibility to arrive when parking is most likely to available. (A variation of this theme is for students to gather or share information about locations where parking is more available.)

This problem—like the others on the list—can also be viewed in terms of institutional responsibility. The institution is responsible for providing sufficient parking for its students. This interpretation of the problem, in turn, is more likely to elicit advocacy and social action problem solving. For example, when insufficient parking is viewed as an institutional deficiency, student social action is seen as a viable strategy. Not only is the problem viewed as outside individual students, but students are also viewed as a class that could benefit from a change in institutional policies and practices.

Each problem in the list of grievances can be subject to this kind of analysis, and unless the course title and description signal the appropriate response, students can determine whether they have a consistent way of construing problems and solutions: individualistically or ecologically. The exercise is not a trait inventory, but a way to activate student thinking about consistencies in their approaches to problem finding and problem solving. It also initiates student thinking about the potential relationship between their predispositions and their receptivity to advocacy and social action approaches.

## Discussion
Class discussion of this exercise should take into consideration the fact that students' predispositions are often attitudes and beliefs they have cherished all their lives. The student whose background has instilled a highly valued internal locus of control ("I am the master of my fate, the captain of my soul") might view the ecological perspective as an

attempt by individuals to avoid personal responsibilities. This stance may not be simply analytical, but emotional and possibly moral.

The usefulness of the activity presented here is that students can relate to the problems they identify personally, and they will notice the different perspectives toward those problems taken by their peers. The objective is to add to or strengthen the students' ecological understanding of personal problems and to recognize how advocacy and social action, as they have been described here, derive from such an understanding.

# References

American Counseling Association. (1995). *Code of ethics and standards of practice*. Alexandria, VA: Author.

Arredondo, P., & Vazquez, L. (2000). *Advocacy: Empowerment strategies from Latino/Latina perspectives* (American Counseling Association Presidential Theme Paper No. 12). Alexandria, VA: American Counseling Association.

Atkinson, D. R., Morten, G., & Sue, D. W. (1993). *Counseling American minorities: A cross-cultural perspective* (4th ed.). Dubuque, IA: William C. Brown.

Avis, J. M. (1991). Power politics and therapy with women. In T. J. Goodrich (Ed.), *Women and power: Perspectives for family therapy*. (pp 183-200). New York: W. W. Norton.

Bennis, W. G., Benne, K. D., Chin, R., & Corey, K. E. (1976). *The planning of change*. New York: Holt Rinehart & Winston.

Brydon-Miller, M. (2001). Education, research, and action: Theory and methods of participatory action research. In D. L. Tolman & M. Brydon-Miller (Eds.), *From subjects to subjectivities: A handbook of interpretive and participatory methods* (pp. 76-94). New York: New York University Press.

Collison, B. B., Osborne, J. L., Gray, L. A., House, R. M., Firth, J., & Lou, M. (1998). Preparing counselors for social action. In C. C. Lee & G. R. Walz (Eds.), *Social action: A mandate for counselors* (pp. 263-277). Alexandria, VA: American Counseling Association.

D'Andrea, M., & Daniels, J. (2000). *Advocacy: Youth advocacy* (American Counseling Association Presidential Theme Paper No. 5). Alexandria, VA: American Counseling Association.

Dobash, R. E., & Dobash, R. P. (1992). *Women, violence, and social change*. New York: Routledge.

Edelman, M. (1974). The political language of the helping professions. *Politics and Society, 4,* 295-310.

Enns, C. (1993). Twenty years of feminist counseling and therapy: From naming biases to implementing multifaceted practice. *The Counseling Psychologist, 21*(1), 3-87.

Galper, J. (1975). *The politics of social services*. Englewood Cliffs, NJ: Prentice-Hall.

Galper, J. (1978). What are radical social services? *Social Policy, 8*(4), 37-41.

Galper, J. (1980). *Social work practice: A radical perspective*. Englewood Cliffs, NJ: Prentice Hall.

Goodrich, T. J. (Ed.). (1991). *Women and power: Perspectives for family therapy*. New York: W. W. Norton.

Goodman, J., & Waters, E. (2000). Advocating on behalf of older adults. In J. Lewis & L. Bradley (Eds.), *Advocacy in counseling: Counselors, clients, and community*. Greensboro, NC: CAPS.

Gould, M. (1986). Self-advocacy: Consumer leadership for the transition years. *Journal of Rehabilitation*, 39-42.

Gruber, J., & Trickett, E. J. (1987). Can we empower others? The paradox of empowerment in the governing of an alternative public school. *American Journal of Community Psychology, 15*(3), 353-371.

Hare-Mustin, R. (1991). Sex, lies, and headaches: The problem is power. In T. J. Goodrich (Ed.), *Women and power: Perspectives for family therapy* (pp. 63-85). New York: W. W. Norton.

Herring, R. (2000). *Advocacy: Advocacy for Native American Indians and Alaska Native clients and counselors* (American Counseling Association Presidential Theme Paper No. 7). Alexandria, VA: American Counseling Association.

House, R. M., & Martin, P. J. (1988). Advocating for better futures for all students: A new vision for school counselors. *Education, 119*(2), 284-290.

Kaslow, N., & Carter, A. (1991). Depressed women in families: The search for power and intimacy. In T. J. Goodrich (Ed.), *Women and power: Perspectives for family therapy* (pp. 166-182). New York: W. W. Norton.

Katz, J. (1985). The sociopolitical nature of counseling. *The Counseling Psychologist, 13*(4), 615-624.

Keiffer, C. H. (1984). Citizen empowerment: A developmental perspective. In J. Rappaport, C. Swift, & R. Hess (Eds.), *Studies in empowerment: Steps toward understanding and action* (pp. 30-38). Alexandria, VA: American Counseling Association.

Kiselica, M. S., & Robinson, M. (2001). Bringing advocacy counseling to life: The history, issues, and human dramas of social justice work counseling. *Journal of Counseling & Development, 79*(4), 387-397.

Larson, L. M., & Besett-Alesch, T. (2000). Bolstering the scientist component in the training of scientist-practitioners: One program's curriculum modifications. *The Counseling Psychologist, 28*(6), 873-896.

Lee, C. C. (1998). Counselors as agents of social change. In C. C. Lee & G. R. Walz (Eds.), *Social action: A mandate for counselors* (pp. 3-14). Alexandria, VA: American Counseling Association.

Lewis, J., & Bradley, L. (Eds.). (2000). *Advocacy in counseling: Counselors, clients, and community*. Greensboro, NC: CAPS.

Lewis, J. A., Cheek, J. R., & Hendricks, C. B. (2000). *Advocacy in supervision*. Philadelphia: Brunner-Routledge.

Lewis, J. A., & Lewis, M. D. (1983). *Community counseling: A human services approach*. New York: Wiley.

Lewis, J. A., Lewis, M. D., Daniels, J., & D'Andrea, M. (1998). *Community counseling: Empowering strategies for a diverse society*. Pacific Grove, CA: Brooks/Cole.

Maxwell, J. A. (1996). *Qualitative research design: An interactive approach*. Thousand Oaks, CA: Sage.

McWhirter, E. H. (1994). *Counseling for empowerment*. Alexandria, VA: American Counseling Association.

Morrill, W. H., Oetting, E. R., & Hurst, J. (1974). Dimensions of counselor functioning. *Personnel and Guidance Journal, 52*, 354-359.

Myers, J. E. (1998). Combating ageism: The rights of older persons. In C. C. Lee & G. R. Walz (Eds.), *Social action: A mandate for counselors* (pp. 137-160). Alexandria, VA: American Counseling Association.

Naples, N. (1998). Women's community activism and feminist activist research. In N. Naples (Ed.), *Community activism and feminist politics: Organizing across race, class, and gender*. New York: Routledge.

Pardeck, J. T. (1988). Social treatment through an ecological approach. *Clinical Social Worker Journal, 16*(1), 92-104.

Pardeck, J. T., & Chung, W. S. (1997). Treating powerless minorities through an ecosystem approach. *Adolescence, 32*(127), 625-634.

Pederson, E. L., Chaikin, M., Koehler, D., Campbell, A., & Arcand, M. (1993). In E. Sutton & A. Factor (Eds.), *Older adults with developmental disabilities: Optimizing choice and change* (pp. 277-325). Baltimore, MD: Paul H. Brookes.

Pinderhughes, E. B. (1983). Empowerment for our clients and for ourselves. *Social Casework, 6*(6), 331-338.

Polkinghorne, D. E. (1984). Further extensions of methodological diversity for counseling psychology. *Journal of Counseling Psychology, 31*, 416-429.

Polkinghorne, D. E. (1991). Two conflicting calls for methodological reform. *The Counseling Psychologist, 19*, 103-114.

Prochaska, J. O., DiClemente, C. C., & Norcross, J. C. (1992). In search of how people change: Application to addiction behaviors. *American Psychologist, 49*(9), 1102-1114.

Prochaska, J. O., DiClemente, C. C., & Norcross, J. C. (1994). *Changing for good: A revolutionary six-stage program for overcoming bad habits and moving your life positively forward*. New York: Avon Books.

Ramm, D. R. (1998). Consider the scientific study of morality. *American Psychologist, 53*(3), 323-324.

Russo, T., & Matchette, J. (1998, April). *Critical approaches to service learning in a counselor training program*. Paper presented to the National Youth Leadership Conference, Minneapolis, MN.

Sue, D. W., & Sue, D. (1999). *Counseling the culturally different*. New York: Wiley.

Toporek, R. (2000). Developing a common language and framework for understanding advocacy counseling. In J. Lewis & L. Bradley (Eds.), *Advocacy in counseling: Counselors, clients, and community* (pp. 5-14). Greensboro, NC: CAPS.

Toporek, R., & Liu, W. M. (2001). Advocacy in counseling: Addressing race, class, and gender oppression. In D. Pope-Davis, L. Hardin, & K. Coleman (Eds.), *The intersection of race, class, and gender in multicultural counseling* (pp. 385–413). Thousand Oaks, CA: Sage.

Walz, G. R. (1997). *Knowledge generalization regarding the status of guidance and counseling.* Washington, DC: Education Trust.

Weinrach, S. G., & Thomas, K. R. (1998). Diversity-sensitive counseling today: A postmodern clash of values. *Journal of Counseling & Development, 76,* 115–122.

Withorn, A. (1984). *Serving the people: Social services and social change.* New York: Columbia University Press.

Chapter 13

# Counseling and Ecological Prevention Practice

*Krista M. Chronister, Benedict T. McWhirter,*
*and Shoshana D. Kerewsky*

---

*Chapter Highlights*

- *Mental health problems occur along a continuum; thus, real-world imple-*
  *mentation of prevention efforts will also form a conceptual and practical*
  *prevention-treatment continuum.*
- *Prevention efforts with an individual or community must include other*
  *systems within the ecology and must address person-environment*
  *interactions.*
- *Increasing critical consciousness is an important and necessary step for*
  *counselors in increasing the relevancy of their prevention efforts and their*
  *multicultural counseling competencies.*
- *Preventive interventions that include the needs, expectations, and practices*
  *of a specific culture or community—and not of the counselor or researcher—*
  *are more likely to be effective.*
- *Preventive interventions should include counselors' efforts to advocate for*
  *individuals and communities at broader levels of the ecology in order to*
  *promote social change.*

---

The purpose of this chapter is to present an ecological model as a framework for guiding prevention efforts in counseling. First, we define prevention as it applies to the counseling profession. Second, we use the ecological model of development as articulated by Bronfenbrenner (1979, 1989) and two case studies to describe the processes and competencies needed for effective prevention practice with individuals and groups. Third, we give special attention to multicultural issues, and to the value and importance of the counselor's role in promoting

315

social change. We refer to the two case studies that follow throughout our discussion of counseling and ecological prevention practice.

## Case Studies

### Case Study 1: Smith Middle School

Blockstown is an urban city with a population of 750,000. In the past 5 years, Blockstown school administrators, teachers, and counselors have recognized a significant and dramatic increase in dating violence among their high school students. They have noted an increase in the number of female students who report experiences of dating violence, the number of physical and nonphysical altercations among students that seem related to dating problems, and the number of injuries female students present with at school (i.e., bruises, scratches).

Blockstown school officials fear that their community may parallel national trends indicating a lowering of the age at which students begin dating, as well as a pattern that shows many adult abusers and survivors of domestic violence have their first experiences with relationship violence during adolescence. In response, Blockstown school officials have sought consultation regarding the implementation of a curriculum intervention program that addresses dating violence earlier in students' development. School officials have chosen Smith Middle School to implement and test this pilot program. Smith Middle School is composed of 1,200 students in grades six through eight (most from lower income families), and 55 teachers, counselors, and school administrators and staff. Blockstown's superintendent and Smith Middle School officials have hired you to create and implement a dating violence prevention program.

As a counseling consultant, what particular issues do you want to address first with students and school officials? What intervention format might you use to teach students and school officials about dating violence? What information and resources would you include in the intervention program? What factors may complicate your work with Smith Middle School students and school officials? Consider these questions as you read.

### Case Study 2: Magdalena

Magdalena is a 27-year-old woman from Mexico who moved to the United States 3 years ago with her husband, Jorge, and their three young children. Magdalena has learned to speak English, but she is shy and insecure about her English skills. Jorge and Magdalena left their families and friends in Mexico so that Jorge might find a better paying job to support their families. Since moving to the United States, Jorge has attained U.S. citizenship and has learned to speak English, but he has had great difficulty finding stable work.

Jorge has been emotionally abusive since he and Magdalena began dating. Despite Jorge's many promises to change, his emotional abuse has grown more severe during their marriage. He constantly criticizes Magdalena's intelligence, appearance, and parenting, and has isolated her from family and friends. He refuses to allow her to apply for U.S. citizenship or work. Jorge also prevents Magdalena from driving their car and refuses to give her enough money to buy sufficient food and clothing for the family. The abuse is most severe when Jorge is between jobs and is drinking all day at home. When Magdalena shares her desire to work and help financially, Jorge often becomes enraged and threatens to report her to immigration services or physically abuses her. Magdalena fears not only for her safety, but also for their children's safety.

Magdalena feels tired, hopeless, and confused about where to turn for support. Last week, she saw a flier for a domestic violence services agency posted on her church bulletin board. Magdalena decided to take a great risk and ask her neighbor to drive her to the domestic violence office so she could speak with someone.

As Magdalena's counselor, what particular issues do you want to address first? What efforts might you make to help Magdalena protect herself and her children from further violence? To what support services and resources would you refer Magdalena? What factors may complicate your work with Magdalena? Consider these questions as you read.

## Prevention Defined

Definitions of prevention have varied over time and across disciplines (e.g., Caplan, 1964; Gordon, 1987; Mrazek & Haggerty, 1994; Romano & Hage, 2000). Although the scope of this chapter does not allow us to review the complete history of prevention, we offer some historical highlights and provide a prevention definition specifically created for the counseling profession. For a more in-depth review of the history of prevention, we refer the reader to Romano and Hage (2000).

Literally, *prevention* means to stop something before it happens (Romano & Hage, 2000). In 1964, Caplan added the categories of primary, secondary, and tertiary prevention. These terms refer to the reduction of new incidence rates of a disorder (primary), prevalence rates for those at risk of developing a disorder (secondary), or the harmful effects of an existing disorder (tertiary). In 1987, Gordon created a different classification system making distinctions among universal, selected, and indicated prevention. This classification system identified targeted populations, including everyone in a population (universal), an individual or subgroup of a population (selected), or only individuals and groups at high risk (indicated). More recently, the Institute of Medicine (IOM) defined prevention efforts as only those that occur before the onset of a disorder (Mrazek & Haggerty, 1994).

There are several criticisms regarding the applicability of these more recognized definitions and classification systems to the prevention of mental disorders (Lorion, Price, & Eaton, 1989; Romano & Hage, 2000). For example, the prevention definitions posited by Caplan (1964) and Gordon (1987) were originally created to classify prevention efforts for physical disorders. Unlike most physical disorders, however, it is more difficult to identify the cause or origin of a psychological disorder and classify complex mental disorder prevention efforts into a single category such as primary or universal prevention. Similarly, the IOM's definition (Mrazek & Haggerty, 1994) has been criticized for using a disease-based prevention model and excluding social and political change—as well as health-promoting interventions—as part of prevention (as cited in Romano & Hage).

Romano and Hage (2000) addressed these criticisms and created a new definition for the prevention of mental disorders. They defined prevention efforts as those having one or more of the following five dimensions: (a) stops (prevents) a problem behavior from ever occurring; (b) delays the onset of a problem behavior; (c) reduces the impact of an existing problem behavior; (d) strengthens knowledge, attitudes, and behaviors that promote emotional and physical well-being; and (e) supports institutional, community, and government policies that promote physical and emotional well-being.

This definition encompasses the goals of primary, secondary, and tertiary prevention practices and also includes risk reduction and health promotion strategies. Moreover, this definition includes prevention efforts within larger social systems and acknowledges the counselor's role as an agent of social change. To engage in prevention efforts along any of these dimensions, however, counselors are challenged to determine what prevention practices and implementation strategies will be most effective with what individuals and communities at what time. These challenges require counselors to consider both individual and context-specific factors, as well as the interaction among these factors, in creating and implementing their preventive interventions (Bogenschneider, 1996; Bronfenbrenner, 1979, 1989; McWhirter, McWhirter, McWhirter, & McWhirter, 2004; Trickett & Birman, 1989).

Prevention efforts are often conceptualized as only those interventions implemented with newborns and young children, and before mental health problems occur. Domestic violence, however, is a complex social problem that requires a multisystemic and developmental approach to prevention (Browne, 1993; Buzawa & Buzawa, 1996; Crowell & Burgess, 1996; Dutton, 1995; Romano & Hage, 2000). For example, educating middle school students about dating violence in an effort to prevent adult domestic violence is a typical example of prevention practice.

The prevention goals of implementing a relationship violence prevention curriculum in a middle school can be classified along the following prevention dimensions: (a) preventing a problem behavior from ever occurring; (b) delaying the onset of a problem behavior; (c) strengthening knowledge, attitudes, and behaviors that promote emotional and physical well-being; and (d) supporting institutional, community, and government policies that promote physical and emotional well-being (Romano & Hage, 2000). Indeed, these efforts are enhanced if related preventive interventions are also implemented at the elementary school level (Stipek, de la Sota, & Weishaupt, 1999; Walker & Epstein, 2001).

Interventions at the individual level that are designed specifically to help adult women leave battery situations are not commonly used in discussions of preventive interventions, but may be classified along the following prevention dimensions: reducing the impact of domestic violence, and increasing a woman's knowledge, attitudes, and behaviors that promote her emotional and physical well-being (Romano & Hage, 2000). These prevention efforts also may include delaying the onset of more complex and severe problem behaviors for women and their children (Romano & Hage, 2000). We selected the social problem of domestic violence and the two case studies presented here to illustrate the real-world prevention–treatment continuum in counseling. That is, mental health problems occur along a continuum from less severe to more severe and acute. Consequently, the implementation of preventive intervention, early intervention, and treatment efforts necessarily form a conceptual and practical continuum as well (McWhirter et al., 2004). In addition, what serves as a treatment intervention for one mental health problem (e.g., working with adult survivors) often serves as a preventive strategy for another problem (e.g., prevention of related child emotional or physical abuse and subsequent potential behavior problems) (McWhirter et al., 2004).

In the next section, we demonstrate the utility of an ecological model as a comprehensive conceptual guide for counselors in meeting the challenges of preparing and conducting prevention efforts with individuals and groups of individuals within their communities. We continue to use the two case studies involving Smith Middle School and Magdalena to highlight different practices counselors may use at different points along the prevention–treatment continuum in a manner consistent with different levels of ecology.

## The Ecological Model

The ecological model is a theory of human development. It posits that individual human development does not occur in isolation, but within multiple, embedded ecological systems (Bronfenbrenner, 1979, 1989). Bronfenbrenner defined these systems as the micro-, meso-, exo-, macro-, and chronosystems—with the *individual* at the center (see Figure 13.1).

The *microsystem* consists of the people and communities with whom an individual comes into direct contact. For example, a child's family, peers, church community, teachers, and doctors are part of the

### Figure 13.1
### Bronfenbrenner's Ecological Model
### (Bronfenbrenner, 1989)

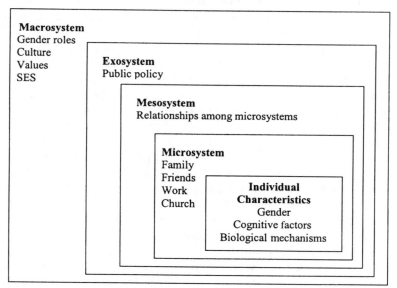

child's immediate environment and may significantly influence his or her development.

The *mesosystem* refers to the interconnections between the different microsystems. Mesosystemic influences include the relationships between a child's parent(s) and teacher, teacher and siblings, and siblings and peers. The ecological model assumes that an individual's development is enhanced if the mesosystem (i.e., the relationships among the microsystems) is positive (Bronfenbrenner, 1979, 1989).

The *exosystem* consists of the interconnections between one or more settings that do not directly involve the individual. Public policy is an excellent example of an exosystemic factor. Public policy decisions regarding educational standards, teacher wages, and health care or school lunch programs have an impact on an individual and his or her microsystems (e.g., family, community, and school), but the individual might not be present in the environments in which public policy decisions are made (e.g., city council, state legislative sessions).

The *macrosystem* represents our social blueprint: cultural values, belief systems, societal structure, gender-role socialization, race relations, and national and international resources (Bronfenbrenner, 1989). Research that examines the relationship between children's aggressive behavior and their exposure to television shows with violent images or themes is an example of the study of macrosystemic influences on individual development (Huesmann, Moise-Titus, Podolski, 2003). An additional concept is the *chronosystem*, which is defined as the development of interconnections among individuals and their environments over time.

There are three explicit assumptions of the ecological model (Bronfenbrenner, 1979, 1989). First, the ecological model assumes that an individual and his or her environment are continually interacting and exerting mutual influence—and, as a result, constantly changing. The environment influences individual development, and in turn, the individual changes and contributes to the environment in which subsequent development occurs. Second, the ecological model assumes that an individual is an active participant in his or her development. That is, the individual is not merely acted upon by the environment, but has the potential to exert influence and power within his or her environment. Third, the ecological model assumes bidirectionality, or the idea that changes in one ecological system may influence changes in systems that are more proximal and distal to the individual. It is apparent, for example, that public policy decisions can impact human development in more immediate or proximal ecological systems, including at the mesosystemic, microsystemic, and individual levels. In the same way, individuals, families, and communities in the micro- and mesosystems can influence public policy decisions (exosystem) by writing their government representatives, speaking at public forums, or protesting. The example of how public policy decisions are made illustrates bidirectionality and the manner in which factors in every system within the ecology can effect change in another system.

## Using the Ecological Model as a Conceptual Framework for Prevention Practice

The assumptions of the ecological model have important implications for prevention practice. The model's primary consideration is that prevention efforts with an individual or community must include other systems within the ecology and address person–environment interactions. Consequently, as counselors we cannot effect change in one system without effecting change in other systems. Failure to consider person–environment interactions in prevention practice leads to interventions that are, at best, ineffective or inefficient and that may also be quite harmful to our clients ( McWhirter, 1994, 1997; McWhirter & McWhirter, 1998). Moreover, more effective preventive counseling involves engaging in a self-examination process in which we explore the nature of our own role in creating social change or, conversely, in perpetuating social systems and inequities that increase client dependency and risk (McWhirter, 1997; Prilleltensky, 1997; Prilleltensky & Nelson, 2002). We highlight these notions again when applying the model to our case studies.

The ecological model is a framework that counselors may use to identify and classify the multiple contextual factors influencing individual development and to design preventive interventions to effect change across multiple systems within the ecology. The ecological model is also consistent with an important empowerment approach to counseling, defined by McWhirter (1994) as

> the process by which people, organizations, or groups who are powerless or marginalized (a) become aware of the power dynamics at work in their life context, (b) develop the skills and capacity for gaining some reasonable control over their lives, (c) which they exercise, (d) without infringing on the rights of others, and (e) which coincides with actively supporting the empowerment of others in their community. (p. 12)

McWhirter's definition illustrates that counseling for empowerment requires consideration of contextual influences on individuals' development, including their beliefs about themselves and others, and their capacity to effect changes in their lives.

We propose that the ecological model is an excellent framework for counselors to systematically examine the contextual influences and power dynamics at work in their clients' lives, and to create and implement preventive interventions that empower these individuals to effect change across multiple ecological systems. We use the prevention of domestic violence to illustrate the link between prevention practice and the ecological model, and to outline how prevention practice is enhanced when counselors address person–environment interactions and use the strengths and experiences of those individuals and communities for whom their prevention efforts are created.

## Best Practices in Ecological Prevention

Best practices in ecological prevention include addressing individual and contextual factors that have an impact on client development; collaborating with clients to create and implement effective preventive interventions across multiple ecological systems; and using ideas, strategies, and resources from other disciplines (see chapter 1). In this section, we refer back to our case studies and the prevention of domestic violence to describe the best counseling practices for ecological prevention. Please refer also to Table 13.1, which outlines best practices in prevention from an ecological perspective using Smith Middle School (Case Study 1) as the example.

### Smith Middle School
School-based prevention efforts require an understanding of the school and community environments and working within these contexts to define the prevention aim and program purpose and content. Such efforts are likely to be most effective when the individual and social development of adolescents is considered at each level of ecology. Teen dating violence is similar to adult domestic violence in terms of the power and control issues at the root of the violence, in addition to how abuse escalates over time, the types of abusive behavior, and the emotional effects of violence on young women (Morales & Gutierrez, 1998). Unique aspects of teen dating violence and adolescent development must also be considered to create and implement an effective teen dating violence prevention program. For example, females experiencing teen dating violence often attend the same school as their abusive partners; they do not typically seek help from parents and other adults; and teens may not have the same legal options for protection that are available to adults (Levy, 1998). Apart from these characteristics, little is known about preventing teen dating violence because it has been so

323

**Table 13.1**

**Best Practices in Prevention Across
Levels of Ecology: Smith Middle School**

| Ecological Level | Examples of Best Prevention Practice With Smith Middle School |
|---|---|
| Macrosystem | • *Identify and address influence of adolescents community, culture, gender roles, media, peers, and societal messages about sex and dating*<br>• *Facilitate counselor awareness of how adolescent development and urban culture may influence effectiveness of traditional therapy approaches* |
| Exosystem | • *Identify ecological influence of educational and school policies on curriculum, availability of counselors, and campus safety*<br>• *Identify relationship violence resources for adolescents and their families*<br>• *Facilitate counselor, school, and students working together for social change regarding relationship violence public policy and the provision and allocation of resources to youth* |
| Mesosystem | • *Identify and facilitate students' connections with community resources*<br>• *Include family, teachers, school officials, and community members in prevention program*<br>• *Identify and consider mesosystemic relationships and influences* |
| Microsystem | • *Facilitate students' awareness and understanding of healthy and unhealthy relationships*<br>• *Facilitate students' abilities to identify emotional, mental, physical, and spiritual dating violence*<br>• *Facilitate students' awareness and identification of ecological factors, across all system levels, impacting their individual and social development*<br>• *Facilitate counselor critical consciousness, self-reflection, and power analysis, across all ecological system levels* |
| Individual | • *Facilitate students' awareness of their strengths, skills, and power to make changes within their relationships*<br>• *Facilitate students' identification and examination of their own academic, personal, and interpersonal goals* |

understudied. In fact, in a review of 1,168 articles on youth violence from 1980 to 1999, only 1% of the studies focused on assessing dating violence, 5% focused on preventing it, and none were found focused on dating violence treatment (Acosta, Albus, Reynolds, Spriggs, & Weist, 2001). What we do know includes some of the following characteristics; we draw on related research to complement our discussion.

***Microsystemic level interventions.*** Prevention curriculum components at the microsystemic level may include increasing the students' awareness of themselves, dating, and violence as well as how their relationships with family, peers, and the community have influenced their beliefs and choices. Prevention programs at the microsystemic level also may contain any number of foci, including but not limited to increasing

324

students' competencies in the areas of self-expression, assertiveness, resistance and refusal skills, problem solving, and conflict resolution (Wolfe, Wekerle, & Scott, 2003). Moreover, these programs provide students with the information, skills, and resources that empower them to build healthy relationships, resist negative peer pressure, and make positive changes in their school and family environments (McWhirter, 1994; McWhirter et al., 2004). These components reflect the primary principles of the ecological model—that is, students learn they are continually interacting with their environments, exerting mutual influences, and being active participants in their own development.

An example of effective prevention for teen dating violence that includes consideration of contextual factors and intervention across different ecological levels may be found in the literature on teen pregnancy and sexually transmitted disease (STD) prevention. In a review of programs on preventing teen pregnancy and improving teens' sexual behavior (i.e., increasing safer sex through consistent use of condoms, delaying age of first intercourse, using contraceptive methods other than condoms) the National Campaign to Prevent Teen Pregnancy (2001) found that the best and most efficacious programs shared 10 necessary characteristics. Programs that fail to include even one of these 10 characteristics tend to be significantly less effective. These program characteristics are related to prevention of dating violence because they similarly relate to increasing and improving adolescent girls' knowledge about themselves and effectiveness in making personal and interpersonal decisions. As such, they are indicated prevention efforts because they target a high risk population—adolescent girls (Gordon, 1987).

Included in the 10 characteristics of efficacious teen pregnancy prevention programs are

- reduction of one or more sexual behaviors leading to pregnancy or HIV/STD infection;
- delivery and consistent reinforcement of a clear message about abstaining from sexual activity and/or using contraception;
- provision of basic, accurate information about the risks of teen sexual activity and about ways to avoid intercourse or use protective methods against pregnancy and STDs;
- inclusion of activities that address social pressures from peers influencing sexual behavior;
- provision of examples of and practice with communication, negotiation, and refusal skills;
- incorporation of behavioral goals, teaching methods, and materials appropriate to age, sexual experience, and student culture; and

- selection of adequately trained teachers and peer leaders who believe in the program. (National Campaign to Prevent Teen Pregnancy, 2001)

The effectiveness of programs that consistently maintain these characteristics are fairly well demonstrated. Such programs also respond directly to some of the common problems faced in work with adolescents. For example, adolescents typically do not seek information and support from their parents and other adults when faced with a difficult interpersonal situation; young teens often want and need more independence and strive to solve problems by themselves or with peers; and many adolescents fear that if they were to tell their parents or other adults about a relationship problem, such as an abuse experience with someone they are dating, their independence and control with future decisions might be severely restricted. A program that includes the characteristics just described may be effective in preventing dating violence because it provides young people with skills and information in a safe environment and supports communication and decision making about personal and interpersonal choices and relationships within their microsystems. See Table 13.1 for a summary of preventive interventions at the individual and microsystemic levels of ecology.

***Mesosystemic level interventions.*** Interventions at the mesosystemic level may include increasing students' identification of people and communities that are sources of support as well as increasing their use of these available resources. Teachers, families, school administrators, and community members may play an active role in the creation and implementation of the prevention curriculum. For example, school officials and community members might give presentations, facilitate discussions, and build mentoring relationships with students as a means for improving communication and providing network support. In addition to the characteristics just listed, parents and other family members might also play an active role in organizing curriculum activities or meeting with school officials to show support for their children and teenagers. Prevention at the mesosystemic level will be enhanced by building stronger relationships among students, families, teachers, school administrators, and other community leaders and members (Lutenbacher, Cooper, & Faccia, 2002). These relationships should be based on consistent and regular communication. Consistent communication among adults in the system helps create an environment that will increase young adolescents' attempts to seek support if they have experienced or witnessed dating violence, and may be key to providing young people with the necessary information, skills, and support to recognize and deal with a problem before it becomes a pattern. Working as a community to build stronger mesosystemic relationships illustrates bidirectionality: the power of individuals and communities to mutually influence each other, and in this case, to effect positive development.

Program components at the mesosystemic level may also address peer relationships. The importance of recognizing the role of peers in the development of problem behavior among at-risk youth (e.g., violence, drug and alcohol use, delinquency), and how to engage peers in prevention and intervention efforts when working with children and adolescents, has been clearly demonstrated throughout the prevention and intervention literature (e.g., Dishion, & Andrews, 1995; Dishion, Patterson, Stoolmiller, & Skinner, 1991; Oetting & Beauvais, 1987). A dating violence prevention curriculum might foster student awareness of their power to influence their own development and contexts by encouraging them to brainstorm how their peers might use their strengths and abilities to foster healthy relationship norms in their school.

Conducting prevention efforts at the mesosystemic level also requires an interdisciplinary approach, using the strengths and resources of an entire community to support adolescents' healthy development. Programs that integrate existing community personnel and programs can be particularly effective (Lutenbacher, Cooper, & Faccia, 2002). For instance, in communities where school funding has been reduced or reallocated away from counseling and preventive education, community agencies may serve as an important resource in improving children's interpersonal skills and decision-making abilities to prevent them from entering poor relationships. With the current reduction in funding in Oregon schools, for example, the community Sexual Assault Support Services (SASS) agency has initiated and implemented preventive education programs that are offered to elementary schools in at least one school district. These programs are designed developmentally. Instruction in earlier grades (e.g., fourth–fifth) focuses on general issues of improving personal safety, lessons on appropriate touch, setting boundaries with friends, trusting one's own feelings, communicating feelings, learning how to support a friend, and learning about sexual anatomy. Lessons for older children (e.g., middle school students) also adds content on sexual abuse, power dynamics in relationships, sexual assaults, resistance and refusal skills specific to sexual scenarios, and so forth. These themes and content clearly support interpersonal and dating violence prevention because they focus on metathemes related to building skills useful in many situations and environments. In addition, these programs represent another example of thinking and acting ecologically because they improve school, community, and family links that are critical for all prevention work (McWhirter et al., 2004); in other words, they provide effective prevention services related to a specific problem. See Table 13.1 for a summary of preventive interventions at the mesosystemic level of ecology.

***Exo- and macrosystemic level interventions.*** Addressing exo- and macrosystemic level factors in a dating violence prevention program is essential and involves increasing students' awareness of the effects of culture, gender role socialization, socioeconomic status, religion, and other larger contextual influences on their development and the incidence of dating violence. This process of increasing one's awareness is defined as *critical consciousness*, which is composed of two specific and overlapping processes: power analysis and critical self-reflection (McWhirter, 1997). Power analysis refers to a student's examination of how power is distributed and used in a given situation or context in terms of race/ethnicity, gender, disability status, sexual orientation, age, experience, family positions (McWhirter, 1997). Critical self-reflection involves increasing awareness of one's privilege, power, strengths, weaknesses, culture, values, biases, assumptions, and worldviews (McWhirter, 1997). Together, engaging in power analysis and critical self-reflection may facilitate students' awareness of their interpersonal interactions and relationships at the micro-, meso-, exo-, and macrosystemic levels, as well as the way in which their privilege or lack of privilege, skills, and power within a cultural and social context influence their personal assumptions and relationships (McWhirter, 1997, 2001).

Increasing middle school students' critical consciousness of exo- and macrosystemic factors may include facilitating discussions about how the media and living in an urban community impact their beliefs about themselves, gender roles, relationships, and violence. Students may also be asked questions about the strengths, supports, and barriers they encounter as young adolescents from lower socioeconomic backgrounds and what power they have to make changes in their relationships, school, and community.

Preventive program components at the exo- and macrosystemic levels also include community involvement, social activism, and development of critical consciousness by counselors, family and community members, and school personnel. For example, it is important for counseling professionals to take a stand on issues critical to the individuals and groups with whom they are working (Blustein, 2001; Fassinger, 2001; McWhirter, 2001; Prilleltensky, 1997; Prilleltensky & Nelson, 2002). When working with middle school students, for instance, this activism might include being informed about community resources for young adolescents and advocating for school legislation to fund relationship education and violence prevention programs. This level of intervention—engaging in community action to improve the lives of clients and to help clients improve their own lives—represents the fifth aspect of prevention in Romano and Hage's (2000) prevention definition: to "support institutional, community, and government policies that promote physical and emotional well-being" (p. 741). This dimension links very strongly to the goal of the World Health Organization (1999), which has focused recently on providing education in life skills as a universal preventive measure for children and adolescents in nations throughout the world—another excellent example of exosystemic and macrosystemic factors.

Development of critical consciousness by counselors and other community members is not part of the ecological model. It is a construct and process that we have added to the ecological prevention framework because we believe it is essential for counselors to consider and reflect upon their role in their clients' ecology and in promoting social change. The counseling relationship, however, is a microsystemic influence, and counselors are challenged to examine their own power and privilege in the counseling relationship, which can positively or negatively influence their clients' lives. A counselor may use his or her role to the benefit of students by helping them gain skills and build supportive relationships. Counselors also may use their power to the detriment of children and adolescents with whom they work—usually unknowingly—by creating, for example, a prevention curriculum that is narrow in focus, culturally incongruent with middle school students' worldviews, or multiculturally insensitive, or that perpetuates gender bias or a sense of inequality that enhances risk for young people to become engaged in destructive and violent relationships. See Table 13.1 for a summary of preventive interventions at the exo- and macrosystemic levels of ecology.

### Magdalena

We now turn to Magdalena's story (Case Study 2) and consider ecological prevention efforts with an individual domestic violence survivor. Considering the treatment–prevention continuum, Magdalena's story falls closer to the treatment intervention end of the continuum than prevention work at Smith Middle School. The ecological model, however, can again be used to systematically apply ecological prevention principles to the counseling relationship and toward the prevention of further domestic violence, in addition to the prevention of domestic violence across generations. Refer to Table 13.2, which presents a worksheet for conceptualizing Magdalena's circumstances, strengths, and weaknesses from an ecological perspective.

***Microsystemic level interventions.*** Domestic violence preventive interventions with Magdalena at the microsystemic level might include safety planning as well as individual mental health counseling. From an empowering counseling approach that considers all levels of ecology, Magdalena and her counselor might collaborate to create safety plans for when Jorge becomes physically violent and an explosion occurs—when she is preparing to leave, and after she has left (Gelles, 1997; Kirkwood, 1993; Koss, 1990; Morales & Gutierrez, 1998; Walker, 1994). Safety

## Table 13.2

### Client Conceptualization Worksheet
### Across Levels of Ecology: Magdalena

Using client intake information and additional information such as family genograms, identify at least two or three risk and resilience factors for your client at each ecological level.

After identifying these factors, design a multilevel, multisystems intervention that addresses the client's presenting concerns by utilizing or increasing resilience factors and decreasing or resolving risk factors identified at each ecological level.

| Ecological Level | Risk Factors | Resilience Factors |
|---|---|---|
| Macrosystem | • *Latina in U.S.*<br>• *Majority culture's negative attitudes toward women who do not leave battering situations.* | • *Developing critical consciousness of overlapping and diverging gender roles in U.S./Mexican cultures.*<br>• *Sustaining religious and spiritual beliefs.* |
| Exosystem | • *Policies and practices related to citizenship.*<br>• *Not able to access existing welfare programs for micro/ mesosystem reasons (e.g., husband won't provide wage information).* | • *Domestic violence statutes in her jurisdiction.*<br>• *School breakfast and lunch programs are available for children.* |
| Mesosystem | • *Geographically isolated from extended family.*<br>• *Husband won't let her socialize with neighbors or church friends without him.* | • *Able to ask neighbor to drive her to domestic violence services office.*<br>• *Has relationships with friends and neighbors that could be incorporated into a safety plan for self and children.* |
| Microsystem | • *Husband is emotionally, financially, and physically abusive.*<br>• *Husband will not allow her to apply for U.S. citizenship.* | • *Loves her children.*<br>• *Has neighbors and church friends.* |
| Individual | • *Insecure about English (second language).*<br>• *Feels tired and hopeless.* | • *Is feeling more empowered since seeking intervention services.*<br>• *Speaks English.* |

planning for domestic violence situations might address identifying support networks in the larger community, opening and closing bank accounts, changing door locks, keeping a written account of domestic violence events, and learning self-defense strategies (Morales & Gutierrez, 1998; Walker, 1994). In addition to facilitating awareness of the oppressive nature of an abusive situation, it is important for counselors to facilitate women's awareness of the strengths and skills they possess that have helped them survive domestic violence in the past. A focus only on Magdalena's experiences of abuse and oppression might leave her feeling victimized and helpless, rather than empowered and hopeful that she can make changes for her future and her children's future.

*Mesosystemic level interventions.* Many women hesitate to leave an abusive situation because they do not want to take their children away from the other parent or fear that leaving the abusive situation will create conflict between her partner and family members or friends (Masaki & Wong, 1997). As such, preventive interventions should also attend to mesosystemic factors that influence a woman's decision to leave. Preventive interventions within Magdalena's mesosystem may include facilitating her connections with her communities: families, schools, churches, support groups, shelters, hospitals, advocacy centers, mental health agencies, and employment and welfare services. Counselors must be active and not only provide women with a list of resources, but also serve as a liaison by providing specific names of contacts within organizations and by helping women set up meetings and contacts (Gelles, 1997; Kirkwood, 1993; McWhirter, 1994; Walker, 1994). Counselors also may assist battered women with financial and legal planning. This assistance may include providing information directly about federal and state emergency grants, employment opportunities, and legal rights and procedures for obtaining restraining orders and child custody.

*Exo- and macrosystemic level interventions.* Prevention practices with Magdalena in the exo- and macrosystems might include facilitating her critical consciousness of the strengths, supports, and barriers that her Mexican heritage, age, gender, religion, and sociopolitical history provide, as well as her role in maintaining certain systemic supports, barriers, beliefs, and values. As Magdalena becomes more critically conscious, she will gain a more realistic and accurate awareness of her locus in relationships and society. She will also gain the capacity to analyze the causes and consequences of her reality, compare herself and her situation with other situations and possibilities, and feel able to transform her own life (Freire, 1970; Martín-Baró, 1994; Comas-Diaz, 1994). Furthermore, counselors' critical consciousness and social activism at the exo- and macrosystems include staying informed about domestic violence legislation, court proceedings, victim services, and law enforcement systems, as well as voting on these and other related issues (McWhirter, 1994).

The preventive interventions just discussed reflect our assumptions, based on the ecological model, that Magdalena is developing within multiple contexts, that she can direct her own development, and that she has the power to effect change in her environment. Next, we consider critical consciousness and multicultural competence, and how they relate to both case examples.

## Critical Consciousness and Multicultural Competence

Increasing critical consciousness is an important and necessary step for counselors in increasing their multicultural counseling competencies and in identifying their roles and power within an ecological framework. Multicultural counseling competency has been characterized as (a) counselor awareness of his or her own assumptions, values, and biases; (b) understanding the worldviews of culturally different clients; and (c) developing culturally sensitive and appropriate interventions and techniques (Sue, Arredondo, & McDavis, 1992). Counselors must examine their own cultural assumptions, biases, and worldviews as well as the impact of these worldviews on each client, the ecological systems in which their clients are embedded, and their approach to prevention practice. A critically conscious counselor also will gain the capacity to reflect critically on his or her role in maintaining or perpetuating unjust social systems. Our case studies help illustrate the importance of critical consciousness in prevention practice for both the client and counselor.

When working with middle school students of color from lower socioeconomic backgrounds in an urban setting, it is critical that a dating violence prevention curriculum address racism, relationships among students and police, gang violence, and cultural beliefs such as peer and racial/ethnic loyalty. It is irresponsible for counselors to focus merely on individual students and encourage them to simply say "no" to engaging in violent behavior without considering community norms and young adolescents' survival strategies (Kozol, 1995). Counselors also must address these issues when working with battered women of color. Women survivors of domestic violence encounter numerous barriers associated with language, socioeconomic status, immigration status, level of acculturation, and ethnic identity conflict (Chronister & McWhirter, in press; Kanuha, 1994; Loue & Faust, 1998). For example, Magdalena's English skills are limited and she is not a U.S. citizen. These factors significantly influence how safe Magdalena feels in coming forward to seek help and use social services, how clearly she is able to understand her options and receive help from an agency that does not have staff members who speak Spanish, and what social services and government programs are accessible to her as an immigrant.

Functioning with cultural competence also requires working interdisciplinarily—that is, collaborating with other professionals across disciplines. The case studies of Smith Middle School and Magdalena clearly illustrate the importance of an interdisciplinary approach to ecological prevention practice. In each of these cases, counselors might use the strengths of clergy, elders, and extended family within the client's ethnic communities to assist with identifying and addressing important cultural issues in the counseling process.

Attention to human diversity and cultural competence also requires understanding the specific challenges of nonethnic minority groups and applying this knowledge to prevention practice. Dating violence prevention programs, for example, need to consider how difficult it might be for young adolescents who identify as lesbian or gay to report dating violence and to access support networks that are typically more easily available to adolescents in heterosexual dating relationships. Similarly, for adult lesbians in abusive relationships, it is important for counselors to address heterosexism and homophobia as well as the attitudes among many social service agencies, law enforcement groups, and legal systems that lesbian battery is not as serious or harmful because the abuser is a woman (Kanuha, 1994). In fact, lesbians may be more at risk of battery by a partner because, compared with heterosexual couples, odds are higher that one member of a lesbian couple has experienced victimization by family violence or sexual abuse (Kerewsky & Miller, 1995). Both of those factors are highly correlated with being in an abusive relationship as an adult.

Similarly, women with physical and cognitive disabilities, which often may be the result of years of abuse, may also fear discrimination based on their disability status. They may delay using services such as advocacy offices and shelters because provisions, such as wheelchair accessibility or modified reading materials and forms, are not available.

Given the wide range of issues related to human diversity that must be considered with each client, counselors are challenged to reexamine and think critically about their approach to preventive intervention. For example, counselors may assume that a dating violence prevention curriculum needs to focus on increasing students' communication skills with family, teachers, and police, but they may fail to consider young adolescents' relationships and experiences with these groups of people. Lack of attention to details, as in these situations, places an adolescent at even higher risk. Likewise, counselors may assume that the ideal goal for Magdalena is for her to leave Jorge. For Magdalena, living independently away from her current cultural and ethnic community might not be an option she is willing to consider and prosecuting her case in court might violate specific cultural norms regarding family loyalty and privacy. Traditional prevention efforts that focus solely on the individual typically will not work for someone with Magdalena's ecological context.

In summary, prevention practice cannot address person–environment interactions across multiple contexts without including the experiences and knowledge of the individuals and communities that make up each level of the ecological system. Preventive interventions that include the experiences of targeted populations are more likely to be multiculturally sensitive because they have been created based on the needs, expectations, and practices of a specific culture or community and not of the counselor or researcher. In turn, prevention efforts that are multiculturally sensitive are likely to lead to improved individual and community investment in the prevention efforts, since greater aspects of the client's ecology will be more fully integrated into action.

## Conclusion

Throughout this chapter, we elaborate on the ecological model as a framework for guiding prevention efforts in counseling. The case studies of Smith Middle School and Magdalena help illustrate this content. Ecological prevention practice assumes that Smith Middle School students and Magdalena, respectively, are interacting, constantly changing, and mutually influencing the contexts within which they are living. As such, a counseling relationship with young adolescents and with an adult survivor of domestic violence should be collaborative and use the skills, competencies, and knowledge of each community and client in creating and implementing preventive intervention efforts across all levels of their ecologies.

We also highlight the importance of counselors engaging in critical consciousness. This allows us to examine our own role in perpetuating unjust social and service systems and the importance of integrating multicultural counseling competencies into our prevention and intervention work as fundamental to an ecological prevention framework. These skills are not peripheral, but central to best prevention practices. In addition, we emphasize the value of the counselor's role in promoting social change as one way to address exo- and macrosystemic factors that negatively influence clients, and the importance of always using an ecological framework for conceptualizing and conducting prevention work. By describing potential relationship violence prevention efforts with young adolescents in a school setting, as well as with an individual survivor, we hope you are inspired by the complexity of ecological prevention practice and its importance for counseling.

## Learning Activities

1. Table 13.1 provides an example of how to use the ecological model to develop appropriate prevention strategies at each ecological level. In small groups, choose and describe a situation in your community that is similar to the Smith Middle School example. Trade scenarios with another group and develop prevention strategies using Table 13.1 as a model.

2. Table 13.2 provides an example of how to consider an individual client's risk and resilience factors at all levels of ecology. With a partner, identify prevention efforts that might occur in Magdalena's community over the next 5 years. How might each prevention intervention, or failure to intervene, affect Magdalena's risk and resilience factors at each level? How might they affect other members of her family?

3. How have prevention efforts influenced your life? Research and list major prevention initiatives beginning a year before you were born and continuing to the present. For example, you might have received tobacco education in middle school. Create a master worksheet showing the effects of these efforts on your own risk and resilience factors at each level of ecology. It may help to talk to a parent or adult who knew you as a child. Write a short reflection paper about this activity, including your thoughts on how your culture, gender, socioeconomic status, or other characteristics may have influenced which prevention efforts you were exposed to and which you were not.

## References

Acosta, O. M., Albus, K. E., Reynolds, M. W., Spriggs, D., & Weist, M. D. (2001). Assessing the status of research on violence-related problems among youth. *Journal of Clinical Child Psychology, 30,* 152–160.

Blustein, D. L. (2001, March). *Social action at the community level.* Paper presented at the biannual conference of the Society for Vocational Psychology, Houston, Texas.

Bogenschneider, K. (1996). An ecological risk/protective theory for building prevention programs, policies, and community capacity to support youth. *Family Relations, 45*, 127-138.

Bronfenbrenner, U. (1979). *The ecology of human development.* Cambridge, MA: Harvard University Press.

Bronfenbrenner, U. (1989). Ecological systems theory. *Annals of Child Development, 6*, 187-249.

Browne, A. (1993). Violence against women by male partners: Prevalence, outcomes, and policy implication. *American Psychologist, 48*, 1077-1087.

Buzawa, E. S., & Buzawa, C. G. (Eds.). (1996). *Do arrests and restraining orders work?* Thousand Oaks, CA: Sage.

Caplan, G. (1964). *Principles of preventive psychiatry.* New York: Basic Books.

Chronister, K. M., & McWhirter, E. H. (in press). Women, domestic violence, and career counseling: An application of social cognitive career theory. *Journal of Counseling & Development.*

Comas-Diaz, L. (1994). An integrative approach. In L. G. Comas-Diaz & B. Greene (Eds.), *Women of color: Integrating ethnic and gender identities in psychotherapy* (pp. 287-318). New York: Guilford Press.

Crowell, N. A., & Burgess, A. W. (Eds.). (1996). *Understanding violence against women.* Washington, DC: National Academy Press.

Dishion, T. J., & Andrews, D. W. (1995). Preventing escalation in problem behaviors with high-risk young adolescents: Immediate and 1-year outcomes. *Journal of Consulting and Clinical Psychology, 63*, 538-548.

Dishion, T. J., Patterson, G. R., Stoolmiller, M., & Skinner, M. L. (1991). Family, school, and behavioral antecedents to early adolescent involvement with antisocial peers. *Developmental Psychology, 27*, 172-180.

Dutton, D. G. (1995). *The domestic assault of women: Psychological and criminal justice perspectives.* Vancouver: University of British Columbia Press.

Fassinger, R. (2001, March). *Social action at the national level: On dismantling the Master's house.* Paper presented at the biannual conference of the Society for Vocational Psychology, Houston, Texas.

Freire, P. (1983). *Pedagogy of the oppressed.* (M. B. Ramos, Trans.). New York: Continuum. (Original work published 1970)

Gelles, R. J. (1997). *Intimate violence in families.* Thousand Oaks, CA: Sage.

Gordon, R. (1987). An operational classification of disease prevention. In J. A. Sternberg & M. M. Silverman (Eds.), *Preventing mental disorders* (pp. 20-26). Rockville, MD: U.S. Department of Health and Human Services.

Huesmann, L. R., Moise-Titus, J., & Podolski, C. (2003). Longitudinal relations between children's exposure to TV violence and their aggressive and violent behavior in young adulthood: 1977-1992. *Developmental Psychology, 39*(2), 201-221.

Kanuha, V. (1994). Women of color in battering relationships. In L. G. Comas-Diaz & B. Greene (Eds.), *Women of color: Integrating ethnic and gender identities in psychotherapy* (pp. 428-454). New York: Guilford Press.

Kerewsky, S. D., & Miller, D. (1995). Lesbian couples and childhood trauma. *Journal of Feminist Family Therapy, 7*(3/4), 115-133.

Kirkwood, C. (1993). *Leaving abusive partners*. London: Sage.

Koss, M. P. (1990). The women's mental health research agenda: Violence against women. *American Psychologist, 45*, 374-380.

Kozol, J. (1995). *Amazing grace: The lives of children and the conscience of a nation*. New York: Crown.

Levy, B. (1998). *Dating violence: Young women in danger* (2nd ed.). Seattle, WA: Seal Press.

Lorion, R. P., Price, R. H., & Eaton, W. W. (1989). The prevention of child and adolescent disorders: From theory to research. In D. Shaffer, I. Philips, & N. B. Enzer (Eds.), *Prevention of mental disorders, alcohol and other drug use in children and adolescents* (OSAP Prevention Monograph 2, pp. 55-123). Rockville, MD: U.S. Department of Health and Human Services, Office for Substance Abuse Prevention.

Loue, S., & Faust, M. (1998). Intimate partner violence among immigrants. In S. Loue (Ed.), *Handbook of immigrant health* (pp. 521-544). New York: Plenum Press.

Lutenbacher, M., Cooper, W., & Faccia, K. (2002). Planning youth violence prevention efforts: Decision making across community sectors. *Journal of Adolescent Health, 30*(5), 346-354.

Martín-Baró, I. (1994). Writings for a liberation psychology. In A. Aron & S. Corne (Eds.). Cambridge, MA: Harvard University Press.

Masaki, B., & Wong, L. (1997). Domestic violence in the Asian community. In E. Lee (Ed.), *Working with Asian Americans* (pp. 439-451). New York: Guilford Press.

McWhirter, E. H. (1994). *Counseling for empowerment*. Alexandria, VA: American Counseling Association.

McWhirter, E. H. (1997). Empowerment, social activism, and counseling. *Counseling and Human Development, 28*, 1-14.

McWhirter, E. H. (2001, March). *Social action at the individual level: Fostering critical consciousness*. Paper presented at the biannual conference of the Society for Vocational Psychology, Houston, Texas.

McWhirter, B. T., & McWhirter, E. H. (1998, Spring). An ecological model of counseling psychology training. *Prevention and Public Interest Special Interest Group Newsletter, 5*.

McWhirter, J. J., McWhirter, B. T., McWhirter, E. H., & McWhirter, R. J. (2004). *At-risk youth: A comprehensive response* (3rd ed.). Pacific Grove, CA: Brooks/Cole.

Morales, J., & Gutierrez, T. (Eds.). (1998). *Womenspace: Friends and family packet*. Eugene, OR: Womenspace.

Mrazek, P. J., & Haggerty, R. J. (Eds.). (1994). *Reducing risks for mental disorders: Frontiers for preventive intervention research*. Washington, DC: National Academy Press.

National Campaign to Prevent Teen Pregnancy. (2001, May). *Emerging answers: Research findings on programs to reduce teen pregnancy.* Washington, DC: Author.

Oetting, E. R., & Beauvais, F. (1987). Peer cluster theory, socialization characteristics, and adolescent drug use: A path analysis. *Journal of Counseling Psychology, 34,* 205–213.

Prilleltensky, I. (1997). Values, assumptions, and practices: Assessing the moral implications of psychological discourse and action. *American Psychologist, 52*(5), 517–535.

Prilleltensky, I., & Nelson, G. (2002). *Doing psychologically critically: Making a difference in diverse settings.* New York: Palgrave Macmillan.

Romano, J. L., & Hage, S. M. (2000). Prevention and counseling psychology: Revitalizing commitments for the 21st century. *The Counseling Psychologist, 28,* 733–763.

Stipek, D., de la Sota, A., & Weishaupt, L. (1999). Life lessons: An embedded classroom approach to preventing high-risk behaviors among preadolescents. *Elementary School Journal, 99*(5), 433–451.

Sue, D. W., Arredondo, P., & McDavis, R. J. (1992). Multicultural counseling competencies and standards: A call to the profession. *Journal of Counseling & Development, 70,* 477–486.

Trickett, E. J., & Birman, D. (1989). Taking ecology seriously: A community development approach to individually based preventive interventions in schools. In L. A. Bond & B. E. Compas (Eds.), *Primary prevention and promotion in the schools* (pp. 361–390). Newbury Park, CA: Sage.

Walker, L. A. (1994). *Abused women and survivor therapy. A practical guide for the psychotherapist.* Washington, DC: American Psychological Association.

Walker, H. M., & Epstein, M. H. (Eds.). (2001). *Making schools safer and violence free: Critical issues, solutions, and recommended practices.* Austin, TX: PRO-ED.

Wolfe, D. A., Wekerle, C., & Scott, K. (2003). Dating violence prevention with at-risk youth: A controlled outcome evaluation. *Journal of Consulting and Clinical Psychology, 71*(2), 279–291.

World Health Organization. (1999). *Partners in life skills education.* Geneva, Switzerland: World Health Organization, Department of Mental Health.

Afterword

# Implications and Future Directions

## *Ellen P. Cook and Robert K. Conyne*

As you have read, ecological counseling is a multifaceted approach that pays attention to the meaning people derive from their contextualized person–environment interactions. We have tried to explain this understanding of ecological counseling through sections of the book devoted to conceptual foundations and to applied interventions, often with examples. In this final discussion, we consider the significance of the ecological counseling approach to us and to you, the reader. We begin by looking back on some of what we have learned from this process, and then turn to whether ecological counseling works. We still have many questions that need research, as you shall see.

## Meaningfulness of the Ecological Counseling Perspective

To borrow a truism, a good counseling perspective should comfort the afflicted (counselor) and afflict the comfortable. That is, it should provide some workable ideas for dealing with difficult professional situations or issues, yet should also challenge some of our familiar ways of seeing and doing things.

The ecological counseling perspective has done precisely that for us. As we noted in the preface, our counseling program embraces this perspective as a guiding vision for our training, beginning with our vision statement: "To obtain national excellence in implementing an ecological counseling perspective through service to diverse populations, emphasizing underserved groups." Adopting this vision gave us a language to coordinate our highly individualized professional interests, and articulate a shared-training focus previously missing, or perhaps implicit. Our meaning making crystallized for the better.

Faculty and students use this vision statement as a template for charting faculty development, scholarship, and service activity. In our teaching, we created six new doctoral courses that are explicitly ecological in their orientation, while infusing this same orientation within several master's courses. Yet, as Geoffrey Yager (one of our faculty members) was able to show in chapter 7 ("Training and Supervision") incorporation of an ecological orientation need not mandate a total overhaul of what exists. As a group, we faculty discovered how an ecological perspective can be infused naturally within ongoing master's-level course activities without much disruption. We also significantly disrupted our doctoral training program by intentionally recreating it around an ecological orientation. We eliminated several courses in lieu of two new doctoral seminar series (six courses) that focus on ecological counseling, and we use problem-based learning (PBL) extensively as an instructional method, since it synchronizes well with the ecological orientation.

The process of translating ecological ideas into counseling practice definitely challenged our comfortable ways of viewing the purposes and processes of counseling. Interdisciplinary literature repeatedly reminded us how narrow our views can be.

It is fortunate we counselors love a good challenge, which is probably why we—and you—chose this career in the first place. We counselors also are a practical sort. Ideas must work successfully in our daily practice. How well does the ecological perspective work? Anyone who has read at least some of the preceding chapters is likely to answer, "It all depends."

## The Effectiveness of Ecological Counseling

Within an ecological perspective, questions about effectiveness or validity cannot be answered independent of the context and meaning making attending it. That is, it depends on what you mean by the question and in what context.

From our own professional experience, we find this perspective to be helpful. It enhances our program as a whole, as we described earlier. Students also reported this perspective to be valuable in integrating material from a variety of courses (e.g., multicultural counseling, theory, career development, program development) and in sharpening their case conceptualization skills. We hope these consequences also extend to you.

A different type of answer to the effectiveness question is provided by research. Counselors typically are trained to have a healthy respect for the power of empirical research to establish the true value of ideas.

Although ideas in this book are founded in a body of knowledge that was researched extensively (e.g., developmental and community psychology), the packaging of these ideas into the ecological counseling framework is new and offers fertile ground for research.

In chapter 1, you were introduced to both the simplicity and the complexity inherent within ecological counseling. Lewin's basic ecological formula, $B = f(P \times E)$, reminds us that, in statistical terms, the main effect is in the interaction (cf. Bronfenbrenner, 1977). In addition, these P $\times$ E interactions are set within dynamic contexts from which people derive meaning. The research and evaluation challenge is to develop designs that increasingly are sensitive to the relevant aspects of a particular ecology.

Research provides only one type of answer to the effectiveness question. Quantitative research is based on a certain philosophy about the nature of knowing (see chapter 4 by Neufeldt and Nelson), and by its very nature cannot answer all questions counselors might have about being effective change agents. No study in the world can tell us ahead of time if a particular technique will work with a particular client problem. Research-based conclusions can provide generalizations that serve as hypotheses for our work with such particulars. It is likely (or not) that this strategy will work. The complex contexts, interactions, and associated meaning-making that keep our work fresh on a daily basis also keep it somewhat unpredictable.

## Research Questions to Explore

Despite (or maybe because of) the challenges involved with researching ecological counseling, we asked our authors to develop model research questions that emerged from their chapter's focus. We list just a few, to provide you with a glimpse of some ripe questions that need to be pursued:

- How can the relative contributions of person, environment, and person $\times$ environment be measured? How can ecological concordance be operationalized, and would we know it when we see it? How does an ecological perspective influence counseling practice? For example, we do not know what types of clients might benefit from this approach, or if other counselors even find it attractive compared with any of a myriad other possible counseling frameworks. Do ecological counselors become more involved than other counselors with system and system-change efforts? (Bob Conyne and Ellen Cook, chapter 1).

- Consider the probability that people who differ by gender, race, or socioeconomic class view differently the behavioral metaphors that relate to them. Think about how to identify these metaphors (interviews, surveys) and how to determine their impact (focus groups, standardized instruments). Sketch out a research proposal to answer these questions, and discuss it with a colleague or professor. (Edwin Herr, chapter 2)

- The ecological approach outlined in chapter 3 suggests that relationships between people and environments are the primary reality of the social world. If this is the case, then this approach suggests that counselors use these relational variables in research. Research could focus on the technical questions inherent in measuring such relationships, as well as their relative value as predictors of counseling outcomes. For instance, one might explore the effects of participating in different fields, dominant ideologies, popular culture, and mass media on clients' construction of themselves and their problems, as well as the solutions to those problems. (Joseph Stewart-Sicking, chapter 3)

- Researchers now know that psychotherapy, regardless of its theoretical base, generally results in positive outcomes; however, it would be interesting to study how clients' worldviews change as a result of working with ecological counselors who understand constructivist ideas. This could be done through questionnaires or qualitative interviews. A research program might, for example, conduct a qualitative study that consists of interviewing clients before and after participating in ecological counseling to determine whether (a) they have come to view their experiences in a more contextualized way; and if so, (b) what aspects of perceived embeddedness are most salient. (Susan Allstetter Neufeldt and Mary Lee Nelson, chapter 4)

- What kinds of research methods most appropriately fit ecological counseling? How are these research methods different from conventional research approaches? (Ellen Cook, Bob Conyne, Cheryl Savageau, and Mei Tang, chapter 5)

- For which sorts of client problems (i.e., associated with disruptions of the biological substrata, drive dysregulation, personality, or with the person's lived experience) is the ecological view of psychotherapy most (or least) clearly suited? (F. Robert Wilson, chapter 6)

- Consider the variety of ideas that are included in chapter 7, "Training and Supervision." In a small group of five or six people, discuss the ideas of greatest interest to the group. Select one approach for further exploration. Taking this one potential intervention, generate a research study to test its effectiveness. Make certain your group addresses this research idea with a clear and specific objective, reproducible treatment, and measurable outcomes. (Geoffrey Yager, chapter 7)

- Maslow's hierarchy of needs is argued as fundamental to a person involved in one-on-one counseling (i.e., people transitioning from their basic needs to self-actualization). Describe the connection that can be made between his theory and ecological considerations for the members involved within an ecologically centered group. (Fred Bemak and Bob Conyne, chapter 8)
- Accurate and timely documentation is essential to the ability of an agency to continue the mission of the organization in the community. Discuss methods of tracking documentation in an agency. How can an agency administrator be certain that all documentation is up-to-date, complete, and valid prior to an audit by a funding authority? (William O'Connell and Alan Mabry, chapter 10)

These are just a few of the myriad questions we need to explore to better understand and apply ecological counseling. We also would be wise to examine how ecological counseling might fit with our own worldview and way of working.

## Ecological Counseling and Us

We encourage you to evaluate, in terms of both process and outcome, whether the ideas discussed in this book improve the ecological concordance experienced in your daily work. Does the ecological counseling framework seem like a good match to you? Make sense to your clients? Assist you in structuring the counseling process in a meaningful way? Enhance the range of options you explore together? Fit with the practice parameters set by your work setting? Encourage broader applications of counseling to other levels? Help empower your clients? Add to how successful you feel in your work?

In addition, we ask you to consider the meaningfulness of the ideas to you. Of course, if we did not do a good job of clarifying these ideas for you, it probably does not mean much at all! Because of the integrative nature of our work, it is likely that at least some of the ideas seemed familiar and important. Your reaction to the book also reflects how you construct the meaning of your professional life. How well does this framework fit your notions of a counselor's role, the implicit blueprint for behavior you have developed to guide your professional role performance? Does it fit your personality style set, the ways you interact with clients, your skills set? Does it resonate with your basic assumptions about the way the world works? Some readers may be drawn to the metaphors of humans as growing things; others may find such metaphors simplistic or misleading. In disagreeing with us, do you find your own thinking sharpened?

We want to communicate with you about these and other related kinds of matters. We have established three ways for such discussions to occur on an ongoing basis. Our electronic mailing list (Eco-Counseling@listserv.uc.edu) allows members to share information. Our Web site (www.ecologicalcounseling.org) permits many interesting activities to occur among those of us involved in ecological counseling. Further, the Center for Ecological Counseling has been established at the University of Cincinnati College of Education, where you can find external grants, research projects, and related opportunities. Send an e-mail to Bob Conyne at conynerk@email.uc.edu to start a conversation, and feel free to explore the Web site.

Whether or not you ultimately adopt the ecological perspective, we hope you have reflected on what you find meaningful and valid in your professional work. If you have done so, we consider ourselves successful in providing the challenge needed for growth, as noted in chapter 1. We hope you will continue to find intellectual stimulation in this book, and that you will enrich our professional community by sharing your ideas.

## Reference

Bronfenbrenner, U. (1977). Toward an experimental ecology of human development. *American Psychologist, 32,* 515–531.

# Index

Holloway, E. L., 191
Homosexual dating violence, 333
Horowitz, L. M.,, et al., 148
House, R. M., & Martin, P. J., 300
Husserl, Edmund, 91

Immigration. *See* Diversity
Implicit meaning, 21-22
Individual interventions, 126
Individualism, 13, 96, 293
Industrial urbanization, transition to, 53-54
Integration approach, 10-11, 68. *See also* Objective and subjective reality, relationship between
agency-structure integration theories, 75-80
deep ecology and, 204, 205t8.1
Interactional nature of ecological counseling, 12-13
career counseling and, 225
Interdependent nature of ecological counseling, 29, 271
Interdisciplinary nature of ecological counseling, 8, 42
career counseling and, 224-225
prevention practice and, 327
Interpersonal assessment, 115, 148-149
in problem formulation, 151-152
Interpersonal problems, treatment of, 156
Interventions in ecological counseling, 25-26, 123-128. *See also* Ecological psychotherapy
career counseling and, 228-229, 236-237
case conceptualization and, 97-102
case study of selecting, 134-136
community interventions, 127-128
contextual levels of, 126-128
environmental interventions, 81-82, 124-126

group interventions, 126-127
individual interventions, 126
organizational interventions, 127, 265-288. *See also* Organizational interventions
parsimonious interventions, 26-27
at personal levels, 81-82
values issues in, 120-123
Intrapersonal assessment, 115, 146-147
in problem formulation, 150
Intrapersonal problems, treatment of, 155-156
Inventory of Interpersonal Problems, 148
Israel and immigrants' loss of cultural identity, 48

Job stress, 54

Kasambira, K. P., & Edwards, L., 17, 267
Keiffer, C. H., 296
Kelly, G., 21
Kelly, J. G., et al., 271
Knowledge and empowerment, 297
Knowledge economy, 50
Krieshok, T. S., 224
Krumboltz, J. D., 9, 221
Kunkel, J. H., 203

Language, nature and use of, 73-75
Language game, 73
Lazarus, A., 152, 153
Leary, T., 148
Lee, C. C., 300
Lee, M., 148
Leigh, H., & Reiser, M. F., 152
Lent, R. W., Brown, S. D., & Hackett, G., 221
Lesbian dating violence, 333
Levenson, R. W., et al., 97
Lewin, K., 6, 40, 145, 341
Lewis, J., & Bradley, L., 289, 305